LearningExpress®'s

GMAT® EXAM SUCCESS

In Only 4 Steps!

LearningExpress®'s

GMAT® EXAM SUCCESS

In Only 4 Steps!

Elizabeth Chesla
and Colleen Schultz

LearningExpress®
NEW YORK

Library of Congress Cataloging-in-Publication Data:
Chesla, Elizabeth L.
GMAT exam success in only 4 steps / Elizabeth Chesla and Colleen Schultz—1st ed.
p. cm.
Includes bibliographical references.
ISBN 1-57685-472-8
1. Graduate Management Admission Test—Study guides.
2. Management—Examinations, questions, etc. I. Schultz, Colleen.
II. Title.
HF1118.C44 2003
650'.076—dc21 2003009065

Printed in the United States of America
9 8 7 6 5 4 3 2 1
First Edition

ISBN 1-57685-472-8

For more information or to place an order, contact LearningExpress at:
55 Broadway
8th Floor
New York, NY 10006

Or visit us at:
www.learnatest.com

About the Authors

Elizabeth Chesla is the author of *TOEFL Exam Success, ACT Exam Success, GED Success, Reading Comprehension Success, Write Better Essays,* and many other writing and reading guides and test preparation books. She lives in South Orange, New Jersey.

Colleen Schultz is a math teacher from Binghamton, New York. She is a contributing writer for *501 Math Word Problems, 501 Quantitative Comparison Questions,* and an item writer for several high-stakes math tests.

Contents

PART I ▶ Preparing for the GMAT

CHAPTER

1 About the GMAT Exam

Planning to apply to a graduate business or management degree program? Then you need to find out all you can about the GMAT® exam so you can do your best on the exam. This chapter will tell you everything you need to know to get started. You will learn how the test is structured and scored, how to register, and what procedures and regulations to expect at the testing center.

A graduate degree in business or management can transform your professional life, opening the door to promotions, new opportunities, and new careers. For better or for worse, which business school you attend depends to some degree upon how well you do on the Graduate Management Admissions Test® (GMAT®).

Like the SAT® exam, ACT Assessment®, and GRE® test, the GMAT exam is a standardized test designed to help schools determine how well you might succeed in their graduate program. Of course, the GMAT exam is just *one* of the tools schools use to assess a candidate's knowledge and skills, and it is by no means a definitive measure. But it is an important test, and because your scores can determine your eligibility for certain programs and give you an edge over other candidates, it is important that you do well on the exam.

The GMAT exam is sponsored by the Graduate Management Admission Council® (GMAC®), a nonprofit association of representatives from business schools around the world. Nearly 2,000 business schools use the GMAT exam, which is developed and administered by the Educational Testing Service® (ETS®), the same organization that develops and administers a number of other standardized tests including the SAT and TOEFL® exams. The majority of people taking the GMAT exam seek to enter MBA programs, but an increasing number of other graduate business and management programs are now offered, and many of these programs also use the GMAT exam to assess the qualifications of applicants.

On the Road to a Graduate Degree

Although the MBA is still the most popular graduate business degree, a growing number of other graduate-level business and management programs are becoming available. Taking the GMAT exam can help you apply for programs that offer several different graduate degrees, including the following:

- Master of Business Administration (MBA)
- Master of Science in Management
- Master of Public Administration (MPA)
- Master of Science in Financial Engineering

▶ An Overview of the GMAT Exam

Nearly 50 years ago, the GMAC was founded with the goal it maintains today: to develop a standardized assessment tool for business school candidates. Although the GMAT exam has evolved over the years, the three-and-a-half-hour exam still tests candidates in three main areas, measuring analytical writing, verbal, and quantitative skills.

The Analytical Writing Assessment (AWA)

The first part of the GMAT exam, the Analytical Writing Assessment (AWA), is designed to measure your ability to analyze ideas and to write clearly and effectively about those ideas. You will be asked to write two separate essays: one that analyzes an *issue* and one that analyzes an *argument.* You will have 30 minutes for each essay.

In the Analysis of an Issue section, you will be presented with a short passage (one paragraph) about an issue, such as whether new technologies create or destroy more jobs or whether education is the most important key to success. You will be asked to *take a position* on this issue and *explain* your position. In the Analysis of an Argument section, you will be presented with a short argument (again, just one paragraph) and be asked to *critique* that argument. In this essay, you should not present your own point of view but rather assess the logic of the argument that has been presented.

In both cases, the topics will be general enough for every test taker to write about. Prior knowledge of the subject matter may be helpful, but it is not required. It is more important to show your ability to take and support a position and your ability to analyze the effectiveness of an argument.

The Quantitative Section

The Quantitative section is the second part of the test and includes 37 multiple-choice questions covering two areas of mathematics: data sufficiency and problem solving. You will have 75 minutes to answer these questions.

The problem solving questions will constitute approximately 60% of the exam (22 questions). The problems will test your knowledge of basic math facts and skills covered in high school, including arithmetic,

GMAT Exam Facts

- Over 1,700 schools/programs use GMAT scores in the admissions process.
- The first GMAT exam was developed and administered nearly 50 years ago.
- In 2002, over 150,000 people took the GMAT exam in the United States.
- In 2002, over 75,000 people took the GMAT exam in locations outside the United States.
- Nearly 7% more GMAT exams were given in 2002 than in 2001 in the United States.
- Over 4% more GMAT exams were given elsewhere in the world in 2002 than in 2001.
- Approximately 20% of people who take the GMAT exam take it more than once. Most repeat testers take the test two or three times.

algebra, geometry, word problems, and interpreting charts and graphs. These questions will emphasize your understanding of mathematical concepts, although you will also need to know basic math procedures in order to select the correct answer.

The data sufficiency questions constitute the remaining 40% of the test and are quite different in nature. For these questions, you do not actually need to solve a problem or make a calculation. Instead, you will be presented with two items of information and a question. You must determine whether the information presented is sufficient to accurately answer the question or if you need more data to solve the problem. The answer choices will ask you to identify which item of information is insufficient if more data is indeed required.

The Verbal Section

The third and final part of the GMAT exam is the Verbal section. You will have another 75 minutes to answer 41 multiple-choice questions. These questions cover three areas: reading comprehension, critical reasoning, and sentence correction. Approximately one-third of the questions will fall into each category.

The reading comprehension questions will be based on short passages (150 to 350 words) about topics ranging from the social sciences to the physical and biological sciences to business, the arts, and humanities. You may be asked about the main idea of the passage, the author's support for that main idea, argumentative strategies, specific facts and details in the text, and inferences that can be drawn from the passage. You can expect the passages to be rather sophisticated, much like the reading material you will be exposed to in business school.

The critical reasoning questions present you with a short reading passage (50 to 100 words) that makes an argument about a general topic. You will be asked about the structure of the argument, including its conclusion and assumptions; about the quality of the argument, including its strengths and weaknesses; and about plans of action based upon the argument, including what actions are appropriate and effective based on the text. Again, this is great training for the business world.

The sentence correction questions present you with a sentence with part or all of the sentence underlined. You must choose the answer that best expresses the idea of the sentence. To determine the best answer, you will need to consider the grammar and usage, diction, sentence structure, sentence logic, and tone.

What the GMAT Exam Is and Is Not

Like all standardized tests, the GMAT exam is just one measure of your potential success in a graduate business or management program. A strong correlation can be made between high performance on the GMAT exam and success in the first year of business school. However, the exam is designed to measure a targeted set of knowledge and skills, and does not take into account other factors that are essential to academic success.

The GMAT exam is designed to measure the following:

- your ability to take a position on an issue and support it
- your ability to critique an argument
- your ability to organize ideas and convey them clearly in writing
- your ability to express your ideas in logical, correct, and effective sentences
- your ability to conduct basic mathematical operations
- your ability to determine what data is necessary to solve problems, especially those you might encounter in real business situations
- how well you understand what you read
- your ability to identify the logic and assumptions behind an argument
- your knowledge of techniques and strategies for effective writing
- your knowledge of the conventions of standard written English

The GMAT exam is not designed to measure the following:

- what you know about business or technology
- your job skills and experience
- your computer skills
- how well you study or manage your time
- your ability to manage others
- your interpersonal skills
- how well you learned content from your specific undergraduate or other degree areas
- other important character traits, such as your level of motivation, creativity, and self-discipline

► Computer-Adaptive Test (CAT)

Computer technology has transformed standardized tests in many ways. In the past, people who took the GMAT exam would all receive the same test (or one of several versions of the same test). Now, with its new computer-adaptive format, the GMAT exam's Quantitative and Verbal sections present each test taker with a unique test designed to more accurately measure his or her ability in the subject.

On the GMAT exam, your questions will be drawn from a pool of possible questions, beginning with a question of moderate difficulty. This process of dynamic question selection will continue throughout the entire test. Each question will be selected based upon the level of the previous question and whether or not

Why a CAT?

The GMAC has switched the GMAT exam from a paper-based exam to a CAT for several reasons. One reason is that computer tests are cheaper to develop, administer, and score than traditional paper exams. Another reason is that computer-adaptive exams help maintain the confidentiality of test items and prevent cheating on the exam. Because no two test takers ever have the same test, it is very difficult for individuals to assist each other during the exam.

More importantly, for business schools, the CAT (at least ostensibly) provides a more accurate measure of a student's verbal and quantitative ability than paper-based exams. For test takers anxious to know their scores, the CAT provides an instant (but unofficial) score for the Verbal and Quantitative sections of the exam.

you answered that question correctly. The test continuously adjusts to your skill level. The computer-adaptive test (CAT) is designed to adjust the level of difficulty of the questions to the performance of the test taker. This means that if you answer a question of medium difficulty correctly, the next question will probably be more difficult. However, if you answer it incorrectly, the next question will probably be easier. On a CAT, you earn more credit for answering a hard question correctly than for answering an easy question correctly.

However, the questions will not increase in difficulty infinitely if you continue to answer all questions correctly, or at least the level will not increase at the same rate. The degree of change will be significantly lower because the program considers your answers to every question you have answered so far, not just the current question. The more questions you answer, the more knowledge about your skill level the computer has, and the less dramatic the change in level will be as you proceed through the exam. Indeed, by the fifth or sixth question, the CAT is likely to have honed in on the skill level it believes is appropriate for you. Thus, an important test-taking strategy for the GMAT exam CAT is to answer the first five or six questions correctly. Doing so will set your questions at a higher level for the exam, enabling you to earn more credit for each correct answer.

In the Quantitative and Verbal sections, you must answer each question in the order in which it is presented. Unlike a paper-based exam, the computer-based exam does not allow you to skip questions and come back to them later; you must answer as you go. You also cannot change your answer to a previous question or see the questions that follow.

Because the test is timed, you must be sure not to spend too much time on any one question. On a CAT such as the GMAT exam, your best bet is to take an educated guess at questions you cannot answer. If you can eliminate one or two choices, you dramatically increase your chances of answering correctly and can then move on to the next question. This is important because, as you will see in the scoring section, the number of questions you answer is a key factor in your score.

▶ Preparing for the Computer-Based GMAT Exam

Taking a computer-based test is a very different experience from taking a traditional paper-based exam. Although the Verbal and Quantitative sections require very little computer skill, you will need some basic computer experience. More important, you need at least minimal word-processing skills to complete your

Practice Your Computer Skills

On the GMAT computer-based test, you will need to know the following:

- how to use a mouse
- how to enter an answer
- how to move to the next question
- how to use a word processor (for typing your AWA essays)
- how to use the HELP function

The GMAC offers a free tutorial to help you become comfortable with the computer skills you will need for the GMAT exam. You can download this software from the GMAT website at www.mba.com/mba/TaketheGMAT/ToolsToHelpYouPrepare/GMATPrepProducts/GMATTutorialsSoftware.htm.

NOTE: The tutorial is not compatible with Macintosh® computers.

AWA essays. You are already under enough pressure to try to write two essays in an hour. If you are not comfortable typing, and if you do not know basic word-processing functions such as how to delete or move text, you may have a difficult time writing a successful essay.

If you are not experienced with computers, then part of your GMAT exam preparation time must include learning computer skills. Here are some specific tips to help you improve your computer skills to reach peak performance on the GMAT exam:

- Practice using a mouse. Get comfortable with the movement of the arrow and clicking around on the computer screen.
- Learn how to move up and down a page. Practice using the scroll bar and the arrow keys.
- Get a typing tutorial. You can learn proper hand and finger positions that will help you type faster. One website that offers help is www.typing-tutorial.com.
- Learn to highlight, delete, and copy and paste text within a document. Get comfortable with the backspace, delete, and arrow keys so you can move around quickly within a document. Practice typing and changing text so that you can be sure not to delete text that you want to keep.
- Practice typing your essay on the computer. Use the sample topics listed in Part III and on the GMAT website at www.mba.com/mba/TaketheGMAT/Tools/AWATopics2001.htm. Set a timer so you get used to the 30-minute time limit.

The GMAC offers its own GMAT computer tutorials to help you develop the computer skills you need for the exam. You can download these tutorials at www.mba.com/mba/TaketheGMAT/ToolsToHelpYouPrepare/GMATPrepProducts/GMATTutorialsSoftware.htm.

On Your Score Report

Your official GMAT score report will include four scores:

SCORE	RANGE
Verbal	0–60
Quantitative	0–60
Total	200–800
AWA	0–6

How the GMAT Exam Is Scored

Your GMAT score report will actually include four scores: a Verbal section score, a Quantitative section score, a Total score, and an AWA score. Your report will show these scores for the three most recent exams within the last five years. It will also include information you provided to the GMAC, including your gender, date of birth, Social Security number, undergraduate institution, major, date of graduation, and intended area of graduate study.

Verbal and Quantitative Scores

Your Verbal and Quantitative section scores will range between 0 to 60. This number will be computed based on a formula that considers the number of correct answers, the number of incorrect answers, the number of questions answered, and the level of difficulty of the questions answered.

Because the questions on the Quantitative and Verbal sections are weighted, answering a difficult question correctly will count more than answering an easy question correctly. That is why it is so important, as we noted earlier, to answer the first few questions correctly to help set a higher level of difficulty for your exam.

In the Quantitative and Verbal sections, your score is determined by:

- how many questions you answer
- how many of those questions you answer correctly
- the level of difficulty of each question you answer correctly

Total Score

The Total score is a combination of your Verbal and Quantitative scores scaled to a range between 200 to 800. According to the GMAC, two-thirds of GMAT Total scores are between 400 to 600.

AWA Score

Both of your AWA essays will be scored holistically by two separate readers on a scale of 0 to 6. This means that readers will rate each essay based on its overall effectiveness, not just its grammatical correctness. Specifically, readers will be looking for the following:

- the level of critical thinking evident in your ideas
- effective organization
- sufficient development of ideas
- strong and sufficient support of ideas
- effective word choice and sentence structure
- clear and controlled sentences
- a command of the conventions of standard written English

An important note about your readers: One reader will be a college or university professional specially trained to assess GMAT essays. The other reader, however, will probably be a computer. Since 1999, GMAC and the ETS have been using E-rater® to score GMAT essays. E-rater is a program that evaluates essays based on organization, word choice, sentence structure, and other key factors. You will learn more about E-rater and the scoring of the AWA in Chapter 14. At this point, you can be comforted by this fact: According to the GMAC, E-rater and human readers give essays the same rating, on average, 87% to 94% of the time.

If a discrepancy of more than one point appears between the two readers, your essay will be read by a third independent reader—a human.

Once both essays are scored, the numbers will be averaged to determine your AWA score. Here is an example:

	READER 1	READER 2	READER 3	AVERAGE
Analysis of an Issue	5	5	N/A	5
Analysis of an Argument	2	4	3	3
AWA Score				4

When to Expect Your Score

You will receive unofficial Verbal, Quantitative, and Total scores at the completion of your GMAT CAT. You can expect to receive official Verbal, Quantitative, and Total scores along with your AWA score via mail approximately two weeks after your exam.

Canceling Your Score

At the end of your exam, but before you see your unofficial Verbal and Quantitative section scores, you will have the opportunity to cancel your test scores. If you opt to cancel your scores, the schools you selected to receive your score report will receive a cancellation notice, and the cancellation will be noted on all future score

Does Every Question Count?

If you answer all of the questions in each multiple-choice section, your final score will not be the percent of the 75 questions you answered correctly. That is because the questions are weighted and because not all of the questions are scored. Several questions in the test bank are included for research purposes only. The ETS includes these questions to determine whether a new question for a future exam is sufficiently clear.

Do not bother trying to figure out which questions are "real" and which are research questions. Just assume all questions are "real" and do your best on all of them. The time allotted for each section is designed for you to answer 75 questions total, and your score will be based only on your answers to the active test questions. So don't worry; a few research questions on your exam will not hurt your score in any way.

reports. Once you cancel, *you cannot reinstate your scores.* Once you view your scores, *you cannot cancel.* You should therefore be very confident that you performed poorly on the exam before you elect to cancel your scores. Please note that your testing fee *will not be refunded* if you cancel. After all, you did take the exam.

If you decide *not* to cancel, you can then see and print your unofficial Verbal, Quantitative, and Total scores. You will receive an official score report in approximately two weeks, as mentioned previously. The institutions you selected should also receive your scores at approximately the same time.

Appealing Your AWA Score

As detailed as the AWA scoring rubric may be for human readers, rating an essay is inherently subjective and certainly far more subjective than scoring a multiple-choice exam. Although E-rater may be successful, it is possible for a highly effective essay (especially if it is unconventional) to receive a low E-rater score. If you believe that your AWA essay(s) merits a higher rating, you may ask the ETS to rescore your essays for a fee of $45. Your request must be made within six months of the date you took the exam.

Be aware, however, that you should request a rescore only if you are very confident that your essay did not receive the score it deserved. Your rescored results are final, whether they are better or worse than your original score, and you cannot request another rating. Your revised score will be sent to you and the institutions that received your original score report approximately three weeks after your rescoring request is received.

To request a rescoring, you must write, call, or fax the following address/numbers with your name, date of birth, GMAT appointment/registration number, Social Security number, and the reason you feel your essay should be rescored:

Phone: 609-771-7330
Fax: 609-883-4349
Mail: GMAT Rescoring Service
Educational Testing Service
P.O. Box 6102
Princeton, NJ 08541-6102

▶ Getting Your Scores to Schools

Of course, the reason you are taking the GMAT test in the first place is to get your scores to the schools to which you will apply. Your testing fee includes the cost of sending your score report to up to five schools. You can select these schools on the day of your scheduled exam. Before your test, make sure you get the four-digit **institution codes** for those schools and bring those codes with you to the testing center. Make sure you have the right code for each program; large colleges and universities may have different codes for separate schools within the system.

If you want to send your report to more than five schools, or if you want to add a school after your test day, you can do so for an additional $25 per school. Print a copy of the Additional Score Report Request Form from www.mba.com or call 800-GMAT-NOW to request this form. You can submit the form by phone, fax, or mail:

Phone: 609-771-7330
Fax: 609-883-4349
Mail: GMAT
Educational Testing Service
P.O. Box 6104
Princeton, NJ 08541-6104

Your score report will be sent to the new recipient within approximately two weeks from when ETS receives your request.

▶ Retaking the Exam

If you are not satisfied with your scores or think you can do better with a little more study or practice, you may retake the GMAT exam—in fact, you may retake the exam up to five times in any given year, as long as you do not take the test more than once a month.

When you arrive to retake the GMAT exam, you can select the schools you want to receive your new test scores. Your score report to these institutions will include the score report from your most recent exam and those from the dates from your two most recent previous exams (if applicable) within the last five years.

If for some reason you want to take the test more than five times in a year, you may appeal to the GMAC in writing. Your letter or e-mail should explain why you want to take the exam more than five times; the dates and locations of your previous exams; and your full name, address, phone number, and fax/e-mail if available. Mail or e-mail this request to

Should You Retake the Test?

Because you will be familiar with the format and content of the GMAT exam after you take the exam, chances are you can significantly improve your score if you retake the test. According to the GMAC, most people improve their Total score by approximately 30 points the second time they take the exam. So, if you take the test, study the material you realized you did not know well enough during the exam, and then retake the GMAT exam, you should be on your way to a significantly higher score.

But do not plan on gaining another 30 points by taking the test a third time. GMAC statistics show that score improvements are typically much lower after the second exam.

E-mail: fifthtest@gmac.com
Mail: GMAT Fifth Testing Request
Graduate Management Admissions Council
Suite 1100
1750 Tysons Boulevard
McLean, VA 22102

▶ GMAT Testing Center Rules and Regulations

Like all standardized tests, the GMAT exam must be taken under very specific conditions that are standard for all testing centers. Because everyone who takes the exam takes it under the same conditions, business schools can feel more confident in comparing the GMAT scores of their applicants.

Test center regulations for the GMAT exam are numerous and very specific, and violation of the regulations can lead to expulsion from the testing center and cancellation of your test scores. *Read this section carefully* to be sure that you do not inadvertently violate any regulations.

Present Valid Identification

When you sign in at the testing center, you must present valid identification. Each form of identification must contain your name, a recent photograph, and your signature. An ID without all three elements *is not acceptable,* with the following possible exception: Test administrators are authorized, under certain conditions, to accept IDs that contain a physical description in lieu of a photograph. Your identification must contain the following:

- your name (use this name when you register; your ID and your registration name must match exactly)
- a recent and recognizable photograph
- your signature

Letter of Identity Confirmation

If you lack a valid ID with your photograph, you may present a letter from your college or university attesting to your identity. The letter must be from an official from the college or university you attend(ed) and must include the following:

- your name
- a recent and recognizable photograph of you
- your signature
- the college/university official's signature and job title, along with the institution's seal (if available)

These letters are valid for up to one year.

It is important that the name on your ID be *the same name you provide when you register for the test.* For example, if you register for the test as Rajita Aggarwal, but your ID says Rajita Aggarwal-Samson, your identification may be questioned and you might not be permitted to take the test.

Test administrators will accept the following valid forms of ID:

- a current passport (valid passports are required for test takers in India, Pakistan, and Bangladesh; expired passports are not acceptable anywhere)
- a current driver's license (expired driver's licenses are not valid ID)
- a national identity card
- a military ID card
- a student ID card*
- an employee ID card*
- a letter from your college or university attesting to your identity

*You must present a *second* form of ID from the previous list with one of these forms of ID. A driver's license alone will be sufficient; however, if you have an employee ID card as your primary ID, you will also need a student ID or letter in order to enter the exam.

Social Security cards, credit cards, and bank cards are *not* acceptable forms of identification for the GMAT exam.

At the testing center, you may also be asked to verify your identity with a fingerprint, photograph, videotape, or other form of electronic identity confirmation. If you refuse to participate in electronic identity verification you will forfeit your right to take the exam, and your testing fee will not be refunded.

The GMAC is very serious about proper identification. If you do not present valid ID or agree to additional identity verification, you will not be admitted, and your test fee will be forfeited. The ETS may also determine that your ID was invalid *after* you take the exam. In that case, your test scores will be canceled and

What You Need to Bring to the Testing Center

On the day of your scheduled exam, bring the following items:

- proper identification
- names of the schools that you would like to receive your score reports
- your authorization voucher, if you registered via mail

Paper and pencils will be provided for you at the testing center; do not bring your own.

cancellation notices will be sent to all of the schools that receive your scores. Your testing fee will not be reimbursed.

Make sure you arrive early for the exam to allow sufficient time for the verification of your identity.

If you have any questions about GMAT registration, testing centers, scores, or any other matters relating to the GMAT exam, contact ETS-GMAT Customer Service at gmat@ets.org, or 800-GMAT-NOW, or 703-749-0131.

Confidentiality Agreement

In addition to providing the proper identification, you must also sign a **confidentiality agreement**—your promise not to reveal specific details about the contents of the GMAT exam you will take. If you do not sign this agreement, you will not be permitted to take the test, and your test fee will not be refunded.

Exam Procedures and Regulations

At the GMAT testing center, you will be given an individual computer workstation for your exam. You will also have access to a small locker or other limited space for your personal belongings. Purses, backpacks, cell phones, and other personal items are *not* permitted in the testing room and must be left in your locker. You will not be able to access items in your locker during the exam or breaks.

Your test administrator will supply you with several sheets of scratch paper at the start of the exam. If you need additional sheets, need help with your computer, have technical difficulties with your machine, or need any other assistance, you must raise your hand to notify the test administrator. *Do not leave your seat* except in an emergency. If you leave your seat during the exam session, the timing of the section you are taking will continue, and you will not be granted extra time to complete the test.

Once you have arrived and signed in and until you sign out, you must follow several regulations.

During the test sessions and during the breaks, you may *not*

- use testing aids of any kind, including notes, calculators, dictionaries, or translators
- exceed the scheduled five-minute breaks between sections
- communicate with anyone about the content of the exam
- leave the test center

Technical Difficulties

Although the old paper exams could not adapt to your level as you took the test, they had one sure advantage: No technical difficulties occurred. If you have any problems with your computer as you are taking the exam, raise your hand for assistance from the test administrator. If the technical difficulties cannot be immediately repaired and you are unable to complete your exam, you will be permitted to reschedule your test and take another exam free of charge. If you decide not to retake the test, you will be reimbursed for your testing fee.

- use telephones or cell phones
- remove scratch paper from the testing room (all scratch paper must be returned at the end of the test session)
- remove or attempt to remove, or reproduce or attempt to reproduce, any test questions from the testing center
- give or attempt to give, or receive or attempt to receive, unauthorized help
- create a disturbance or behave in a disruptive manner

You may eat and drink *only* during the scheduled breaks, and if you wish to step outside for a cigarette, you must let the test administrator know and stay in the immediate vicinity of the testing center. Failure to follow any of these rules may result in your dismissal from the exam.

▶ Registering for the GMAT Exam

Registering for the GMAT exam is easy. Once you choose your testing center and determine which of the available testing dates and times best suits your schedule, you can schedule your exam online, by phone, or via fax. A complete list of testing centers and their contact information is available on the GMAT website at www.mba.com/mba/TaketheGMAT/Tools/TestCenterList.htm. You will need Adobe Acrobat Reader to download the list. You can also download the GMAT Information Bulletin; pages 10 through 16 include list of national and international testing centers and their phone numbers.

You can register for the GMAT exam in several ways:

- **By phone.** Call 800-GMAT-NOW (800-462-8669) or 800-529-3590 for TTY or call your selected testing center directly.
- **By mail.** Call 800-GMAT-NOW to request a **Voucher Request Form**, or print the form from the GMAT website at www.mba.com/mba/TaketheGMAT/Tools/VoucherRequestForm.htm.

No Testing Aids Allowed!

The following items are considered testing aids and are not permitted in the testing room during the exam sessions:

- notes
- calculators
- dictionaries or thesauruses
- translators
- personal data assistants (PDAs)
- rulers or other measuring devices
- stopwatches or watch alarms
- telephones or cellular phones
- pagers or beepers
- photographic devices
- stereos or radios

You will be given pencils and scratch paper at the testing center, so don't bring your own pens, pencils, or blank paper into the testing room; if you do, you will be asked to store them in your locker until the test is over.

Send your completed form and testing fee to:
GMAT
Educational Testing Service
P.O. Box 6103
Princeton, NJ 08541-6103

- **Online.** Register directly on the website www.mba.com. Click on "Take the GMAT" and then "Scheduling a GMAT Appointment." You will need a valid Visa®, MasterCard®, or American Express® card to pay your $200 registration fee.

Again, whether you register by mail, phone, or computer, *make sure you register with the name that is printed on the ID you will take to the testing center.* If your registration name and ID do not match—for example, if you make a spelling error when you type in your registration online—you may not be permitted to take the exam, and your testing fee will not be refunded.

Registering for the GMAT Exam outside the United States

How you register for the GMAT exam outside of the United States, U.S. territories, Puerto Rico, or Canada depends upon the kind of testing center you choose. Three kinds of international testing centers are available—permanent, mobile, and supplementary. Each has a different registration procedure.

Permanent centers offer the GMAT CAT year-round. You can register for the test at a permanent center via phone, fax, mail, or Internet. To schedule by phone, call the Regional Registration Center (RRC) for your desired testing center (phone numbers for RRCs are listed on the Testing Center Locations List). You must call at least three days before your desired test date, and payment by credit card is required at the time of your call.

Follow the Rules

A considerable portion of this section has been dedicated to rules. This is because GMAT testing center regulations must be followed very carefully. If you violate any regulations during the exam, you may be dismissed by the test administrator, and your violation will be reported to the ETS. Consequences may include the cancellation of your test scores and forfeiture of your testing fee. If your violation is serious enough—for example, if you attempt to use testing aids or remove test questions from the testing room—you could even be barred from future exams.

To register by mail, download the International Test Scheduling Form from www.mba.com/mba/TaketheGMAT/Tools/InternationalTestSchedulingForm.htm (or call 800-GMAT-NOW to request this form) and return it with your payment to the RRC for your testing center.

To register by fax, send your completed International Test Scheduling Form and your credit card information to the fax number for your testing center RRC.

Mobile centers are temporary and offer the GMAT CAT on a limited schedule. You can register for the test at a mobile center by mail, phone, or fax. Follow the instructions provided for permanent centers.

Supplementary centers offer the paper-based GMAT exam only once or twice each year. To register for the test at one of these sites, you must complete a Supplementary Test Center Preregistration Form and send it (via fax or mail) to the ETS by the appropriate deadline. You can download this form at www.mba.com/mba/TaketheGMAT/Tools/SupplementaryTestCenterPreregistrationForm.htm or request it from 800-GMAT-NOW. This form reserves you a place at the testing center for the exam. Do not include payment with this form. After the ETS receives your request, you will receive a packet of information with details about the testing center location and information about the paper-based exam.

Nonstandard Testing Accommodations

Test takers with disabilities can arrange for several nonstandard testing accommodations for the exam. These accommodations include the following:

- extended (but not unlimited) testing time
- additional breaks during exam sections and/or extended breaks between sections
- adjusted background and foreground colors (for CAT only)
- a recorder or writer of answers
- a sign language interpreter for spoken directions
- audio cassette, Braille, or large-print GMAT formats

GMAT Information Bulletin

The GMAC offers a print version of most of the GMAT information available on its website at www.mba.com. You can download this bulletin at www.mba.com/mba/TaketheGMAT/Tools/GMATBulletin2002.htm or call 800-GMAT-NOW to request the brochure.

Test takers may also request a Kensington® Trackball mouse, a HeadMaster Plus™ mouse, an Intellikeys® keyboard, or ZoomText®. If you request an alternate format GMAT exam, you will receive special instructions for your non-CAT version of the test.

To register for nonstandard testing accommodations, you must obtain the GMAT Supplement for Test Takers with Disabilities form and follow the instructions for registration in that bulletin. You can download the form from www.mba.com or request a copy from:

E-mail: gmat@ets.org
Phone: 609-771-7780
Fax: 609-771-7165
TTY: 609-771-7714
Mail: GMAT Disability Service
Educational Testing Services
P.O. Box 6054
Princeton, NJ 08541

Rescheduling or Relocating Your GMAT Appointment

You may need to reschedule your GMAT appointment date, time, or testing center location for many reasons. You can reschedule by phone or online at www.mba.com (see page 15 for details). You must reschedule at least seven days before your appointment date or else your testing fee will be forfeited. The rescheduled date must also be within a year of the original scheduled exam. The GMAC charges a $40 fee for rescheduling. This fee is paid at the time of rescheduling, so you must have a credit card ready when you call or go online.

Canceling Your GMAT Appointment

If you want to cancel your GMAT appointment and do so within seven days of your scheduled exam, you will receive a partial refund of $80. If you cancel any time closer to the test date, you will not be refunded any portion of your testing fee. You can cancel by phone or online at www.mba.com.

GMAT Fees	
GMAT	$200
Rescheduling exam	$40
Canceling exam	$80 refund
Additional school report	$25 per school

▶ Paying for the GMAT Exam

The GMAC charges $200 for the GMAT. Payment is due *in full* at registration; partial payments are not accepted. In the United States, payment may be made by cash,* check, credit card, or money order (checks must be drawn on funds from a U.S. bank). In Canada, *cash payments are not accepted*; registrants must pay by credit card, check, money order, bank drafts, money orders, or UNESCO coupons. Please note that appointments are automatically cancelled if your credit card is declined. Checks should be made payable to ETS-GMAT; they may *not* be postdated.

That should do it for administrative matters. Now it is time to review study skills and create a study plan so that you can maximize your GMAT preparation time.

*Cash payments may be made in U.S., Canadaian, Australian, Hong Kong, New Zealand, or Singapore dollars. British pounds, Danish and Norwegian kroners, euros, Japanese yen, Swiss francs, and Swedish krona are also accepted.

CHAPTER

2 Study Skills

Thomas Edison said, "Genius is 1% inspiration, 99% perspiration." Here is our take on that: "GMAT® exam success is 1% inspiration, 99% *preparation*." As with so many other things in life, the more prepared you are, the more you are likely to succeed. Whether that preparation involves practicing skills, researching information, memorizing lines, or developing a presentation, you make success possible by doing whatever you can to be ready for the situation.

Where Do I Start?

Chances are you already have a crowded to-do list, and you may be wondering how you will fit in the time you need to prepare for the GMAT exam. You have a life outside your plans for business school that may include work and family obligations, and you may already be in school, so you don't have an unlimited amount of time to prepare. The key is to maximize the study time you *do* have.

To study means "to give one's attention to learning a subject; to look at with careful attention." Notice that the word *attention* comes up twice in this definition. How you study is as important as how much time you spend studying. To study effectively, you need to focus all your attention on the material, so the preparation time you do have must be quality time. This section of the book will help you determine the study strategies that are right for you. It also will provide you with techniques for overcoming the two most common roadblocks to successful studying: anxiety and distraction.

Visualize Your Future

If you are ready to prepare for the GMAT exam, you have probably already researched several business schools and selected the programs that interest you most. Perhaps you are attracted to a particular program because it offers a unique course program or concentration, or you are impressed with the work of certain faculty members and would like to study with them. Maybe you know the reputations of particular programs and want the career opportunities they can offer. You may desire to go to a school close to where you live or to one that offers weekend or online courses.

If you have not investigated your options, now is the time to do so. You can search online for information, contact schools directly, and ask reference librarians to help you search. Keep an open mind—at this stage, it cannot hurt to explore any program that piques your interest. One excellent business school resource is GMAC's MBA Pathfinder™, a program that helps you objectively compare programs and consider important factors such as elective course work and faculty teaching styles. You can search business schools through Pathfinder at www.mba.com.

As you narrow your options to one or a few schools, you will want to learn as much about the particular program(s) as you possibly can. Perform Internet searches for all faculty members to learn more about their particular areas of interest. Skim through whatever course syllabi, student projects, and graduate student resources the program has posted online so you can compare your top choices and have an edge when you submit application materials and go in for interviews.

If at all possible, visit the campuses of your top two or three choices. In addition to helping you choose wisely, the information you gather on a visit is valuable input to help you form a visual image of yourself in business school. Visualization is a powerful tool that motivates you to make your dreams a reality.

Once you know where you want to be, spend a little time envisioning yourself there. What are you doing? Giving a presentation? Engaging in a conversation with an admired professor? Listening to an inspired lecture? Go over your vision, keep it in your mind, and use it to reinforce your resolution to study. Sticking to a study plan can be a real challenge. You would often rather be doing other things, and unforeseen obstacles may present themselves. You may be overwhelmed at times with the size of the task, or you may be anxious about your chances for success. These are all common problems. This book will show you how you can overcome them.

A Reality Check

The actor and comedian Jim Carrey is reported to have written himself a check for a million dollars when he was still struggling and broke. He carried that check in his wallet for years. Whenever he felt discouraged, he would take out the check and look at it. He visualized receiving a million-dollar check for his work one day. Carrey made that million-dollar paycheck part of his reality, and reality added a few extra zeros for him.

▶ I Need a Plan

You already know a great deal about studying. You could not have gotten this far, to the doorstep of business school, without effective study skills. The following pages will help you fine-tune your study methods so that you can make the most efficient use of your time.

The key to success in this endeavor, as in so many, is to take things one step at a time. Break this giant task down into manageable pieces. Your first step in successful studying is to create a study plan.

What Should I Study?

First, you must decide what you need to study. You may want to start with the pretests at the beginning of Parts II, III, and IV to help you assess your strengths and weaknesses. Make a list of each type of question and how well you scored on it, and analyze your list. What kinds of questions did you miss? What patterns do you see? Do you need to work on sentence correction questions? Word problems or data sufficiency? Do critical reasoning questions throw you for a loop? In your practice analytical essays, did you organize your thoughts well and convey them clearly? Did you take a clear position on the issue and effectively analyze the argument? It can be difficult to judge your own writing accurately so get feedback from someone whose opinions you trust and respect so you can better identify your writing strengths and weaknesses. Most importantly, do not forget to give yourself credit for the questions you answered correctly.

Once you are aware of what you know and what you still need to work on, you can effectively prioritize whatever study time you have available. Remember, no matter how you scored on the pretests and no matter what your weaknesses are, you will get better with practice. The more you study and the more effectively you work, the higher you will score on the actual exam.

How Do I Find the Time to Study?

Now is the time to create a realistic study schedule. You might be thinking that your life is too full without cramming in study time, too. But maybe you have more time available than you think. Think about your typical daily and weekly activities and determine when you have free time to devote to studying. Do not forget the short stretches—the 10 minutes here, the 15 minutes there. Sometimes you can do your best studying in short bursts. If you cannot seem to find the time, ask yourself what is more important to you in the long run than achieving your goals. Your life may seem quite full, but you are bound to spend some time at less productive activities, such as watching television. You could use this time to help make your dreams a reality.

Four Sources of Practice Tests

1. The next three sections of this book begin with a short diagnostic pretest and end with multiple-choice practice questions. Answers and explanations for each question are provided within each section.
2. When you register for the GMAT exam, you will receive PowerPrep® software on a CD-ROM. PowerPrep includes hundreds of practice questions and answers in the same format as the actual GMAT exam as well as a CAT tutorial and math review. You can also download PowerPrep by becoming a registered user of www.mba.com. (No registration fee is required.)
3. The GMAC's *Official Guide for GMAT Review, 10th Edition* contains over 1,400 actual GMAT exam questions with explanations by the test developers. You can purchase this book from the GMAT exam website at www.mba.com/mba/TaketheGMAT/ToolsToHelpYouPrepare/GMATPrepProducts/OfficialGuide.htm.

I Deserve a Reward

One excellent way to keep yourself motivated is to set up a system of rewards. Write down a list of things you enjoy; they will be the rewards to give yourself when you reach certain study goals. For example, if you keep your commitment to study for an hour in the evening, you can reward yourself by watching your favorite television show. If you stay on track all week, you can indulge in a Sunday afternoon banana split. Think carefully about what truly motivates you—only *you* know what will keep you on task—and use this strategy throughout your preparation time.

What's My Style?

Another way to make your study time more effective is to think about how you learn the best. We all have certain modes that we employ to make it easier to learn and remember information. Are you a **visual** learner, an **auditory** learner, a **kinesthetic** learner, or a combination of two or all three? Here are some questions to help you determine your dominant learning style(s):

1. If you have to remember an unusual word, you most likely
   a. picture the word in your mind.
   b. repeat the word aloud several times.
   c. trace out the letters with your finger.

2. When you meet new people, you remember them mostly by
   a. their actions and mannerisms.
   b. their names (faces are hard to remember).
   c. their faces (names are hard to remember).

Go with Your Learning Style

Visual learner

- Form images in your mind.
- Use color codes.
- Use flashcards.

Auditory learner

- Say things out loud.
- Record tapes for yourself.
- Explain things to others.

Kinesthetic learner

- Write it down.
- Walk or move around as you study.
- Act it out.

3. In class you like to
 a. take notes, even if you do not reread them.
 b. listen intently to every word.
 c. sit up close and watch the instructor.

A visual learner would answer **a, c,** and **c.** An auditory learner would answer **b, b,** and **b.** A kinesthetic learner would answer **c, a,** and **a.**

Visual learners like to read and are often good spellers. They may find it hard to follow oral instructions, or even to listen, unless there is something interesting to watch. When visual learners study, they often benefit from graphic organizers such as charts and graphs. Flashcards often appeal to them and help them learn, especially if they use colored markers, which will help them form images in their mind as they learn words or concepts.

Auditory learners, by contrast, like oral directions and may find written materials confusing or boring. They often talk to themselves and may even whisper aloud when they read. They like being read aloud to. Auditory learners will benefit by saying things aloud as they study and by making tapes for themselves and listening to them later. Oral repetition is also an important study tool. Making up rhymes or other oral mnemonic devices will also help them study, and they may like to listen to music as they work.

Kinesthetic learners like to stay on the move. They often find it difficult to sit still for a long time and will often tap their feet and gesticulate a lot while speaking. They tend to learn best by doing rather than observing. Kinesthetic learners may want to walk around as they practice what they are learning, because using their body helps them remember things. Taking notes and making flashcards are important ways of reinforcing knowledge for the kinesthetic learner.

It is important to note that most people learn using a mixture of styles, although they may have a distinct preference for one style over the others. Determine which is your dominant style, but be open to strategies for all types of learners.

▶ I Need a Place

So far, you have gathered information about the GMAT exam and about graduate programs, taken pretests to determine what you need to learn, and thought about techniques that will help you better absorb what you are learning. Now it is time to think about where you are going to work and what kinds of things will enhance your learning experience.

You know that in order to do your best work, especially when you are studying, you need to be focused, alert, and calm. Your undivided attention must be on the task at hand. That means you have to use a lot of forethought when setting up your study time and environment.

Five Questions about Setting

Ask yourself the following questions to determine the study environment that will be most effective for you:

1. *Where do I like to work? Where do I feel comfortable and free from distractions?*

   If you have a desk in your living space, you may be used to studying there, or maybe you usually work at the dining room table or the kitchen counter. If your usual spot is well lit and set up for your comfort and convenience, with all your study materials at hand, then it is an obvious choice for you. However, sometimes it can be hard to avoid distractions in shared living areas.

   If you share a living space, you may find it best to study away from home, perhaps at the local library or coffee shop, or to schedule your study time when you know your study area will be quiet. If you are currently in school, remember that you are adding your GMAT exam preparation time to your usual study schedule. Will this create any scheduling conflicts with your normal study space?
2. *What time of day is best for me to study? When am I most alert and focused? Are there potential conflicts with other duties or family members that need to be addressed?*

   If you are a morning person, it might make sense for you to get up an hour or so earlier than normal while you are preparing for the GMAT exam. Early mornings are often a time of relative quiet, when you can work without interruptions.

   If you do not think so well in the early morning, you can schedule another time of the day as your GMAT exam study time. Just be sure you do not push yourself to stay up extra late in order to study. Studying is only productive if you are focused, and it is difficult to focus when you are tired. (Do not count on caffeine to keep you alert. Caffeine is only a temporary solution that can exacerbate the problem.)

   It is wise to establish a consistent time for study if possible (e.g., Monday through Friday morning from 7:00 A.M. to 7:30 A.M. and Saturday mornings 9:00 A.M. to 12:00 P.M.). Make sure the people around you are aware that this is your study time. You can expect more support for your efforts if you

When Can I Study?

Use this table to determine the times during the week that are available to you for studying. Be sure to respect your sleep time—the more rest you have, the better you will learn and retain information.

	MONDAY	TUESDAY	WEDNESDAY	THURSDAY	FRIDAY	SATURDAY
6:00 A.M.						
6:30 A.M.						
7:00 A.M.						
7:30 A.M.						
8:00 A.M.						
8:30 A.M.						
9:00 A.M.						
9:30 A.M.						
10:00 A.M.						
10:30 A.M.						
11:00 A.M.						
11:30 A.M.						
12:00 P.M.						
12:30 P.M.						
1:00 P.M.						
1:30 P.M.						
2:00 P.M.						
2:30 P.M.						
3:00 P.M.						
3:30 P.M.						
4:00 P.M.						
4:30 P.M.						
5:00 P.M.						

(continued)

When Can I Study?

	MONDAY	TUESDAY	WEDNESDAY	THURSDAY	FRIDAY	SATURDAY
5:30 P.M.						
6:00 P.M.						
6:30 P.M.						
7:00 P.M.						
7:30 P.M.						
8:00 P.M.						
8:30 P.M.						
9:00 P.M.						
9:30 P.M.						
10:00 P.M.						
10:30 P.M.						
11:00 P.M.						
11:30 P.M.						

let family members and friends know you are working to achieve a goal and that you need to stay focused. Be sure to let them know you appreciate their support when you receive it.

Set aside a time to study on the same day of the week and time of the day you have scheduled to take the exam. This is the very best time to prepare for the GMAT exam, especially in the weeks leading up to the test. If you practice taking the test and work on improving your skills on that day and at that time, your mind and your body will be ready to operate at peak efficiency when you really need them. For example, if you are scheduled to take the GMAT exam on Saturday morning, get into the habit of studying for the test during the actual testing hours.

3. *How do sounds affect my ability to concentrate? Do I prefer silence? Does music enhance my concentration?*

Some people need relative quiet in order to study because most noises distract them. If you are one of these people, you know it by now, and you have a repertoire of strategies that help you achieve the level of silence you need. Earplugs can be a real blessing. Make sure your study place and time can accommodate your need for quiet.

Maybe you do not mind a little noise; perhaps you even like music playing in the background while you study. Research has shown that the music of Mozart enhances math performance. Similar results have not been shown for other kinds of music, but if you have music that you know helps you relax and focus, then make sure that music is on hand when you study. If you have never tried studying to classical music, especially Mozart, now is a good time to try. If you do not think it enhances your concentration, then go back to techniques you already know work for you. The important thing is to be aware of the effect sound has on your ability to concentrate. It does not do any good to sit in front of the books and sing along with your favorite CD.

4. *Is the light right? Does my study space have adequate lighting?*

Study lighting needs to be bright enough to read by comfortably. Lighting that is too dim can cause eyestrain and headaches, and can make you sleepy. Lighting that is too bright, though, can make you uncomfortable and make it difficult to relax and focus. You can't control the lighting in many situations, including the exam room itself, but you can create a lighting situation that's right for you when you study.

Experts say the best light for reading comes from behind, falling over your shoulder onto your book. If that isn't a possibility for you, then at least make sure the light falls onto your books, not into your eyes.

5. *What about food? Should I snack while I study? If so, on what?*

Only you can answer these questions. Does food energize you, or does it slow you down while you digest? If you are not sure, pay attention to how your brain and body feel after eating. After a big meal, many people feel sluggish and sleepy as the blood from their brain and muscles goes to the stomach to aid in digestion. If the only time you have to study is right after dinner, you may want to pass on the second helpings and even on dessert so that you will be more alert.

On the other hand, it is also difficult to concentrate when you are hungry. If it has been a while since your last meal, you may want to snack before or as you study. Generally speaking, snacks are fine. However, you want to avoid two categories of foods: sugary snacks (candy, cookies, and ice cream) and caffeinated drinks (coffee, colas, and nonherbal teas).

Sugar surges into your bloodstream quickly, making you feel temporarily energized, but it leaves your bloodstream just as quickly and you experience a rebound effect of feeling more tired than ever. Try keeping track of this effect sometime. See if you can determine how long it takes you to crash after a dose of sugar.

Caffeine is another trickster. In moderation, it produces an effect of alertness, but it is easy to cross the line into being jittery, which makes it hard to focus and be productive. Also, if you consume caffeine in the evening, it can interfere with a good night's sleep, leaving you feeling tired instead of well rested in the morning. It is best to stay away from caffeinated drinks after lunchtime.

▶ The Right Tools

You can spend hours trying to put a nail through a piece of wood with a rock, or you can get the job done in a few minutes with a hammer. The right tools can make all the difference, especially if your time is limited. Fortunately, you already have one of the most important tools for the GMAT exam: this book, which tells you all about the GMAT exam and the information and skills you need to be successful on the exam. You may also want to use the *Official Guide for GMAT Review, 10th Edition,* which is the best source for retired GMAT exam questions. In addition, check out the Skill Builder in Focus series from LearningExpress. Each of these books is designed to help you build proficiency in specific skills tested either directly or indirectly on the GMAT exam:

- *501 Reading Comprehension Questions*
- *501 Grammar and Writing Questions*
- *501 Vocabulary Questions*
- *501 Writing Prompts*
- *501 Challenging Logic and Reasoning Problems*
- *501 Algebra Questions*
- *501 Geometry Questions*
- *501 Math Word Problems*

You should also assemble some other important study tools and keep them in your GMAT exam study area:

- a good dictionary, such as *Merriam-Webster's Collegiate® Dictionary, Tenth Edition*
- a notebook or legal pad dedicated to your GMAT exam notes
- pencils (and a pencil sharpener) or pens
- a highlighter, or several in different colors
- index or other note cards
- paper clips or sticky note pads for marking pages
- a calendar or personal digital assistant (PDA)

Take the time to choose tools that you will enjoy using; they can be a small daily reward for doing your work. Buy the type of pens you like the most and select items in your favorite colors.

Information Gathering

As you gather your tangible tools, you also need to gather your intangible tools: the information you need about the exam so that you can study the right material in the right way at the right time. If you have not already done so, read Chapter 1 of this book to learn about the GMAT exam. Chapter 1 discusses what kind of test it is, what you need to do to register, when you can take the test, what the testing center will be like, and what your scores mean. Part I will also tell you where you can take the GMAT exam, when you should register, how much it costs, and what you can and cannot take with you to the exam.

In addition, Parts II, III, and IV describe in detail the kinds of questions to expect on the GMAT exam and provide you with study tips and strategies for answering them correctly. Obviously, you need to know this information to create an effective study plan.

Before you begin to work out a study schedule, spend a few days or a week or two going through this book, especially the introduction to each section so that you can get a better feel for the exam. For instance, you will learn that critical-reasoning skills are important to your success on both the Verbal section and the Analytical Writing Assessment. If your pretest scores were weak in this area, you may decide to allow extra time for critical-reasoning skills review.

▶ The Study Plan

You have thought about how, when, and where you will study; you have collected your tools and gathered essential information about the GMAT exam. Now, you are ready to flesh out your study plan. Here are the steps:

1. *If you have not done so already, take a practice test.* You can use the pretests at the beginning of Parts II, III, and IV of this book or take one or more of the tests in the *Official Guide for GMAT Review, 10th Edition.* To create an effective study plan, you need to have a good sense of exactly what you need to study.

2. *Analyze your test results.* How did you do? What areas seem to be your strengths? Your weaknesses? Remember that these are just diagnostic tests at this point, so if your results are not as good as you had hoped, do not be discouraged. You are committing to this study plan because you are going to improve your score. Fear and worry are your enemies here; let go of them. Just look at each question as you score it. Why did you answer that question correctly? Did you know the answer or were you guessing? Why did you miss that question? Was there something you needed to know that you did not know? If so, what was it? Make a list of the things you need to know and how many questions you missed because you didn't know them. Think of how your score will improve as you learn these things.

   As you review your practice test results, note whether you missed any questions because you misunderstood the question. This is actually a common problem with the kinds of questions on the GMAT exam, especially the reading comprehension and critical reasoning questions, which often ask for exceptions, and the data sufficiency questions, which are very unusual in their construction. In addition, in general, the language and style of the questions can sometimes seem difficult and unfamiliar. You may become confused, and if you do not understand the question, your chances of answering correctly are not good.

Six Steps to Successful Studying

1. Take a practice test.
2. Analyze your results.
3. List your strengths and weaknesses.
4. Determine your time frame.
5. Break down week-by-week goals.
6. Study! Stick to your plan.

The good news is that, with practice, you will become much better at understanding these kinds of questions. If misreading was the reason why you missed some of the questions, that is actually a good thing. Your preparation time will start paying off immediately.

Did you make a careless mistake on any of the questions? Careless mistakes include marking the wrong bubble and simple misreading, such as mistaking one word or number for another. If you are making careless mistakes, you need to work on focusing. Again, that gets easier with practice.

3. *Make a list of your strengths and weaknesses.* This will point you in the right direction. Use your analysis of why you missed the questions you missed. Now you know what specific math, verbal, and writing skills you need to work on, and you know what test-taking skills you need to improve. Do not forget to congratulate yourself for the areas in which you did well.

4. *Determine your time frame.* Decide how much time you can devote each day and each week to your GMAT exam preparation. Use the chart you filled out on pages 27–28. How many weeks are there until the exam? Be realistic about how much time you have available—life will go on, with all its other demands—but do not forget to note when you have a few extra minutes. You will learn how to make good use of small windows of opportunity.

   Once you know how much time you have, estimate how long you need to work on each specific task you have set for yourself. You may find it useful to break down the Verbal section by question type (reading comprehension, critical reasoning, and sentence correction) and the Quantitative section by subjects, such as arithmetic, geometry, algebra, and data analysis. You may have to prioritize your work in various areas, depending on how much time you have to prepare and in which areas you can most improve your score.

5. *Break it down.* Plan your studying week by week with specific interim goals. For example, "learn everything by April 1" is not a useful plan. But if you plot specific learning goals for each type of question in the Verbal and Quantitative sections throughout the month, then your study plan will be a truly useful study guide.

   Let's say, for example, you have ten weeks until your test date. One way to set up your study schedule is shown on the next page.

When Life Gets in the Way . . .

It's important to stick to your study plan, but sometimes life will get in the way, and you will get off schedule. When this happens—and it almost certainly will—don't despair. Don't let the fact that you have fallen a little behind cripple you so that you fall even more behind. Instead, just keep going. Adjust your schedule to fit your new time frame and do what you can to make up for lost time by squeezing in another hour of study here or there. It may mean you will have to sacrifice some leisure time, but remember what you are working for. A little more sacrifice now can get you much closer to your ultimate goal.

Week One	Learn about and practice reading comprehension skills.
Week Two	Learn about and practice critical reasoning skills.
Week Three	Continue with critical reasoning. Do extra work in *501 Challenging Logic and Reasoning Problems*.
Week Four	Learn about and practice sentence correction skills. Continue with critical reasoning.
Week Five	Learn about the AWA section and review effective writing skills. Practice writing Analysis of Argument essays.
Week Six	Practice writing Analysis of Issue essays. Review all Verbal section skills.
Week Seven	Learn about and practice problem solving skills.
Week Eight	Learn about and practice data sufficiency skills.
Week Nine	Do two practice tests from the *Official Guide for GMAT Review, 10th Edition.*
Week Ten	Review any question types you do not understand. Get lots of rest!

Naturally, if you have longer than ten weeks to prepare, your weekly schedule will be broken up differently. (And good for you for starting ahead of time!) You may want to work on all your skills each week, making progress simultaneously on all fronts. That is fine too. Adjust the schedule accordingly. Your schedule will also be different if you have less than ten weeks, or if you are a whiz with numbers, but have trouble with analytical writing.

6. *Just Do It!* Stick to your plan. It is easy to say, but difficult to do. How can you stay motivated? How do you follow your schedule so that you do not fall behind? How do you keep from thinking about other things when you are supposed to be working? These are the really big questions, and there are no easy answers. The following sections discuss some tried and true techniques for maintaining self-motivation. Now you have to see what works for you.

▶ You Are Worth It: Motivational and Relaxation Techniques That Work

Whenever you find yourself tempted to give up your hard work for an hour or two of entertainment, remind yourself that many people never reach their goals because they seem so far away and difficult to achieve. It is important that you break down your preparation for the GMAT exam into small, manageable steps. It's also important to keep in mind why you are working so hard.

Remember your visualization about business school? The more often you practice that visualization, the more real it becomes to you. The more real it is, the more clearly you will see that your goal is within your grasp. Just stick to your plan, and take things one day at a time.

Sometimes your study plans are derailed for legitimate reasons. You get sick; a family member needs your help; your teacher or boss assigns a project that takes more time than you expected. Life happens, but don't let it discourage you; just pick up where you left off. Maybe you can squeeze in a little extra study time later. Keep working toward your goal.

One Step at a Time

Many people get discouraged when the task seems too big; they feel that they will never get to the end. That's why it's a good idea to break down all big undertakings, such as this one, into smaller, manageable tasks. Set small goals for yourself, such as "this week I will learn logical fallacies." "Learning logical fallacies" is a much more manageable task than "preparing for the GMAT exam"—even though it moves you in the same direction. Establish positive momentum and maintain it, one step at a time. That is how you get where you want to go.

Because You Deserve It

Don't forget to reward yourself for your progress. Your daily reward can be a small one, such as sending off a few chatty e-mails or paging through your favorite magazine. Your weekly reward might be something larger, such as buying a CD you have wanted or renting a favorite film. Your biggest reward, of course, is being able to live out the dreams you have visualized.

Reach Out

Another way to motivate yourself is to get other people to help you. Everybody likes being asked to help someone—it makes those around you feel important, especially when they are being approached for their expertise in a particular area. You will often be more motivated when studying means you also get to be with people whose company you enjoy.

You may want to form a study group with one or more of your friends. Maybe reading comprehension just comes naturally to you, but you struggle with math. Chances are you have a friend who is a math whiz, but who may need help with reading comprehension skills. You could agree to get together once a week or so for a tutoring and drilling session. You take one subject to study and explain, while your friend explains a different subject to you. Now you are benefiting from your friend's expertise, reinforcing what you know by explaining it to someone else, having more fun than you would on your own, and helping yourself (and your friend) stay motivated to study.

Motivation Technique

We all need positive feedback. When you could use some motivational help, say the following out loud (be specific):

My goal is to ______________________________

I am working to achieve my goal.

I will succeed because I am working toward my goal.

A family member or a roommate could also help. If you are working on building your vocabulary, for example, why not make up some flashcards with word roots or prefixes and suffixes, and ask your roommate or a family member to work with you?

Thought Police

Finally, as you struggle to stay motivated, it helps to check in periodically with your thoughts—the things you sometimes find yourself thinking when you should be focusing on your work. If you are thinking, "Oh boy, I'll have that last piece of chocolate when I finish this!" or "Columbia has never seen an MBA student like me" when you sit down to study, you are in good shape. If you are thinking "That TV show I really like is on now," or "I could get in a few hoops before dark," you could be headed for trouble. It's not that there's anything wrong with television or basketball; it is just that you promised yourself you would work right now. Often, just noticing these deviant thoughts is enough to keep them in check. "Good try," you can tell yourself, "but you have other commitments, buster!"

If this doesn't work and you are still tempted to ignore your scheduled study time, sit down and think for a moment about why you are working so hard. Use your visualization. Promise yourself a bigger reward than usual when you finish your work. You can do it because you *want* to do it. This is the person you want to be: disciplined, focused, and successful.

Another strategy is to trick yourself into a study mode. Start with something easy, such as a brief review of what you have already learned. Starting with a quick and easy task will often ease you into the work and motivate you to continue with your self-assigned task of the day. A review will also reinforce what you already know.

Take Care of Yourself

You may have noticed that the last thing on the sample study plan is "get lots of rest." During the last few days before the exam, you should ease up on your study schedule. The natural tendency for many people is to cram. Maybe that strategy has worked for you with other exams, but it is not a good idea with the GMAT exam. For one thing, the GMAT exam is a three-and-a-half-hour test, and you need to be well rested to do your best. For another thing, cramming tends to raise your anxiety level, and your brain doesn't do its best work when you are anxious. Anxiety produces a fight-or-flight response that sends blood away from the brain to the arms and legs, in case we need to defend ourselves or run away. Without a good supply of oxygen-carrying blood,

Stay Away from Cramming!

By creating a study plan, you can avoid cramming, a study technique that will only make you more anxious. If you wait until only a week or two before the exam to prepare, you won't be able to review all of the material and practice the questions enough to perform your best on the exam. If you stay up late night after night trying to get everything done, you will be too tired to study effectively.

Instead, create a study plan that spaces out your learning goals. Give yourself plenty of time to learn and time to review.

your brain won't be able to think as well as it should be able to. So it's important to reduce your anxiety about the GMAT exam by relaxing and changing your anxious attitude to one of calm self-assurance.

How to Relax

If you want to do productive work the night before the GMAT exam, spend the time working on your confidence ("I have worked hard and will do well."). Visualize your business school environment—really see yourself there. Here are some other relaxation techniques you can use if you find yourself feeling anxious at any time before or during the GMAT exam:

1. *Breathe.* When most people think about breathing, they think about breathing in. However, when you want to relax, it's more important to focus on breathing out. You want to be sure you are exhaling completely. It's also important to breathe deeply and to use abdominal breathing rather than shallow chest breathing. Try this: Place one hand on your stomach and the other hand on your chest. Sit up straight. Now inhale deeply through your nose. Try to move your stomach as much as possible and your chest as little as possible. Exhale and feel your stomach deflate. Again, your chest should hardly move. Count slowly as you breathe to make sure you spend at least as much time breathing out as you do breathing in. This kind of breathing relaxes you. It gets rid of carbon dioxide that can otherwise get trapped in the bottom of your lungs. You can practice this deep breathing anytime, anywhere you need to relax.
2. *Tense and relax your muscles.* As your anxiety mounts, your muscles tense, just in case they are going to be called on to fight or flee. Of course, in the case of the GMAT exam, you have to fight with your brain, and running away would result in a very low score. So the best thing you can do is to relax. It can be hard to know which muscles are tensed. Many people hold tension in their shoulders or their jaws and are never even aware it's there. It's helpful to start with your toes and work your way up through all the muscle groups, first tensing (really tightly!) and then relaxing each muscle group. (Tense your toes, and relax. Tense your feet, and relax. Tense your calves, and relax . . .) Don't forget your facial muscles, especially your jaw.
3. *Visualize.* This is a different exercise from your graduate school visualization. This time, imagine yourself in a favorite place, a place you find especially soothing and pleasant. It could be a real place or one found only in your imagination. Focus on the sensations of your special place—what does it feel like,

Three Relaxation Techniques

1. Breathe deeply and completely.
2. Imagine yourself in a special, soothing place.
3. Tense and relax your muscles.

look like, or sound like? You want to feel like you are really there. Take a few minutes to just relax in this place. It's there for you any time you need it, and it will always help you be calm and focused.

▶ Learning Strategies and Test-Taking Techniques

Sometimes you just get lucky, and this is one of those times. Why? Because the following study techniques are also strategies that will help you when you take the GMAT exam. The more you practice them before the exam, the more natural they will be on test day.

Be an Active Reader

Being an active reader means *interacting* with what you read. Ask questions. Make notes. Mark up passages. Don't be a passive reader, just looking at words. Be a thinker and a doer. This is not only a study strategy; it's also an important technique for the GMAT exam's reading comprehension questions and an essential skill in graduate school. Of course, for the GMAT CAT, you won't be marking on the actual passage, which will be displayed onscreen. Therefore, you may want to practice making notes on a separate piece of paper as you read. You should jot down key words, main ideas, and your own reactions to and questions about what you read. On test day, you will write on the scratch paper provided by the test center. You are allowed as much of this paper as you need, so use it.

Ask Questions

When you read a passage, such as the ones on the GMAT exam, ask yourself the following questions:

1. What is this passage about?
2. What is the main idea?
3. What is the author's point of view or purpose in writing this?
4. What is the meaning of this word in this sentence?
5. Is the author stating a fact or expressing an opinion?
6. Is this sentence part of the main idea, or is it a detail?
7. How does the author support the argument?
8. Why does the author draw this particular conclusion?
9. What does this passage suggest about the topic/the author/the future?

The more difficult the passage is, the more crucial it is that you ask these questions (and even more questions) about anything you don't understand. Think about a question as a clue to the answer. When you have asked the right questions, you are halfway to the right answer. These are the kinds of questions you will need to ask in order to answer the exam questions correctly. In business school, you will use the same questioning technique to help you comprehend densely written material (of which you will see plenty). It's essential that you practice asking and answering these questions. Quickly—what is the main idea of this passage?

Until you become very skilled at asking and answering questions about what you have read, it's a good idea to actually write questions out for yourself. For one thing, the act of writing helps you remember what questions to ask, especially for kinesthetic and visual learners. If you are an auditory learner, you will want to repeat them aloud as you write.

Mark It Up

Assuming the book belongs to you, get in the habit of highlighting and underlining when you read. When you open your book, pick up your pen, pencil, or highlighter. When you see a main idea, mark it. If you come across an unfamiliar word or a word used in an unfamiliar context, mark it. However, the trick is to be selective. If you are marking too much of the passage, important information and key ideas will not stand out. You need to practice distinguishing between main and supporting details. (You will learn how in Chapter 5.)

You can practice asking questions and marking main ideas and supporting details by going through the sample test passages in this book and in *Official Guide for GMAT Review, 10th Edition.* Check yourself by looking at the questions about those passages. How well do your ideas match up with the questions about the passages? Check the answers. Were you correct? If not, why not?

On the GMAT CAT, you will write the key words and ideas on your scratch paper. You may want to prepare by practicing this technique as you study for the test. Of course, you will also want to practice it with any borrowed books you use, such as library books.

Make Notes

Don't just *take* notes; *make* them. Making notes requires you to think about what you are reading. Asking questions, such as the ones mentioned previously, is one way to make notes. Another kind of note-making involves recording your reactions to what you are reading. For example, you may disagree with an author's opinion; if so, write down your reaction. Be sure to say why you disagree or agree, or why you are confused. When you read the kinds of challenging materials you will find on the GMAT exam and in graduate school, it should be more like a conversation between you and the author than an author's monologue. So what if the author can't hear you? You can still hold up your end of the conversation. It will be more interesting for you, and you will get more out of what you read.

Make Connections

Another way of interacting with the material you study is to relate it to what you already know. For example, if you are trying to learn the word *demographic*, you may know that *demo*-cracy refers to government run by the *people*, while *graphic* refers to *information*, written or drawn. Then you can remember that *demographic* has to do with information about people.

Making connections differentiates *remembering* from *memorizing*. In the short run, it may seem easier to just memorize a word or a fact, but unless you understand what you are learning—unless you have connected it to what you already know—you are likely to forget it again. Then you will have wasted your study time and failed to improve your test score. Memorized information gets stored in your short-term memory, which means it's forgotten within a few days or even a few hours. Your long-term memory has to file new information to fit in with your existing information. That means you have to create connections to what you already know.

Find Patterns

Success on the Quantitative section of the GMAT exam does not depend on math skills more advanced than algebra; it depends on how well you use basic math as a logical tool. One way to start practicing math logic is to look for patterns in the questions on the practice tests you take. As you look for patterns, you will see that the same kinds of questions appear in different guises. You may realize, for example, that you will be asked about the properties of triangles or about solving inequalities. Then you can practice the kinds of questions you have had difficulty with and learn to master them.

Math is easily learned when you find patterns and make connections that are meaningful for yourself. When you encounter the same type of question on the GMAT exam, you will know how to tackle it and find the right answer.

Break It Up

Just as you do not train to run a marathon by waiting until the last minute and then running twenty miles a day for five days before the race, you cannot effectively prepare for the GMAT exam by waiting until the last minute to study. Your brain works best when you give it a relatively small chunk of information, let it rest and process, and then give it another small chunk.

When you are studying the 24 Rules for Grammar and Style in Chapter 7, for example, don't try to memorize the whole list at once. The most efficient way to learn these rules is to break your list into several smaller lists of five or six rules each and learn one group of rules before tackling the next. Making some kind of connection among the rules in each list will help you remember them. For example, you can group rules about sentence structure together or rules about agreement and consistency. If you decide to review vocabulary, learn words in small chunks, preferably groups of four or five words. Can you relate those five words in some way? If not, can you make up an amusing sentence that uses all five words? Doing this kind of creative work is more fun than rote memorization, and it is easier to learn when you are actively engaged with the material you are studying.

Flashcards are a great study aid for the GMAT exam. The act of writing on the cards engages your kinesthetic learning ability. Seeing the cards uses your visual learning, and reading the cards aloud sets up auditory learning. Flashcards are also extremely portable and flexible in the ways they can be used and help

Five Times to Use Flashcards

1. During commercial breaks
2. While working out on a stationary bike
3. Just before you go to sleep
4. Whenever someone else is willing to help you
5. Any time you have a minute or more

you work on small chunks of material at a time. For example, you can pull them out while you wait for the bus or look through a few while eating breakfast.

Remember, your brain works best when you give it small, frequent assignments and then give it time to process each one. Recent scientific studies show that sleep, especially, helps the brain process what it has learned. In other words, if you study before bed, when you wake up, you will know more than you did before you went to sleep. It's just one more reason for getting a good night's rest.

On the actual exam, it is important to give yourself permission to take a mini-break whenever you need it. If you need to stretch after every question, that's okay. A quick stretch or a deep breath and forceful exhalation can do wonders to keep you focused and relaxed.

▶ Testing Psychology

As you already know, it's important to review reading comprehension techniques, improve your critical reasoning skills, review the rules of grammar and style, practice your writing skills, and brush up on your math as you prepare for the GMAT exam—but it's not sufficient to do *only* these things. Like all standardized tests, the GMAT exam also measures your test-taking skills. In this section, you will learn some of the best test-taking strategies for success on the GMAT exam, including approaches to the AWA. Strategies for each type of question will be discussed in more detail in Parts II, III, and IV of this book.

Get Familiar with the Exam to Combat Fear

In the previous section, you learned that fear (or anxiety) is your enemy on the GMAT exam. What happens when you are feeling fearful or anxious? Your heart starts pounding, sending blood away from your brain to your limbs. Maybe you start feeling a little light-headed, a little disconnected, or even a little woozy. Are you in good condition for test taking then? Of course not!

There is much truth in the saying that we fear what we don't understand. Therefore, the best way to overcome the anxiety that keeps you from doing your best on the GMAT exam is to learn as much as you can about the test. The more you know about what to expect, the more practice you have with the exam, the more relaxed you will be, and the better you will perform on test day.

Taking practice tests and working with the tips and strategies in this book will help you immensely. You will get used to the kinds of questions on the GMAT exam and learn how to maximize your chances of answering them correctly. You will build on what you already know and enhance the skill sets you need for GMAT exam success. By the time you enter the testing center, you will be familiar with the format of the test and prepared for the length of the exam with strategies to help you succeed.

► How to "De-stress"

It's one thing to be told not to worry, and another thing to *actually* not worry. How can you stop yourself from worrying? You can start by replacing worried and anxious thoughts and actions with positive ones. The following sections examine some techniques.

Nip It in the Bud

What are you worried about? Maybe you are worried that you don't have enough time to prepare for the test or perhaps you are afraid you won't do well on the exam. That leads to anxiety about not getting into the right business school. Pretty soon, you are convinced your life is basically ruined, so why not just turn on the TV and resign yourself to a low-paying, dead-end job? Sounds silly when you put it that way, right? But fear has a way of escalating when you do not control it.

The best way to beat test anxiety is to *prevent* it. Don't let it get a good grip on you. Whenever you catch yourself worrying or thinking anxious thoughts about the GMAT exam, firmly tell yourself that you have nothing to worry about because you are preparing for GMAT exam success. Of course, for that strategy to work, you have to establish and stick to your study plan. Therefore, beating test anxiety is made up of two components: *thinking* and *doing.*

Face Your Fears

Different people have different ways of manifesting test anxiety. You may deal with anxiety by working yourself into a frenzy, limiting yourself to six hours of sleep, and refusing to engage in leisure activities so you can get more work done. Meanwhile, your anxiety level mounts. Or you may take the opposite approach and put off work because the task seems so large and the time available so short. Of course, the more you procrastinate, the shorter the time becomes. You end up feeling more anxious so you avoid working and your anxiety level mounts. These two approaches are like two sides of the same coin, and the denomination of the coin is *fear.* Before you can get productive work done, you have to face your fears. Admitting that you are worried about the GMAT exam is the first step toward overcoming those fears.

It can be helpful to write about your anxiety. Start with the basic fear: You are worried you don't have enough time to prepare. Once you have written that fear down, you can come up with a way to eliminate it. Prioritize what you want to study so that you work on the most important skills first. (Start by working your way through this book.) Look at your schedule again. Where can you squeeze in more study time? Remember that flashcards can be studied any time you have one free minute!

Rules of the GMAT Exam Game

1. During test preparation, pretend you are actually taking the test.
2. During the actual test, pretend you are just practicing.

Maybe you've already allowed your anxieties to roam out of bounds by speculating about what would happen if you don't do well on the GMAT exam. Now you are seeing that this is a mistake, so go ahead and write down your fears of failure. What would happen? Would low scores keep you out of business school? No. Perhaps you wouldn't get into your first choice program, but some things in life can't be predicted. If you think hard enough, you can surely remember a time when things didn't work out the way you wanted them to, but they turned out for the best anyway. It's good to make plans and work to achieve your goals, but it's also important to put your goals and plans in perspective.

If you didn't get into your first choice school would you be a less-worthy person? No. Would your family stop loving you? No. Would the world come crashing down around you? Of course not.

Thinking about your fears in this way helps keep them in perspective. You know the GMAT exam is serious business; that's why you are preparing for it. But if you can persuade yourself to think about it as a game you want to play (see the sidebar above), you can control your fear and replace it with a simple, burning desire to win. You have nothing to be afraid of now. You just practice and prepare so that you will succeed on the test.

Just Do It

Half the battle with test anxiety is how you *think* about the test and what kinds of messages you are giving yourself about the exam. The other half is what you *do* to prepare. These two halves are interrelated: If you are paralyzed by negative thoughts ("I'm not ready; I don't have enough time; I'm not smart enough; I don't want to think about the GMAT exam"), you are going to have a hard time getting yourself to do the work you need to do.

On the other hand, if you can somehow get yourself to stop thinking those unproductive thoughts, you can start preparing. The very act of doing something makes you feel better and leads to more positive thoughts, which makes it easier to continue working.

Therefore, it makes sense to just begin work. Start by making a study plan based on the times you have available to study and on your assessment of your practice test results (see the section "The Study Plan" earlier in this chapter). Creating a study plan is easy. You have time to do it. Once you have it in place, you just follow it. You choose success. If you have not already made your study plan, what are you waiting for?

Once you have created a study plan, stick to it as though you had no choice. Of course, you do have a choice. You are choosing how you want your future to unfold. You are doing this for yourself.

► Stay Healthy

If you were preparing to run a marathon, you would be thinking about how to take care of your body. You would want to eat well, get enough rest, and condition your body for its endurance test. Taking the GMAT exam is much like running a marathon. You will need to perform at your mental maximum for three and a half hours on test day. Your body and your mind both need to be ready. Here are the basics of caring for your marathon machine:

1. *Get enough rest.* Some people need more sleep than others. You know how much sleep you need to feel rested. Is it eight hours, or do you need more? Is six enough, or does that make you feel like a zombie the next day? Regardless of your individual need, make sure that you leave yourself enough time every day to get enough sleep. It's also important to remember that too much sleep can leave you feeling as groggy as too little sleep. Get the amount you need to feel rested and no more. The best time of the week to study for the GMAT exam is Saturday morning, so do not sleep through that valuable time. If you regularly get up on Saturday morning and sit down to take a practice test, when exam day comes, you will be ready to do your very best.

   If you find yourself having trouble sleeping, first establish a bedtime routine. Maybe a warm bath or a glass of warm milk helps you relax. Whatever you do, do not get interested in a good book just before bed. Anxious thoughts can also keep you awake, so bedtime is a good time to practice a calming visualization or a series of visualizations using the techniques previously discussed.

   Finally, if nothing seems to be helping you fall asleep, just get up and study. If you cannot sleep, you might as well be productive.
2. *Eat well.* Athletes have to pay attention to what they eat. A marathon runner, for example, maintains a healthy diet during training as well as just before the race. Your brain also needs good food to function at its peak.

   A well-balanced diet based on the food pyramid will keep your body and brain in top form. You are better off avoiding fast food laden with grease, sugar, and empty calories. Rather than junk food snacks, try substituting the following:

INSTEAD OF	EAT
donuts	low-sugar, multigrain cereal
chips	carrot sticks
cookies	natural granola bar
ice cream	low-fat yogurt
soda	fruit juice
coffee	herbal tea

Take Care of Your Body

- Get enough sleep.
- Eat healthy foods.
- Exercise regularly.

Remember that caffeine interferes with sleep when consumed past mid-afternoon. It is also an additive substance that tricks you into feeling more alert. If you feel that you need coffee, maybe what you need is more rest.

3. *Exercise.* Unless you have a daily workout routine, you may not be meeting your body's need for exercise. Our bodies appreciate a good aerobic workout every day. Exercise helps you sleep more soundly and feel more relaxed throughout the day. Vigorous exercise is a great way to combat anxiety because it releases endorphins, the body's natural feel-good chemical.

   Light exercise, such as a walk, can also double as study time. You can study your flashcards during a walk around the neighborhood. You can record an audio tape for yourself to listen to as you run through the park. Get in the habit of identifying times you can double up on studying and another activity to maximize your productivity.

   If you take care of your body and brain by getting enough sleep, eating healthily, and exercising adequately, your body and brain will take good care of you on the GMAT exam. You are in training now: Get with the program.

▶ Multiple-Choice Strategies

As we noted earlier, the GMAT exam, like all standardized tests, will not only measure your academic knowledge and skills, but it will also measure your test-taking skills. Fortunately, you can use specific strategies on standardized tests to help you determine the right answers to multiple-choice questions on the exam.

Avoid Distracters

Except for the two essays in the AWA section, all of the questions on the GMAT exam are multiple-choice questions. The good news about multiple-choice questions is that they provide you with the answer. The bad news is that ETS® almost always provides *distracters* in addition to the correct answer. Distracters are wrong answers designed to look like possible right answers. In the Quantitative and Verbal sections of this book, you will find detailed strategies for separating the correct answers from the distracters. Here is an overview of the basic technique:

1. *Read the question carefully.* Be sure you know *exactly* what is being asked. Many test-takers miss questions on the GMAT exam because they try to answer a question other than the one that is being asked. In particular, look for wording such as "All of the following conclusions can logically be drawn from

the passage EXCEPT." Train yourself to notice any word in the question that is in all capital letters. Such a word will often completely change the meaning of the question. In the previous example, if you did not notice the word *EXCEPT*, you will look for answers that are logical conclusions drawn from the passage when you should be looking for the one answer that is *not* a logical conclusion you can draw from the text.

2. *Write down the key words and phrases in the question.* These are words and phrases that help you pick the one correct answer. Think of them as clues, and think of yourself as a detective who must examine each question closely for clues to the correct answer. For example, if you have a reading comprehension passage about improvements in bicycle safety and then the question "The modern bicycle has all the following safety features EXCEPT," the key words are *modern*, *safety features*, and *EXCEPT*. After you mark these words and phrases, look in the passage for the safety features of the modern bicycle. Then choose the answer that is *not* mentioned in the passage as a safety feature of the modern bicycle.
3. *Rule out incorrect answers.* In the previous example, as you identify safety features of the modern bicycle from the passage, you will mark them off as choices. Because this is such a helpful technique, you will want to seriously consider setting up your scratch paper with choices **a** through **e**. If you actually mark an answer as you eliminate it from your choices, you will know it is not the answer and will not waste time mistakenly considering it again. You may only be able to eliminate one or two incorrect answers, but every wrong answer you eliminate increases your chances of picking the correct answer.
4. *Watch out for absolutes.* The ETS, through years of practice, has become very skillful at encouraging test takers to choose the wrong answer when they are not sure of the right one. Fortunately for you, several categories of distracter answers tend to recur on the GMAT exam. One type of distracter uses an absolute word such as *always, never, all,* or *none* within an answer. Although it is *possible* to find a correct answer that uses such an absolute, if you are unsure, it is wise to avoid an answer that uses one of these words. You will learn in Parts II and IV how to identify other types of distracters and eliminate them from your answer choices.

To Guess or Not to Guess?

On the old paper-based exams, if you did not know the answer to a question, you could skip it and come back to it later. But because the GMAT exam is a CAT, you must select an answer before you can move on to the next question. If you do not know the answer to a question, then you *have to* guess to move on. But guess wisely. No matter what the question, you should be able to eliminate one or two options. If you must guess between two or three possible answers instead of five, you dramatically increase your chances of answering correctly.

▶ The Endgame

If you are reading these words several weeks or more before you take the GMAT exam, you may want to bookmark this page and come back to it the week before the test (got your sticky notes handy?). Your study routine during the last week before the exam should vary from your study routine of the preceding weeks.

The Final Week

Exactly one week before you take the GMAT exam is a good time for your final practice test. Then you can use the next few days to wrap up any loose ends. You should also read back over your notes on test-taking tips and techniques at this time.

During the final week, however, it is also a good idea to cut back on your study schedule. Cramming on grammar rules and math concepts or frantically writing essays now will only make you feel less prepared and more anxious. As mentioned previously, anxiety is your enemy when it comes to test taking. It is also your enemy when it comes to restful sleep, and it's extremely important that you be well rested and relaxed on test day.

You want to substitute more visualization and relaxation for studying. Visualize yourself sitting at the computer in the testing center, working your way through the exam in a calm and focused manner, buoyed by the confidence that you have prepared for this exam. You remain confident even though you don't know all the answers. When you don't know an answer, you apply the techniques you practiced as you worked your way through this book. Picture yourself smiling and stretching as you finish the exam, feeling good about the work you have done. Then imagine the reward you have waiting for yourself after the test. Don't forget to tell yourself out loud, especially if you are an auditory learner, how proud you are of your hard work and how confident you are of your success. If you sound unsure of yourself at first, repeat your words until you sound convincing—then you will believe yourself.

During that last week before the exam, make sure you know where you are taking the test. If it is an unfamiliar place, take a test drive so you will know how much time you need to get there, where you can park, and how far you will have to walk from the parking lot to the testing center. Do this in order to avoid a last-minute rush to the test and any additional anxiety.

Be sure you get adequate exercise during this last week. It will help you sleep soundly, and exercise also helps rid your body and mind of the effects of anxiety. However, don't tackle any new physical skills or overdo any old ones. You don't want to be sore and uncomfortable on test day.

Check to see that your test appointment confirmation and your forms of personal identification are in order and ready to go. You will not need anything else because you are not allowed to bring anything in with you to the testing area.

T Minus One

It's the day before the GMAT exam. You have done your preparation, and you are as ready as you are going to be. Here are some dos and don'ts for this final part of the countdown:

Do

1. Relax!
2. Find something amusing to do the night before—watch a good movie, have dinner with a friend, or read a good book.
3. Get some light exercise. Walk, dance, swim, or do yoga.
4. Get all of your test materials together: confirmation of your appointment and proper identification.

5. Practice your visualization of GMAT exam success.
6. Go to bed early. Get a good night's sleep.

Don't

1. Study. You have prepared. Now relax.
2. Party. Keep it low key.
3. Eat anything unusual or adventurous—save it!
4. Try any unusual or adventurous activity—save it!
5. Allow yourself to get into an emotional exchange with anyone—a sibling, a friend, a parent, or a significant other. If someone starts something, remind him or her that you have a GMAT exam to take tomorrow and need to postpone the discussion so you can focus on the test.

Test Day

On the day of the test, get up early enough to allow yourself extra time to get ready. If you have a morning appointment, set your alarm and ask a family member or friend to make sure you are up. Even if your appointment is later, make sure you don't sleep longer than you usually do. Too much sleep can actually make you feel tired all day.

Eat a light, healthy breakfast, even if you usually don't eat in the morning. If you do usually eat breakfast, eat whatever you normally eat. Remember that sugary things are likely to let you down during the exam. Protein, which can be found in eggs and cheese, is more apt to keep on giving your brain fuel throughout the test. If you do not normally drink coffee, don't do it today. If you do normally have coffee, have one cup. More than that may make you jittery.

If you have scheduled an afternoon test, eat a light but satisfying lunch. Be sure not to stuff yourself before going in. Digestion drains blood from your brain, so it is best to eat at least an hour before exam time. Again, it's best to eat protein because that will give you sustained energy. Stay away from sugar—you can always promise yourself a sweet treat after the test.

Give yourself plenty of time to get to the testing center and avoid a last-minute rush. Plan to get to there at least ten to fifteen minutes early.

Once you are settled at your computer, you will have as much time as you need to run through the testing procedures. They will be identical to the ones you have practiced in PowerPrep®. Your timed exam will start only when you are ready to begin. Just before you begin the actual test is a good time to visualize success one more time. Remember to breathe. Inhale fully into your abdomen and exhale at least as fully. If you feel your body tensing up, practice your relaxation exercises by tensing and releasing muscle groups to help them relax. Breathe.

Once the exam begins, quickly skim the directions. You will already know what to do, so a quick scan of the directions to make sure nothing has changed is all you need.

Remember not to spend too much time on questions you do not understand; you want to answer every question presented to you. On the other hand, take your time on the first ten to fifteen questions. You want to answer them correctly so that the computer will place you in the highest possible range.

You can hide the onscreen clock if you want to, but do check it periodically in each section to see how you are doing on time. You don't want to suddenly realize you have only five minutes and a lot of unanswered questions.

If you find yourself getting anxious during the test, remember to breathe. If you need to, take a minute or two to slip into your relaxation visualization or your visualization of success. You have worked hard to prepare for this day. You are ready.

After the GMAT Exam

Celebrate! Reward yourself for a job well done.

▶ In a Nutshell

As you go through this review book, as you make your study plan, and as you prepare to take the GMAT exam, always remember why you are doing these things. You are doing them for your future and for your dreams, whatever they may be. Whenever you hit a snag, when you feel weary and unmotivated and are tempted to give up, remember why you committed yourself to this path. Call up the vision of yourself, with an MBA or other business school degree in hand, living your dreams. Only you can make that vision a reality, but this book is here to help you take your first step. Read on.

PART

II The GMAT Verbal Section

CHAPTER

3 Verbal Pretest

The Verbal section of the GMAT® exam is the last part of the test, but it is the first section covered in this book because many of the concepts and skills you need to do well on the Verbal section are also important to your success on the Analytical Writing Assessment (AWA) section. In the following chapters, you will learn all about the Verbal section: what this portion of the test is like, what kinds of questions to expect, and how to tackle those questions. You will also review the core skills you will need for each type of question and specific tips and strategies to use on the exam.

Before you begin this section, take a few minutes to do the pretest that follows. The passage and questions on the pretest are the same types you will find on the GMAT exam. When you are finished, check the answer key carefully to assess your results. Your pretest score will help you determine how much preparation you need and the areas in which you need the most careful review and practice.

▶ Pretest

The Verbal section pretest contains 20 multiple-choice questions—approximately half the number of questions you will see on the actual exam. To practice the timing of the GMAT exam, take approximately 37 minutes to complete the pretest. Record your answers on the answer sheet provided on this page. Make sure you mark your answer clearly in the circle that corresponds to the question.

Remember that the GMAT exam is a CAT, so you will not be able to write anywhere on the exam. To mimic the exam environment, do not write on the pretest pages. Make any notes or calculations on a separate piece of paper.

ANSWER SHEET

1.	ⓐ	ⓑ	ⓒ	ⓓ	ⓔ	8.	ⓐ	ⓑ	ⓒ	ⓓ	ⓔ	15.	ⓐ	ⓑ	ⓒ	ⓓ	ⓔ
2.	ⓐ	ⓑ	ⓒ	ⓓ	ⓔ	9.	ⓐ	ⓑ	ⓒ	ⓓ	ⓔ	16.	ⓐ	ⓑ	ⓒ	ⓓ	ⓔ
3.	ⓐ	ⓑ	ⓒ	ⓓ	ⓔ	10.	ⓐ	ⓑ	ⓒ	ⓓ	ⓔ	17.	ⓐ	ⓑ	ⓒ	ⓓ	ⓔ
4.	ⓐ	ⓑ	ⓒ	ⓓ	ⓔ	11.	ⓐ	ⓑ	ⓒ	ⓓ	ⓔ	18.	ⓐ	ⓑ	ⓒ	ⓓ	ⓔ
5.	ⓐ	ⓑ	ⓒ	ⓓ	ⓔ	12.	ⓐ	ⓑ	ⓒ	ⓓ	ⓔ	19.	ⓐ	ⓑ	ⓒ	ⓓ	ⓔ
6	ⓐ	ⓑ	ⓒ	ⓓ	ⓔ	13.	ⓐ	ⓑ	ⓒ	ⓓ	ⓔ	20.	ⓐ	ⓑ	ⓒ	ⓓ	ⓔ
7.	ⓐ	ⓑ	ⓒ	ⓓ	ⓔ	14.	ⓐ	ⓑ	ⓒ	ⓓ	ⓔ						

▶ Reading Comprehension

Directions: Questions 1–6 are based on the following passage. Read the passage carefully and then choose the best answer to each question. Answer the questions based upon what is stated or implied in the reading passage.

In Ursula LeGuin's short story "The Ones Who Walk Away from Omelas," everyone in the city of Omelas is happy—everyone, that is, except the child who is kept locked in a basement closet. The child is left entirely alone and neglected except for occasional visits from the citizens of Omelas. They come at a certain age as a rite of initiation, to learn the secret of the happiness they enjoy. They come to learn that their happiness has a price: the suffering of an innocent child. In the end, most people stay in Omelas; but a few, unable to bear the fact that they are responsible for the suffering of that child, reject this utopia built upon a utilitarian morality.

Utilitarianism is an ethical theory based upon the belief that happiness is the ultimate good and that people should use happiness as the measure for determining right and wrong. For utilitarians, the right thing to do is that which will bring about the greatest amount of happiness for the greatest number of people. Furthermore, utilitarianism argues that the *intention* of people's actions does not matter; only the *consequences* of their actions are morally relevant, because only the consequences determine how much happiness is produced.

Although many useful social policies and much legislation are founded on this "greatest good" philosophy, utilitarianism can be problematic as a basis for morality. First, happiness is not so easy to quantify, and any measurement is bound to be subjective. Second, in a theory that treats everything except happiness as *instrumentally* rather than *intrinsically* valuable, anything—or, more importantly, *anyone*—can (and should) be treated as a means to an end, if it means greater happiness. This rejects the notion that human beings have their own intrinsic value. Further, utilitarianism puts the burden of the happiness of the masses on the suffering of the few. Is the happiness of many worth the suffering of a few? Why do those few deserve to suffer? Isn't this burden of suffering morally irresponsible? This is the dilemma so brilliantly illustrated in LeGuin's story.

1. Which of the following best sums up the author's opinion of utilitarianism?
- **a.** It is an ethical theory.
- **b.** It is the ethical theory that people should all live by.
- **c.** It is a useful but problematic ethical theory.
- **d.** It does not adequately measure happiness.
- **e.** It underestimates the intrinsic value of human beings.

2. According to the passage, in utilitarianism
- **a.** only intentions have moral significance.
- **b.** consequences are important, but intentions are more important.
- **c.** intentions and consequences are equally important.
- **d.** intentions are important, but consequences are more important.
- **e.** only consequences have moral significance.

3. The author summarizes LeGuin's story primarily to
- **a.** show how good the story is.
- **b.** get readers interested in the story.
- **c.** illustrate the power of words.
- **d.** illustrate the central problem with utilitarianism.
- **e.** illustrate a utilitarian utopia.

4. From the passage, it can be inferred that the author
- **a.** may use utilitarianism occasionally but not as a guiding moral principle.
- **b.** would never use utilitarianism to make a decision about what is right or wrong.
- **c.** uses utilitarianism regularly to make moral decisions.
- **d.** believes utilitarianism is a good basis for social policy.
- **e.** thinks most people do not really understand utilitarianism.

5. From the author's summary of LeGuin's story, the reader can infer that
- **a.** most people in Omelas are utilitarians.
- **b.** most people in Omelas reject utilitarianism.
- **c.** everyone in Omelas is happy.
- **d.** the child willingly sacrifices himself for others.
- **e.** LeGuin is a popular science-fiction writer.

6. Utilitarianism could best be expressed in which of the following formulas?

X = action

Y = consequences that create happiness

Z = consequences that create unhappiness

a. Do X if $Y = Z$.
b. Do X if $Y \leq Z$.
c. Do X if $Y \geq Z$.
d. Do X if $Y > Z$.
e. Do X if $Y < Z$.

▶ Critical Reasoning

Directions: For each question, select the best answer from the choices given.

7. Unemployment in Winston County has risen only 4% since I took office. Under my predecessor, unemployment rose 14%. Clearly, my economic policies are far more effective.

Which of the following must be true in order for this argument to be valid?

a. Winston County's population dropped significantly during the current administration.
b. The national unemployment rate increased by 12% during the previous administration but only 2% during the current administration.
c. Key socioeconomic variables such as the state of the national economy and the demographics of Winston County are comparable for each administration.
d. Key policy changes, such as increased job training for the unemployed, were implemented under the current administration.
e. Tax incentives have been implemented to bring new businesses to Winston County.

8. Morning Glory, the coffee shop on the corner, has lost nearly 50% of its business because a national retail coffee chain opened up a store down the street. Instead of closing up shop, the owner of Morning Glory plans to draw in customers by offering coffee, tea, and pastries at much lower prices than the national coffee chain.

The owner's plan of action is based on all of the following assumptions EXCEPT

a. some customers will choose the coffee shop that offers the lowest price.
b. the quality of Morning Glory's coffee is comparable to that of the national coffee chain.
c. Morning Glory can afford to cut its profit margin in order to lower prices.
d. Morning Glory's customers are very loyal.
e. the national coffee chain will not lower its prices in order to compete with Morning Glory.

9. When romance novels were located in the back of the bookstore, they accounted for approximately 6% of total sales. Since we moved romance novels close to the front of the store and put several books on display, sales of romance novels have increased to 14% to 18% of total sales.
All of the following conclusions can logically be drawn from this argument EXCEPT
a. customers who bought one romance novel are likely to come back for another.
b. customers are more likely to buy books located near the front of the bookstore than at the back.
c. the display caught the interest of people who might not have otherwise purchased a romance novel.
d. customers believe that bookstores put their best books near the front of the store.
e. sales of romance novels may increase even more if the section were moved all the way to the front.

10. With more and more classes being offered online, more and more students will earn their degrees in virtual universities. Students in California will graduate from schools in New York without ever leaving their state. Because online courses offer flexibility without geographic boundaries, virtual degrees will be in greater demand, and colleges and universities should invest the bulk of their resources in developing online degree programs.
All of the following, if true, are valid objections to this argument EXCEPT
a. online courses are more time consuming for faculty to develop than regular courses.
b. many students need the ability to attend class outside of regular classroom hours.
c. some students prefer the traditional classroom to the virtual classroom.
d. not every course is suitable for an online environment.
e. there is no way to ensure the authenticity of a student's work in an online environment.

11. Property values in South Orange, New Jersey, have nearly doubled in the last six years. South Orange is located in Essex County, 17 miles from New York City.
Which of the following, if true, best explains the results described in the statement?
a. the proximity of South Orange to New York City
b. the completion of a direct rail line to New York City
c. the addition of 240 housing units in South Orange
d. improved schools and a renovated downtown in South Orange
e. the relocation of a major technical corporation to Union, New Jersey, two miles from South Orange

12. One out of four heart surgery patients at St. Vincent's dies from complications during surgery. Only one out of six heart surgery patients at St. Mary's dies from complications during surgery. If you need heart surgery, make sure you go to St. Mary's, not St. Vincent's.
Which of the following, if true, is the best reason to reject this argument?
a. St. Vincent's specializes in heart surgery for elderly and high-risk patients.
b. St. Mary's surgical equipment is more up to date than St. Vincent's.
c. St. Vincent's has the most renowned heart surgeon in the country on its staff.
d. St. Vincent's offers flexible payment options for balances not covered by insurance.
e. Two doctors who used to work at St. Mary's now work at St. Vincent's.

13. DNA evidence has increasingly been used in court to prove guilt and to exonerate the innocent. Because so many convicted felons have been cleared by DNA evidence, all cases in which someone was convicted largely on circumstantial evidence should be called into question and reviewed. Which of the following, if true, would most strengthen this argument?

a. One in three convictions today rests largely on DNA evidence.
b. DNA evidence is admissible even after the statute of limitations has expired.
c. Of every ten cases in which DNA evidence becomes available post-conviction, five convictions are overturned.
d. DNA evidence is 99.8% accurate.
e. DNA evidence is very difficult to falsify or tamper with.

► Sentence Correction

Directions: The following questions each present a sentence, part or all of which is underlined. Beneath the sentence you will find five ways of phrasing the underlined portion. The first choice repeats the original; the other four choices present different options for phrasing the underlined text. Determine which choice *best* expresses the idea in the underlined text. If you think the original is best, choose option **a.** These questions test both the correctness and overall effectiveness of expression. In choosing your answer, pay attention to grammar, sentence construction, and word choice and style. The correct answer is free of grammatical errors, clear, precise, and concise.

14. Despite growing evidence of global warming; 34 different states plan to develop nearly 100 new coal-burning electric plants in the next decade.

a. warming; 34 different states
b. warming. Thirty-four different states
c. warming: 34 different states
d. warming, 34 different states
e. warming, for 34 different states

15. Suggested by new research is the fact that people who achieve phenomenal success do so, not only by visualizing their success in future endeavors, but also, by recalling their past successes, creating a tremendous surge in confidence.

a. Suggested by new research is the fact that people who achieve phenomenal success do so, not only by visualizing their success in future endeavors, but also, by recalling their past successes, creating a tremendous surge in confidence.
b. New research suggests that people that achieve phenomenal success visualize their success in future endeavors and also recall their past successes to create a tremendous surge in confidence.
c. New research suggests that the achievement of phenomenal success by persons is accomplished not only by the visualization of success in future endeavors but also by the recollection of past successes, which creates a tremendous surge in confidence.

d. New research suggests that people who achieve phenomenal success do so not only by visualizing their success in future endeavors but also by recalling their past successes, creating a tremendous surge in confidence.

e. New research suggests that people who achieve phenomenal success do so not only by visualizing their success in future endeavors, but also they recall their past successes, creating a tremendous surge in confidence.

16. Creating a fundamental shift in American foreign policy and establishing a "policy of containment" that framed our foreign policy as a battle between the forces of good (America and other democratic societies) and evil (the Soviet Union and other communist nations), was the 1947 Truman Doctrine.

a. Creating a fundamental shift in American foreign policy and establishing a "policy of containment" that framed our foreign policy as a battle between the forces of good (America and other democratic societies) and evil (the Soviet Union and other communist nations), was the 1947 Truman Doctrine.

b. The 1947 Truman Doctrine created a fundamental shift in American foreign policy, establishing a "policy of containment" that framed our foreign policy as a battle between the forces of good (America and other democratic societies) and evil (the Soviet Union and other communist nations).

c. Creating a fundamental shift in American foreign policy was the Truman Doctrine, which was put forth in 1947, and which established a "policy of containment" that framed our foreign policy as a battle between the forces of good (America, along with other democratic societies) and the forces of evil (the Soviet Union, along with other communist nations).

d. The 1947 Truman Doctrine created a fundamental shift in American foreign policy, establishing a "policy of containment" that framed our foreign policy as a battle between American and other democratic societies, which it considered the forces of good, and the Soviet Union and other communist nations, which it considered the forces of evil.

e. A fundamental shift in American foreign policy was created in 1947 by the Truman Doctrine, which importantly established a "policy of containment," a policy that framed our foreign policy in terms of a battle between good and evil, with the good forces being America and other democracies and the evil forces being the Soviet Union and other communist nations.

17. The first science-fiction novel, Mary Shelley's Frankenstein, actually contains very little science, but it masterfully explores the social and moral repercussions of what might happen if certain scientific advances were possible.

a. but it masterfully explores the social and moral repercussions of what might happen

b. but it explores in a masterful way the social and moral repercussions of what might happen

c. but, exploring the social and moral repercussions, it masterfully considers what might happen

d. but it masterfully explores repercussions, social and moral in nature, of what might happen

e. but it masterfully explores what are the social and moral repercussions

18. The most important issue relating to computer technology and the Internet is the right of individual privacy, this includes the privacy of our personal data and our actions in cyberspace.

a. Internet is the right of individual privacy, this includes the privacy
b. Internet is the right of individual privacy, being the privacy
c. Internet is the right of individual privacy, including the privacy
d. Internet is the right of individuals to have privacy, and included in this consideration is the privacy
e. Internet is an individual's right to privacy. Including the privacy

19. While diabetes does not interfere with digestion, on the other hand, it does prevent the body from converting an important product of digestion, *glucose*, which is commonly known as sugar, into energy.

a. While diabetes does not interfere with digestion, on the other hand, it does prevent the body from converting an important product of digestion, glucose, which is commonly known as sugar, into energy.
b. Diabetes does not interfere with digestion, but it does prevent the body from using glucose, which is commonly known as sugar, which is a product of digestion and which is converted into energy.
c. Commonly known as sugar, glucose is an important product of digestion, which is prevented from being converted by the body into energy by diabetes, although diabetes does not interfere with digestion.
d. Diabetes does not interfere with digestion, but it does prevent the body from converting an important product of digestion, glucose (commonly known as sugar), into energy.
e. Diabetes does not interfere with digestion, but glucose (commonly known as sugar) is an important product of digestion and is unable to be converted into energy by the body because of the disease.

20. With an increasing amount of vegetarians, more stores are beginning to stock their shelves with standard vegetarian fare, such as soy milk and tofu.

a. With an increasing amount of vegetarians
b. With the number of vegetarians on the rise
c. With the number of vegetarians, which is on the rise
d. Increasingly, there are more and more vegetarians, so
e. Increasing in number are vegetarians, so

▶ Answer Explanations

1. c. The author is critical of utilitarianism, but she also includes evidence that it is a useful theory. LeGuin's story, for example, shows how the sacrifice of one can create the happiness of many. The author also notes that "many useful social policies and much legislation are founded on" utilitarianism, demonstrating that it is a useful ethical theory. The word choice throughout also indicates that the author feels that this ethical theory has both positive and negative aspects. For example, she calls it "problematic," but not "wrongheaded" or "faulty." She calls the problem of the suffering of the few for the happiness of the many a "dilemma," not a "flaw" or "failure." She asks questions rather than making statements about the immorality of utilitarian choices. Choice **a** is incorrect because it simply states a fact from the essay; it does not express an opinion. The author clearly states that "there are several serious problems with utilitarianism as a basis for morality," so choice **b** is incorrect. Although the statements in choices **d** and **e** are true and clearly stated in the text, these are *specific* criticisms of utilitarianism and do not *sum up* the author's opinion of this ethical theory.

2. e. In the second paragraph, the author states that "only the *consequences* of [people's] actions are morally relevant, because only the consequences determine how much happiness is produced."

3. d. LeGuin's story illustrates the problem with utilitarianism by describing how one person (the child) lives in misery so that others can be happy. The author explains that "utilitarianism puts the burden of the happiness of the masses on the suffering of the few" and then states that this problem is "so brilliantly illustrated in LeGuin's story." Choice **a** is incorrect because the author does not comment on or make any inferences about the overall quality of the story; she only comments on it in relation to its demonstration of the dilemma of utilitarianism. Readers may be interested in the story after reading this passage (choice **b**), but again, the purpose of including the story is made evident by the last sentence in the passage. The author does not quote directly from the story, and she is clearly not summarizing it to illustrate the power of words, so choice **c** is incorrect.

4. a. The author is critical of utilitarianism and admits it has several problems, but she does not reject it as an ethical theory. In fact, she concedes that it is useful in creating social policies and legislation. Therefore, the most logical inference is that she may use utilitarianism occasionally but not as a guiding moral principle. Choices **b** and **c** are therefore incorrect. Choice **d** is incorrect because nothing in the passage indicates how she feels about utilitarianism as a basis for social policy. The passage does not state that she believes most people do not really understand utilitarianism, so choice **e** is incorrect.

5. a. The author states that "most people stay in Omelas" after they have visited the child. This indicates that they understand and have accepted the utilitarian nature of their society. Only a few walk away and reject the society, so choice **b** is incorrect. The summary clearly states that everyone *except* the child and the ones who are "unable to bear the fact that they are responsible for the suffering of that child" are happy, so choice **c** is incorrect. No evidence indicates that the child willingly sacrifices himself for others (choice **d**). The passage makes no reference to LeGuin's popularity or success as a science-fiction writer, so choice **e** is incorrect.

6. d. The basic principle of utilitarianism as explained in the passage is that people should do "that which will bring about the greatest amount of happiness for the greatest number of people." Therefore, humans should choose actions that will have more happy consequences (Y) than unhappy consequences (Z); Y must be greater than (>) Z.

7. c. In order for the two administrations to be compared, the socioeconomic variables must be comparable. If Winston County's economy had relied largely upon a factory that closed down during the previous administration, then the unemployment rate would necessarily rise considerably following that event. The state of the national, state, and local economies and the demographic makeup of

Winston County (e.g., no significant increase or decrease in population) need to be nearly identical for the speaker to make a fair comparison and claim that his or her policies are more effective. If Winston County's population dropped significantly (choice **a**), it could explain why the unemployment rate dropped as well—but it does not support the speaker's claim that his or her policies "are far more effective." Choice **b**, which reflects the state of the national economy, also offers an explanation for the change in unemployment rates in Winston County, again contradicting the speaker's claim that his or her economic policies made the difference. If the speaker had implemented key policy changes (choice **d**) or tax incentives (choice **e**), they could have significantly reduced unemployment. However, the unemployment rates still cannot be compared unless other variables are comparable.

8. **d.** The owner's plan—to lower prices to attract customers—assumes that some customers will choose the lower price (choice **a**), that the quality of Morning Glory's products is comparable to its competitor (choice **b**), that Morning Glory can afford to offer lower prices (choice **c**), and that its competitor will also not lower its prices (choice **e**). The plan does not rest on any assumptions about the loyalty of Morning Glory customers (choice **d**). Indeed, there is evidence that the customers are *not* loyal, because Morning Glory has already lost 50% of its business.

9. **a.** The significant increase in sales after the relocation of the books indicates that customers are more likely to buy books at the front of the store (choice **b**) and that the display may have caught the interest of people who might not otherwise purchase a romance novel (choice **c**). It is also logical to conclude that sales would further increase if the books were moved even farther toward the front of the store (choice **e**). Choices **b** and **e** and the increase in sales all suggest that customers believe the best books are near the front of the store (choice **d**). The only conclusion that cannot logically be drawn from this scenario is that customers will come back to purchase more romance novels (choice **a**). The data does not indicate repeat purchases for customers.

10. **b.** All of the choices except **b** offer reasons why online degree programs are problematic, suggesting that resources should not be focused on developing online degree programs. Choice **b** offers support for the argument by stating that the flexibility of online classes will attract students who would not normally be able to attend regular classes.

11. **b.** The direct rail line is the most logical explanation for an increase in property values. The proximity to New York City in itself (choice **a**) would not necessarily increase property values, but the addition of public transportation that provides direct access to the city would make the town a more desirable place to live. When a place becomes more desirable, real-estate values increase. Choice **c**, the addition of housing units, is likely an *effect* of the direct rail line and an increase in the desirability of the location. The improvement of the schools and the renovation of the downtown (choice **d**) may or may not be related to the increase in property values. It would be logical to conclude that funds for improving the schools and downtown could be gleaned from additional resources from increased property taxes, another *effect* of increased property values. The relocation of a major corporation to a neighboring town (choice **e**) could account for the increased desirability of property in South Orange, but the direct access to the city is a more compelling reason. Perhaps a few hundred persons may work in the corporation, but many thousands are likely to want an easy commute to the city.

12. **a.** Statistics can be very deceiving. In this case, based only on the numbers, St. Mary's seems like a safer place to undergo heart surgery. But what you do not know about St. Mary's and St. Vincent's can lead you to make a poor choice. If St. Vincent's specializes in heart surgery for elderly and high-risk patients (choice **a**), then it is logical that it would have a higher rate of mortality among its patients. Indeed, given this fact, the difference in mortality rates may make a case for going to St. Vincent's instead of St. Mary's. Assuming you are not an elderly or high-risk patient, to make an informed choice, you would need statistics about St. Vincent's mortality rates for surgery on patients who are not elderly or high risk. Up-to-date equipment is important (choice **b**), but the condition of the patients prior to surgery and the skill of the surgeons are more important considerations. The fact that St. Vincent's has the best heart surgeon in the country (choice **c**) is compelling, but it does not contradict the statistics. The payment options (choice **d**) are irrelevant if you do not survive the surgery, and there can be many reasons why the doctors who worked at St. Mary's are now at St. Vincent's (choice **e**), so you cannot consider this factor without more information.

13. **c.** The fact that would most strengthen this argument is the percentage of cases in which DNA evidence overturned prior convictions. If half of all cases resulted in erroneous convictions that were later cleared by DNA evidence, then that should certainly draw other convictions into doubt. The fact that one in three of today's convictions rest on DNA evidence has no bearing on prior convictions, so choice **a** is incorrect. Similarly, the admissibility of DNA evidence (choice **b**) has no bearing on the quality of prior convictions. That DNA evidence is accurate (choice **d**) and difficult to tamper with (choice **e**) strengthens the argument for the use of DNA evidence in court, but it does not directly strengthen the argument that prior convictions should be called into doubt.

14. **d.** *Despite growing evidence of global warming* is a dependent clause that should be followed by a comma when preceding an independent clause (*34 different states . . .*). Choice **a** is incorrect because a semi-colon should not be used between a dependent and independent clause. Choice **b** creates a sentence fragment because the dependent clause is set off as a separate sentence. Choice **c** incorrectly uses a colon, which should only be used to introduce lists, quotations, or explanations. Choice **e** creates an illogical sentence that uses both *despite* and *for*, confusing the relationship between the two clauses.

15. **d.** This version states the idea clearly, correctly, and concisely, using parallel structure. Choice **a** is bulky and awkward with its opening phrase *suggested by new research is the fact that*; it also has several superfluous commas. Choice **b** incorrectly uses *that* instead of *who* to refer to *people*, and while it is not wordy, it is not as fluent as choice **d**. Choice **c** is wordy, relying on bulky passive constructions and prepositional phrases. Choice **e** is incorrect because it lacks parallel structure.

16. **b.** This version is the most active and direct, starting with the agent of action (the Truman Doctrine) and clearly and concisely stating the effects of the doctrine. Choices **a** and **c** awkwardly put the action before the subject, and choice **c** also breaks up the two actions, interrupting the fluency of the sentence. Choice **d** uses two bulky *which* clauses, rather than the more concise parenthetical phrases of choice **b**. Choice **e** begins with a passive construction and is both wordy and redundant.

17. **a.** This is the most concise, precise, and correct choice. Choice **b** is wordy, using the phrase *in a masterful way* instead of *masterfully*. Choice **c** uses awkward word order that requires the addition of a verb (*considers*) because *explores* is moved to before the subject. Choice **d** is wordy as the result of moving *social and moral* from their position directly before the noun they modify. Choice **e** awkwardly places *what are* after *explores* and deletes the important idea of possibility conveyed by *of what might happen*.

18. **c.** Choice **a** is a run-on sentence and is therefore incorrect. Choice **b** uses *being* in an awkward and grammatically incorrect manner. Choice **d** is unnecessarily wordy, and choice **e** replaces the comma with a period and creates a sentence fragment.

19. **d.** This is the most concise and fluent version. Choice **a** incorrectly uses the transitional phrase *on the other hand*, and because it puts *which is commonly known as sugar* into a nonrestrictive clause immediately after the appositive *glucose*, the sentence may be confusing. Choice **b** is grammatically correct but quite awkward, using *which* three times in one sentence. Choice **c** inverts the sentence, making it less direct and therefore less clear. Choice **e** is correct but less direct and slightly more wordy than **d** because it uses the passive construction (*converted by the body*).

20. **b.** Choice **b** presents the most concise and fluent version. Choice **a** incorrectly uses *amount* instead of *number*. Choice **c** is unnecessarily wordy, using the nonrestrictive phrase *which is on the rise* instead of *on the rise*. Choice **d** is also unnecessarily wordy and less direct. Choice **e** is awkward, with an inverted word order.

▶ Pretest Assessment

How did you do on the pretest? If you answered nearly all of the questions correctly, congratulations. If you missed more than three questions, chances are most of your incorrect answers were in one category. Perhaps your reading comprehension skills are strong, but you need to focus on building your critical-reasoning skills. Clearly, the more questions you got wrong in each section, the more time you should devote to your review of that material.

It is difficult to scale your performance on this pretest to its actual GMAT equivalent because the GMAT CAT factors in both the number of questions answered and the level of difficulty of each question to determine your score. However, a simple percentage of correct answers in each category should give you a good indication of how you might perform on the Verbal section. If you missed three or more questions in any section, you will probably need several weeks of concentrated study to do well on those questions during the actual exam.

CHAPTER

4

What to Expect on the GMAT Verbal Section

The GMAT® Verbal section actually covers a rather varied and complex set of knowledge and skills. In this chapter, you will learn all about the Verbal section, including what types of questions it includes and what kinds of skills it measures.

Based on the title "Verbal section," you might expect this portion of the exam to measure your oral communication skills or your ability to express yourself effectively in writing. But that is not quite what the Verbal section is about. It is designed to measure three rather different groups of skills. The questions on the GMAT Verbal section can be divided into the following categories:

- **reading comprehension questions** that test your ability to read and understand sophisticated written texts
- **critical reasoning questions** that test your reasoning skills and ability to evaluate arguments
- **sentence correction questions** that test your knowledge of standard written English and the elements of effective writing

The 41 multiple-choice questions in the Verbal section are divided evenly among these three types. Each category contains approximately 13–14 questions, and you will have 75 minutes to complete this portion of the test.

► Reading Comprehension Questions

You have probably taken many tests with reading comprehension questions in your academic career, and you probably have a good idea what to expect from this portion of the Verbal section. You will be given between three and five reading passages of 150 to 350 words each. You will then be asked a series of multiple-choice questions about each passage. Each question will have five answer choices; you must choose the best answer.

Types of Passages

The reading comprehension passages on the GMAT exam are usually academic in nature. They may cover any topic from the physical or life sciences, social sciences, humanities, or business, but you do *not* need to be familiar with the topic to be able to answer the questions. The questions test what you understand and can logically infer from the information in the text, not what you may already know about the topic.

The writing in these passages is serious and sophisticated. You can expect college-level material of the sort you might see in graduate school. Most passages will contain between four and seven paragraphs and are about 150 to 350 words long. You will typically be asked three to five questions about each passage.

The passages on the GMAT exam are either **informative** or **argumentative**. An informative passage might, for example, explain Einstein's theory of relativity, evaluate its impact on science and society, or discuss how current findings in physics are forcing a revision of Einstein's theory. An argumentative passage, on the other hand, might argue that Einstein's theory of relativity is the most important scientific discovery of the twentieth century; that the theory of relativity dramatically altered humans' understanding of themselves, their place in the universe, and their relationships to each other; or that a revision of the theory of relativity will encourage more research in the existence of other dimensions. Some passages are *both* informative and argumentative. For example, a passage may explain the theory of relativity in the first three paragraphs and argue in the last three that it is the most important scientific discovery of the twentieth century.

Types of Questions

The GMAT Verbal section has essentially four types of reading comprehension questions:

- **Basic comprehension** questions test your ability to understand the words and ideas expressed in the passage. You may be asked about the main idea of the text or the best way to paraphrase a definition or key concept discussed in the passage. Questions 1 and 2 from the pretest are examples of basic comprehension questions.
- **Analysis** questions test your ability to see the structure of a passage and the relationship between the ideas in the passage. You may be asked to identify the main idea, to distinguish between main and supporting ideas, to identify the strongest support, or to identify the organizational pattern of the text. You may also be asked about the effect of the organization or other techniques or the relationship between ideas discussed in the text. Question 3 from the pretest is an example of an analysis question.
- **Inference** questions test your ability to draw logical conclusions based upon the facts and ideas expressed in the passage. You may be asked how the author might feel about a related subject, for

example, or why the author includes certain passages or uses certain techniques in the text. Questions 4 and 5 from the pretest are examples of inference questions.

- **Quantitative interpretation** questions test your ability to understand quantitative concepts expressed in textual (as opposed to graphic) form and interpret the numerical data to draw conclusions about the text. For example, you may be asked which prediction about the subject is most logical based on the quantitative information in the passage or to use that information to determine which aspect or feature of the subject has a particular characteristic (e.g., "Which experiment resulted in the most dramatic change for participants?"). Question 6 from the pretest is a quantitative interpretation question; it asks how the idea expressed in the text might be represented in quantitative form.

▶ Critical Reasoning Questions

Although many standardized test questions indirectly test critical thinking skills, the kind of critical reasoning questions you will find on the GMAT exam may be new to you. As you saw on the pretest, each critical reasoning question presents you with a short argument followed by a question stem and five multiple-choice options. The exam contains approximately 13–14 critical reasoning questions. If the pretest was your first experience with this type of question, do not worry. By the end of this section, critical reasoning questions and the skills you will need to answer these questions correctly should be very familiar to you.

Types of Passages

Critical reasoning questions, like reading comprehension questions, are based upon reading passages about a wide range of topics, but they have a few important differences. For one thing, the critical-reasoning passages are much shorter—only one or two paragraphs—and each passage only has one question. More importantly, each passage presents an argument (or at least part of an argument). Some of these arguments will be logical and well reasoned; others will be built upon faulty logic or invalid assumptions. As with the reading comprehension passages, you do not need to know anything about the topic discussed in the passage in order to answer the question correctly. In fact, sometimes your knowledge of the topic can interfere with making the correct choice. It may lead you to choose an answer that is not supported by the information in the passage.

Types of Questions

To measure your critical thinking skills, the GMAT exam presents you with three types of critical reasoning questions:

- **Structure** questions test your ability to recognize basic argument structure. For example, you may be asked to identify the conclusion, premises, or underlying assumptions of an argument. Questions 9 and 11 from the pretest are structure questions.

Common Question Stems

Because critical reasoning questions may be new to you, their format might take some getting used to. The following is a sampling of the kind of stems you might see on critical reasoning questions:

- All of the following are valid objections to the argument EXCEPT
- The statements, if true, best support which of the following assertions?
- If the information in the statement is true, which of the following must also be true?
- If the information in the statement is true, all of the following statements must also be true EXCEPT
- The argument is based upon all of the following assumptions EXCEPT
- All of the following conclusions can reasonably be drawn from the argument EXCEPT
- Which of the following, if true, would most strengthen the argument?
- Which of the following, if true, would most seriously weaken the argument?

- **Evaluation** questions test your ability to measure the effectiveness of an argument and recognize common errors in reasoning. You might be asked to identify factors that would strengthen or weaken the argument, for example, or which aspect of the argument rests on faulty logic. Questions 7, 10, 12, and 13 from the pretest are evaluation questions. The majority of critical reasoning questions on the GMAT exam will probably fall into this category.
- **Extension** questions test your ability to determine effective and appropriate plans of action. You may be asked to evaluate the effectiveness and appropriateness of a proposed plan of action or to identify what assumptions underlie a particular proposal. Question 8 from the pretest is an extension question.

► Sentence Correction Questions

Sentence correction questions should return you to more familiar ground, as you are likely to have seen questions of this sort on previous standardized tests. This last group of 13–14 questions presents you with sentences that sound like they have been excerpted from newspaper or magazine articles, academic journals, or nonfiction books or textbooks. In other words, the sentences will likely be serious and complex. Once again, the passages can be about any topic, but you do not need to know anything about the topic to answer the question correctly.

For each question, part or all of the sentence is underlined. You must determine which of the five multiple-choice answers is the most correct and effective way to express the idea in the underlined portion of the sentence.

Types of Questions

Sentence-correction questions are designed to measure two related but distinct aspects of effective writing: *grammar* and *style.* These questions test your ability to identify and correct errors in standard written English and your understanding of what makes effective writing on the *sentence level only.* In contrast, the AWA tests your ability to write effectively on three levels: the essay level, the paragraph level, and the sentence level. Although the AWA requires you to actually write your own essay, in this section, you do not have to write your own sentences. You do *not* need to identify errors in mechanics, including spelling, capitalization, or punctuation, *except* as punctuation affects sentence boundaries and clarity. For example, you will not find sentences with misspelled words, improper capitalization, or misused hyphens or apostrophes, but you will find sentences that use a comma when a period should be used or sentences that misuse semicolons—punctuation issues that deal with establishing the right relationship between clauses and answers.

- **Grammar** questions test your knowledge of the rules and conventions of standard written English, including correct sentence structure, idioms, and parallel structure. You will need to determine whether sentences have errors such as run-ons or fragments, inconsistent verb tense, or unparallel structure. You will *not* need to identify errors in mechanics, including punctuation, spelling, or capitalization. These skills are not tested on the GMAT exam.
- **Style** questions test your ability to identify sentences that are clear, precise, and concise. You will see many versions of sentences that are wordy, redundant, vague, awkward, and/or ambiguous. You will need to determine which version expresses the idea with the most clarity, precision, and concision.

These three types of questions will be presented in random order throughout the exam. Thus, your GMAT exam may begin with three or four questions based on a reading comprehension passage, then a sentence correction question, then two critical reasoning questions followed by another sentence correction question and reading comprehension passage.

CHAPTER

5 Reading Comprehension

In business school, you will be expected to read quite a lot—and much of what you read will be quite sophisticated. But the skills you need to comprehend these texts are the same skills you have been using for years. This section will review those essential reading comprehension skills and discuss how you can apply them to the GMAT® Verbal section.

Active Reading

Strong reading skills begin with *how* you read. People often think that reading is a passive activity—after all, you are just sitting there, looking at words on a page. But reading should actually be a highly active exercise in which you *interact* with the text. Whenever you read—for the GMAT exam, for class, or for pleasure—these active reading strategies can dramatically increase your comprehension of texts.

Preview and Review

Although it only takes a few seconds to **preview** a reading-comprehension passage, it can make a tremendous difference in how much you understand from the text. Before you begin reading, quickly *scan* the text. As you

Learn a Word a Day

Want to build your vocabulary? Try setting your Internet browser homepage to one of these word-a-day websites:

- www.mywordaday.com
- www.dictionary.com/wordoftheday/
- www.oed.com/cgi/display/wotd
- www.nytimes.com/learning/students/wordofday/
- www.wordsmith.org/awad

skim through the passage, you will see how the text is broken up and get a sense of what the passage is about. You will get a feel for how the writer has organized his or her ideas and the main point that will be developed in the text. You will notice key words and ideas, especially those that are boldfaced, bulleted, boxed, or otherwise highlighted in the text.

Previewing works by planting context and comprehension clues in your mind. If you have a rough sense of what is ahead, you will be more prepared to absorb and understand the text when you return for a more careful read. The same principle is true for just about any discipline or skill. If you know what to expect, you will be more comfortable and alert when you take on that task—and that means you will perform it better.

When you finish a careful reading, quickly skim through the text once more. This review will help you get a better sense of the whole—the controlling idea of the passage, the overall organization, and the connections between ideas in the text. You can see the emphasis of the passage and the writer's tone. A quick review will also help you better understand and remember key terms and ideas in the text.

Expand Your Vocabulary

Although the GMAT exam does *not* directly test your vocabulary, it does use texts that include sophisticated terms. Thus, the stronger your command of English words, the easier it will be to comprehend what you read. After all, you need to know what all the words in a sentence mean to fully understand what someone is saying, and understanding a key word or phrase can change your understanding of a whole passage.

One of the best ways to build your vocabulary is to *always* look up words you do not know. Whenever possible, have a dictionary with you when you read. Circle and look up any unfamiliar words right away. (Circling them makes them easier to find if you lose your place.) Write the meaning of the word in the margin so you will not have to look up the meaning again if you forget it; it will always be there for you to refer to. If you do not own the book, write the vocabulary word and its definition in a notebook. Keep your own vocabulary log and review it periodically to seal those words and their meanings in your memory.

If you do not have a dictionary with you, try to figure out what the word means from its **context**. What clues does the author provide in the sentence and surrounding sentences? At a minimum, you should usually be able to determine whether the word is positive or negative. (For example, in the sentence *The negotiations were stymied by the union's refusal to consider an alternate benefits package*, you can tell that *stymie* is not a good thing, even if you do not know exactly what the word means.) Mark the page or write down the word somewhere so you can look it up later. See how closely you were able to guess its meaning. The more you practice determining meaning from the context, the more accurately you will be able to guess at those meanings and understand material at test time.

Mark Up the Text

As you read, mark up the text (or notepaper if the text does not belong to you). This includes the following three strategies:

- Highlight or underline key words and ideas.
- Take notes.
- Make notes.

See pages 138–139 to review these important active reading strategies.

Of course, on the GMAT CAT, you cannot mark up the computer screen, but you *can* take effective notes on scratch paper. Take notes as you read, marking down key words and ideas as you go. Write down the main idea of each paragraph in the text so you can form a rough outline of the passage. This will help you see its structure and the relationship of ideas in the essay. Notes on the utilitarianism passage from the pretest, for example, might look like the following:

- Omelas: *child sacrificed 4 happiness of others*
  a few reject this society
- Utilit'ism: *happiness ultimate good*
  right = greatest happiness 4 greatest #
  only consequences matter
- Probs: *happiness subjective, how to measure*
  people as means to end
  burden of happiness on few who must suffer

Notice how these notes outline the passage, highlighting the main points of each paragraph. This makes it much easier (and faster) to find the correct answer.

As you read passages on the GMAT exam, you can make notes about your own reactions to the text, but be sure to use these notes only as a means of deepening your understanding of the material. On the GMAT exam, the reading comprehension questions are strictly limited to your understanding of the material in the passage. You will *not* be asked your opinion of the ideas in the text. *Do not let your personal reaction to the material influence your answer choice.* Use only what is written in the passage to determine the correct answer. For example, if you reacted to the story of Omelas by thinking "I feel sorry for the child, but if no one else suffers, that is a sacrifice worth making," don't let your positive view of utilitarianism cloud your understanding of the author's view of utilitarianism. The questions are about what the *author* thinks and conveys in the passage.

▶ Finding the Main Idea

Standardized reading comprehension tests always have questions about the main idea of the passage, and for good reason: The main idea is the key concept or thought that the writer wants to convey in the text.

People often confuse the *main idea* of a passage with its *topic*, but they are two very different things. The topic or subject of a passage is *what the passage is about.* The main idea, on the other hand, is *what the writer wants to say about that subject.* For example, take a look at this paragraph from the pretest:

> Although many social policies and much legislation is founded on this "greatest good" philosophy, there are several problems with utilitarianism as a basis for morality. First, happiness is not so easy to quantify, and any measurement is bound to be subjective. Second, in a theory that treats everything except happiness as *instrumentally* rather than *intrinsically* valuable, anything—or, more importantly, *anyone*—can (and should) be treated as a means to an end, if it means greater happiness. This rejects the notion that human beings have their own intrinsic value. Further, utilitarianism puts the burden of the happiness of the masses on the suffering of the few. Is the happiness of many worth the suffering of a few? Why do those few deserve to suffer? Isn't this burden of suffering morally irresponsible? This is the dilemma so brilliantly illustrated in LeGuin's story.

This paragraph is *about* "problems with utilitarianism," but that does not adequately convey the main idea. The main idea must say something more and make a specific assertion about that subject. You could say a lot about this topic: "There are not any problems with utilitarianism," for example, or "The problems with utilitarianism are an acceptable tradeoff for happiness," or "The problem with utilitarianism is its mathematical approach to happiness." In this paragraph, the writer makes her assertion (the main point) in the first sentence:

> Although many social policies and much legislation is founded on this "greatest good" philosophy, t*here are several problems with utilitarianism as a basis for morality.*

A sentence like this—one that clearly expresses the main idea of a paragraph—is the **topic sentence.** A sentence that expresses the main idea of a longer text (an essay) is the **thesis statement.** Of course, main ideas are not always stated in topic sentences or thesis statements, and in much of what you read, main ideas will be inferred. That scenario will be dealt with in a moment.

Whether explicit or implied, a main idea must be sufficiently general to hold together all of the ideas in the passage. Indeed, everything in the passage should work to explain, illustrate, or otherwise support the main idea. Thus, you can think of the main ideas as an umbrella that covers (encompasses) all of the other ideas in the passage. For example, look at the following choices for the main idea of the utilitarianism paragraph:

a. Utilitarianism is problematic because it treats people as a means to an end.
b. Utilitarianism requires that a few suffer so that many can be happy.

Topic vs. Main Idea

- The topic/subject is what the passage is about.
- The main idea is the overall fact, feeling, or thought a writer wants to convey about his or her subject.

c. Utilitarianism is flawed as a foundation for moral action.
d. Utilitarianism is often used to determine social policy.

The only answer that can be correct is **c**, because it is the only idea that is general enough to hold together all of the information in the paragraph. Choices **a** and **b** are both too specific to be the main idea; they are not broad enough to cover all of the ideas in the passage, which discusses three different problems with utilitarianism, including the problems cited in choices **a** and **b**. Choice **d** is a contrasting idea used to introduce the main idea of the sentence, and how utilitarianism is used to determine social policy is not even discussed in this paragraph, so the idea expressed in **d** certainly does not hold together the entire paragraph. Only choice **c** is general enough to cover every sentence in the paragraph. It makes a general statement that all of the sentences in the paragraph work to support.

The kind of texts you will see on the GMAT exam—and, in fact, most of the texts you will read in graduate school—will follow this basic pattern of **general idea → specific support**. That is, the writer will state the main idea he or she wants to convey about the topic and then provide support for that idea, usually in the form of specific facts and details. This works on both the paragraph and essay level. That is, in an essay, each paragraph should work to support the overall main idea (thesis) of the text. But each paragraph should also have its own main idea (in support of the thesis), and each sentence within that paragraph should work to support that main idea. This can be outlined as follows:

Thesis: overall main idea (general assertion about subject)
Paragraph 1
Main idea (general assertion in support of thesis)
Supporting sentence (specific fact or detail supporting main idea)
Supporting sentence (specific fact or detail supporting main idea)
Supporting sentence (specific fact or detail supporting main idea)

Paragraph 2
Main idea (general assertion in support of thesis)
Supporting sentence (specific fact or detail supporting main idea)
Supporting sentence (specific fact or detail supporting main idea)
Supporting sentence (specific fact or detail supporting main idea)
Supporting sentence (specific fact or detail supporting main idea)

Paragraph 3
Main idea (general assertion in support of thesis)
Supporting sentence (specific fact or detail supporting main idea)
Supporting sentence (specific fact or detail supporting main idea)

Of course, not all texts will have such a clear-cut organization, but this is the basic underlying structure of most nonfiction writing.

Distinguishing Main Ideas from Supporting Ideas

When you are dealing with short passages like those you will find on the GMAT exam, you can often distinguish between a main idea and a supporting idea by asking the following question: Is the sentence making a *general statement*, or is it providing *specific information*? In the following passage, for example, most of the sentences are too specific to be the main idea of the passage. Only one sentence—the second—is general enough to serve as an umbrella or net for the whole paragraph.

> A dyad is a face-to-face relationship between two people. Human beings are drawn to dyadic relationships, and many social theorists believe that humans are incapable of having triadic relationships (relationships consisting of three equal partners). They believe that the introduction of a third individual to a dyad either (a) strengthens the original dyad, thereby excluding the newcomer, or (b) creates a new dyad between the new arrival and one of the original dyad members, thereby excluding the other original dyad member.
>
> It is this unique feature of human interaction that can create stress when a new baby is introduced into a relationship between two parents or caregivers. When the new baby arrives, the result is usually the creation of a new dyad between the baby and its primary caregiver. Establishing such a relationship is, of course, imperative to the baby's development. However, the partner left out of this new, loving dyad may feel a sense of abandonment or even harbor a secret resentment. It is, therefore, important for the parents to carve out time alone together, so they can re-establish their original dyadic relationship—if only temporarily.

Notice how the second sentence makes a general claim about dyads: that social theorists believe humans are incapable of having triadic relationships. Then the rest of the sentences in the passage provide details and specific facts that support the main idea. Indeed, the entire second paragraph, with its example of the mother-father-child triad, supports this assertion. Notice that the first sentence of the second paragraph is also the topic sentence of that paragraph: *It is this unique feature of human interaction that can create stress when a new baby is introduced into a relationship between two parents or caregivers.* All of the sentences in that paragraph support the idea that a baby creates stress in the original dyad.

Locating the Main Idea

When main ideas are stated in thesis statements or topic sentences, they are often located at the beginning of the passage or paragraph. However, thesis statements are sometimes found at the end of the introductory paragraph of an essay. Topic sentences are often the first sentence in a paragraph because writers often follow

Transitional Words

Writers often provide clues that can help you distinguish between main ideas and their support. The following transitions are some of the most common words and phrases used to introduce specific examples:

for example	for instance	in particular
in addition	furthermore	some
others	specifically	

Look for these transitions to help distinguish between main and supporting ideas.

the general (specific principle for organizing ideas and information, but this is certainly not always the case. Sometimes writers begin with specific supporting ideas and lead up to the main idea. In this case, the topic sentence would probably be at or near the end of the paragraph, as in the following revision of the second paragraph from the dyad passage:

> When a new baby is introduced into a relationship between two parents or caregivers, the result is usually the creation of a new dyad between the baby and its primary caregiver. Establishing such a relationship is, of course, imperative to the baby's development. However, the partner left out of this new, loving dyad may feel a sense of abandonment or even harbor a secret resentment. *This unique feature of human interaction can create stress between the members of the original dyad.* It is therefore important for the parents to carve out time alone together so they can re-establish their original dyadic relationship—if only temporarily.

Of course, sometimes a topic sentence is neither at the beginning of a paragraph nor at the end, but rather somewhere in the middle; other times, the passage does not have a topic sentence at all. But that does not mean the paragraph does not have a main idea; it just means that the author has chosen not to state that idea explicitly. Skilled writers know the power of suggestion, and they know they can get an idea across without directly saying it.

Most questions about determining the main idea on the GMAT exam will probably ask you to identify the overall main idea of the passage, not just the main idea of a paragraph. Writers often state their overall main idea, but thesis statements (especially in test passages) are not quite as common as topic sentences in paragraphs. You will often have to look carefully at the answer options and decide which of those ideas best encompasses all of the ideas in the passage. You can ask yourself these questions to help determine the best answer for main idea questions:

- Which option states an idea that sums up all of the ideas in the passage?
- Which idea can serve as a net or umbrella for the passage, including all of the ideas that are discussed?
- What do all of the sentences in the passage add up to?

Vocabulary Words for the GMAT Exam

As noted earlier, vocabulary is not tested directly on the GMAT **exam,** but your knowledge of vocabulary will be tested indirectly by your ability to understand passages on the exam. Because of the academic nature of the passages on the test, you can expect to find the following types of words:

- words about **ideas**: for example, *contention, extrapolate, fallacy,* and *substantiate*
- words about **actions**: for example, *coalesce, levy, mediate, placate, sanction,* and *stipulate*
- words about **attitudes**: for example, *belligerent, complaisant, impetuous, pedestrian,* and *wary*
- words about **communication** and **expression**: for example, *aver, diatribe, euphemism,* and *mandate*

You will not be expected to know specific business-related terms beyond those in a general college-level vocabulary. For example, you should know what the term *arbitrate* means, but you will not be expected to know the meaning of *arbitrage*.

To build your vocabulary for the GMAT **exam, do the following:**

- Practice determining the meaning of unfamiliar words in context.
- Maintain your own vocabulary list and review it regularly.
- Study prefixes, suffixes, and word roots. Many GMAT-level words have Latin or Greek word roots, and knowing these word bases and common beginnings and endings can give you an edge in determining the meaning of unfamiliar words. Chapter 10 includes a list of some of the most common prefixes, suffixes, and word roots.

▶ Distinguishing between Fact and Opinion

Often, your ability to answer a reading comprehension question correctly will depend upon your ability to distinguish between fact and opinion. You may need to determine whether an author *thinks* something is true or whether the author *knows* something to be true to determine the main idea or draw logical conclusions about the text.

First, here is a quick review of definitions. A **fact** is something *known* for certain to have happened, to be true, or to exist. An **opinion**, on the other hand, is something *believed* to have happened, to be true, or to exist.

The key difference between fact and opinion lies in the difference between *believing* and *knowing*. Opinions may be *based* on facts, but they are still what people think and believe, not what they know. Opinions are debatable; facts are not. Two different people would have a hard time debating a fact, but they could debate forever about which opinion is more valid. Note that people can also debate about how to *interpret* facts, but they would have to agree on the facts themselves.

Fact or Opinion?

A good test for whether something is fact or opinion is to ask yourself two questions:

- Can this statement be debated?
- Is this something known to be true?

If you can answer yes to the first question, it is probably an opinion. If you can answer yes to the second question, it is probably a fact.

In addition, consider the nature of the claim. If the statement is *prescriptive*—if it is describing what someone should or ought to do—then the statement is an opinion, as in the following examples:

- You *should* try advertising on the radio.
- We *ought* to offer a better severance package.
- I *had better* confirm this appointment before I book a flight.

Words that show *judgment* or *evaluation*, like *good, bad, interesting*, and *important,* usually also signal an opinion. Here are some examples:

- She is a *great* motivator.
- This was the *most significant* development in the history of science.
- The debate between the candidates was *fascinating*.

Consider this example:

Employee benefits should include coverage for "alternative medicines" such as acupuncture and massage therapy.

This statement is clearly debatable and could be argued either way. In an effective argument, this opinion would be *supported by* and *based upon* facts. For example, if you had chronic back pain that was not alleviated by traditional medical approaches but that disappeared after three weeks of acupuncture, you could use this fact to support your opinion. In addition, you could cite the fact that the alleviation of pain saved your insurance company hundreds to thousands of dollars in additional visits to back pain specialists and other medical practitioners. You might also cite statistics, such as a recent survey that showed more than 60% of patients with chronic back pain reported relief after one month of acupuncture. These facts, which are nondebatable, would support your opinion, making it more reasonable and therefore more valid.

It is easy to see how this information is relevant to the critical-reasoning questions (which ask you to evaluate arguments) and the AWA questions (which ask you to write your own argument). It is also relevant to reading comprehension questions because knowing the author's opinion and how the author supports that opinion can help you draw appropriate conclusions from the text. You can then answer questions such as the following:

The passage implies that the author

a. has insurance that covers alternative treatments.
b. believes alternative treatments are more effective than traditional medicine.
c. has other medical problems besides back pain.
d. believes alternative treatments are best for psychosomatic disorders.
e. thinks covering alternative treatments could save insurers millions of dollars.

The correct answer is **e**—an opinion based on the facts of her experience of relief after a few treatments, ending her medical costs for that ailment; the fact that so many others experienced the same kind of quick relief; and the simple fact of the exorbitant costs of specialty treatments and extended care.

▶ Identifying Specific Facts and Details

On standardized tests, you will often be asked to identify specific facts and details from what you read. The idea behind this kind of question is not for you to *memorize* everything in the passage. Rather, these questions test (1) how carefully you read and (2) your ability to know where to look for specific information within a passage. If you read carefully, you are more likely to draw logical conclusions from the text; and if you know where to look for specific information, you are more likely to have a good understanding of how the text is organized and the relationship between ideas in the text. Thus, although these questions may seem unsophisticated, they lay the groundwork for more sophisticated reading skills. For example, take another look at the following paragraph and question from the pretest:

> Utilitarianism is an ethical theory based upon the belief that happiness is the ultimate good and that people should use happiness as the measure for determining right and wrong. For utilitarians, the right thing to do is that which will bring about the greatest amount of happiness for the greatest number of people. Furthermore, utilitarianism argues that the *intention* of people's actions does not matter; only the consequences of their actions are morally relevant, because only the *consequences* determine how much happiness is produced.

According to the passage, in utilitarianism

a. only intentions have moral significance.
b. consequences are important, but intentions are more important.
c. intentions and consequences are equally important.
d. intentions are important, but consequences are more important.
e. only consequences have moral significance.

Using Text Clues

To find specific facts and details, use the following two guidelines:

- Look for ***key words*** in the question to tell you exactly what information to look for in the passage.
- Think about the ***structure*** of the passage and where that information is likely to be located.

This basic comprehension question asks you to find a specific fact or detail. The best way to find this kind of information in a text is to use the key words from the question and the structure of the passage as your guide. In this example, the only key word in the question is *utilitarianism.* The question does not mention the story or *problems,* which indicates that the answer must be in the section of the text that explains utilitarianism. If the question had asked about the *consequences* of utilitarianism, the answer would be even easier to find, because you could quickly find the section of the passage that discusses the consequences of utilitarianism. You don't have to reread the entire passage—in fact, you can't, because you will run out of time for other questions—but a scan should quickly find your key word(s) and the answer.

In addition, you can use the structure of the passage to help you find the correct information. Even a preview of the passage reveals that the first paragraph is about the story of Omelas, the second about utilitarianism in general, and the third about the problems with utilitarianism (the author's opinion). Thus, the structure alone would tell us to look for the answer to the question in the second paragraph.

▶ Essay Types and Organizational Patterns

In all forms of art, structure is intimately connected to meaning. Writing is no exception. Even in the driest of academic articles, form helps convey meaning, and writers use organizational patterns that help reflect their ideas.

As noted previously in Chapter 4, the reading comprehension passages on the GMAT exam are either argumentative or informative in nature. These are very general categories, and the types of essays you will see on the GMAT exam can be further characterized based on their purpose:

- **Classification.** The goal of this type of passage is to describe different kinds or types of a certain something. For example, a passage might describe the three types of flora found in the Everglades.
- **Illustration.** The goal of this type of passage is to present specific facts, details, and examples that illustrate a particular theory, idea, or phenomenon. For example, the utilitarian passage in the pretest uses LeGuin's story to illustrate the central moral dilemma of a utilitarian society.
- **Persuasion.** This type of text argues a specific position or point of view and aims to convince readers that this position or point of view is valid. For example, a passage may argue that all high school curricula should include mandatory community service.
- **Analysis.** This type of text takes an idea or issue and breaks it down into its parts so that readers can better understand and evaluate the subject. For example, a passage analyzing a proposed development

project might discuss the scope of the project, the different stages of development, and the costs and benefits of the project.

- **Evaluation.** The goal of this type of passage is to assess the effectiveness of something. For example, a passage might evaluate the success of a recent merger.

Organizational Patterns

When writers write, they generally use several main organizational patterns. These basic patterns help writers organize their ideas effectively. The following are the four most common patterns:

- chronological order
- order of importance
- comparison and contrast
- cause and effect

Writers often use one pattern as an overall organizing principle and then use a combination of patterns throughout the text. For example, an article about ethical theories might use comparison and contrast as its overall organizing principle and also use order of importance when listing key similarities and differences.

Chronological Order

When writers use *time* to organize their ideas, it is called **chronological order**. They describe events in the order in which they did happen, will happen, or should happen. Much of what you read is organized in this way, including historical texts, instructions and procedures, and essays about personal experiences.

Order of Importance

This organizational pattern arranges ideas by *rank* instead of time. That is, the first idea is not what *happened* first; it is the idea that is *most* or *least important.* Writers can start with the most important idea and then work down the line to the least important. Or they can do the opposite: Start with the least important idea and build up to the one that is the most important.

Organizing ideas from the most important to the least important puts the most essential information first. Writers often do this when they are offering advice or when they want to be sure readers get the most important information right away. Newspaper articles, for example, generally use this structure, beginning with the most important information (the *who, what, when, where,* and *why* about the event) so readers do not have to read the whole article to get those facts.

When writers move from the least to the most important, they save their most important idea or piece of information for last. Writers often use this approach when they are presenting an argument. This is because this kind of structure is usually more convincing than a most-to-least organization. The more controversial the argument, the more important this structure. In an argument, you need to build your case piece by piece and win your readers over point by point. If your less important points make sense to the reader, then your more important points will come off stronger. As the saying goes, writers often "save the best for last" because that is where "the best" often has the most impact.

Comparison and Contrast

When we **compare** two or more things, we show how they are similar; when we **contrast** them, we show how they are different. This organizational technique provides a way to classify or judge the items being analyzed. By placing two (or more) items side by side, for example, you can see how they measure up against each other. How are they similar or different? And why does it matter? For example, how is utilitarianism different from other ethical theories, such as deontology?

Remember that whenever an author compares and contrasts two or more items, he or she is doing it for a reason. The author wants to point something out by putting these two items side by side. For example, by comparing utilitarianism and deontology, the author might want to show how one theory is more appropriate for social policies, whereas the other is more appropriate for determining individual actions. Be on the look out for this main idea in any comparison and contrast.

Cause and Effect

Another common organizational pattern is cause and effect. A **cause** is a person, thing, action, or event that makes something happen (creates an effect); an **effect** is an event or change created by an action (or cause). A passage about cause explains *why* something took place—for example, what caused the Industrial Revolution? A passage about effect, on the other hand, explains *what happened after* something took place—for example, what happened as a result of the Industrial Revolution? How did it affect the economy? Daily life? Education?

On the GMAT exam, you are not likely to see any question directly asking "What type of passage is this?" or "Which organizational pattern does the passage use?" However, you may see questions that ask, "What is the author's main purpose in writing this passage?" (a question clearly related to the structure of the essay). Furthermore, understanding these basic essay types and patterns will help you identify the writer's main idea, locate supporting facts and details, and draw logical inferences from the text.

Transitions

Transitions are an essential element of effective writing, and they are important clues to organizational patterns and meaning. Transitions signal the relationships between ideas, connecting ideas within sentences and between sentences, within paragraphs and between paragraphs. They tell us the order in which things happened, whether one idea is more important than another, and how one item is similar to or different from something else.

For example, notice how transitions guide us through the following paragraph:

> (1) Why do we punish those who commit crimes? (2) There are two main theories of punishment: retribution and deterrence. (3) The first, retribution, argues that people who commit crimes deserve to be punished and that the punishment should fit the crime. (4) In other words, it is an "eye for an eye" philosophy. (5) Deterrence theory, on the other hand, posits that punishing offenders will help prevent future crimes.

The transitions here show us that sentence 4 offers an explanation for sentence 3 and that sentence 5 offers an idea that contrasts with the idea in sentence 3.

Certain transitions work best for specific functions. For example, *for example* is a great transition to use when introducing a specific example. Here is a brief list of some of the most common transitional words and phrases to watch for—and to use in your own writing.

IF YOU WANT TO	USE THESE TRANSITIONAL WORDS AND PHRASES		
introduce an example	for example in other words in fact	for instance in particular first (second) of all	that is specifically
show addition	and again	in addition moreover	also furthermore
show emphasis	indeed	in fact	certainly
acknowledge another point of view	although despite	though even though	granted
show rank	more importantly most importantly	above all first, second, third	first and foremost
show cause	because	since	created (by)
show effect	therefore consequently	hence as a result	so
show comparison	likewise in the same way	similarly in a like manner	like just as
show contrast	unlike whereas but in contrast	however instead on the contrary yet	on the other hand rather conversely
show the passage of time	then after meanwhile eventually in the meantime	next before while finally immediately	later during soon afterward suddenly

▶ Making Inferences

Inferences are conclusions that we draw based upon evidence. For example, if you look up at the sky and see heavy black clouds, you might logically infer that it is going to rain. Reading-comprehension questions like those you will see on the GMAT exam will often ask you to draw conclusions based upon what you read in the passage. The key to drawing the right conclusions (making the right inferences) is the same as the key to finding the meaning of unfamiliar vocabulary words. You have to look for clues in the context. These clues include details, actions, and ideas described in the text (what has been stated, proposed, asked, and asserted); sentence structure; and word choice.

Making logical inferences is largely a matter of looking objectively at the evidence in the passage. Remember, you are not being asked what *you* think about the writer or the passage but what is implied *by* the passage. What do the ideas and words add up to? What does the evidence suggest? For example, take a look at the following description:

> Dennis was scared. His knees were weak. He looked down . . . the water was 20 feet below. He looked up again, quickly. He tried to think of something else. He tried to reassure himself. "It's only 20 feet!" he said aloud. But that only made it sound worse. Twenty feet!

The writer could have said, "Dennis was scared. He was afraid of heights." Instead, the writer *suggests* how Dennis feels through details (his knees were weak), repetition (20 feet), and the short, choppy sentence structure that reflects the panic Dennis is feeling.

Word Choice

The best clues to the meaning often come from the specific words a writer chooses to describe people, places, and things. The writer's word choice (also called **diction**) can reveal a great deal about how he or she feels about the subject.

By looking closely at word choice, you will find clues that can help you better understand the text. Word choice clues can come in the following forms:

- particular words and phrases that the author uses
- the way those words and phrases are arranged in sentences
- word or sentence patterns that are repeated
- important details about people, places, and things

To see how word choice reveals the writer's attitude, read the following two sentences:

a. Higgins proposed a revolutionary idea.
b. Higgins proposed a radical idea.

It is not hard to see the difference between these sentences. In sentence **a**, the writer calls Higgins's idea *revolutionary*, whereas the writer of sentence **b** calls the idea *radical.* Although the sentences are similar, their word choice conveys two very different attitudes about Higgins's idea. Both writers agree that Higgins's idea is something unusual and different from the norm. But the way in which it is unusual differs significantly between sentences. A *revolutionary* idea is unusual in that it is new and unlike ideas that came before; it changes things dramatically. A *radical* idea, however, is unusual because it is extreme. From the word choice, one can infer that the writer of sentence **a** feels very positive about Higgins's proposal, whereas the writer of sentence **b** feels concerned about the extreme nature of Higgins's plan. The writers do not need to spell out their feelings for you because their *word choices* make their positions clear.

Denotation and Connotation

Even words that seem to mean the same thing have subtly different meanings and sometimes not-so-subtle effects. For example, look at the words *dangerous* and *perilous.* If you say "The situation is *dangerous*," that means one thing. If you say "The situation is *perilous*," that means something a little bit different. That is because *dangerous* has a different **connotation** than *perilous.* Connotation is a word's *suggested* or implied meaning; it is what the word makes you think or feel. *Dangerous* and *perilous* have nearly the same **denotation** or dictionary definition—in fact, each word is used in the definition of the other. But *perilous* suggests more threat of harm than *dangerous. Peril* has a more ominous ring to it than *danger* and suggests a more life-threatening situation. *Perilous* and *dangerous,* therefore, have different connotations, and the word you choose to describe the situation can indicate a lot.

Euphemisms and Dysphemisms

Another way writers use word choice to reveal their feelings is through the use of **euphemisms** and **dysphemisms**. A euphemism is a neutral or positive word used in place of something negative. A common example is to substitute the phrase *passed on* or *departed* for *died.* A dysphemism, on the other hand, uses a negative word or phrase (instead of something neutral or positive), such as saying *croaked* or *kicked the bucket* for *died.* To cite a business example, "I've been let go" is a euphemism and "I've been axed" is a dysphemism for "I've been fired."

Question 1 from the pretest requires you to make an inference using many different clues from the passage.

Which of the following best sums up the author's opinion of utilitarianism?

a. It is an ethical theory.
b. It is the ethical theory that we should all live by.
c. It is a useful but problematic ethical theory.
d. It does not adequately measure happiness.
e. It underestimates the intrinsic value of human beings.

To find the correct answer—choice **c**—we must look at what is stated in the passage and how those ideas are stated. The summary of "The Ones Who Walk Away from Omelas," for example, shows how the sacrifice of one can create the happiness of many and how most of the citizens accept this price for their happiness. This tells us that the theory is not one to be rejected outright. But because there *is* that one person suffering, and because some people *do* walk away, this also tells us that there is something wrong with this utopia. The author also states that "many social policies and much legislation is founded on" utilitarianism, which reveals that it is a useful ethical theory. The word choice throughout also suggests that the author sees both positive and negative aspects of utilitarianism. For example, she calls the theory *problematic*, but she does not use stronger words such as *wrongheaded* or *faulty*. She calls the problem of the suffering of the few for the happiness of the many a *dilemma*, not a *flaw* or *failure*. And she asks questions rather than making statements about the immorality of utilitarian choices, suggesting that this is a very complex moral issue.

A Note about Quantitative Analysis Questions

A small minority of reading-comprehension questions on the GMAT exam are quantitative-analysis questions that ask you to draw conclusions from a *discussion* of numbers or statistics in the text. Don't let the numbers throw you off. These questions are still inference questions. The only difference is that the main evidence you need to use to draw your conclusion is the quantitative information provided in the text. (And don't worry—you won't be expected to perform any complex mathematical computations. You will only need to do very simple arithmetic, if you need to do any math at all.)

CHAPTER

6 Critical Reasoning

The term **critical reasoning** describes a set of analytical skills that enable people to make effective arguments and evaluate arguments made by others. Sometimes critical reasoning is merely a matter of common sense. For example, if there is a hurricane outside, but I say it's a good day to go for a walk and get some fresh air, you know something is wrong with my argument. But written and spoken arguments are often much more complicated, and the ability to think critically and judge the effectiveness of an argument is not only important to your success on the GMAT® exam—it's also critical to your success in the business world. This section reviews the basic structure of arguments and guidelines for evaluating arguments, especially arguments like the ones you will encounter on the GMAT exam.

▶ Elements of an Argument

Although arguments often end up in heated debate, you don't need to shout or elevate your blood pressure to have an argument. In fact, you don't even need another person to argue with. In the realm of critical reasoning, an **argument** is a set of claims with a premise(s) and a conclusion. A **claim** is a statement (as opposed to a question or interjection) with a truth value—it is either true or false (although you may not know which). The **conclusion** of the argument is its main claim—what the arguer wants us to see, do, or

Argument = Conclusion (main claim) + Premise(s) (supporting claim[s])

believe. The **premise** is the claim or claims that provide *support* or *reasons to accept* the conclusion. To make an argument, you must articulate at least two claims, and at least one of the claims must offer (or attempt to offer) support for the conclusion.

Here are some examples. The conclusion of each argument is underlined:

I do not see Xiomara anywhere. <u>She must not have arrived yet.</u>

<u>You should spend ten minutes each day doing yoga.</u> Deep breathing and stretching will improve your health and mood, and they are easy to fit into your day.

<u>A flat tax is the answer to our tax troubles.</u> It would treat everyone fairly and would dramatically simplify the tax code. This would make filing taxes easier and make many Americans feel better about giving their money to the government.

Notice that this last argument offers several premises to support its conclusion:

1. A flat tax would treat everyone fairly.
2. A flat tax would simplify the tax code.
3. A flat tax (because it would simplify the tax code) would make filing taxes easier.
4. A flat tax (because it would treat everyone fairly) would make Americans feel better about paying taxes.

Of course, the more reasonable the premises and the more premises offered, the more convincing and effective the argument. You will see an example of this in a moment.

It will often be clear which of the claims in an argument is the conclusion, but many times you will need to consider the argument carefully to determine the main claim. The following conclusion and premise indicators can help.

CONCLUSION INDICATORS	PREMISE INDICATORS
thus	since
therefore	because
hence	for
this shows/suggests/implies/proves that	in view of the fact that
consequently	
so	
accordingly	

► Complicating Arguments

The previous examples of arguments are quite simple, and many arguments—including many of those you will encounter on the GMAT exam—are far more complex. Within arguments, you will often find two factors that complicate arguments:

1. The conclusion of one argument serves as the premise for another.
2. The conclusion and/or one or more premises are unstated.

The conclusion of one argument serves as the premise for another. Like essays, arguments are often richly layered. For example, look at the following argument:

You should present our position to the board. The board members trust you because they have known you for years, and you know our position better than anyone.

The claim *the board members trust you* actually serves as both the premise for the conclusion *you should present to the board* and the conclusion for a second argument: *The board members trust you* (conclusion) because *they have known you for years* (premise). This might be represented as follows:

conclusion → premise/(becomes) conclusion → premise

Sometimes this argument construction will be easy to detect; other times quickly mapping out the argument can help. To do this, put brackets [] around each claim (remember that each sentence can have more than one claim). Then determine which of those claims is the main claim—the overall point of the argument. Just as an essay may have many main ideas (a main idea for each paragraph), it also has an overall main idea. Similarly, an argument can have many different conclusions that are part of a larger argument, and the argument should have one main claim (the overall conclusion). Label this main claim C1 (conclusion 1). Then look carefully at the premises. Do they directly support C1? If so, label them P1 (premises that support C1). But if they do not directly support C1, then you might have a secondary (or tertiary, etc.) conclusion. For example, *they have known you for years* doesn't directly support the claim *you should present our position to the board.* Thus, you need to find the claim it *does* directly support (*the board members trust you*) and label that claim C2. Thus, the claim *the board members trust you* is labeled both P1 and C2, and *they have known you for years* is labeled P2 (premise supporting C2). Meanwhile, *you know our position better than anyone* directly supports C1, so it is labeled P1:

C1 P1/C2
[You should present our position to the board.] [The board members trust you] because
P2 P1
[they have known you for years] and [you know our position better than anyone.]

Here is another example:

P3
[With more and more classes being offered online, more and more students will soon earn their degrees
P3
in virtual universities.] [Already, students in California are graduating from schools in New York without ever
P2/C3
leaving their state.] Because [online courses offer flexibility without geographic boundaries],
P1/C2 C1
[virtual degrees will be in ever greater demand], and [colleges and universities should invest the bulk of their resources in developing online degree programs.]

In this argument, the final claim is the overall conclusion, the main claim of the argument.

Identifying the main claim (which we will refer to simply as the conclusion for the rest of this section) is a critical skill on the GMAT exam. You must be able to identify the conclusion to effectively evaluate an argument, and you need to be able to see when the conclusion is in fact missing from an argument. This is the second complication:

The premise and/or conclusion of an argument is unstated. These arguments are common both in real life and on the GMAT exam. The problem with an argument that contains unstated premises and conclusions is that it leaves room for the premise or conclusion to be misunderstood. For example,

You should turn her in for cheating. She violated the honor code.

This argument has an **unstated premise**—a key idea that links the conclusion and premise together. In order for this argument to be clear and strong, you need to know the unstated assumption that makes this argument possible:

People who violate the honor code should be turned in.

This could be stated in a slightly different way, but the assumption behind this argument is now clear. This is crucial because unless you understand all of the premises upon which an argument is based, you cannot effectively evaluate that argument and determine whether or not it is valid.

Here is another example of an argument with an unstated premise:

We should offer online classes because other schools are now offering online classes.

At first glance, this might seem like a simple case of poor logic, an "everyone else is doing it" approach. But if you recognize the unstated assumption, then this is a much stronger argument:

We need to do what other schools are doing to stay competitive.

Finding an Unstated Premise

When you are presented with an argument that has an unstated premise, you need to determine what claim would link the existing premise and conclusion together. What must be true (assumed) in order for the conclusion to be true? This missing premise is a necessary transition or bridge between the premise and conclusion, one that probably makes the conclusion true. For example, look at the following argument:

P C
[Ellen plagiarized.] [She should be punished.]

An argument that jumps from premise to conclusion like this is called a ***non sequitur*** (jumping to conclusions). This can be corrected by stating the premise that links the conclusion and premise:

P P C
[Ellen plagiarized.] [Plagiarism is wrong.] [Therefore, she should be punished.]

Here is another example. Notice how the unstated premise links the premise to the conclusion in the second version:

I promised to clean the garage on Saturday. I better clean the garage on Saturday. (non sequitur)
I promised to clean the garage on Saturday. People should keep their promises. I better clean the garage on Saturday. (logical, complete argument)

Not every argument with an unstated premise is a non sequitur, but you should follow essentially the same process to determine and evaluate unstated assumptions. Take another look at question 8 from the pretest, for example. This question asks you to determine which assumption the conclusion is *not* based upon:

8. Morning Glory, the coffee shop on the corner, has lost nearly 50% of its business because a national retail coffee chain opened up a store down the street. Instead of closing up shop, the owner of Morning Glory plans to draw in customers by offering coffee, tea, and pastries at much lower prices than the national coffee chain.

The owner's plan of action is based on all of the following assumptions EXCEPT

a. some customers will choose the coffee shop that offers the lowest price.
b. the quality of Morning Glory's coffee is comparable to that of the national coffee chain.
c. Morning Glory can afford to cut its profit margin in order to lower prices.
d. Morning Glory's customers are very loyal.
e. the national coffee chain will not lower its prices in order to compete with Morning Glory.

The first step to tackling this question is to clearly identify the core argument. This plan of action could be reworded as follows:

P C
[Its prices will be lower than the national coffee chain's], so [Morning Glory will stay in business].

Now, this argument has several unstated assumptions. To answer the question, you need to identify which one is *not* a logical connection between the premise and the conclusion. You can simply insert each choice between the premise and conclusion to see if it forms a logical link:

P P
[Its prices will be lower than the national coffee chain's] and [ ] so
C
[Morning Glory will stay in business].

Broken down in this manner, it should be easy to see that all of the assumptions except **d** form a logical link between premise and conclusion. If customers are loyal, they will continue to patronize Morning Glory, whether or not their prices are lower. This is the only assumption that does not fit the argument.

Determining an Unstated Conclusion

Determining the unstated conclusion of an argument is like finding an implied main idea. In a reading passage, you would ask the following questions: What overall impression do the examples and ideas in the text add up to? What idea or concept do the ideas from the text support? Similarly, in critical reasoning, you must ask the following questions:

- What do these premises add up to?
- What idea or claim does this evidence amount to?
- If these premises are true, what else then is also likely to be true?

For example, look at the following passage:

Rajita paid $35 for her scarf at Hanson's on sale. The same scarf is $20 (regular price) at Lambert's and only $18 (regular price) at Sam's.

Which one of the following conclusions can be logically drawn from the passage?
a. Rajita does not know where to shop.
b. There is no Sam's or Lambert's in Rajita's area.
c. You will probably pay more for most items at Hanson's than at Lambert's or Sam's.
d. Sam's sale prices are always the best.
e. Rajita bought the scarf at Hanson's because she was already there buying other things.

All of these choices *could* be true, but only one is likely to be true *based on the evidence in the passage.* Maybe Rajita doesn't know where to shop (choice **a**); maybe she has no idea that Lambert's and Sam's have the same merchandise at better prices. But there is no evidence of this in the passage. The same is true of choices **b, d,** and **e**; they may be true, but there is no evidence in the passage. (We know Sam's regular price for the scarf is the best, but we don't know if Sam's sale prices are always better than Lambert's.) Only choice

c is a logical conclusion based on the passage. If Hanson's *sale* price is $35, nearly twice the price for the same merchandise from Sam's, you will probably pay more for most items at Hanson's.

On the exam, you will also see questions where several conclusions can be drawn from a series of premises, and you must determine which of the conclusions presented is *not* logical based on the evidence (premises) provided. This was the case with question 9 from the pretest:

9. When romance novels were located in the back of the bookstore, they accounted for approximately 6% of total sales. Since we moved romance novels close to the front of the store and put several books on display, sales of romance novels have increased to 14% to 18% of total sales.

All of the following conclusions can logically be drawn from this argument EXCEPT

a. customers who bought one romance novel are likely to come back for another.
b. customers are more likely to buy books located near the front of the bookstore than at the back.
c. the display caught the interest of people who might not have otherwise purchased a romance novel.
d. customers believe that bookstores put their best books near the front of the store.
e. sales of romance novels may increase even more if the section were moved all the way to the front.

To answer this question correctly, you must evaluate each option in light of the evidence. In this case, the only conclusion that does not logically follow from the premises is **a.** The significant increase in sales after the relocation of the books indicates that customers are more likely to buy books at the front of the store (choice **b**) and that the display may have caught the interest of people who might not otherwise purchase a romance novel (choice **c**). It is also logical to conclude that sales would further increase if the books were moved even farther toward the front of the store (choice **e**). Choices **b** and **e** and the increase in sales all suggest that customers believe the best books are near the front of the store (choice **d**). The only conclusion that cannot logically be drawn from this scenario is that customers will come back to purchase more romance novels (choice **a**). There is no evidence here for this conclusion; nothing in the data indicates repeat purchases for customers.

▶ Evaluating Arguments

Many GMAT critical reasoning questions will ask you to *evaluate* an argument. This usually means you will have to assess the logic of the argument and/or the effectiveness of the evidence provided in support of the conclusion. To do this, you need to consider three elements of effective arguments:

- **Qualifiers.** Does the argument allow for exceptions, or make an absolute claim?
- **Evidence.** Does the argument provide strong evidence to accept the claim?
- **Logic.** Does the argument present *reasonable* premises, or is it based on faulty logic?

Qualifiers

Qualifiers are words and phrases that limit the scope of a claim to help make an argument more **valid** (more likely to be true). For example, take a look at the following arguments:

1. Don't believe anything politicians say. All politicians are corrupt.
2. Don't believe most of what politicians say. Most politicians are corrupt.
3. Be careful believing what politicians say. A lot of politicians are corrupt.

Which argument is the strongest? Although argument 1 is the most assertive, it's also the *weakest* argument. It is the *least* likely to be true because it uses absolute terms (*anything* and *all*) in both its conclusion and premise. Argument 2 is much stronger because it uses the word *most* to qualify its conclusion and premise. But it is still telling you to disbelieve most of what politicians say, and even the most corrupt politicians probably don't lie most of the time. It still asserts that most politicians are corrupt, a claim that will likely be difficult to prove. Argument 3 may seem the weakest because of its qualifiers, but it is actually the strongest because it is the most plausible argument of the three. It is the most likely to be true.

The following words and phrases can significantly strengthen arguments by qualifying them:

- few
- rarely
- some
- sometimes
- in some cases
- it is possible
- it seems
- it may be
- many
- routinely
- most
- often
- one might argue
- perhaps
- possibly
- possibly
- for the most part

It might seem that adding qualifiers is a way of copping out, but they are quite necessary for logical arguments. Arguments that lack appropriate qualifiers dig their own graves, because an absolute statement almost always has an exception. And if it has an exception, the claim becomes false, rendering the entire argument invalid.

With this knowledge, it should be easier to answer a question such as the following:

I should not bother getting Hal a birthday gift this year. He is never happy with anything he gets from anybody.

Which of the following statements would most strengthen the speaker's argument?

a. Hal is simply impossible to please.
b. At least he is never been happy with a gift from me, and I have tried just about everything.
c. Besides, Hal does not need anything—he already has everything he wants.
d. Hal is disgusted with our consumption-obsessed culture.
e. Hal even complains about gift certificates.

The best choice is **b**, the only statement that offers qualifiers to make the argument more likely to be true (and therefore stronger). In **b**, the speaker limits Hal's discontent with gifts to the gifts given by the speaker. The speaker also says she has tried *just about* everything, a qualifier that allows for the possibility that she simply has not been able to find the right gift. Thus, choice **b** actually strengthens the argument.

Evidence

A good argument will provide strong evidence of its conclusion. This means that there is *sufficient* evidence (this often means more than just one premise) and that the evidence provided in support of the conclusion is *strong* (reasonable and convincing).

Many types of evidence can be provided, including the following:

- observations
- interviews
- surveys and questionnaires
- experiments
- personal experience
- expert opinion

Each type of evidence has its strengths and potential weaknesses. Surveys, for example, can give you great statistics and quotes to offer as evidence, and they tend to sound convincing, since they often provide hard numbers that seem objective. But survey results are often less objective than they seem because the results depend upon how well (or how poorly) the survey was designed and implemented. For example, if you only survey two people, your results are probably quite meaningless. If you design my survey so that the questions push respondents to answer in a certain way (loaded questions), then your survey results will probably be quite biased. Similarly, observations have empirical power, but observations can be flawed, and people have been known to see what they want to see.

Evaluating Evidence

When you are presented with evidence in argument, you should ask several important questions:

- Is there **sufficient evidence** to accept the conclusion?
- Is the evidence **relevant** to the conclusion?
- Does the evidence come from an **unbiased source**?
- Is the evidence **logical**?

Is There Sufficient Evidence to Accept the Conclusion?

The more that is at stake in the conclusion (the more controversial it is, the more risk you take in accepting the argument), the more evidence you should have before accepting the claim.

For example, in the DNA argument from the pretest, which we will return to in a moment, the stakes are very high—the conclusion asks us to agree that thousands of convictions should be reviewed and potentially overturned on the likelihood that many innocent people are serving time in prison. This is a serious matter, so the amount of evidence should be plentiful.

Is the Evidence Relevant to the Conclusion?

For example, if you are arguing that colleges and universities should offer more classes online, the following evidence might be compelling, but it is not relevant:

At one campus, 68% of students said they spent an average of two to three hours online each day.

The following item of evidence, however, *is* relevant:

According to a survey of students at three large state universities, 72% of students stated that they would be "very interested" in taking courses online.

Does the Evidence Come from an Unbiased Source?

Bias is a strong inclination or preference for one person, position, or point of view over others. As discussed earlier, surveys can be loaded so that the answers will favor particular responses; similarly, experts may not be objective because they have something to gain from espousing a particular point of view. You need to consider the potential bias of a source when you consider evidence in an argument. For example, take a political science professor who is asked to evaluate a candidate for a local election. Many factors can bias the professor's assessment of the candidate's merits, including whether or not the professor has any personal or professional relationship with the candidate; whether or not they have had past experiences with each other and of what sort; whether or not they belong to the same political party; and whether or not any potential rewards might befall the professor should the candidate win. The following question addresses this kind of problem:

City Treasurer: Vote Carson for Governor. Carson knows what it takes to turn the state's economy around. He will create jobs and improve education. Carson knows how to get things done.

Which of the following provides the best reason to reject the treasurer's argument?

a. The treasurer belongs to the same political party as Carson.
b. The treasurer has known Carson for less than one year.
c. The treasurer once lost an election against Carson.
d. The treasurer has been promised a position in Carson's cabinet if he wins.
e. The last candidate the treasurer backed lost the election.

Choice **d** indicates that the treasurer has a real stake in Carson's winning the election; if Carson wins, he will be on the governor's payroll. Maybe he does believe that Carson can turn the state around, but because his potential for bias is so high, voters would be wise not to let this politician influence their feelings about Carson and seek other evidence that Carson would (or would not) be a good governor.

Credibility

Sources are credible if they:

- have expertise in the subject matter (based upon their experience, education, reputation, recognition, and achievements).
- are free from bias.

Is the Evidence Logical?

Logical means *reasonable*, based on good common sense, not emotional. It is logical, for example, to conclude that if it is snowing outside, it is cold. It is *not* logical to assume that it will stop snowing if you wish for it hard enough. It *is* logical to argue that you should exercise because it will make you feel better—logic does not discount emotions—but it is *not* logical to argue that you should not help your brother because you are angry with him. Feeling better about yourself *is* a good reason to exercise; you are doing something in order to feel a positive and healthy emotion. Not helping your brother because you are angry, however, is not logical. You need to provide logical reasons for whether or not you should help your brother. Not helping your brother because the last two times you helped him he broke your glasses in half is logical!

Logical Fallacies

Logical fallacies are errors in reasoning that all too often find their way into arguments. Dozens of fallacies exist, but the ones you are most likely to encounter on the GMAT exam are also the ones you are most likely to encounter in everyday life:

- comparing apples to oranges
- appeal to emotion
- bandwagon "everyone else is doing it" appeal
- straw man
- red herring
- slippery slope
- begging the question
- ad hominem

Also, fallacies exist specifically for causal arguments and explanations. These will be addressed in the section "Common Flaws in Causal Arguments" later in the chapter.

Comparing Apples to Oranges

Jonas has an apple in one hand and an orange in the other. "Look how much redder the apple is than the orange," he says. "And the orange is so much more orange."

Well, *of course* an apple is redder and an orange more orange. It is rather absurd to be making such a comparison because even though apples and oranges are both fruit, they are not the same *kind* of fruit. If you were to compare a Fuji apple to a gala apple, or a naval orange to a clementine, *then* you would have a legitimate comparison. But comparing two things that do not fit in the same category makes for an illogical comparison.

It is obvious here, but in many arguments, you may have to look harder to detect an apples-to-oranges comparison. Two questions from the pretest can help demonstrate how common this fallacy is and how to identify it.

7. Unemployment in Winston County has risen only 4% since I took office. Under my predecessor, unemployment rose 14%. Clearly, my economic policies are far more effective.
Which of the following must be true in order for this argument to be valid?
a. Winston County's population dropped significantly during the current administration.
b. The national unemployment rate increased by 12% during the previous administration but only 2% during the current administration.
c. Key socioeconomic variables such as the state of the national economy and the demographics of Winston County are comparable for each administration.
d. Key policy changes, such as increased job training for the unemployed, were implemented under the current administration.
e. Tax incentives have been implemented to bring new businesses to Winston County.

The problem here is that unless key variables that affect unemployment are the same during these two administrations, this is a case of comparing apples to oranges. For example, if the predecessor was in office during a deep national recession, no matter how good his economic policies were, he would experience a higher unemployment rate. If Winston County's economy had been supported largely by a factory that shut down during the predecessor's administration, that might also explain a significantly higher unemployment rate. The national recession and the factory closing would both have a huge impact on the county's unemployment no matter who was in office. Without knowing that the variables are nearly the same or without making allowances for differences in those variables, one must assume this is a case of comparing apples to oranges.

The same is true for the question about where to go for heart surgery:

12. One out of four heart surgery patients at St. Vincent's dies from complications during surgery. Only one out of six heart surgery patients at St. Mary's dies from complications during surgery. If you need heart surgery, make sure you go to St. Mary's, not St. Vincent's.
Which of the following, if true, is the best reason to reject this argument?
a. St. Vincent's specializes in heart surgery for elderly and high-risk patients.
b. St. Mary's surgical equipment is more up to date than St. Vincent's.
c. St. Vincent's has the most renowned heart surgeon in the country on its staff.
d. St. Vincent's offers flexible payment options for balances not covered by insurance.
e. Two doctors who used to work at St. Mary's now work at St. Vincent's.

Don't Get Personal

Remember that on the GMAT **exam**, you must assess arguments and answer questions based only on the information presented on the test. For the moment, forget what you might know or how you might feel about the topic or issue. Base your answer only on the argument and evidence in front of you.

The best reason to reject this argument is the one that shows us this is an apples-to-oranges comparison. To make a fair comparison of mortality rates, the patient base for both hospitals would have to be nearly identical. Because the patients at St. Vincent's are already at a higher risk for mortality, their mortality rates are necessarily going to be higher—but that doesn't mean you are less likely to survive surgery there. Assuming you are not an elderly or high-risk patient, to make an informed choice, you would need statistics about St. Vincent's mortality rates for surgery on patients that are not elderly or high risk.

Appeals to Emotion

Arguments that appeal to emotions try to rouse your sense of pity, fear, or anger instead of offering logical reasons for accepting their claim. Here is an example:

Let's go to Morning Glory for coffee. That national coffee chain is putting Morning Glory out of business, and I feel bad for the owner.

Although feeling sorry for the owner is a legitimate emotion, it is not a *logical* reason to go to Morning Glory for coffee. Similarly, see the following argument:

Let's go to Morning Glory for coffee. I'm sick of those big franchises putting the little guy out of business.

The speaker is appealing to your sense of anger, but he is *not* offering any logical reasons for going to Morning Glory. His argument would be much stronger, however, if he simply added a logical premise or two:

Let's go to Morning Glory for coffee. I'm sick of those big franchises putting the little guy out of business. We should support local businesses and help them stay in business.

Bandwagon Appeals

Bandwagon appeals are those fallacies that appeal to the human desire to be accepted and belong. They include arguments of **peer pressure**, **bandwagon** (join the winning side just because it's winning), and **common practice** (it's okay to do it because everyone else does it). Here is an example:

I know I'm not supposed to take anything from the stock room, but no one saw me take it. Besides, everyone steals stuff from the office once in a while.

This argument suggests that because "everyone steals stuff from the office once in a while," it's okay for the speaker to take stuff, too. But just because others do X, that doesn't make X right.

Straw Man

The **straw man** fallacy works by distorting, oversimplifying, exaggerating, or otherwise misrepresenting the opponent's position. For example, in arguing *against* tax reform, you might distort the opponent's position by saying the following:

The people who support tax reform are only out to get a break in their own capital gains taxes.

Even if this is one of the reasons why people support tax reform, it cannot be the only one—after all, something like tax reform is a pretty complicated issue. Furthermore, the straw man portrays the reformers as selfish and greedy—only in it for themselves—which makes it much easier for us to reject their position.

Similarly, if you were to argue *for* tax reform, you might set up a straw man like the following:

The folks who oppose tax reform simply don't want to go to the trouble of restructuring the IRS.

True, restructuring the IRS may be one major concern of the opponents, but is it their only, or even their main, concern? Is that the real reason why they don't support it? Chances are their position stems from a number of issues of which reforming the IRS is only one. Once again, the opponent's position has been misrepresented, making it much easier to reject.

Red Herring

Imagine for a moment a magician on a stage. At the crucial moment of the trick, a puff of smoke appears, and poof—the rabbit appears, the assistant is cut in two, or the box begins to levitate. Whatever trick the magician is performing, and whatever technique he or she uses to distract you—smoke, music, a wave of the hand, and so on—the point is that he or she has misdirected you. The magician has used a technique of distraction to prevent you from seeing what is really happening with his or her hands.

The same thing can be done with arguments. If you want to distract your listeners from the real issue, you can throw in a **red herring** (also called a **smokescreen**)—an *irrelevant issue*—in the hopes that your listeners will follow that trail instead of the original. For example, look how the following argument uses a red herring to throw the reader off track:

Many citizens will be upset by another tax increase, but we have no other choice. Besides, we live in the best county in the state.

This argument claims the tax increase is inevitable, but instead of offering a premise that supports this conclusion, it changes the subject to bring in an irrelevant issue. Whether or not "we live in the best county in the state" has no bearing on the claim that another tax increase is necessary. This red herring attempts to deflect the matter so that the speaker does not have to explain *why* taxes should be higher.

Slobodan Milosevic, the former president of Yugoslavia, attempted to defend himself through red herrings during his 2002 trial at The Hague War Crimes Tribunal. Accused of atrocities in Kosovo, war crimes in Croatia, and genocide in Bosnia, Milosevic repeatedly tried to change the issue by shifting the blame onto his accusers. In his opening defense, Milosevic said, "They [NATO] want to ascribe to me responsibility and accountability for everything that they themselves did and all the crimes that they perpetrated themselves" and that "Our defense was a heroic defense from the aggression launched by NATO." Instead of offering reasons why he should not be found guilty of his alleged crimes, Milosevic was raising other controversial issues (whether NATO and other countries involved in the conflict committed the same crimes, whether NATO launched a criminal attack on Yugoslavia, or whether the Yugoslav defense was "heroic"). He was hoping to throw his accusers off track.

Slippery Slope

The **slippery slope** fallacy presents an *if/then* scenario as an absolute. It argues that *if* X happens, *then* Y will automatically follow. This "next thing you know" argument has one major flaw, however: X does not always lead to Y. You need to look carefully at the argument to determine whether this is false reasoning (slippery slope) or if a direct and plausible cause/effect relationship really exists between X and Y. For example, look at the following argument:

> *If scientists are allowed to experiment with cloning humans, next thing you know, they will be mass producing people on assembly lines. It will be just like* Brave New World!

If scientists were to experiment with cloning human beings, for example, does that necessarily mean that humans will be mass produced on production lines? Definitely not. First of all, it may prove impossible to clone healthy humans successfully, no matter how much scientists experiment. Second, if it is possible, it's a far step from one clone to assembly-line production. Third, if assembly-line production *is* possible, it will probably not be legal, unless the kind of social/political revolution described in the classic science fiction novel *Brave New World* occurs. So although the thought of mass-produced human beings is frightening, it's not logical to restrict experiments because you are afraid of consequences that will probably not occur. You must have other, more logical reasons if you wish to limit that kind of experimentation.

Begging the Question

Another common logical fallacy is **begging the question**. This fallacy is also known as **circular reasoning**, and for good reason: The argument goes in a circle. Notice how the following argument doubles back on itself; the conclusion and premise say essentially the same thing:

Tom:	*"That's not important, Jeb."*
Jeb:	*"Why?"*
Tom:	*"It just doesn't matter."*
Conclusion:	*That's not important.*
Premise:	*It doesn't matter.*

This is begging the question. Instead of progressing logically from conclusion to evidence for that conclusion, Tom's argument gets stuck repeating the conclusion. Like a dog chasing its tail, it goes nowhere.

Here is another example:

I know he is telling the truth because he is not lying.

Again, the argument goes in a circle. The premise repeats the conclusion.

Ad Hominem

Ad hominem is any type of pseudoreasoning that asks you to reject a claim because of its source—not because the source lacks credibility, but because of who or what that source is—a lobbyist, a member of a particular political party, a notorious liar, a gabby next door neighbor, and so on. Hence the name, *ad hominem*, which means "to the man" in Latin. It is a fallacy that attacks the person, not the claim. Here are some examples:

"Oh, don't listen to him. What does he know? He's just a kid."
"Don't believe anything George has to say. He's a liar."
If Wilkins says to vote yes, then I'm voting no. I won't go along with any of her ideas.

The source of a claim is *very* important, and you should always consider the credibility of the source before you accept a claim. *Ad hominem*, however, is different because it asks us to *reject* a claim based on the person who made the claim, not on any merits of the claim itself. You may thoroughly dislike the person who made the claim, but that doesn't mean what that person has to say isn't a good argument or that his or her claim deserves to be automatically rejected.

Any time you automatically reject a claim (or ask someone to reject a claim) because of who said it, you commit the *ad hominem* fallacy. This includes rejecting a claim because it's inconsistent with something the claim maker has said or done. Just because Sally once cheated on an exam, for example, doesn't mean you should reject her claim that it's wrong to cheat. If Sally claims that it's wrong to cheat and continues to cheat herself, then you have every right to call her a hypocrite. But that doesn't mean that her claim—that cheating is wrong—is invalid. Keep in mind that people have the right to change their minds and to reject past beliefs or behaviors.

Now read the following question carefully. Use your knowledge of logical fallacies to answer it correctly.

The national golf tournament should not be open to women. The tournament has traditionally been open to male members only. There is no reason to break with that tradition, just because some people want to be politically correct. Besides, women golfers have their own clubs and tournaments. This is the most renowned tournament, however, and that is exactly why it should remain exclusive. Indeed, the tournament is renowned in part because it is so exclusive. Opening it to women would reduce its importance in the golf world. Worse, allowing women into the event would mean that we would end up having to let everybody play, without restrictions, and that would completely demean the tournament.

Which of the following is the most serious weakness of this argument?

a. It assumes that it is wrong to break tradition.

b. It assumes that women should not have an equal opportunity.

c. It assumes that including women would mean that everyone would have to be included without restriction.

d. It does not acknowledge that men are included in some women's tournaments.

e. It does not explain why the tournament is such a renowned event.

This argument has many problems, including the fact that in general, it does not offer any truly logical reasons to support its conclusion. Of the options given, the best choice is **c**. This assumption is a slippery slope fallacy. Including women would not mean anyone could enter the tournament. This slippery slope is used as a sort of scare tactic to frighten off support for including women in the tournament.

GMAT questions will often ask you to determine what evidence strengthens or weakens an argument or what information would help you better evaluate an argument. Now that you have reviewed the elements of evaluating arguments, take another look at this question from the pretest:

13. DNA evidence has increasingly been used in court to prove guilt and to exonerate the innocent. Because so many convicted felons have been cleared by DNA evidence, all cases in which someone was convicted largely on circumstantial evidence should be called into question and reviewed.

Which of the following, if true, would most strengthen this argument?

a. One in three convictions today rests largely on DNA evidence.

b. DNA evidence is admissible even after the statute of limitations has expired.

c. Of every ten cases in which DNA evidence becomes available post-conviction, five convictions are overturned.

d. DNA evidence is 99.8% accurate.

e. DNA evidence is very difficult to falsify or tamper with.

To answer this question, you need to evaluate each of the options. The key question is which choice is the most relevant to the argument. As discussed earlier in this chapter, this is a controversial conclusion, so it should be backed by very strong evidence. Which of these claims provides the best support for the argument?

The best choice is **c**. The fact that would most strengthen this argument is the percentage of cases in which DNA evidence overturned prior convictions. If a full half of all cases resulted in erroneous convictions that were later cleared by DNA evidence, then that should certainly draw other convictions into doubt. That means that potentially half of all felons have been wrongly convicted. The fact that one in three of today's convictions rest on DNA evidence has no bearing on *prior* convictions, so choice **a** is irrelevant. Similarly, the admissibility of DNA evidence (choice **b**) has no bearing on the quality of prior convictions; it is also irrelevant. That DNA evidence is accurate (choice **d**) and difficult to tamper with (choice **e**) strengthens the argument for the use of DNA evidence in court, but it does *not* directly strengthen the argument that prior convictions should be called into doubt.

Evaluating Explanations

Many of the critical reasoning questions on the GMAT exam will either present a scenario and ask you to determine the best explanation for a phenomenon or offer an explanation and ask you to evaluate that explanation. Some special criteria must be considered when judging an explanation. A good explanation is based on the following criteria:

- **Testable.** An explanation must be subject to testing. If the phenomenon is the only evidence for its existence, then it is a poor explanation. If it cannot be tested for correctness, then you cannot determine whether or not it is correct. If an explanation cannot be verified or refuted under any circumstances, regard it with suspicion.

  Example: *He knew what I was thinking because he has ESP.*

  Although many have tried to prove that extra-sensory perception (ESP) exists, tests remain inconclusive. And how could you test whether or not this was true? If you test him for ESP and he fails, he could claim that he only uses his ESP powers when he wants to. This is an untestable explanation.
- **Noncircular.** If the phenomenon and the evidence/explanation for the phenomenon are essentially the same, then you have a circular (and therefore unacceptable) explanation. (This works just the same as the circular reasoning logical fallacy.) Beware of any explanation that merely restates the phenomenon it is supposed to explain. It may *look* like an explanation because it restates the phenomenon in different words, but no explanation is really being offered.

  Example: *Prices keep going up because of inflation.*

  Inflation means that prices are going up; this doesn't explain why prices are rising.
- **Precise.** If an explanation is excessively vague, it does not really explain the phenomenon.

  Example: *Our society is a mess because of TV.*

  This is an exceptionally vague explanation. What does the speaker mean by "a mess"? What does she mean by "because of TV"?
- **Reliable and relevant.** A reliable explanation is one that people can use to predict other behaviors. If an explanation leads to predictions that turn out to be false, then it is unreliable.

  Example: *The Watsons are always late because they only have one car.*

  Based on this explanation, you would have to expect that every family that has only one car will always be late. Clearly, this will lead to false predictions, proving this is an unreliable explanation. In addition, the fact that the Watsons have only one car is irrelevant to their punctuality. Families with no cars might always be on time; families with four cars might always be late. This is also an irrelevant explanation.

- **Able to explain more phenomena.** Other things being equal, the more phenomena an explanation explains, the better the explanation, especially for scientific theories.

  Example: *Rent is high in this neighborhood because*

  1. *landlords are greedy.*
  2. *there is a new train line that goes directly to the city.*

  Clearly, the second explanation here is better. It can explain more phenomena, such as an increased demand for apartments, an increase in local property taxes, an increase in population, and an increase in upscale retail establishments in the area.
- **Consistent with well-established theory/common knowledge.** Although established theories are not infallible (remember, people once thought the world was flat), you need very powerful evidence to discard them. So, if an explanation conflicts with such a theory, you have good reason to be suspicious. Likewise, if an explanation conflicts with your common knowledge, be on guard. It is probably not a good one.

  Example: *That little girl has tons of freckles, just like her parents. They all must spend way too much time in the sun.*

  Although it's true that sun exposure can cause some people to develop freckles, this explanation goes against the well-established theory of heredity. If a little girl has freckles and her parents also have freckles, it is safe to assume she inherited the freckle gene from her parents.

Returning to the bookstore question about the placement of romance novels, you can further assess the possible conclusions with these criteria for evaluating explanations. You could test all of the choices to see if they are correct, none are circular, and all have explanatory power. But **a**—that customers would come back for another romance novel—is not reliable or relevant to the scenario. Return purchases have nothing to do with the placement of books in the store.

Common Flaws in Causal Arguments

Arguments about cause (why things happen) contain their own types of fallacies that you should watch out for, including the following:

- *post hoc, ergo propter hoc*
- ignoring possible common cause
- assuming common cause
- reversing causation

Post Hoc, Ergo Propter Hoc

Translated from Latin, this means "after this, therefore because of this." This argument assumes that X caused Y just because X preceded Y. For example,

As soon as Thompson took office, the market crashed. He has simply destroyed the economy.

The problem with this argument is that although X (Thompson's taking office) preceded Y (the market crash), that does not mean Thompson *caused* the market crash. The key question to ask is this: Is X the *only relevant change* prior to Y? In this case, definitely not. Many, many other relevant factors could have preceded the market crash. (Besides, it is difficult for a politician to destroy the economy "as soon as" he or she takes office. Common sense tells you it would take some time for a leader's policies to have an impact.)

Ignoring Possible Common Cause

This argument assumes that X caused Y, but maybe X *and* Y were both caused by another factor (W). For example,

I had hives because I had a fever.

Perhaps the fever caused the hives, but maybe the hives *and* the fever were both caused by another factor, such as a virus. Before accepting a causal explanation, ask the following: Could there be an underlying cause for both X and Y?

Assuming Common Cause

This argument assumes that X and Y had a common cause and ignores the possibility of a coincidence. Maybe X and Y are due to different or multiple causes. For example,

On Thursday, there was a black cat sitting in my driveway. That night, I had an accident in my car. On Friday, the cat was there again, and that night, my boyfriend broke up with me. That black cat sure brought me some bad luck.

Besides the fact that this argument does not have much initial plausibility (and requires belief in the superstition that black cats bring bad luck), it fails for several other reasons:

- It ignores the possibility of coincidence.
- It does not consider the fact that a black cat is totally irrelevant to the occurrences.
- It does not consider other possible common causes (maybe the accident and the breakup were both due the speaker's inability to pay attention—to the road and to her boyfriend).
- It does not consider that the two events could have resulted from very different causes (the accident could have been because the speaker was distracted; the breakup could have been caused by an infidelity, a change of heart, and so on).

Reversing Causation

This fallacy confuses cause and effect (the "chicken and the egg" problem), arguing that the effect was really the cause or vice versa. For example,

Lucy feels more confident because she aced her last two exams.

This example could definitely be a case of reversed causation. Maybe Lucy aced her last two exams because she was feeling more confident. You would have to study the situation further to determine which was cause and which was effect. If you suspect reverse causation, consider carefully whether a reversal of cause and effect could have occurred. Is it possible for the alleged cause to actually be an effect, or the effect to really be the cause?

Now take a look at the following question. Use your knowledge of causal argument fallacies to answer it correctly:

> Did you ever notice that successful business people drive expensive cars? If I get myself an expensive car, I will become more successful.
>
> The most serious flaw in this argument is
>
> **a.** it assumes all successful business people drive expensive cars.
> **b.** it reverses cause and effect.
> **c.** it is not a testable explanation.
> **d.** it ignores the possibility of coincidence.
> **e.** it ignores a possible common cause.

The correct answer is **b**: The argument reverses cause and effect. Successful business people can afford expensive cars *because* they are successful; the success comes first, *then* the car. The speaker may be looking at some serious debt if he believes otherwise.

CHAPTER

7 Sentence Correction

Sentence correction questions are designed to measure your knowledge of both grammar and effective style. Chances are you already know most of these rules and guidelines even if you don't know how to articulate them. You can often tell when something *sounds* wrong, even if you don't know exactly *why* it is wrong. That is good news because on the GMAT® exam you do not have to identify the grammar rule that has been broken or what makes the writing ineffective. Rather, you will simply have to identify which sentence is free of errors and written most effectively.

That said, you can still benefit a great deal from a review of the basic rules of grammar and guidelines for effective style, especially if you feel that grammar is not your strong suit. You may find some sections here more basic than you need, but give yourself the opportunity to review everything in this section. You may find that you have forgotten some rules and guidelines, and a review of the rules and terminology can give you more confidence on the exam.

24 Rules for Grammar and Style

Throughout this chapter, you will learn about and review each of these rules in depth. After you have completed the chapter, use the following list as a checklist as you review for the GMAT exam:

1. Follow the basic subject-predicate word order for sentences: subject, verb, indirect object, and direct object.
2. Make sure sentences have both a subject and a predicate *and* express a complete thought.
3. Respect sentence boundaries. Do not let two or more independent clauses run together.
4. Keep modifiers as close as possible to the words they modify.
5. Use parallel structure for any series of actions or items or the *not only/but also* construction.
6. Make sure verbs agree in number with their subjects.
7. Keep verb tenses consistent.
8. Use the correct subject or object form of personal pronouns. Determine whether a pronoun is functioning as a subject or object in the sentence.
9. Use apostrophes with pronouns to show contraction only. Pronouns do not need apostrophes to show possession.
10. Use *who* for people, *that* for things, and *which* for nonessential clauses that do not refer to people.
11. Make sure pronouns agree in number and person with their antecedents.
12. Be consistent in pronoun point of view.
13. Use *less* (meaning a smaller *amount*) for singular nouns representing quantity or degree. Use *fewer* (meaning a smaller *number*) for plural nouns and countable items.
14. Use *good* and *bad* to modify nouns and pronouns; use *well* and *badly* to modify verbs.
15. In comparisons, add *-er* or *-est* to short modifiers. For longer words, use *more/the most* or *less/the least* before the modifier.
16. Do not use double comparisons.
17. Do not use double negatives.
18. Use idioms correctly.
19. Be concise. Avoid unnecessary repetition or wordiness.
20. Be precise. Use exact words.
21. Avoid ambiguity. Make sure word choice and pronoun references are clear and modifiers properly placed.
22. In general, use the active voice.
23. Use variety in sentence structure.
24. Avoid jargon and pretentious language.

▶ Sentence Structure

The best place to begin a grammar review is with the basics of sentence construction. Although you will not need to diagram a sentence on the GMAT exam, understanding the fundamentals of sentence structure can help you better remember the rules of grammar and style.

Sentence structure refers to the way sentences are composed: how subjects, verbs, objects, and modifiers are strung together in clauses and phrases. Awkward or incorrect placement of phrases and clauses can result in sentences that are confusing, unclear, or say things that you do not mean. Indeed, many sentences on the GMAT exam will be wrong precisely because of misplaced sentence elements. Sentence structure is also important to style. If sentence structure is too simple or repetitive, the writing becomes monotonous for the reader. (Style will be addressed later in this section.)

Subjects, Predicates, and Objects

The sentence is the basic unit of written expression. It consists of two essential parts—a **subject** and a **predicate**—and it must express a complete thought. The subject of a sentence tells the reader *who* or *what* the sentence is about—who or what is performing the action of the sentence. The predicate tells the reader something *about* the subject—what the subject is or does. Consider the following sentence:

The clock is ticking.

The word *clock* is the subject. It tells you what the sentence is about—who or what performs the action of the sentence. The verb phrase *is ticking* is the predicate. It tells you the action performed by (or information about) the subject.

The subject of a sentence can be **singular** or **compound** (plural):

I slept all day. (subject: *I*)	*Kendrick and I worked all night.* (subject: *Kendrick and I*)
singular subject	compound subject (two subjects performing the action)

The predicate can also be singular or compound:

I received a bonus. (predicate: *received a bonus*)	*I received a bonus and got a raise.* (predicates: *received a bonus*, *got a raise*)
singular predicate	compound predicate (two actions performed by the subject)

Subject-predicate is the fundamental word order of sentences. When this order is reversed, the result is an awkward and perhaps unclear sentence such as the following:

A bonus I received.

In such a short sentence, the meaning is often clear despite the awkward word order. However, in longer sentences, when the subject and predicate are reversed, the sentence can be quite confusing, as in the following sentence from the pretest:

Creating a fundamental shift in American foreign policy and establishing a "policy of containment" that framed our foreign policy as a battle between the forces of good (America and other democratic societies) and evil (the Soviet Union and other communist nations), was the 1947 Truman Doctrine.

In many sentences, someone or something "receives" the action expressed in the predicate. This person or thing is called the **direct object.** In the following sentences, the subject and predicate are separated by a slash (/) and the direct object is underlined:

I / bought a present. (The present receives the action of being bought.)
Jane / loves ice cream. (Ice cream receives the action of being loved by Jane.)

Sentences can also have an **indirect object**: a person or thing who "receives" the direct object. In the following sentences, the direct object is underlined and the indirect object is in bold:

I / gave ***Sunil*** *a raise.* (Sunil receives the raise; the raise receives the action of being given.)
The student / asked ***the professor*** *a question.* (The professor receives the question; the question receives the action of being asked.)

Rule #1: Follow the basic subject-predicate word order for sentences: subject, verb, indirect object, and direct object.

Independent and Dependent Clauses

A **clause** contains a subject and a predicate and may also have direct and indirect objects. An **independent clause** expresses a complete thought; it can stand on its own as a sentence. A **dependent clause**, on the other hand, cannot stand alone because it expresses an incomplete idea. When a dependent clause stands alone, it results in a **sentence fragment**.

Independent clause:	*She was excited.*
Dependent clause:	*Because she was excited.*

Notice that the dependent clause is incomplete; it needs an additional thought to make a complete sentence:

She spoke very quickly because she was excited.

The independent clause, however, can stand alone. It is a complete thought.

Subordinating Conjunctions

A subordinating conjunction such as the word because makes a dependent clause dependent. Subordinating conjunctions connect clauses and help show the relationship between those clauses. The following is a list of the most common subordinating conjunctions:

after	even though	that	when
although	if	though	where
as, as if	in order that	unless	wherever
because	once	until	while
before	since		

When a clause begins with a subordinating conjunction, it is dependent. It must be connected to an independent clause to become a complete thought:

I never knew true happiness	*until I met you.*
independent clause	dependent clause
After Johnson quit,	*I had to work extra overtime.*
dependent clause	independent clause

Conjunctive Adverbs

A very common grammar mistake is to think that words such as *however* and *therefore* are subordinating conjunctions. But however and therefore belong to a group of words called **conjunctive adverbs**, which also signal relationships between parts of a sentence. When they are used with a semicolon, they can combine independent clauses. The following is a list of the most common conjunctive adverbs:

also	indeed	now
anyway	instead	otherwise
besides	likewise	similarly
certainly	meanwhile	still
finally	moreover	then
furthermore	namely	therefore
however	nevertheless	thus
incidentally	next	undoubtedly

I did not go to the party; <u>instead</u>, I stayed home and watched a good film.
Samantha is a fabulous cook; <u>indeed</u>, she may even be better than Jacque.
I need to pay this bill immediately. <u>Otherwise</u>, my phone service will be cut off.

Compound Sentences and Coordinating Conjunctions

When two *independent clauses* are combined, the result is a **compound sentence** such as the following:

He was late, so he lost the account.

The most common way to join two independent clauses is with a comma and a **coordinating conjunction**: *and, but, or, nor, for, so, yet.* Independent clauses can also be joined with a semicolon if the ideas in the sentences are closely related:

I am tall, and he is short.	[IC, coordinating conjunction + IC]
I am tall; he is short.	[IC; IC]
I was late, yet I still got the account.	[IC, coordinating conjunction + IC]

Sentence Boundaries

Expressing complete ideas and clearly indicating where sentences begin and end are essential to effective writing. Two of the most common grammatical errors with sentence boundaries are fragments and run-ons.

Incomplete Sentences (Fragments)

As stated earlier, a complete sentence must (1) have both a **subject** (who or what performs the action) and a **verb** (a state of being or an action) and (2) express a complete thought. If you don't complete a thought, or if you are missing a subject or verb (or both), then you have an incomplete sentence (also called a sentence **fragment**). To correct a fragment, add the missing subject or verb or otherwise change the sentence to complete the thought.

Incomplete:	Which is simply not true. (No subject. *Which* is not a subject.)
Complete:	*That* is simply not true.
Incomplete:	For example, the French Revolution. (No verb.)
Complete:	The best example is the French Revolution.
Incomplete:	Even though the polar icecaps are melting. (Subject and verb, but not a complete thought.)
Complete:	Some people still do not believe in global warming even though the polar icecaps are melting.

Rule #2: Make sure sentences have both a subject and a predicate and express a complete thought.

Run-On Sentences

A run-on sentence occurs when one sentence "runs" right into the next without proper punctuation between them. Usually, the sentence has no punctuation at all or it has just a comma between the two thoughts (called a comma splice). But commas alone are not strong enough to separate two complete ideas. See the examples of run-ons on the next page.

Let us go it is getting late.
I aced the interview, I should get the job.
Whether or not you believe me it is true, I did not lie to you.

You can correct run-on sentences in five ways:

- with a period
- with a comma *and* a coordinating conjunction: *and, or, nor, for, so, but,* or *yet*
- with a semicolon
- with a dash
- with a subordinating conjunction to create a dependent clause: *although, because, during, while,* and so on

The following is a run-on sentence corrected with each of the previous techniques:

The debate is over, now it is time to vote.

PUNCTUATION	CORRECTED SENTENCE
period	The debate is over. Now it is time to vote.
comma + conjunction	The debate is over, and now it is time to vote.
semicolon	The debate is over; now it is time to vote.
dash	The debate is over—now it is time to vote.
subordinating conjunction	Since the debate is over, it is time to vote.

Rule #3: Respect sentence boundaries. Do not let two or more independent clauses run together.

Phrases and Modifiers

Sentences are often "filled out" by phrases and modifiers. Phrases are groups of words that do not have both a subject and predicate; they might have either a subject or a verb, but not both, and sometimes neither. Modifiers are words and phrases that qualify or describe people, places, things, and actions. The most common phrases are prepositional phrases, which consist of a preposition and a noun or pronoun (e.g., *in the attic*). Modifiers include adjectives (e.g., *slow, blue, excellent*) and adverbs (e.g., *cheerfully, suspiciously*). In the following examples, the prepositional phrases are underlined and the modifiers are in bold:

*He was **very late** for **an important** meeting with **a new** client.*
*He **brazenly** looked through **her** purse when she got up from **the** table to go to **the ladies'** room.*

Placement of Modifiers

As a general rule, words, phrases, or clauses that describe nouns and pronouns should be as close as possible to the words they describe. *The relaxing music*, for example, is better (clearer, more concise, and more precise) than *the music that is relaxing*. In the first sentence, the modifier *relaxing* is right next to the word it modifies (*music*).

When modifiers are not next to the words they describe, you not only often use extra words, but you also might end up with a **misplaced** or **dangling modifier** and a sentence that means something other than what was intended. This is especially true of phrases and clauses that work as modifiers. Take a look at the following sentence:

Whispering quietly, I heard the children stealing cookies from the cookie jar.

Who was whispering quietly? Because the modifier *whispering quietly* is next to *I*, the sentence says that *I* was doing the whispering. But the context of the sentence indicates that it was the children who were doing the whispering. Here are three corrected versions. In the first version, the modifier is moved to its proper place, next to *children*. In the second and third versions, *I* is removed from the sentence to eliminate any confusion:

I heard the children whispering quietly as they stole cookies from the cookie jar.
The children, whispering quietly, stole cookies from the cookie jar.
Whispering quietly, the children stole cookies from the cookie jar as I listened.

Here's another example:

Worn and tattered, Uncle Joe took down the flag.

It's quite obvious that it was the flag, not Uncle Joe, that was worn and tattered. But because the modifier (worn and tattered) isn't right next to what it modifies (the flag), the sentence actually says that Uncle Joe was worn and tattered. Here are two corrected versions. The first simply puts the modifier in its proper place. The second moves the modifier and puts it in a restrictive clause (a *which* clause) that clarifies what is modified:

Uncle Joe took down the worn and tattered flag.
Uncle Joe took down the flag, which was worn and tattered.

Rule #4: Keep modifiers as close as possible to the words they modify.

Parts of Speech: A Brief Review

A word's function and form is determined by its part of speech. The word calm, for example, can be either a verb (calm down) or an adjective (a calm afternoon); it changes to calmly when it is an adverb (they discussed the matter calmly). Be sure you know the different parts of speech and the job each part of speech performs in a sentence. The following table offers a quick reference guide for the main parts of speech.

PART OF SPEECH	FUNCTION	EXAMPLES
noun	names a person, place, thing, or concept	water, Byron, telephone, Main Street, tub, virtue
pronoun	takes the place of a noun so that noun does not have to be repeated	I, you, he, she, us, they, this, that, themselves, somebody, who, which
verb	expresses an action, occurrence, or state of being	wait, seem, be, visit, renew
helping verb (also called auxiliary verb)	combines with other verbs (main verbs) to create verb phrases that help indicate tenses	forms of be, do and have; can, could, may, might, must, shall, should, will, would
adjective	modifies nouns and pronouns; can also identify or quantify	green, round, old, surprising; that (e.g., that elephant); several (e.g., several elephants)
adverb	modifies verbs, adjectives, other adverbs, or entire clauses	dreamily, quickly, always, very, then
preposition	expresses the relationship in time or space between words in a sentence	in, on, around, above, between, underneath, beside, with, upon

Prepositions are extremely important; they help us understand how objects relate to each other in space and time. Recognizing them can help you quickly check for subject-verb agreement and other grammar issues. The following is a list of the most common prepositions. See pages 127–128 for notes about the most common prepositional idioms.

about	above	across	after
against	around	at	before
behind	below	beneath	beside

(continued)

Parts of Speech: A Brief Review

besides	between	beyond	by
down	during	except	for
from	in	inside	into
like	near	of	off
on	out	outside	over
since	through	throughout	till
to	toward	under	until
up	upon	with	without

Parallel Structure

Parallel structure means that words and phrases in a sentence follow the same grammatical pattern. Whenever a sentence has a series of actions, a list of items, or a *not only/but also* construction, it should have parallel structure. Parallelism makes ideas easier to follow and expresses ideas more gracefully. Notice how parallelism works in the following examples:

Not parallel: *We came, we saw, and it was conquered by us.* (The first two clauses use the active *we* + past tense verb construction; the third uses a passive structure with a prepositional phrase.)

Parallel: *We came, we saw, we conquered.* (All three clauses start with *we* and use a past tense verb.)

Not parallel: *Please be sure to throw out your trash, place your silverware in the bin, and your tray should go on the counter.* (Two verbs follow the *to* + *verb* + *your* + *noun* pattern; the third puts the noun first and then the verb.)

Parallel: *Please be sure to throw out your trash, place your silverware in the pin, and put your tray on the counter.* (All three items follow the *to* + *verb* + *your* + *noun* + *prepositional phrase* pattern.)

The following are two more examples of sentences with correct parallel structure:

Hermione's nervousness was exacerbated not only by the large crowd but also by the bright lights. (Each phrase has a preposition, an adjective, and a noun.)

Their idea was not only the most original; it was also the most practical. (Each phrase uses the superlative form of an adjective [see page 126 for more information on superlatives].)

Rule #5: Use parallel structure for any series of actions or items or the *not only/but also* construction.

▶ Grammar and Usage

Grammar and usage refer to the rules that govern the forms of words people use and the special combinations of words that create specific meanings. In this section, you will review the following areas of basic grammar and usage:

- subject-verb agreement
- consistent verb tense
- pronoun cases
- pronoun agreement
- pronoun consistency
- adjectives and adverbs
- idioms

Agreement

In English grammar, agreement means that sentence elements are balanced. Verbs, for example, should agree in number with their subjects. If the subject is singular, the verb should be singular; if the subject is plural, the verb should be plural.

Incorrect:	*Robin want to meet us later.* (singular subject, plural verb)
Correct:	*Robin wants to meet us later.* (singular subject, singular verb)
Incorrect:	*He do whatever he want.* (singular subject, plural verbs)
Correct:	*He does whatever he wants.* (singular subject, singular verbs)

Of course, to make sure subjects and verbs agree, you need to be clear about who or what is the subject of the sentence. This can be tricky in sentences with indefinite pronouns and in inverted sentences. Use the following guidelines for proper subject-verb agreement:

- Remember that *subjects are never found in prepositional phrases,* so the subject must be elsewhere in the sentence. Sometimes the subject is the antecedent of a noun found in a prepositional phrase, as in the following example:

  Only one of the students was officially registered for the class.

  The pronoun *one* is the subject of the sentence, not *students,* because *students* is part of the prepositional phrase *of the students.* The verb must therefore be singular (*was*).
- If a compound, singular subject is connected by *and,* the verb must be plural.

  Both Vanessa and Xui want to join the committee.

- If a compound, singular subject is connected by *or* or *nor,* the verb must be singular.

  Neither Vanessa nor Xiu wants to join the committee.

Verb Review

If English is your second language, a quick review of verb conjugation and usage rules might be in order. Turn to Chapter 11 for an overview of verb forms, a list of irregular verbs, and a review of troublesome verbs such as *lay/lie*.

- If one plural and one singular subject are connected by *or* or *nor*, the verb agrees with the closest subject.

  Neither Vanessa nor the treasurers want to join the committee.
  Neither the treasurers nor Vanessa wants to join the committee.

- In an **inverted sentence**, the subject comes *after* the verb, so the first step is to clearly identify the subject. (Sentences that begin with *there is* and *there are*, for example, and questions are inverted sentences.) Once you correctly identify the subject, then you can make sure your verb agrees. The correct subjects and verbs are underlined in the following examples:

  Incorrect: *There is plenty of reasons to go.*
  Correct: *There are plenty of reasons to go.*

  Incorrect: *Here is the results you have been waiting for.*
  Correct: *Here are the results you have been waiting for.*

  Incorrect: *What is the side effects of this medication?*
  Correct: *What are the side effects of this medication?*

Rule #6: Make sure verbs agree in number with their subjects.

Consistent Tense

One of the quickest ways to confuse readers, especially if you are telling a story or describing an event, is to shift verb tenses. To help readers be clear about when actions occur, make sure verb tenses are consistent. If you begin telling the story in the present tense, for example, stay in the present tense; do not mix tenses as you write. Otherwise, you will leave your readers wondering whether actions are taking place in the present or took place in the past:

Incorrect: *She left the house and forgets her keys again.*
Correct: *She left the house and forgot her keys again.*
Incorrect: *When we work together, we got better results.*
Correct: *When we work together, we get better results.*
When we worked together, we got better results.

Rule #7: Keep verb tenses consistent.

Pronouns

Pronouns, as noted earlier, replace nouns, so you don't have to repeat names and objects over and over. There are several different kinds of pronouns, and each kind of pronoun follows different rules.

Personal Pronouns

Personal pronouns refer to specific people or things. They can be either singular (*I*) or plural (*we*); they can be subjects (*I*) or objects (*me*). Pronouns reflect three points of view: first person (*I, we*), second person (*you*), and third person (*he, she, it, them*).

	SUBJECT	OBJECT	POINT OF VIEW
singular	I	me	first person
	you	you	second person
	he	him	third person
	she	her	third person
	it	it	third person
plural	we	us	first person
	you	you	second person
	they	them	third person

Pronoun mistakes are often made when you use the subject form when you really need the object form. Here are two guidelines to follow:

- **Always use the object pronoun in a prepositional phrase.** Pronouns and nouns in prepositional phrases are always objects:

  He promised to bring a souvenir for Betty and <u>me</u>.
  Please keep this between <u>us</u>.

- Always use the subject pronoun in a *than* construction (comparison). When a pronoun follows *than*, it is usually part of a clause that omits the verb to avoid redundancy:

  I realize that Alonzo is more talented than <u>I</u>. [than I am]
  Sandra is much more reliable than <u>he</u>. [than he is]

Rule #8: Use the correct subject or object form of personal pronouns. Determine whether a pronoun is functioning as a subject or object in the sentence.

Possessive Pronouns

The **possessive pronouns** *its, your, their,* and *whose* are often confused with the contractions *it's (it is* or *it has), you're (you are), they're (they are),* and *who's (who is).* Because writers use apostrophes to show possession in nouns (*Louise's* truck, the *rug's* pattern), many people make the mistake of thinking that pronouns use apostrophes for possession, too. But possessive pronouns *do not* take apostrophes. When a pronoun has an apostrophe, it always shows **contraction.**

POSSESSIVE PRONOUN	MEANING	EXAMPLE
its	belonging to it	The dog chased its tail.
your	belonging to you	Your time is up.
their	belonging to them	Their words were comforting.
whose	belonging to who	Whose tickets are these?

CONTRACTION		
it's	it is	It's time to eat.
you're	you are	You're not going to believe your eyes.
they're	they are	They're getting their tickets now.
who's	who is	Who's got my tickets?

Rule #9: Use apostrophes with pronouns to show contraction only. Pronouns do not need apostrophes to show possession.

The pronouns *who, that,* and *which* are also often confused. The following lists the general guidelines for using these pronouns correctly:

- Use **who** or **whom** when referring to people:

  She is the one who should make that decision, not I.

- Use **that** when referring to things:

  This is the most important decision that she will make as director.

- Use **which** when introducing clauses that are not essential to the information in the sentence (nonrestrictive), *unless* they refer to people. In that case, use **who.**

Contraction Confusion

It is easy to make a mistake with pronouns and contractions because apostrophes are used to show possession of nouns (*Ralph's car*). With pronouns, however, possession does not require an apostrophe. If you get confused, think of a possessive pronoun that doesn't get confused with contractions, such as *my* or *our*. These do not have apostrophes; other possessive pronouns should not either.

Here is one way to remember to use *that* when referring to things: both words begin with the letters *th*.

Sam bought a suit to wear to his new job, which will begin on Monday.
Emily married Sonny, who has been in love with her since first grade.
Antoinette, who is a computer programmer, would be a good match for Daniel.

Rule #10: Use *who* for people, *that* for things, and *which* for nonessential clauses that do not refer to people.

Pronoun-Antecedent Agreement

Just as subjects (both nouns and pronouns) must agree with their verbs, pronouns must also agree with their antecedents—the words they replace. For example, consider the following sentence:

Children will often believe everything their parents tell them.

The word *children* is the antecedent and is replaced by *their* and *them* in the sentence. Because *children* is plural, the pronouns must also be plural.

Indefinite pronouns can also be antecedents. Singular indefinite pronouns require singular pronouns:

Everyone has *his or her* *own reasons for coming.*
Neither of the physicists could explain what she saw.

Plural indefinite pronouns, on the other hand, require plural pronouns, just like they require plural verbs:

both few many several

Both of them have finished their work.
Only a few are still in their original cases.

A Bad Habit

One of the most common mistakes people make when speaking and writing is an error of pronoun-antecedent agreement. You may often say sentences such as the following:

Everyone will receive their scores within two weeks.

Most people make this mistake because it's easier (shorter and faster) to say *their*—but it's not correct. When the antecedent is singular, the pronouns must be singular, too:

Everyone will receive his or her scores within two weeks.

The students will receive their scores within two weeks.

Finally, those pronouns that can be either singular or plural, depending upon the noun or pronoun to which they refer, should take the pronoun that matches their referent. If the antecedent is singular, the pronoun and verb must also be singular. If the antecedent is plural, they must be plural:

all any most none some

All of the chocolate is gone. It was delicious!
All of the cookies are gone. They were delicious!

None of the information is accurate; it's all out of date.
None of the facts are accurate; they are all out of date.

Rule #11: Make sure pronouns agree in number and person with their antecedents.

Pronoun Consistency

Just as you need to be consistent in verb tense, you should also be consistent in your pronoun point of view. A passage that begins in the third-person plural should continue to use that third-person plural point of view.

Incorrect: *We have tested our hypothesis and the team believes it is correct.*
Correct: *We have tested our hypothesis and we believe it is correct.*

Incorrect: *If you prepare carefully, one can expect to pass the exam.*
Correct: *If you prepare carefully, you can expect to pass the exam.*
If one prepares carefully, one can expect to pass the exam.

Rule #12: Be consistent in pronoun point of view.

Adjectives and Adverbs

Adjectives and **adverbs** help give our sentences color; they describe things and actions. Adjectives describe nouns and pronouns and tell us *which one, what kind,* and *how many*:

that book	*romance* novel	*several* chapters
the *other* class	*steep* expense	*multiple* options

Adverbs, on the other hand, describe verbs, adjectives, and other adverbs. They tell us *where, when, how,* and *to what extent*:

flying *south*	arrive *early*	sings *beautifully*	*very* talented
wait *here*	meet *tomorrow*	fight *courageously*	*severely* compromised

Remember to keep modifiers as close as possible to what they modify.

Fewer/Less, Number/Amount

As a rule, use the adjective *fewer* to modify plural nouns or things that can be counted. Use *less* for singular nouns that represent a quantity or a degree. Most nouns to which an *-s* can be added require the adjective *fewer.*

Use less salt this time.	*Use fewer eggs this time.*
I had less reason to go this time.	*I had fewer reasons to go this time.*

Rule #13: Use *less* (meaning a smaller *amount*) for singular nouns representing quantity or degree. Use *fewer* (meaning a smaller *number*) for plural nouns and countable items.

Good/Bad, Well/Badly

These pairs of words—*good/well, bad/badly*—are often confused. The key to proper usage is to understand their function in the sentence. *Good* and *bad* are adjectives; they should only be used to modify nouns and pronouns. *Well* and *badly* are adverbs; they should be used to modify verbs:

I was surprised by how good Sebastian's cake was.
Jennelle hasn't been feeling well lately.
Her experience is good, but she didn't do well in the interview.

Rule #14: Use *good* and *bad* to describe nouns and pronouns; use *well* and *badly* to describe verbs.

Comparisons

An important function of adjectives and adverbs is comparisons. When you are comparing *two* things, use the **comparative form** (*-er*) of the modifier. If you are comparing *more than two* things, use the **superlative form** (*-est*) of the modifier.

To create the **comparative** form, either

- add *-er* to the modifier.
- place the word *more* or *less* before the modifier.

In general, add *-er* to short modifiers (one or two syllables). Use *more* or *less* with modifiers of more than two syllables.

cheaper	*less expensive*
smarter	*more intelligent*

To create the superlative form, either

- add *-est* to the modifier.
- place the word *most* or *least* before the modifier.

Again, as a general rule, add *-est* to short modifiers (one or two syllables). Use *more, most, less,* or *least* with modifiers that are more than two syllables:

Wanda is more experienced than I, but I am the most familiar with the software.
Ahmed is clearly the smartest student in the class.

Rule #15: In comparisons, add *-er* or *-est* to short modifiers. For longer words, use *more/most* or *less/least* before the modifier.

Double Comparisons and Double Negatives

Be sure to **avoid double comparisons.** Don't use both *-er/-est* and *more/less* or *most/least* together.

Incorrect: *She has the most longest hair I have ever seen.*
Correct: *She has the longest hair I have ever seen.*

Incorrect: *Minsun is more happier now.*
Correct: *Minsun is happier now.*

Rule #16: Do not use double comparisons.

Likewise, be sure to avoid **double negatives**. When a negative word such as *no* or *not* is added to a statement that is already negative, it results in a double negative and potential confusion. *Hardly* and *barely* are also negative words. Remember, one negative is all you need:

Incorrect: *He doesn't have no idea what she's talking about.*
Correct: *He doesn't have any idea what she's talking about.*
He has no idea what she's talking about.

Incorrect: *I can't hardly wait to see you.*
Correct: *I can hardly wait to see you.*
I can't wait to see you.

Rule #17: Do not use double negatives.

Idioms

Every language has its share of **idioms**: those odd expressions that have a special meaning not consistent with the literal meanings of the words. For example, to say you are *all ears* certainly does not mean that you are composed entirely of ears; rather, it means that you are listening attentively.

Fluency in idiomatic expressions reflects a comfort with and command of the English language, and that is why some sentence correction questions will test your knowledge of idioms. For example, you might find a sentence correction question such as the following:

I have been so busy because I have had to pick through a slack since Winston quit.

a. had to pick through a slack
b. had to pick the slack
c. had to pick up the slack
d. slacked through the pick
e. been unable to see through the slack

The correct answer is **c**, which correctly uses the idiom *pick up the slack*, meaning *to do someone else's work, or fill in.* All of the other versions use incorrect forms of the idiom.

Prepositional Idioms

Prepositional idioms are the specific word/preposition combinations that English speakers use, such as *take care of* and *according to*. Unless English is your second language, most of these idioms should be part of your everyday vocabulary, but a quick review of the list below may be helpful.

according to	afraid of	anxious about	apologize to (someone)
apologize for (something)	approve of	ashamed of	aware of
	bored with	capable of	compete with

Idiom Review

Many websites offer extensive lists of English language idioms. Try one of these sites for a helpful idiom review:

- Wayne Magnuson English Idioms: home.t-online.de/home/toni.goeller/idiom_wm/index.html
- The Idiom Connection: www.geocities.com/Athens/Aegean/6720

blame (someone) for (something)
complain about
congratulate on
equal to
from time to time
grateful to (someone)
in conflict
in the near future
of the opinion
proud of
respect for
sorry for
tired of
composed of
conscious of
except for
frown on/upon
grateful for (something)
inferior to
interested in
on top of
regard to
responsible for
suspicious of
with regard to
concentrate on
consist of
fond of
full of
in accordance with
insist on/upon
knowledge of
opposite of
related to
satisfied with
take care of
concerned with
depend on/upon
from now on
glance at (something)/glance through (something—e.g., a book)
incapable of
in the habit of
next to
prior to
rely on/upon
similar to
thank (someone) for (something)

Rule #18: Use idioms correctly.

▶ Style

Style refers to the manner in which something is said or done. In writing, style is largely controlled by two elements: sentence structure and word choice. Together, these two elements determine the tone, the level of formality, and the level of detail, creating the overall *feel* of the text—smooth or choppy, formal or informal, juvenile or sophisticated, friendly or sinister. These two elements also exert a great deal of control over the readability and clarity of the text. A sentence that is grammatically correct but that has problems with its style can still be difficult (even impossible) to understand.

To keep sentences clear and effective, writers should follow these guidelines for effective style:

1. Be concise.
2. Be precise.
3. Avoid ambiguity.

4. Use the active voice.
5. Use variety in sentence structure.
6. Avoid jargon and pretentious language.

You will certainly see sentences that violate guidelines 1–4 on the GMAT sentence correction questions. You will probably not see many sentences violating guidelines 5–6, but these style guidelines are nonetheless important and can help you write a better essay on the AWA section.

Be Concise

On the sentence level, in general, *less* is more. The fewer words you use to get your point across, the better. Unnecessary words frustrate readers—they waste time and often cloud meaning. Notice, for example, how cluttered and confusing the following sentence from the pretest is:

Creating a fundamental shift in American foreign policy was the Truman Doctrine, which was put forth in 1947, and which established a "policy of containment" that framed our foreign policy as a battle between the forces of good (America, along with other democratic societies) and the forces of evil (the Soviet Union, along with other communist nations).

Notice the difference in length and clarity after wordiness and redundancy have been eliminated:

The 1947 Truman Doctrine created a fundamental shift in American foreign policy, establishing a "policy of containment" that framed our foreign policy as a battle between the forces of good (America and other democratic societies) and evil (the Soviet Union and other communist nations).

To eliminate wordiness, eliminate clutter and unnecessary repetition in your sentences.

Rule #19: Be concise. Avoid unnecessary repetition or wordiness.

Eliminate Clutter

Avoid the following words, phrases, and constructions that add clutter to your writing.

- **Because of the fact that** is an unnecessary and bulky phrase. *Because* is all you really need:

  Because of the fact that my answering machine is broken, I didn't get her message. (15 words)
  Because my answering machine is broken, I didn't get her message. (11 words)

- ***That, who,* and *which* phrases** often needlessly clutter sentences and can usually be rephrased more concisely. Try turning the *that, who,* or *which* phrase into an adjective:

  It was an experience *that was very rewarding.* (8 words)
  It was a *very rewarding* experience. (6 words)

- **There is, it is.** The *there is* and *it is* constructions avoid directly approaching the subject and use unnecessary words in the process. Instead, use a clear agent of action:

  It was with much regret that I had to postpone my education. (12 words)
  I greatly regretted having to postpone my education. (8 words)
  Regrettably, I had to postpone my education. (7 words)

  There is one more thing I should tell you. (9 words)
  I should tell you one more thing. (7 words)

- The word **that** often clutters sentences unnecessarily. Sentences will often read more smoothly without it:

  I wish *that* I had taken the opportunity *that* I was given more seriously. (14 words)
  I wish I had taken the opportunity I was given more seriously. (12 words)
  I wish I had taken the opportunity more seriously. (9 words)

- **I am of the opinion that, I believe, I feel**, and other similar phrases are unnecessary unless you are distinguishing between what *you* think and what someone else thinks.

  I am of the opinion that the flat tax is a good idea. (13 words)
  I feel that the flat tax is a good idea. (10 words)
  I believe the flat tax is a good idea. (9 words)
  The flat tax is a good idea. (7 words)

AVOID UNNECESSARY REPETITION

When writers are not sure they have been clear, or when they are simply not being attentive to the need for concise writing, they often repeat themselves unnecessarily by saying the same thing in two different ways. This happens in the following example:

The willow beetle is red in color and large in size. (11 words)

Red *is* a color, so it is not necessary to say "in color." Likewise, large *is* a size—so "in size" is a waste of words. Here is the sentence revised:

The willow beetle is red and large. (7 words)

Here's another example of unnecessary repetition:

The Bill of Rights guarantees certain freedoms and liberties to all citizens, rights that cannot be taken away. (18 words)

If it's a guarantee, then those rights cannot be taken away—so the whole second half of the sentence repeats unnecessarily. Similarly, "freedom" and "liberties" are essentially the same thing, so only one of those words is necessary. Here is the revised sentence:

The Bill of Rights guarantees certain freedoms to all citizens. (10 words)

Be Precise

Writing has more impact when it is filled with **exact words and phrases**. This means substituting a strong, **specific** word or phrase for a weak or 2 modified word or phrase. (A modifier is a word that describes, such as *red* balloon or *very juicy* apple.) A lot of wordiness can be trimmed by using exact words and phrases, too. Notice how attention to word choice cuts back on wordiness and creates much more powerful sentences in the following example:

He *walked quickly* into the room.
He *rushed* into the room.
He *raced* into the room.
He *dashed* into the room.
He *burst* into the room.

Each of these verbs has much more impact than the phrase *walked quickly.* These exact verbs create a vivid picture; they tell us exactly how he came into the room.

Exact *nouns* will improve your sentences, too. Here's an example:

The *dog* escaped down *the street.*
The *pit bull* escaped down *Elm Street.*

Again, the specific nouns help us see what the writer is describing—they bring the sentence to life. Adjectives, too, should be precise. Instead of writing

I am *very frightened.*

Try using an exact adjective:

I am *petrified.*

"Petrified" means "very frightened"—and it is a much more powerful word.

Rule #20: Be precise. Use exact words.

Ambiguity

Ambiguous means having two or more possible meanings, so, of course, ambiguous words and phrases interfere with clarity. Ambiguity can be caused by poor word choice, misplaced modifiers, and unclear pronoun references. Take a look at this sentence, for example:

The photographer shot the model.

This sentence can be read in two ways: that the photographer took ("shot") pictures of the model with his camera, or that he shot the model with a gun. You can eliminate this ambiguity by addressing the word choice and revising the sentence as follows:

The photographer took pictures of the model.

Took pictures is not as powerful a phrase as the verb *shot*, but at least no ambiguity appears.

Another type of ambiguity happens when a phrase is in the wrong place in a sentence. For example, look at the following sentence:

The woman ate the sandwich with the blue hat.

Here, the *word order*, not an ambiguous word, causes the confusion; the modifier *with the blue hat* is in the wrong place (a **misplaced modifier**). Did the woman eat her sandwich with her hat? Or was the woman wearing a blue hat as she ate the sandwich? Because the phrase *with a blue hat* is in the wrong place, the sentence becomes unclear. The sentence should be revised to read:

The woman with the blue hat ate the sandwich.

Ambiguity can also result from unclear pronoun references. Pronouns are used to replace nouns (*I*, *you*, *he*, *she*, *it*, *we*, *they*). Here is an example of an unclear pronoun reference:

In Heart of Darkness, *Conrad has Kurtz tell Marlow his revelation right before he dies on the steamboat.*

He **appears twice** in this sentence and **could be referring to** three different people: Conrad, Kurtz, and Marlow. Clearly, this sentence needs to be revised:

In Conrad's Heart of Darkness, *Kurtz tells Marlow his revelation right before he dies on the steamboat.*

Here is another kind of unclear pronoun reference:

It has been years since they tore down that old building.

This is an example of a common pronoun error: using a vague *they* when specific people are behind the action. You may not know exactly who those people are, but you know enough to say something like the following:

It has been years since a demolition crew tore down that building.

People are always behind actions, and your sentences should indicate this.

Rule #21: Avoid ambiguity. Make sure word choice and pronoun references are clear and modifiers are properly placed.

Active and Passive Voice

In most cases, effective writing will use the **active voice** as much as possible. In an active sentence, the subject directly performs the action:

James filed the papers yesterday.
Jin Lee sang the song beautifully.

In a **passive** sentence, on the other hand, the person or thing who actually completes the action of the sentence is put into a prepositional phrase. Rather than performing the action, the true subject is *acted upon*:

The papers were filed by James yesterday.
The song was sung beautifully by Jin Lee.

Active sentences are more direct, powerful, and clear. They often use fewer words and have less room for confusion. However, **sometimes** the passive voice is preferable, such as when the source of the action is not known or when the writer wants to emphasize the recipient of the action rather than the performer of the action:

Protective gear must be worn by everyone entering this building.

As a general rule, however, sentences should be active whenever possible.

Using the **active voice** means making sure a sentence has a clear agent of action and a direct approach. For example, compare the following sentences:

Passive: *The patient was given the wrong prescription.*
Active: *Someone gave the patient the wrong prescription.*

Notice how the active sentence gives readers an agent of action—a person, place or thing that performs the action in the sentence. In the passive sentence, you do not know who gave the patient the wrong prescription; you just know that somehow it happened. The active sentence may not name the someone, but it is a much more direct sentence. The active voice also makes a sentence sound more authoritative and powerful —someone is doing something. In a passive sentence, someone or something has something done to it.

Sometimes using the **passive voice** makes more sense than trying to write an active sentence—like when you do not know the agent of action or when you want to emphasize the *action*, not the *agent*. It is also useful when you desire anonymity or objectivity. The following are two examples:

- The location was deemed suitable by the commission. (Here, the passive voice emphasizes the action of the commission rather than the commission itself.)
- He was fired. (The passive voice provides anonymity by not giving an agent of action. Thus, no one has to take the blame for firing him.)

Rule #22: In general, use the active voice.

Sentence Variety

Although sentence correction passages are only one sentence long, issues of variety in sentence structure may come into play as you consider the various versions of the sentence. **Sentence variety** means that a text uses a combination of sentence structures and patterns, an important element in keeping the writing interesting and effective.

When writers consciously repeat a specific sentence pattern to create rhythm in their writing, this is called **parallelism** (see page 118). Here is an example:

She tried begging. She tried pleading. She even tried bribing. But Anuj would not change his mind.

Notice the pattern in the first three sentences: *she* + *tried* + participle. This pattern is repeated three times, and the result is a certain controlled rhythm to the passage. Thus, parallelism consciously repeats a sentence pattern to create a positive effect. However, that is not always the case, as you can see from the following example:

The plasma membrane is the outermost part of the cell. It isolates the cytoplasm. It regulates what comes in and out of the cytoplasm. It also allows interaction with other cells. The cytoplasm is the second layer of the cell. It contains water, salt, enzymes, and proteins. It also contains organelles like mitochondria.

The sentences have a certain rhythm, but instead of creating energy, it creates monotony. Because the sentence structure has no variety—the sentences are all very simple (no compound or complex sentences) and all start with the subject—the paragraph's rhythm is more like a drone than a conversation. The same paragraph, revised to create sentence variety, is found on the next page.

The plasma membrane, the outermost part of the cell, isolates the cytoplasm. It regulates what comes in and out of the cell and allows interaction with other cells. The second layer, the cytoplasm, contains water, salt, enzymes, and proteins as well as organelles like mitochondria.

This revised version combines sentences and uses introduction phrases and appositives (descriptive words and phrases set off by commas) to vary the sentence structure. The result is a much more engaging paragraph.

Rule #23: Use variety in sentence structure.

Avoid Jargon and Pretentious Language

Two other problems that can interfere with clear, effective writing are **jargon** and **pretentious language.**

Good writers make sure they write in a way that is appropriate for their intended audience. That means they do not use jargon—technical or specialized language—unless they are sure their audience will be familiar with that terminology. For example, you may know what a T-cell count is, but unless your readers have had some experience with physiology, AIDS, or other infectious diseases, chances are they don't know. If you are writing for a general audience, then you should not assume your readers know what you are talking about. The texts you will see on the GMAT exam (and the kind of essay you should write on the AWA) are written for the general reader with a college-level education. These texts (and the essays you write on the AWA) should therefore avoid jargon.

Jargon includes abbreviations and acronyms that are not common knowledge. For example, you may know what RAM is, but you cannot assume your readers do. Always write out what the abbreviation or acronym stands for the first time you use it. Then, going forward, you can use the abbreviation or acronym. Here is an example:

When buying a home computer, you need to consider how much Random Access Memory (RAM) you need. The amount of RAM you should have depends upon what kind of programs your machine will be running.

If you find a sentence with jargon in it, choose a version that replaces the jargon with a general word or phrase that general readers will know or a version that keeps the technical term but defines it, as shown in the following example:

Bobby's T-cell count (the number of infection-fighting white blood cells) has risen dramatically, and he will soon be able to come home.

Pretentious language is another matter. *Pretentious* means showy or pompous. Some people are impressed with big words, as if using more syllables in your sentences makes you seem more intelligent. Sometimes a big, multisyllabic word is the one that most clearly expresses the idea you want to convey, and that is fine. But too often, five-syllable words are misused and end up clouding meaning instead of clarifying it. Clear writing makes a much bigger impression than big words. In any case, sentences like the following are unnecessary:

Utilizing my cognitive facilities, I ruminated upon the matter.
Humankind is able to avail itself of a plethora of opportunities it heretofore was unable to take advantage of.

Instead of sounding impressive, these sentences sound rather foolish. Simple, more direct sentences such as the following do the trick much more effectively:

I thought about it.
People can take advantage of many opportunities that were not available to them before.

If you come across a sentence that sounds like it's trying to impress but doesn't quite make sense, it probably isn't the best version. But don't mistake a sentence with pretentious language for a sentence that uses sophisticated vocabulary. If the sentence is unclear to you because you don't know the meaning of a word, that is one thing. If the sentence seems to misuse a vocabulary word, however, or if it just sounds like it is showing off, then it's probably a matter of pretentious language. As a general rule, don't use a word if you do not know what it means.

Rule #24: Avoid jargon and pretentious language.

By following the 24 rules, you will increase your grammar knowledge along with your GMAT Verbal score.

CHAPTER

8 Tips and Strategies for the Verbal Section

The following section offers specific tips and strategies to use on the Verbal section during the exam. Practice these strategies as you complete the practice exercises in the next chapter.

Remember that the different types of questions will be interspersed throughout the Verbal section. For example, you may start with a set of reading comprehension questions based on a passage, then have a sentence correction question, then have two critical reasoning questions, and then have another reading comprehension passage. Try not to let this distract you. Be prepared to shift gears frequently throughout the exam. To help you focus on each type of question, jot a few notes about key things to remember for each type of question on a piece of scrap paper.

It is important to keep moving, but at the same time, don't sacrifice too much for the sake of speed. If you need to reread a reading comprehension passage in order to answer the questions about it correctly, do so. The extra minute you spend rereading will increase your chance of answering those questions correctly and, therefore, of setting the level of difficulty of your exam at a higher level. Even if you answer fewer questions in the end, the questions that you did answer correctly will carry more weight.

The First Five Questions

Remember that on this CAT your answers to the first five questions in each category will largely determine the level of difficulty of your exam. Take some extra time to make sure you answer these questions correctly.

▶ Reading Comprehension Questions

Smart Approach

Remember that active reading is your best strategy for comprehension. On the exam, read each passage three times:

1. First, **preview**. Scan the passage quickly to get a general sense of the argument and context. This should take less than a minute. Use your finger to guide you down the screen so your eyes keep moving. Do not slip into reading mode if a word or sentence catches your attention. Keep skimming.
2. Second, **read carefully and actively**. Use your scratch paper to take notes about main ideas, connections within the text, key terms, and support. As you read, try to outline the passage.
3. Third, **review** the passage. Scan it again to get a better sense of the whole: the whole argument and the overall organization of the text. This review will also help you better understand key ideas and terms.

You can preview the question stem if you like, but *don't* try to memorize it. More important, *don't waste time reading the question options before you read the passage.* Four of the five are incorrect, and the distracters may actually confuse you as you read.

Other Tips

- Most questions will be about key ideas and issues in a passage, not about minor details. Don't focus on trying to remember specific facts or details as you read. If you outline the passage as you read, you should know where to find specific details if you happen to get such a question.
- Remember that your notes are for your use only. They don't have to be neat, and they don't have to make sense to anyone else except you. Use whatever shorthand or note-taking method you feel comfortable with.
- Read all options carefully. Several of the options may state information that is true based on the passage, but those statements may not answer the question or may not be the *best* answer to the question. Beware of distracters that are true statements drawn from other parts of the text. Because they look familiar, they may seem like the correct answer, but they may not provide the best answer to the question.
- Base your answers *only* on the information provided in the passage. *Don't* answer based upon your own reactions, ideas, or knowledge.

Use Scrap Paper

Use as much scrap paper as you need for notes, outlines, and calculations—whatever you need to do to help you determine the correct answer. If you run out of scrap paper, you can always ask for more.

- Refer to the passage as often as you need to; reread sections or the entire passage if you have to. It is better to take the time to understand a passage so you can answer the questions correctly than to just guess so you can move on to the next passage or question. Remember, the more correct answers you provide at the beginning of the test, the higher the level the CAT will establish for you and the better your potential for a higher score.
- Context clues can help you determine the meaning of unfamiliar words. At a minimum, try to determine whether the unfamiliar word is something positive or negative.
- In a long text, the main idea (if stated) is often located in the first paragraph. Within one paragraph, the main idea (if stated in a topic sentence) is often the first sentence in that paragraph.
- Remember that the main idea must be *general* enough to encompass (hold together) all of the ideas in the passage.
- Remember to distinguish between facts (things *known* to be true) and opinions (things *believed* to be true).
- Use key words and the structure of the passage to locate specific facts and details.
- Remember that a writer's purpose drives every decision a writer makes, including how to organize the text. The overall organizing principle of a passage will reflect the writer's purpose.
- Watch for transitions that suggest the organizational pattern and show the relationships between ideas.
- Make sure your inferences are *logical* and based *only* on the evidence in the text. If you cannot point to evidence in the text itself, your inference may not be valid.
- Look carefully at word choice for clues to the writer's feelings.

▶ Critical Reasoning Questions

Smart Approach

Critical reasoning passages are short, but you need to read the passages very carefully to answer the questions correctly:

1. First, skim through each passage. Then reread the passage at a slow, careful pace.
2. Read the question stem. This will tell you what sort of argument you are dealing with. For example, say the stem asks "Which of the following conclusions can be drawn from the previous passage?" You know you do not need to spend any time searching the passage for the conclusion of the argument. Rather, the question is asking you to pick the best conclusion offered through inference.

Educated Guessing

If you need to guess, make sure it's an educated guess. You should be able to eliminate at least one or two answer choices.

3. Use the question stem as your guide to identify the elements of the argument. For example, if the stem asks about a flaw in the argument, search for a fallacy; if the stem asks about assumptions upon which the argument is based, try to identify in your mind what assumption(s) would make the argument valid. It helps to do this *before* reading the answer choices because the wording of the choices can be confusing. This way, you will know what you are looking for when you read the options.
4. Read each answer choice carefully. Which one seems to best provide you with the correct answer?

Other Tips

- Remember that an argument must have a premise and a conclusion, but the premise or conclusion may be unstated.
- If the premise is missing, ask yourself if any assumptions must be true in order for the argument to be valid. Find the missing link between premise and conclusion.
- Remember that a premise for one conclusion can be the *conclusion* of another argument.
- Conclusions must be based on the evidence in the passage. If an answer choice does not have relevant evidence, it cannot be the correct answer.
- Do not let your opinion on the matter influence your answer selection. *Stick to the statements and claims in the argument that has been presented.*
- Pay extra attention to the question stem. Make sure you are looking for the right kind of answer. Remember, many questions will ask you for the exception.
- You do not need to name the fallacy—you just need to be able to recognize that something is wrong with the argument. Do not worry about classifying the flaw; just identify the problem with the argument's logic.
- Remember that qualifiers strengthen arguments by limiting their scope. For example, stating that "*most* students would benefit from more individualized instruction" is a more accurate (and therefore stronger) statement than "*all* students would benefit from more individualized instruction."
- Keep in mind the four characteristics of good evidence: sufficient, relevant, unbiased, and logical.
- Whenever an argument makes a comparison, check to see if it is an apples-to-oranges comparison.
- Whenever an argument asks you to reject a claim, check to see if it is an *ad hominem* argument (rejecting a claim because of *who* makes the claim, not because of the merits of the claim).
- Watch for arguments that bring in irrelevant issues (red herrings). Premises must be directly related to their conclusions to be logical.
- Whenever a passage offers an explanation, make sure it is a good one: testable, noncircular, precise, reliable, relevant, consistent with established theories, and convincing.

- Whenever you are presented with a causal argument, check for the fallacies of causal reasoning: *post hoc*, reversing causation, ignoring a common cause, and assuming a common cause.

▶ Sentence Correction Questions

Smart Approach

With sentence correction questions, it can be time consuming to read each answer choice to determine which one is best. Use the following steps instead:

1. Reread the original version carefully and *listen* to the sentence in your head. Make sure you *hear* how it sounds; this will often help you identify the error. Even if you do not know the grammar rule or cannot name the grammatical or stylistic problem, you can often tell if something is wrong.
2. Identify the error(s) that is made in that sentence. Is it grammatical or stylistic?
3. Quickly scan the other versions to rule out sentences that make the same mistake.
4. Of the versions that remain, which one most effectively corrects the sentence?
5. Make sure the versions that correct the original error do not insert additional errors.

Seven-Step Checklist

1. Check sentence basics. Locate the subject(s) and verb(s). Is the sentence complete? Are verbs properly formed? Are sentence elements in the proper order (subject, verb, indirect object, and object)?
2. Check for agreement. Do the subject(s) and verb(s) agree? Do pronouns agree with their antecedents?
3. Check for consistency. Are verbs consistent in tense? Is pronoun use consistent?
4. Check for structure. Are items parallel? Are modifiers as close as possible to what they modify?
5. Check for clarity. Are words precise? Are ideas direct (expressed in the active voice, with subject first and then verb)?
6. Check for concision. Are unnecessary words crowding the sentence? Is anything repeated unnecessarily?
7. Check for style. Are idioms used correctly? Does anything else just *sound* wrong?

Other Tips

- Remember, don't worry about vocabulary or mechanics (spelling, punctuation, and capitalization). These kinds of errors are *not* tested on the exam. If you think that a sentence has one of these errors, ignore it and look for another mistake in the sentence.
- Don't bother reading choice **a** on sentence correction questions. It repeats the original version, giving you a *correct as is* choice.
- Remember that some of the original sentences will be correct as is. If you read the sentence and it sounds correct, **a** might be the right answer. If you suspect this is the case, quickly scan choices **b** through **e** to see if any other version expresses the idea more effectively.

- Focus only on the underlined portion because that's where the error lies. Don't get caught up trying to understand the whole sentence, especially if it is long, if only a portion of that sentence is underlined.
- Be wary of long versions. The longer versions are often (but not always) ineffective; they may be redundant, wordy, or poorly constructed.
- Look for words that signal relationships and make connections: subordinating conjunctions, coordinating conjunctions, and conjunctive adverbs. These words help describe the relationship between ideas and determine sentence boundaries and punctuation.
- Incorrect idioms are among the most common errors on the GMAT exam. Be sure not to skip over small words such as prepositions (*to, for, in, of . . .*) as you read. Prepositions are particularly important in idioms, and if you read too quickly, you might not pick up an idiomatic error.

CHAPTER

9 Verb Forms

Verbs are the heart of a sentence. They express the **action** or **state of being** of the subject and indicate what the subject is doing, thinking, or feeling:

> *She yelled out the window.* (action)
> *I am happy to be here.* (state of being)
> *We feel very lucky to be alive.* (state of being)
> *I should ask Winston what he thinks.* (action)

Verbs have five basic forms: infinitive, present tense, present participle, past tense, and past participle. These five forms are used with other *helping verbs* to form other verb tenses, including the future, conditional, and subjunctive mood (see pages 150–151).

- **Infinitive base:** the base form of the verb plus the word *to.*

to go *to be* *to dream* *to admire*

To indicate tenses of regular verbs (when the action of the verb did occur, is occurring, or will occur), use the base form of the verb and add the appropriate tense endings.

- **Present tense:** the verb form that expresses what is happening *now.*

I am sorry you do not play tennis.
Jessica enjoys yoga every morning.

The present tense of regular verbs is formed as follows:

	SINGULAR	PLURAL
first person (I/we)	base form *(believe)* *I believe*	base form *(believe)* *we believe*
second person (you)	base form *(believe)* *you believe*	base form *(believe)* *you believe*
third person (he/she/it, they)	base form + *-s/-es (believes)* *she believes/he believes*	base form *(believe)* *they believe*

- **Present participle:** the verb form that describes what is happening *now.* It ends in *-ing* and is accompanied by a helping verb, such as *is.*

Jessica is doing a difficult yoga pose.
The leaves are falling from the trees.

NOTE: Words that end in *-ing* don't always function as verbs. Sometimes they act as nouns called **gerunds**. They can also function as adjectives called **participial phrases**.

Present participle (verb):	*He is loading the boxes into the car.*
Gerund (noun):	*This parking area is for loading only.*
Participial phrase (adjective):	*The loading dock is littered with paper.*

You will learn more about gerunds later in this section.

- **Past tense:** the verb form that expresses what happened in the *past.*

It snowed yesterday in the mountains.
I felt better after I stretched and did some deep breathing.

- **Past participle:** the verb form that describes an action that happened in the past and is used with a helping verb, such as *has, have,* or *had.*

It has not snowed all winter.
I have waited as long as I can.

▶ Regular Verbs

Most English verbs are regular—they follow a standard set of rules for forming the present participle, past tense, and past participle:

- The present participle is formed by adding *-ing.*
- The past and past participle are formed by adding *-ed.*
- If the verb ends with the letter *e*, just add *d.*
- If the verb ends with the letter *y*, for the past tense, change the *y* to an *i* and add *-ed.*

Here are some examples:

PRESENT	PRESENT PARTICIPLE	PAST	PAST PARTICIPLE
ask	asking	asked	asked
dream	dreaming	dreamed	dreamed
protect	protecting	protected	protected
spell	spelling	spelled	spelled
whistle	whistling	whistled	whistled

A handful of English verbs have the same present, past, and past participle form. Here is a partial list of those verbs and two examples:

SAME PRESENT, PAST, AND PAST PARTICIPLE FORM		
bet	hit	set
bid	hurt	shut
burst	put	pread
cost	quit	upset
cut	read	

Present: *I <u>read</u> the newspaper every morning.*
Past: *I <u>read</u> the newspaper yesterday morning.*
Past participle: *I <u>have read</u> the newspaper every morning since 1992.*

Present: *Please <u>set</u> the table for dinner.*
Past: *He <u>set</u> the table for dinner.*
Past participle: *He <u>had</u> already <u>set</u> the table for dinner.*

▶ Irregular Verbs

About 150 English verbs are *irregular*. They don't follow the standard rules for changing tense. These irregular verbs can be divided into three categories:

- irregular verbs with the same *past* and *past participle* forms
- irregular verbs with three distinct forms
- irregular verbs with the same *present* and *past participle* forms

The following table lists the most common irregular verbs.

SAME PAST AND PAST PARTICIPLE FORMS

PRESENT	PAST	PAST PARTICIPLE
bite	bit	bit
dig	dug	dug
bleed	bled	bled
hear	heard	heard
hold	held	held
light	lit	lit
meet	met	met
pay	paid	paid
say	said	said
sell	sold	sold
tell	told	told
shine	shone	shone
shoot	shot	shot
sit	sat	sat
spin	spun	spun
spit	spat	spat
creep	crept	crept

PRESENT	PAST	PAST PARTICIPLE
deal	dealt	dealt
keep	kept	kept
kneel	knelt	knelt
leave	left	left
mean	meant	meant
send	sent	sent
sleep	slept	slept
spend	spent	spent
bring	brought	brought
buy	bought	bought
catch	caught	caught
fight	fought	fought
teach	taught	taught
think	thought	thought
feed	fed	fed
flee	fled	fled
find	found	found
grind	ground	ground

THREE DISTINCT FORMS

PRESENT	PAST	PAST PARTICIPLE
begin	began	begun
ring	rang	rung
sing	sang	sung
spring	sprang	sprung

PRESENT	PAST	PAST PARTICIPLE
do	did	done
go	went	gone
am	was	been
is	was	been
see	saw	seen
drink	drank	drunk
shrink	shrank	shrunk
sink	sank	sunk
stink	stank	stunk
swear	swore	sworn
tear	tore	torn
wear	wore	worn
blow	blew	blown
draw	drew	drawn
fly	flew	flown
grow	grew	grown
know	knew	known
throw	threw	thrown
drive	drove	driven
strive	strove	striven
choose	chose	chosen
rise	rose	risen
break	broke	broken
speak	spoke	spoken
fall	fell	fallen

PRESENT	PAST	PAST PARTICIPLE
shake	shook	shaken
take	took	taken
forget	forgot	forgotten
get	got	gotten
give	gave	given
forgive	forgave	forgiven
forsake	forsook	forsaken
hide	hid	hidden
ride	rode	ridden
write	wrote	written
freeze	froze	frozen
steal	stole	stolen

SAME PRESENT AND PAST PARTICIPLE FORMS

PRESENT	PAST	PAST PARTICIPLE
come	came	come
overcome	overcame	overcome
run	ran	run

In English, as in many other languages, the essential verb *to be* is also highly irregular:

SUBJECT	PRESENT	PAST	PAST PARTICIPLE
I	am	was	have been
you	are	were	have been
he, she, it	is	was	has been
we	are	were	have been
they	are	were	have been

▶ Helping Verbs

Helping verbs (also called **auxiliary verbs**) are essential to clear communication. They enable us to indicate exactly when an action took place or will take place and suggest very specific meanings, such as the subject's ability to perform an action or intention to do something. Helping verbs are used to form the future (e.g., *will call*) and conditional tenses:

Future: *I will call you tomorrow with the results.*
Conditional: *If the results were promising, Jamal would have requested another.*

The following table lists the helping verbs, their forms, and their meanings. Review this table carefully; a helping verb can often significantly change the meaning of a sentence.

PRESENT AND FUTURE	PAST	MEANING	EXAMPLES
will, shall	would	intention	*She will meet us at the hotel.* *They said they would call first.*
can	could	ability	*I can be there in ten minutes.* *Rose could only find one glove.*
may, might, can, could	could, might	permission	*May I tag along?* Could *we get together after the meeting?*
should	should + have + past participle	recommendation	*We should leave before the snow starts.* *They should have known better.*
must, have (to)	had (to)	necessity	*I must go to the dentist.* *I had to draw two models.*
should	should + have + past participle	expectation	*They should be on the next train.* *They should have been on that train.*
may, might	might + have + past participle	possibility	*They may be lost.* *They might have gotten lost.*

▶ Subjunctive Mood

The subjunctive mood is one of the verb forms that is often forgotten in conversation and is therefore often neglected in writing. Like helping verbs, the subjunctive is used to express a specific meaning, indicating something that is wished for or that is contrary to fact. It is formed by using *were* instead of *was* as in the following examples:

If she were a little more experienced, she would get the promotion. (She is not a little more experienced.)
If I were rich, I would travel the world. (Unfortunately, I am not rich.)
If you were in my shoes, you wouldn't say such a thing. (You are not in my shoes.)

▶ Troublesome Verbs

Three verb pairs are particularly troublesome:

lie / lay
sit / set
rise / raise

The key to knowing which verb to use is remembering which verb takes an object. In each pair, one verb is **transitive**—an object receives the action—whereas the other is **intransitive**—the subject itself receives or performs the action. For example, *lie* is intransitive; the subject of the sentence performs the action on itself: *I will lie down.* The transitive verb *laid,* on the other hand, is an action that the subject of the sentence performs upon an object: *He lay the baby down in the crib.* In the following examples, the subjects are in bold and the objects are underlined:

lie: to rest or recline (intransitive—subject only)
lay: to put or place (transitive—needs an object)

I *will lie down for a while.*
Will ***you*** *please lay the papers on the table.*

sit: to rest (intransitive—subject only)
set: to put or place (transitive—needs an object)

Why don't ***we*** *sit down and talk this over?*
He *will set the record straight.*

rise: to go up (intransitive—subject only)
raise: to move something up (transitive—needs an object)

The ***sun*** *will rise at 5:48 A.M. tomorrow.*
He *raised the rent to $750 per month.*

The basic forms of these verbs can also be a bit tricky. The following table shows how each verb is conjugated.

PRESENT	PRESENT PARTICIPLE (WITH *AM, IS,* AND *ARE*)	PAST	PAST PARTICIPLE (WITH *HAVE, HAS,* AND *HAD*)
lie, lies	lying	lay	lain
lay, lays	laying	laid	laid
sit, sits	sitting	sat	sat
set, sets	setting	set	set
rise, rises	rising	rose	risen
raise, raises	raising	raised	raised

▶ Gerunds and Infinitives

Gerunds look like verbs because they end in *-ing*, but they actually function as nouns in sentences:

Tracy loves camping.

Here, the *action* (verb) Tracy performs is *loves.* The *thing* (noun) she enjoys is *camping.* In the following sentence, however, *camping* is the *action* Tracy performs, so it is functioning as a verb, not as a gerund:

Tracy is camping in the Pine Barrens next week.

Words ending in *-ing* can also function as adjectives:

Some of our camping gear needs to be replaced before our trip.

This means is that you cannot count on word endings to determine a word's part of speech; you must look instead at how the word is functioning in the sentence.

Infinitives are the base (unconjugated) form of the verb preceded by *to*: *to be, to delay, to manage*, and so on. They are often part of a verb chain, but they are not the main verb (main action) of a sentence:

Priya likes to write poems.

In this example, *likes* is the main verb; what Priya likes (the action she likes to take) is *to write* poems.

When to Use Infinitives and Gerunds

In many situations, you may be uncertain whether to use an infinitive or a gerund. Which is correct: *I like to swim* or *I like swimming*? In this case, both are correct; *like, hate,* and other verbs that express preference can be followed by either a gerund or infinitive. But other verbs can only be followed by one or the other. Here are a few helpful guidelines:

- Always use a **gerund** after a preposition:

  Keza thought that by taking the train, she would save money and time.
  Noriel was afraid of offending her host.

- Always use a **gerund** after the following verbs:

admit	dislike	practice
appreciate	enjoy	put off
avoid	escape	quit
cannot help	finish	recall
consider	imagine	resist
delay	keep	risk
deny	miss	suggest
discuss	postpone	tolerate

  We should discuss buying a new computer.
  I am going to quit smoking.

- In general, use an **infinitive** after these verbs:

agree	decide	need	refuse
ask	expect	offer	venture
beg	fail	plan	want
bother	hope	pretend	wish
claim	manage	promise	

  Aswad promises to be back by noon.
  Fatima failed to keep her promise.

- When a noun or pronoun immediately follows these verbs, use an **infinitive**:

advise	command	force	remind	want
allow	convince	need	require	warn
ask	encourage	order	tell	
cause	expect	persuade	urge	

  *I would like **you** to reconsider my offer.*
  *The committee needs **Tom** to organize this event.*

CHAPTER

10 Prefixes, Suffixes, and Word Roots

A familiarity with common prefixes, suffixes, and word roots can dramatically improve your ability to determine the meaning of unfamiliar vocabulary words. The following tables list common prefixes, suffixes, and word roots; their meanings; an example of a word with that prefix, suffix, or word root; the meaning of that word; and a sentence that demonstrates the meaning of that word. Refer to this chapter often to refresh your memory and improve your vocabulary.

Prefixes

A prefix is a syllable added to the *beginning* of a word to change or add to its meaning. The following table lists some of the most common prefixes in the English language. They are grouped together by similar meanings.

PREFIX	MEANING	EXAMPLE	DEFINITION	SENTENCE
uni-	one	unify (v)	to form into a single unit; to unite	The new leader was able to **unify** the three factions into one strong political party.
mono-	one	monologue (n)	a long speech by one person or performer	I was very moved by the **monologue** in Scene III.
bi-	two	bisect (v)	to divide into two equal parts	If you **bisect** a square, you will get two rectangles of equal size.
duo-	two	duality (n)	having two sides or parts	The novel explores the **duality** of good and evil in humans.
tri-	three	triangle (n)	a figure having three angles	In an isosceles **triangle**, two of the three angles are the same size.
quadri-	four	quadruped (n)	an animal with four feet	Some **quadrupeds** evolved into bipeds.
tetra-	four	tetralogy (n)	series of four related artistic works	"Time Zone" was the fourth and final work in Classman's **tetralogy**.
quint-	five	quintuplets (n)	five offspring born at one time	Each **quintuplet** weighed less than four pounds at birth.
pent-	five	pentameter (n)	a line of verse (poetry) with five metrical feet	Most of Shakespeare's sonnets are written in iambic **pentameter**.
multi-	many	multifaceted (adj)	having many sides	This is a **multifaceted** issue, and we must examine each side carefully.
poly-	many	polyglot (n)	one who speaks or understands several languages	It is no wonder he is a **polyglot**; he has lived in eight different countries.

PREFIX	MEANING	EXAMPLE	DEFINITION	SENTENCE
omni-	all	omniscient (adj)	knowing all	Dr. Perez seems **omniscient;** she knows what all of us are thinking in class.
micro-	small	microcosm (n)	little or miniature world; something representing something else on a very small scale	Some people say that Brooklyn Heights, the Brooklyn district across the river from the Wall Street area, is a **microcosm** of Manhattan.
mini-	small	minority (n)	small group within a larger group	John voted for Bridget, but he was in the **minority;** most people voted for Elaine.
macro-	large	macrocosm (n)	the large scale world or universe; any great whole	Any change to the **macrocosm** will eventually effect the microcosm.
ante-	before	anticipate (v)	to give advance thought to; foresee; expect	His decades of experience enabled him to **anticipate** the problem.
pre-	before	precede (v)	to come before in time or order	The appetizers **preceded** the main course.
post-	after	postscript (n)	message added after the close of a letter	His **postscript** was almost as long as his letter!
inter-	between	intervene (v)	to come between	Romeo, trying to make peace, **intervened** in the fight between Tybalt and Mercutio.
inter-	together	interact (v)	to act upon or influence each other	The psychologist took notes as she watched the children **interact.**
intra-	within	intravenous (adj)	within or into a vein	She could not eat and had to be fed **intravenously** for three days.
intro-	into, within	introvert (n)	a person whose attention is largely directed inward, toward himself or herself; a shy or withdrawn person	Unlike his flamboyant sister, quiet Zeke was a real **introvert.**

PREFIX	MEANING	EXAMPLE	DEFINITION	SENTENCE
in-	in, into	induct (v)	to bring in (to a group)	She was **inducted** into the honor society.
ex-	out, from	expel (v)	to drive out or away	Let us **expel** the invaders!
circum-	around	circumscribe (v)	to draw a line around; to mark the limits of	She carefully **circumscribed** the space that would become her office.
sub-	under	subvert (v)	to bring about the destruction of, overthrow; to undermine	His attempt to **subvert** my authority will cost him his job.
super-	above, over	supervisor (n)	one who watches over	Alex refused the promotion to **supervisor** because he did not feel comfortable being his friends' boss.
con-	with, together	consensus (n)	general agreement	After hours of debate, the group finally reached a **consensus** and selected a candidate.
non-	not	nonviable (adj)	not able to live or survive	The farmer explained that the seedling was **nonviable.**
in-	not	invariable (adj)	not changing	The weather here is **invariable**—always sunny and warm.
un-	not, against	unmindful (adj)	not conscious or aware of; forgetful	For better or worse, he is **unmindful** of office politics.
contra-	against	contradict (v)	to state that (what is said) is untrue; to state the opposite of	I know we do not have to agree on everything, but she **contradicts** *everything* I say.
anti-	against, opposite	antipode (n)	exact or direct opposite	North is the **antipode** of south.
counter-	against, opposing	counter-productive (adj)	working against production	Complaining is **counter-productive.**
dis-	away,	dispel (v)	to drive away	To **dispel** rumors that I was quitting, I scheduled a series of meetings for the next three months.

PREFIX	MEANING	EXAMPLE	DEFINITION	SENTENCE
dis-	not, opposite of	disorderly (adj)	not having order; messy, untidy, uncontrolled, or unruly	Two people were hurt when the crowd became **disorderly** during the protest.
mis-	wrong, ill	misuse (v)	to use wrongly	She **misused** her authority when she reassigned Charlie to a new team.
mal-	bad, wrong	maltreat (v)	to treat badly or wrongly	After the dog saved his life, he swore he would never **maltreat** another animal.
mal-	ill	malaise (n)	feeling of discomfort or illness	The **malaise** many women feel during the first few months of pregnancy is called *morning sickness*.
pseudo-	false, fake	pseudonym (n)	false or fake name	Mark Twain is a **pseudonym** for Samuel Clemens.
auto-	by oneself or by itself	automaton (n)	a robot; a person who seems to act mechanically and without thinking	The workers on the assembly line looked like **automatons**.
co-	together with, jointly	cohesive (adj)	having a tendency to bond or stick together; united	Though they came from different backgrounds, they have formed a remarkably **cohesive** team.

▶ Suffixes

A suffix is a syllable added to the *end* of a word to change or add to its meaning. The following table lists some of the most common suffixes in the English language. They are grouped together by similar meanings.

SUFFIX	MEANING	EXAMPLE	DEFINITION	SENTENCE
-en	to cause to become	broaden (v)	to make more broad; to widen	Traveling around the world will **broaden** your understanding of other cultures.
-ate	to cause to be	resuscitate (v)	to bring or come back to life or consciousness; to revive	Thanks to a generous gift from an alumnus, we were able to **resuscitate** the study-abroad program.
-ify/-fy	to make or cause to be	electrify (v)	to charge with electricity	The singer **electrified** the audience with her performance.
-ize	to make, to give	alphabetize (v)	to put in alphabetical order	Please **alphabetize** these files for me.
-al	capable of, suitable for	practical (adj)	suitable for use; involving activity, as distinct from study or theory	He has years of **practical**, on-the-job experience.
-ial	pertaining to	commercial (adj)	of or engaged in commerce	**Commercial** vehicles must have special license plates.
-ic	pertaining to	aristocratic (adj)	of or pertaining to the aristocracy	Though he was never rich or powerful, he has very **aristocratic** manners.
-ly	resembling, having the qualities of	tenderly (adv)	done with tenderness; gently, delicately, and lovingly	He held the newborn baby **tenderly** in his arms.
-ly	in the manner of	boldly (adv)	in a bold manner	Despite his fear, he stepped **boldly** onto the stage.
-ful	full of	meaningful (adj)	significant; full of meaning	When Robert walked into the room with Annette, she cast me a **meaningful** glance.

SUFFIX	MEANING	EXAMPLE	DEFINITION	SENTENCE
-ous, -ose	full of	humorous (adj)	full of humor; funny	His **humorous** speech made the evening go by quickly.
-ive	having the quality of	descriptive (adj)	giving a description	The letter was so **descriptive** that I could picture every place he had been.
-less	lacking, free of	painless (adj)	without pain; not causing pain	The doctor assured me that it is a **painless** procedure.
-ish	having the quality of	childish (adj)	like a child; unsuitable for a grown person	He did not get the job because of his **childish** behavior during the interview.
-ance/ -ence	quality or state of	tolerance (n)	willingness or ability to tolerate a person or thing	He has a high level of **tolerance** for rudeness.
-acy	quality or state of	indeterminacy (n)	state or quality of being undetermined (without defined limits) or vague	The **indeterminacy** of his state ment made it impossible to tell which side he was on.
-tion	act, state, or condition of	completion (n)	the act of completing; the state of being completed or finished	The second siren signaled the **completion** of the fire drill.
-or/-er	one who does or performs the action of	narrator (n)	one who tells the story; gives an account of	A first-person **narrator** is usually not objective.
-atrium/ -orium	place for	arboretum (n)	a garden devoted primarily to trees and shrubs	They built a deck with an **arboretum** for their bonsai tree collection.
-ary	place for, pertaining to	sanctuary (n)	a sacred place; refuge	With three noisy roommates, Ellen frequently sought the quiet **sanctuary** of the library.
-cide	kill	pesticide (n)	substance for killing insects	This **pesticide** is also dangerous for humans.

SUFFIX	MEANING	EXAMPLE	DEFINITION	SENTENCE
-ism	quality, state, or condition of; doctrine of	optimism (n)	belief that things will turn out for the best; tendency to take a hopeful view of things	Her **optimism** makes people want to be around her.
-ity	quality or state of	morality (n)	state or quality of being moral	He argued that the basic **morality** of civilized societies has not changed much over the centuries.
-itis	inflammation of	tonsillitis (n)	inflammation and infection of the tonsils	Her **tonsillitis** was so severe that doctors had to remove her tonsils immediately.
-ment	act or condition of	judgment (n)	ability to judge or make decisions wisely; act of judging	He exercised good **judgment** by keeping his mouth shut during the meeting.
-ology	the study of	zoology (n)	the scientific study of animal life	She took a summer job at the zoo because of her strong interest in **zoology**.

► Common Latin Word Roots

Many words in the English language derive from Latin. The following table shows the original Latin words that are used to create various English words. The Latin words serve as roots, providing the core meaning of the words; prefixes, suffixes, and other alterations give each word its distinct meaning. The word roots are listed in alphabetical order.

ROOT	MEANING	EXAMPLE	DEFINITION	SENTENCE
amare	to love	amorous (adj)	readily showing or feeling love	She told him to stop his **amorous** advances, as she was already engaged.
audire	to hear	audience (n)	assembled group of listeners or spectators; people within hearing	The **audience** was stunned when the game show host slapped the contestant.

ROOT	MEANING	EXAMPLE	DEFINITION	SENTENCE
bellum	war	belligerent	inclined to fight; hostile, aggressive	The citizens feared that their **belligerent** leader would start an unjust war.
capere	to take	captivate (v)	to capture the fancy of	The story **captivated** me from the beginning; I could not put the book down.
dicere	to say, speak	dictate (v)	to state or order; to say what needs to be written down	She began to **dictate** her notes into the microphone.
duco	to lead	conduct (v)	to lead or guide (thorough)	He **conducted** a detailed tour of the building.
equus	equal	equilibrium (n)	a state of balance	I have finally achieved an **equilibrium** between work and leisure.
facere	to make or do	manufacture (v)	to make or produce	The clothes are **manufactured** here in this factory.
lucere	to light	lucid (adj)	very clear	No one could possibly have misunderstood such a **lucid** explanation.
manus	hand	manicure (n)	cosmetic treatment of the fingernails	To take care of her long finger-nails, she gets a **manicure** every week.
medius	middle	median (adj)	middle point; middle in a set of numbers	The **median** household income in this wealthy neighborhood is $89,000.
mittere	to send	transmit (v)	to send across	The message was **transmitted** over the intercom.
omnis	all; every	omnipresent (adj)	present everywhere	That top-40 song is **omnipresent**; everywhere I go, I hear it playing.
plicare	to fold	application (n)	putting one thing on another; making a formal request	His loan **application** was denied because of his poor credit history.

ROOT	MEANING	EXAMPLE	DEFINITION	SENTENCE
ponere/ positum	to place	position (n)	the place a person or thing occupies	Although he is only 22, he holds a very powerful **position** in the company.
protare	to carry	transport (v)	to carry across	The goods will be **transported** by boat.
quarere	to ask or question	inquiry (n)	act of inquiry, investigation, or questioning	The **inquiry** lasted several months but yielded no new information.
scribere	to write	scribe (n)	person who makes copies of writings	The **scribe** had developed thick calluses on his fingers from years of writing.
sentire	to feel	sentient (adj)	capable of feeling	No **sentient** beings should be used for medical research.
specere	to look at	spectacle (n)	striking or impressive sight	The debate was quite a **spectacle**—you should have seen the candidates attack one another.
spirare	to breathe	respiration (n)	the act of breathing	His **respiration** was steady, but he remained unconscious.
tendere	to stretch	extend (v)	to make longer; stretch out	Please **extend** the deadline by two weeks so we can complete the project properly.
verbum	word	verbatim (adv)	word for word	The student failed because she had copied an article **verbatim** instead of writing her own essay.

▶ Common Greek Word Roots

Many other English words are derived from the ancient Greek language. The following table shows the Greek words that are used to create various English words. The Greek words serve as roots, providing the core meaning of the words; prefixes, suffixes, and other alterations give each word its distinct meaning. The word roots are listed in alphabetical order.

ROOT	MEANING	EXAMPLE	DEFINITION	SENTENCE
bios	life	biology (n)	the science of living organisms	He is majoring in **biology** and plans to go to medical school.
chronos	time	chronological (adj)	arranged in the order in which things occurred	The story is confusing because she did not put the events in **chronological** order.
derma	skin	dermatology (n)	branch of medical science dealing with the skin and its diseases	She has decided to study **dermatology** because she has always been plagued by rashes.
gamos	marriage, union	polygamy (n)	the practice or custom of having more than one spouse or mate at a time	Throughout history, certain cultures have practiced **polygamy**, but it is uncommon today.
genos	race, sex, kind	genocide (n)	deliberate extermination of one race of people	The recent **genocide** in Bosnia has created a sharp increase in the number of orphaned children.
geo	earth	geography (n)	the study of the Earth's surface; the surface or topographical features of a place	The **geography** of this region made it difficult for the different tribes to interact.
graphein	to write	calligraphy (n)	beautiful or elegant handwriting	She used **calligraphy** when she addressed the wedding invitations.
krates	member of a group	democrat (n)	one who believes in or advocates democracy as a principle of government	I have always been a **democrat**, but I refuse to join the Democratic Party.
kryptos	hidden, secret	cryptic (adj)	concealing meaning; puzzling	He left such a **cryptic** message on my answering machine that I don't know what he wanted.
metron	to measure	metronome (n)	device with a pendulum that beats at a determined rate to measure time/rhythm	She used a **metronome** to help her keep the proper pace as she played the song.

ROOT	MEANING	EXAMPLE	DEFINITION	SENTENCE
morphe	form	polymorphous (adj)	having many forms	Most mythologies have a **polymorphous** figure, a "shape shifter" who can be both animal and human.
pathos	suffering, feeling	pathetic (adj)	arousing feelings of pity or sadness	Willy Loman is a complex character who is both **pathetic** and heroic.
philos	loving	xenophile (n)	a person who is attracted to foreign peoples, cultures, or customs	Alex is a **xenophile**; I doubt he will ever come back to the States.
phobos	fear	xenophobe (n)	person who fears or hates foreigners or strange cultures or customs	Don't expect Len to go on the trip; he is a **xenophobe**.
photos	light	photobiotic (adj)	living or thriving only in the presence of light	Plants are **photobiotic** and will die without light.
podos	foot	podiatrist (n)	an expert in diagnosis and treatment of ailments of the human foot	The **podiatrist** saw that the ingrown toenail had become infected.
psuedein	to deceive	pseudonym (n)	false name	Was George Eliot a **pseudonym** for Mary Ann Evans?
pyr	fire	pyromaniac (n)	one who has a compulsion to set things on fire	The warehouse fire was not an accident; it was set by a **pyromaniac**.
soma	body	psychosomatic (adj)	of or involving both the mind and body	In a **psychosomatic** illness, physical symptoms are caused by emotional distress.

ROOT	MEANING	EXAMPLE	DEFINITION	SENTENCE
tele	distant	telescope (n)	optical instrument for making distant objects appear larger and nearer when viewed through the lens	While Galileo did not invent the **telescope**, he was the first to use it to study the planets and stars.
therme	heat	thermos (n)	insulated jug or bottle that keeps liquids hot or cold	The **thermos** kept my coffee hot all afternoon.

CHAPTER

11 Verbal Section Practice Test

The following Verbal section practice test contains 75 multiple-choice questions that are similar to the questions you will encounter on the GMAT® exam. These questions are designed to give you a chance to practice the skills you have learned in a format that simulates the actual exam. Answer these practice questions carefully. Use the results to assess your strengths and weaknesses and determine which areas, if any, you need to study further.

▶ One Practice Test or Two

With 75 questions, this practice section has nearly twice the number of questions you will see on the actual exam. To practice the timing of the GMAT exam, complete the entire practice section in 137 minutes (2 hours and 17 minutes).

ANSWER SHEET

1.	a	b	c	d	e	26.	a	b	c	d	e	51.	a	b	c	d	e
2.	a	b	c	d	e	27.	a	b	c	d	e	52.	a	b	c	d	e
3.	a	b	c	d	e	28.	a	b	c	d	e	53.	a	b	c	d	e
4.	a	b	c	d	e	29.	a	b	c	d	e	54.	a	b	c	d	e
5.	a	b	c	d	e	30.	a	b	c	d	e	55.	a	b	c	d	e
6	a	b	c	d	e	31	a	b	c	d	e	56	a	b	c	d	e
7.	a	b	c	d	e	32.	a	b	c	d	e	57.	a	b	c	d	e
8.	a	b	c	d	e	33.	a	b	c	d	e	58.	a	b	c	d	e
9.	a	b	c	d	e	34.	a	b	c	d	e	59.	a	b	c	d	e
10.	a	b	c	d	e	35.	a	b	c	d	e	60.	a	b	c	d	e
11.	a	b	c	d	e	36.	a	b	c	d	e	61.	a	b	c	d	e
12.	a	b	c	d	e	37.	a	b	c	d	e	62.	a	b	c	d	e
13.	a	b	c	d	e	38.	a	b	c	d	e	63.	a	b	c	d	e
14.	a	b	c	d	e	39.	a	b	c	d	e	64.	a	b	c	d	e
15.	a	b	c	d	e	40.	a	b	c	d	e	65.	a	b	c	d	e
16.	a	b	c	d	e	41.	a	b	c	d	e	66.	a	b	c	d	e
17.	a	b	c	d	e	42.	a	b	c	d	e	67.	a	b	c	d	e
18.	a	b	c	d	e	43.	a	b	c	d	e	68.	a	b	c	d	e
19.	a	b	c	d	e	44.	a	b	c	d	e	69.	a	b	c	d	e
20.	a	b	c	d	e	45.	a	b	c	d	e	70.	a	b	c	d	e
21.	a	b	c	d	e	46.	a	b	c	d	e	71.	a	b	c	d	e
22.	a	b	c	d	e	47.	a	b	c	d	e	72.	a	b	c	d	e
23.	a	b	c	d	e	48.	a	b	c	d	e	73.	a	b	c	d	e
24.	a	b	c	d	e	49.	a	b	c	d	e	74.	a	b	c	d	e
25.	a	b	c	d	e	50.	a	b	c	d	e	75.	a	b	c	d	e

Record your answers on the answer sheet provided on this page. Make sure you mark your answer clearly in the circle that corresponds to the question.

Remember that the GMAT exam is a CAT, and you will not be able to write anywhere on the exam. To mimic the exam environment, do not write on the test pages. Make any notes or calculations on a separate piece of paper. Remember that the types of questions will be mixed throughout the exam. However, the following practice questions are grouped by type so that you can assess your strengths and weaknesses as you answer each type of question.

▶ Reading Comprehension

Directions: Questions 1–25 are based on the following reading passages. Read each passage carefully and then choose the best answer to each question. Answer the questions based upon what is stated or implied in the reading passage.

Questions 1–4 refer to the following passage.

For many years, there has been much hand-wringing over the fate of Social Security once the baby boomers reach retirement age. Baby boomers, people born between 1946 and 1964, represent the largest single sustained growth of population in the history of the United States. It is the sheer enormity of this generation that has had economists worried as retirement beckons. According to the U.S. Census Bureau, by 2020, an estimated 80,000,000 Americans will have reached or surpassed the conventional age of retirement. With so many boomers retiring and drawing benefits but no longer paying into Social Security, many fear that the Social Security fund itself could go bankrupt.

However, a study released by the American Association for Retired Persons (AARP) that examined baby boomers' plans for retirement found that for the most part, this generation is not expected to adhere to the conventional retirement scheme, a fact that may please the worriers in Washington, DC.

In its survey, the AARP broke baby boomers into different categories based on their financial standing, degree of preparedness for retirement, and optimism toward the future. The AARP found that of all groups surveyed, only 13% planned to stop working altogether once they reached retirement age; the remaining 87% planned to continue working for pay. The reasons to continue working varied among the different groups. For some, the plan to continue working is a financial decision. Between 25% and 44% of respondents reported they are not financially prepared to retire and will therefore continue working past retirement age. For the remainder of those planning to work past their mid to late 60s, the decision is based on long-held goals to start a business and/or the desire to stay active in their industry or community.

Eventually, most baby boomers will need to stop working as they progress into their 70s, 80s, and beyond. But with such large numbers planning to continue working, thereby continuing to pay into the Social Security fund, perhaps Social Security will be able to withstand the end of the baby boom and continue to be a safety net for future generations.

1. Which of the following titles would be most appropriate for this passage?

a. The AARP and Social Security
b. Baby Boomers Bankrupt Social Security
c. Baby Boomers Will Work for Pay Beyond Retirement
d. Worries about Social Security May Be Unfounded
e. Economists Fear Baby Boomers' Impact on Social Security

2. According to the author, baby boomers are not likely to bankrupt the Social Security fund primarily because

a. the government has raised the official age for retirement.
b. most baby boomers are financially prepared for retirement.
c. most baby boomers plan to work past retirement age.
d. most baby boomers are active in their communities.
e. most baby boomers will not need supplemental income.

3. The author cites statistics from the AARP survey primarily to

a. support the assertion that baby boomers are the largest group of retirees in U.S. history.
b. show that baby boomers will not retire en masse as feared.
c. suggest that better financial planning is needed for the elderly.
d. show how optimistic baby boomers are about their future.
e. show the correlation between retirement age and optimism.

4. It can be inferred from the AARP survey results that

a. many baby boomers do not have adequate savings.
b. many baby boomers are afraid of retirement.
c. most baby boomers are unaware of the actual cost of retirement.
d. few baby boomers are realistic about their retirement goals.
e. politicians do not understand the baby boom generation.

Questions 5–9 refer to the following passage.

The Florida panther, known for its distinctive characteristics, including a kinked tail and cowlicks, is nearing extinction with the help of scientists and government officials. Though once abundant in Florida, by the end of the twentieth century, only approximately 30 Florida panthers remained. Efforts to preserve the panthers had focused on shielding them from human encroachment with the hope that they could develop sustainable numbers to survive as a species. However, pressure from development caused officials to grow impatient and shift their strategy and goals.

In 1995, new breeds of female panthers were brought to Florida from Texas to bolster the population. The change has been dramatic. In 1990, 88% of the panthers in Florida had the distinct kinked tail. By 2000, five years after the introduction of the Texas panthers, not a single kitten born to the Texas females had a kinked tail. The breed known as the Florida panther is now on an expedited, ineluctable road to extinction—with the assistance of wildlife protection agencies.

If the goal was to have any kind of panther in Florida, it has been realized. Since the introduction of the Texas panthers, the panther population in Florida has risen to approximately 80 mixed-breed panthers. However, this "success" could portend a tragic trend in wildlife management in the United States. We cannot and should not create genetically mixed species as a means of achieving a compromise between the needs of development and a species' survival. This type of species tampering is a perversion of the ideal of wildlife management and will irrevocably transform our national landscape.

5. The primary goal of this passage is to
   a. demonstrate the fragility of an endangered species.
   b. demonstrate the importance of effective wildlife management.
   c. argue that mixing species to ensure a species' survival is wrong.
   d. demonstrate the effectiveness of mixing species.
   e. limit development in areas with endangered species.

6. The author supports the central idea of this passage primarily by
   a. contrasting the Florida panther with the Texas panther.
   b. showing how interbreeding has destroyed the Florida panther species.
   c. attacking government wildlife protection policies.
   d. showing how human encroachment has depleted Florida's panther population.
   e. describing the history of panthers in the United States.

7. It can be inferred from the passage that
   a. extinction is preferable to mixing species.
   b. wildlife protection and development are completely incompatible.
   c. wildlife protection agencies are in the pocket of development corporations.
   d. scientist and government officials are equally disappointed with the results of the experiment.
   e. there are alternatives to interbreeding, but they take longer.

8. The author suggests that blame for the extinction of Florida panthers rests chiefly upon
   a. government officials who bowed to pressure from developers.
   b. developers who encroached upon protected areas.
   c. scientists who suggested interbreeding as a solution.
   d. advocates of species preservation.
   e. wildlife agencies that did not act sooner to protect the panther population.

9. The passage suggests that the author
   a. is a former member of the Wildlife Protection Agency.
   b. is willing to compromise if it means the survival of a species.
   c. is afraid that species tampering will become the norm in wildlife preservation management.
   d. believes the government has encouraged species tampering as a means of conducting genetic experiments.
   e. believes that "sustainable numbers" statistics are not realistic and lead to the expedited extinction of species.

Questions 10–14 refer to the following passage.

Using art to condemn the moral shortcomings of society is nothing new. English artist William Hogarth (1697–1764) was renowned for prints that revealed the moral lapses of eighteenth-century England. Despite the fact that Hogarth enjoyed the patronage of England's wealthier citizens, he did not shrink away from producing scathing depictions of all levels of English society.

In the ten-print series *Industry and Idleness,* Hogarth presents two apprentices who begin working side by side only to arrive at vastly different ends. The first apprentice is portrayed as a morally incorruptible, diligent worker. He is promoted, marries his boss's daughter, and achieves great distinction and financial success. The other apprentice does little work and engages in many unsavory activities. He is fired from his apprenticeship and continues down a path of illicit behavior and corruption. The series comes to a climax when the two former coworkers are reunited with the industrious apprentice—now elevated to alderman—standing in judgment of the idle coworker brought before him for murder. The idle apprentice is sentenced to death and executed, whereas the industrious apprentice goes on to become Lord Mayor of London.

Among Hogarth's most popular series was *The Rake's Progress*, which tells the story of wealthy Tom Rakewell. In the first of eight prints, Tom inherits a large sum of money that he foolishly spends on enhancing his image and prestige in superficial ways. His prodigal ways lead to his rapid decline as he is arrested for debt and in return marries an old maid for her money. He begins gambling, is imprisoned, and eventually goes insane in Bedlam. Tom's descent and desperate outcome, like many of Hogarth's subjects, is tied directly to moral corruption and poor self-discipline.

It is interesting that Hogarth's prints were extremely popular in his day. Whatever the moral shortcomings of eighteenth-century England, its citizens welcomed Hogarth's social critiques and harsh judgments.

10. According to the passage, Hogarth's prints
- **a.** portrayed many different kinds of moral corruption.
- **b.** focused on the weak and disenfranchised.
- **c.** were extremely controversial.
- **d.** often offended his wealthy patrons.
- **e.** are extremely valuable today.

11. The passage suggests that Hogarth's work is important because
- **a.** Hogarth developed the technique of story-telling through prints.
- **b.** Hogarth defied authorities and convention by depicting the life of common criminals.
- **c.** it reveals the hardships of life in eighteenth-century England.
- **d.** it provides a critical view of the moral shortcomings of Hogarth's society.
- **e.** it demonstrates that art is an important medium for social change.

12. The description of *Industry and Idleness* suggests that

- **a.** people in eighteenth-century England were too quick to judge each other.
- **b.** the moral choices people make determine whether they will succeed or fail.
- **c.** apprentices often engaged in immoral behavior in Hogarth's time.
- **d.** successful politicians are morally incorruptible.
- **e.** the moral apprentice feels sorry for his former coworker.

13. Based on the passage, which of the following best expresses the main lesson of Hogarth's work?

- **a.** If you are diligent and industrious, you will achieve great distinction.
- **b.** Wealth leads to moral corruption.
- **c.** Do not judge others until you have walked in their shoes.
- **d.** Some people are born immoral and cannot be changed.
- **e.** Wise choices and self-discipline can keep us from moral lapses.

Questions 14–17 refer to the following passage.

The labor market is changing yet again. Increasingly, American business is turning to interim staffing to cover a greater number of its employment vacancies. Once interim (or temporary) staffing was reserved for the lower-level positions requiring little training, such as an envelope stuffer, receptionist, day laborer, and the like. Today, however, a more highly trained professional is being sought for interim work. It is not uncommon to find computer programmers, writers, marketing professionals, CPAs, and even chief financial officers working in an interim capacity. The reasons for these changes in staffing norms is generated at both the employer and employee level.

Employers are pushing the drive toward interim staffing in order to maintain maximum flexibility. Companies can be more innovative and flexible in their planning cycles if they have the option to hire employees on an as-needed basis. Additionally, employers save money using interim staffers, as they are not required to provide health insurance to temporary workers and they are not obligated to pay severance when the job terminates.

Employees, too, are pushing the trend toward interim staffing. Increasingly, professionals are seeking more flexibility in their work schedules—often in response to family obligations. No longer does the permanent 9 to 5, Monday through Friday schedule work for everyone. By working interim, employees can work when it fits *their* schedules.

However, interim staffing is not for everyone. Organizations whose workflow requires continuity of personnel may find interim staffing an impediment to productivity. Likewise, employees who need a steady source of income or who require the health insurance and other benefits provided by permanent employers may find the unpredictability in interim work problematic.

14. According to the passage, the main benefit to employers of interim staffing is
- **a.** cost savings from not having to provide benefits.
- **b.** constant influx of new ideas.
- **c.** flexibility in hiring.
- **d.** flexibility in scheduling.
- **e.** a more highly trained interim employee pool.

15. The main purpose of this passage is to
- **a.** convince employers to use interim staffing.
- **b.** explain the difference between temporary and permanent staffing.
- **c.** explain which companies benefit most from interim staffing.
- **d.** explain why interim staffing has become popular with employers and employees.
- **e.** convince employers that interim employees also deserve health benefits.

16. Given the author's purpose, which of the following would most enhance this passage?
- **a.** an interview with an interim employee
- **b.** statistics illustrating the increased emphasis on interim staffing
- **c.** a discussion of whether interim employees deserve benefits
- **d.** examples of positions that are not good for interim employees
- **e.** statistics illustrating how much a company can save by using interim employees

17. From the passage, it can be inferred that
- **a.** interim employment is appealing to many segments of the labor market.
- **b.** interim employees are often less qualified than permanent employees.
- **c.** because of cost savings, interim employees will eventually overtake most permanent positions.
- **d.** because of scheduling flexibility, more permanent employees will opt for interim positions.
- **e.** interim staffing is itself a temporary solution to fluctuations in the labor market.

Questions 18–22 refer to the following passage.

Today, children whose parents are deemed incapable of caring for them are put into foster care. These children are moved into strangers' homes, where they are cared for until their own parents can regain custody, which may not happen for years, if it happens at all. Although it means well, the current foster care program is so poorly funded, staffed, and managed that it cannot ensure the safety and well being of the children in the system.

The laudable idea behind foster care is that children will fare best if placed in a family setting until they can be reunited with their parents, even if it is a family of strangers. However, while in foster care, children typically get shuffled between many different foster homes, preventing them from developing long-term, supportive relationships with their foster families. Foster care placements can also force siblings to be separated, further isolating these vulnerable children. When a child is moved to a new foster home, he or she may also have to enroll in a new school, a disruptive process that has a negative impact on the child's education. The bureaucracy that oversees this system is overwhelmed to the point that social workers are unable to adequately screen potential foster parents and keep accurate track of the children placed in foster care.

There must be a better means of caring for these children. Perhaps it is time to consider creating special group homes as a means of providing these children with stable and safe environments. A child could live in one group home for the duration of his or her time in foster care and be supervised by a team of social workers and other lay people. Children would receive proper meals and healthcare, attend the same school, and develop relationships with others experiencing the trauma of being separated from their parents. In addition, social workers and staff would have daily access to these children, enabling them to better determine if a child has a special physical or psychological need and arrange for the necessary services.

Would this approach be perfect? No, but it would solve many of the problems that plague the current system. For some, the idea of a government agency housing, clothing, and feeding needy children may sound extreme, but it only suggests that we provide these children with the same basic necessities that we give to prison inmates.

18. Which of the following best expresses the main idea of this passage?

a. The current foster care system is a failure.
b. Government-run group homes would be a better option than foster care.
c. Group homes for children are similar to prisons.
d. Children in foster care need more stability.
e. No childcare system is perfect.

19. According to the passage, a group home system has all of the following advantages over the current foster care system EXCEPT

a. children would be reunited with their parents more quickly.
b. it is easier to keep track of children in the system.
c. children would have daily contact with social workers.
d. children would stay in the same school.
e. children would have better access to special services.

20. The passage suggests that the idea of creating group homes in lieu of foster care

a. is long overdue.
b. is the only viable option to foster care.
c. is likely to meet with much resistance.
d. should be researched extensively.
e. is a basic right that should not be denied to children in need.

21. It can be inferred from the passage that the author
- **a.** was once in prison.
- **b.** believes foster care parents are often too lenient.
- **c.** was a foster child.
- **d.** believes prison inmates are treated better than some children in foster care.
- **e.** believes group homes are essentially prisons for children.

22. The passage states that
- **a.** children in group homes would get a better education than children in foster care.
- **b.** children in group homes would have more individual attention than children in foster care.
- **c.** children in groups homes would find comfort in being with other children who have been taken from their parents.
- **d.** group homes are more cost effective than foster care.
- **e.** a group home system is less likely to be bogged down by bureaucracy.

Questions 23–25 refer to the following passage.

Polycystic ovarian syndrome, or PCOS (aka Stein-Leventhal disease), is a condition that affects between 6% and 20% of women in the United States. It is a little understood syndrome that often goes undetected and is frequently misdiagnosed. PCOS produces tiny cysts on the surface of a woman's ovaries. These cysts are undeveloped follicles (eggs) that inexplicably fail to release through the ovarian wall as part of the menstrual cycle. Some researchers believe the eggs fail to release from the ovary because of the presence of male hormones in the blood. However, new research is indicating that PCOS is related to insulin resistance. Unfortunately, the cysts themselves are only a small part of this syndrome.

PCOS can present a variety of symptoms, including hair growth on the face and chest, stubborn acne, hair loss, obesity, irregular menses, infertility, and an increased risk of diabetes. Many of these symptoms impact a woman's physical appearance and her self-esteem. If left untreated, women suffering from PCOS may experience greater levels of stress and depression.

A woman exhibiting any of these symptoms should contact her physician to determine if she has PCOS. Although there is no cure for PCOS, a number of different treatments can stop or reverse many of the symptoms.

23. According to the passage, many women who have PCOS
- **a.** are unable to have children.
- **b.** have an excess of male hormones in their blood.
- **c.** overreact to the symptoms.
- **d.** cannot afford proper treatment.
- **e.** do not even know they have the disease.

24. The passage suggests that the most damaging aspect of misdiagnosed or untreated PCOS is often
- **a.** infertility caused by the cysts.
- **b.** health problems caused by weight gain.
- **c.** psychological ailments, including anxiety and depression.
- **d.** skin rashes and acne.
- **e.** the sudden onset of diabetes.

25. The author implies that PCOS is often misdiagnosed because
- **a.** doctors often ignore the symptoms.
- **b.** many symptoms could be symptomatic of many other illnesses.
- **c.** insufficient attention is given to women's healthcare issues.
- **d.** the symptoms are similar to the symptoms of diabetes.
- **e.** doctors believe the symptoms are psychosomatic.

▶ Critical Reasoning

Directions: For each question, select the best answer from the choices given.

26. Without a doubt, one of America's greatest science-fiction writers is Kurt Vonnegut, who has written dozens of stories and novels, including the masterpiece *Slaughterhouse Five.* Yet for decades, Vonnegut denied that what he was writing was science fiction. Today, however, Vonnegut embraces his rightful place as a master of the genre.

All of the following, if true, are helpful in accounting for the phenomenon described in this passage EXCEPT
- **a.** early in Vonnegut's career, science fiction was largely considered by critics to be an inferior genre.
- **b.** Vonnegut did not want to be pigeonholed as a science-fiction writer.
- **c.** as a young author, Vonnegut's favorite writers were all science-fiction writers.
- **d.** science fiction has become a legitimate literary genre.
- **e.** science fiction has become an increasingly popular genre (for readers and writers alike) because of the increased importance of science and technology in our lives.

27. The greatest failure of modern American society is its rejection of the extended family. It is no wonder our society is so violent and so many Americans feel a deep sense of isolation and overwhelming stress.

This argument is based on all of the following assumptions EXCEPT
- **a.** Americans value *in*dependence more than *inter*dependence.
- **b.** people who live in extended families feel less stress.
- **c.** a large percentage of Americans feel isolated and alone.
- **d.** living in an extended family engenders a strong sense of belonging.
- **e.** deep feelings of isolation and overwhelming stress lead to antisocial and violent behavior.

28. The original *Star Wars* film (1977), in which Luke Skywalker saved Princess Leia and battled against the evil Empire, was followed by two equally successful sequels—*The Empire Strikes Back* and *Return of the Jedi.* Nearly 25 years later, the *Star Wars* prequels have arrived, and they are even more successful than the original series. The prequels (*The Phantom Menace, Attack of the Clones,* and the soon-to-be-released *Episode III*) have shattered box office records, filling theaters with audiences of young children, teenagers, and adults alike.

Which of the following conclusions can properly be drawn from this statement?

a. The prequels are better than the original and its sequels.
b. The prequels have been marketed more effectively than the original and its sequels.
c. The *Star Wars* films have phenomenal special effects.
d. Fans of the original films have always wanted more *Star Wars* stories.
e. The themes and epic struggles of the *Star Wars* movies appeal to viewers of all generations.

29. For years, Americans have been told to stay away from fat. Feeding the market of those anxiously watching their waistlines, food manufacturers have filled grocery store shelves with low-fat and fat-free foods. Now, however, some researchers are blaming the fat-free craze for the American crisis of obesity. Foods without fat, they argue, leave us feeling unsatisfied and craving even more food. As a result, we end up eating a whole bag of low-fat potato chips when we would have only eaten half a bag of regular (fat-laden) potato chips.

Which of the following is the most logical conclusion that can be drawn from the passage?

a. Avoid a no-fat diet, but eat low-fat foods.
b. You will likely eat less if you eat foods with fat.
c. Potato chips of any sort are unhealthy.
d. The key to weight management is to avoid cravings.
e. Fat-free foods should be banned from stores.

30. Nearly a decade ago, researchers at Brandeis University conducted an interesting experiment with small robots. The robots were programmed to get as many individual points as possible by finding small metal pucks and taking them to a nest in a corner of the lab. Robots were rewarded with points whenever they found a puck. But their excessive self-interest led to poor performance as robots repeatedly interfered with one another and battled over pucks. Researchers then reprogrammed the robots to share information: Robots would announce when they found a puck and listen to what other robots had to say. The robots were able to gather twice as many pucks as they had before they were reprogrammed.

Which of the following conclusions can be drawn from the experiment described in this passage?

a. Robots can be taught human behaviors.
b. The robots were poorly programmed in the first experiment.
c. The researchers were shocked by the difference in results between the two experiments.
d. Sharing information can dramatically improve the productivity of a group.
e. Self-interest leads to unproductive behavior.

31. The late 1990s saw the comeback of many rock-n-roll bands that had enjoyed great fame in the 1960s and 1970s, but had fallen into relative obscurity in the 1980s and early 1990s. Bands such as Santana and Aerosmith released new albums at the end of the millennium and embarked on worldwide tours to sold-out audiences.

Which of the following, if true, best explains the phenomenon described in this passage?

a. Not much good rock-n-roll was produced in the late 1990s.
b. These bands were able to blend elements of classic rock with the new sound of the late 1990s to appeal to a wide audience.
c. The late 1990s saw an increasing nostalgia for the peace-loving era of the 1960s and early 1970s.
d. The bands simply got better with age.
e. A new generation of listeners discovered classic rock.

32. Two small-business owners, Jensen and Ling, could not be more different. Jensen is easy going, easy to talk to, good at delegating responsibility, and quick to acknowledge the contributions of others. Ling, however, is often high strung, generally unfriendly, and unable to give up any authority; she is determined to be involved in every decision. This explains why Jensen's business is successful while Ling's business has failed.

The conclusion of this argument is based upon all of the following assumptions EXCEPT

a. the personality of a business owner is the main factor in the success of the business.
b. a business leader with Jensen's type of personality is more effective than one with Ling's personality.
c. Jensen and Ling were in direct competition with each other.
d. Jensen and Ling had similar educational backgrounds and a comparable level of business experience.
e. Jensen and Ling had comparable businesses operating under comparable circumstances.

33. Although no conclusive scientific evidence proves that angels exist, many highly intelligent and respectable people believe they exist and have even claimed to have spoken with angels. It is therefore reasonable to assume that angels do exist, but we just don't have the means to prove their existence.

All of the following, if true, are valid objections to this argument EXCEPT

a. even people who are usually honest lie on occasion.
b. well-respected people often have deep religious beliefs, so they are likely to believe in angels, even if evidence suggests angels do not exist.
c. respectable people often want to be seen as highly moral people, and contact with angels would make them seem "chosen."
d. many people believe that angels are messengers of God, and a belief in angels therefore provides evidence of their belief in God.
e. people who claim to see angels provide very similar descriptions of the angels.

34. In 1980, 18% of American families lived under the poverty line. In 1990, only 12% of families lived under the poverty line. But that doesn't mean fewer families were living in poverty. Indeed, the statistics hide the fact that *more* families were actually living in destitution. The difference in percentages appears because the poverty line was redefined and the income level was *reduced.* Thus, many families were above the poverty line even though they did not earn any more income.

Which of the following statements, if true, would most strengthen this argument?

a. This kind of statistical manipulation is appalling.
b. A nationwide recession occurred in 1980 and an economic boom occurred in the 1990s.
c. Republicans were in power in 1980, whereas Democrats were in power in 1990.
d. The poverty line is regularly adjusted (income level raised) to account for inflation.
e. The number of welfare recipients in 1990 was 11% higher than in 1980.

35. Kylie eats at Moe's Diner every Thursday, but last Thursday she ate at Joe's. On Friday, she was sick to her stomach. It must have been the food at Joe's.

Which of the following is the best criticism of this argument?

a. It does not take into consideration other possible causes.
b. It confuses cause and effect.
c. It assumes that she would not have gotten sick eating the same food at Moe's.
d. It does not identify the specific type of illness.
e. It does not describe how long the illness lasted.

36. Brianais has been feeling jittery over the last three weeks. She has also been putting in extra hours at work, sometimes pulling double shifts. To stay alert, she has been drinking six or seven cups of coffee a day rather than her usual two or three cups. The jitters are interfering with her ability to do her work, so she has decided to stop drinking coffee altogether to eliminate the jitters.

All of the following are valid criticisms of Brianais's plan of action EXCEPT

a. the jitters may be due to lack of sleep, not excessive caffeine.
b. the jitters may be worsened by her total withdrawal from caffeine.
c. Brianais has never had the jitters before.
d. Brianais only gets the jitters when she drinks too much coffee.
e. the jitters may be caused by anxiety due to personal problems or stress at work.

37. Pop singer Clive Jones has been nominated for six Grammy Awards, and his new album is enjoying its eighth consecutive week at number one on the charts. It is safe to say that Jones is today's best pop artist.

Which of the following assumptions is most pivotal to this argument?

a. Jones's previous albums were also chart-toppers.
b. Jones's next album will outsell his current release.
c. Grammy nominations and record sales are accurate measures of an artist's greatness.
d. Jones will win several of the Grammy Awards for which he has been nominated.
e. Jones is popular with both fans and music critics.

38. Anuj wants to lose about 15 pounds. He knows several people who have lost 10 to 20 pounds in just one month with a particular over-the-counter diet pill. Anuj plans to buy the diet pill in order to lose 15 pounds in the same time period.

Based on the previous information, for Anuj's plan to succeed, which of the following must be true?

a. Anuj's body type, exercise regimen, and diet must be similar to those of the people who lost 15 pounds with the pill.
b. Anuj must avoid certain foods that may counteract the effectiveness of the pill.
c. Anuj must take the diet pill at the same time every day.
d. Anuj must adjust his diet to include more protein and fewer carbohydrates.
e. Anuj must monitor his weight loss very carefully.

39. In her old apartment, Hermione had trouble sleeping. She had difficulty falling asleep and would wake up several times in the night. Since Hermione moved from that apartment into her new home, she has been sleeping better. She is able to fall asleep quickly and usually stays asleep through the night.

All of the following, if true, could account for the phenomenon described in the passage EXCEPT

a. Hermione had loud neighbors when she lived in the apartment.
b. Hermione was suffering from anxiety about buying a house and moving.
c. Hermione discovered that she was allergic to cats and gave her cat away when she moved.
d. Hermione's apartment building was constructed prior to 1940, when stricter building codes were put into law.
e. Hermione was having difficulties in her relationship with her boyfriend right before she moved.

40. Toby has breakfast at Good Eats Diner every morning before work. He always orders the same thing: two eggs over easy with three strips of extra crispy bacon, unbuttered wheat toast, and a large coffee. Today, he ordered a bagel with light cream cheese and a large orange juice. Something must be wrong with Toby.

All of the following, if true, are also plausible explanations for Toby's behavior EXCEPT

a. Toby has decided to limit the cholesterol in his diet.
b. a new cook started at Good Eats today.
c. Toby simply wanted a change of pace.
d. Toby has gone on a diet.
e. Toby has decided to become a vegetarian.

41. Zsa Zsa has just opened a beauty salon in her neighborhood. The neighborhood already has two salons—one that caters mostly to older women and one that seems to cater to a general clientele. Zsa Zsa has decided to cater to young clientele to create a niche for herself in the neighborhood.

Zsa Zsa's plan of action is based on all of the following assumptions EXCEPT

a. enough young people live in the neighborhood to establish a large enough client base.
b. Zsa Zsa can provide the styles and services that will appeal to younger customers.
c. younger clients in Zsa Zsa's neighborhood will be able to afford her services.
d. Zsa Zsa will establish friendly relationships with the owners of the other salons.
e. young clients desire services and styles that are not available at the other salons.

42. Mary Shelley's 1818 classic *Frankenstein* has been the most-taught novel on college campuses in the country for the past 10 years. This is due primarily to the worries about scientific responsibility brought on by the recent surge of advances in science and technology, especially biotechnology.

Which of the following statements, if true, would be most helpful in evaluating this argument?

a. *Frankenstein* is considered the first science-fiction novel.
b. Most people who have not read the novel mistakenly assume that Frankenstein is the monster, not the scientist who *created* the monster.
c. In the novel, Victor Frankenstein creates a monster and then abandons it, refusing to take responsibility for his creation.
d. In the novel, Frankenstein's creature causes a great deal of destruction because he is constantly rejected by others.
e. Most Americans are opposed to cloning human beings.

43. *Arthur*: Do animals have rights? Well, they have feelings, and I think if you can feel pain, you do have some rights, particularly the right *not* to have pain inflicted on you.
Brandon: Animals like lions would kill me if they were hungry for food. That inflicts pain on me, all right!

Which of the following is the best criticism of Brandon's response?

a. He assumes that because some animals kill humans, humans have a right to kill those animals.
b. He does not give specific examples to support his position.
c. He attacks Arthur rather than addressing the issue.
d. He takes an absolute position without allowing for exceptions.
e. He brings in a different issue rather than addressing the question of whether or not animals have rights.

44. People who own dangerous pets such as poisonous snakes or ferocious dogs are morally and legally responsible for their pet's actions. If someone is hurt by such a pet, the owner should be held 100% accountable.

All of the following statements, if true, would strengthen this argument EXCEPT

a. the physical whereabouts of pets are completely under the control of their owners.
b. a pet is the legal property of a person, and people are responsible for damages inflicted by their property.
c. a pet is like a young child in that its whereabouts must constantly be controlled and behaviors trained and monitored.
d. pet owners cannot completely control their pets' behaviors.
e. a dangerous pet is no different from a dangerous weapon, and it must be cared for accordingly.

45. Since Lotta came out of her shell, she has made a lot of new friends.

Which of the following is the best criticism of this statement?

a. Lotta may have come out of her shell *because* she made new friends.
b. Lotta may have come out of her shell because of accomplishments at her new job.
c. Lotta may not have very close relationships with any of these new friends.
d. Lotta often has periods of introversion.
e. Lotta is a very likeable person.

46. All across Europe, midwives are the most common choice for prenatal care and delivery. In America, however, midwives are the minority, with most women choosing obstetricians to help them deliver their babies. But using midwives could save millions of dollars a year in healthcare costs.

All of the following information would be helpful in evaluating this argument EXCEPT

a. a comparison of the cost of an obstetrician birth and a midwife birth.
b. a comparison of the percentage of costly procedures such as episiotomies and Caesarian sections in midwife- and obstetrician-led births.
c. a description of the author's experience with a midwife.
d. a comparison of the procedures in an obstetrician birth and midwife birth.
e. a description of how midwives are used in healthcare systems in other countries.

47. Increasing the speed limit to 65 miles per hour or more on highways is dangerous and only leads to more accidents. Whenever the highway speed has been increased, accident rates have increased in that state. Maine raised its turnpike speed to 65 mph in November, and more fatal accidents occurred in December than any other month in the year. Highway fatalities in December and January combined were up 18% from November.

All of the following are valid criticisms of this argument EXCEPT

a. it does not explain why the speed limit was originally set at 55 mph.
b. it does not specify whether the accident rate increase was in accidents only on the highways where the speed limit was increased or on all highways.
c. it does not consider other possible causes for increases in accidents, such as winter weather driving conditions in Maine.
d. it only cites statistics for one state.
e. it does not acknowledge that speed is not the only cause of accidents.

48. Don't be surprised if we have an unusually cold winter this year. The last time we had a very cold winter was 12 years ago, and the last time before that was 12 years earlier, and the time before that was also 12 years earlier. Brace yourself for another cold one.

Which of the following would most strengthen this argument?

a. a chart showing the average temperature of winters over the last 11 years.
b. a chart comparing the actual winter temperatures to predictions for the last 36 years.
c. a chart with the average winter temperatures for the last 36 years.
d. weather predictions from the National Weather Center.
e. a discussion of weather patterns that create colder winters.

49. The main principle of *feng shui* is that our environment must be ordered to permit and encourage the free flow of energy. One of the fundamental steps is to eliminate clutter, which blocks the flow of energy.

Based upon the previous information, which of the following statements is also likely to be true?

a. Proper ventilation will improve the flow of energy.
b. Objects should be dispersed as evenly as possible around the room.
c. Square objects should be placed in corners.
d. Walls should be kept bare except for mirrors.
e. Light colored paints are best.

50. Of course, the Task Force on Crime is going to conclude that crime is on the way up. If they conclude it's on the way down, they would have to disband, wouldn't they?

Which of the following assumptions is most pivotal to this argument?

a. The Task Force is more concerned with its own existence than with carrying out its mission.
b. The Task Force is led by an adversary of the speaker.
c. The speaker was not asked to serve on the Task Force.
d. The speaker's leadership ability will be questioned by the findings of the Task Force.
e. The Task Force wants to hire more police officers and other law enforcement personnel.

▶ Sentence Correction

Directions: Each of the following questions presents a sentence, part or all of which is underlined. After the sentence, you will find five ways of phrasing the underlined portion. The first choice repeats the original; the other four choices present different options for phrasing the underlined text. Determine which choice *best* expresses the idea in the underlined text. If you think the original is best, choose option **a.** These questions test both the correctness and overall effectiveness of expression. When choosing your answer, pay attention to grammar, sentence construction, and word choice and style. The correct answer is the one that is clear, precise, concise, and free of grammatical errors.

51. <u>Presumed to be genetic or partially genetic in origin, about three in every 100 children are born with a severe disorder.</u>

a. Presumed to be genetic or partially genetic in origin, about three in every 100 children are born with a severe disorder.
b. Born with a severe disorder presumed to be genetic or partially genetic in origin, are about three in every 100 children.
c. About three in every 100 children are born with a severe disorder presumed to be genetic or partially genetic in origin.
d. About three in every 100 children, presumed to be genetic or partially genetic in origin, are born with a severe disorder.
e. Severe disorders that are presumed to be genetic or partially genetic in origin are found in about three in every 100 children who are born.

52. By using tiny probes as neural prostheses, surgeons may be able to restore nerve function in quadriplegics and make the blind see or the deaf hear.

- **a.** By using tiny probes as neural prostheses,
- **b.** Through the use of tiny probes used as neural prostheses,
- **c.** By using tiny probes, which will function as neural prostheses;
- **d.** As neural prostheses, and by using tiny probes,
- **e.** Since the use of tiny probes as neural prostheses,

53. The situation is too serious to guess hazardously, we need more data to draw a real conclusion.

- **a.** to guess hazardously, we need
- **b.** to hazard a guess; we need
- **c.** to be hazardous with a guess; we need
- **d.** to hazard guessing, we need
- **e.** for guessing hazardously; we need

54. Medical waste is generally collected by gravity chutes, carts, or pneumatic tubes, each of which have their own advantages and disadvantages.

- **a.** Medical waste is generally collected by gravity chutes, carts, or pneumatic tubes, each of which have their own advantages and disadvantages.
- **b.** Collected by gravity chutes, carts, or pneumatic tubes, each of which has its own advantages and disadvantages, is medical waste.
- **c.** Medical waste is generally collected by gravity chutes, carts, or pneumatic tubes are also used, each of which has its own advantages and disadvantages.
- **d.** Medical waste is generally collected by gravity chutes, carts, or pneumatic tubes, each of which has its own advantages and disadvantages.
- **e.** There are advantages and disadvantages for each means of collection of medical waste, including gravity chutes, carts, and pneumatic tubes.

55. Because the Dvorak keyboard puts vowels and other frequently used letters right under the fingers on home row, where typists make 70% of their keystrokes, people can type 20% to 30% faster and make 50% less errors.

- **a.** people can type 20% to 30% faster and make 50% less errors.
- **b.** people can type making 50% less errors and 20% to 30% faster.
- **c.** people can type 20% to 30% faster and make 50% fewer errors.
- **d.** people can type faster (20% to30%), making errors less than 50% of the time.
- **e.** people can type 20% to 30% faster while making 50% errors less.

56. In order for us within our society to be able to make decisions about the kinds of punishments we impose upon those criminals who are convicted of crimes, we must first understand why we punish criminals.

a. In order for us within our society to be able to make decisions about the kinds of punishments we impose upon those criminals who are convicted of crimes, we must first understand why we punish criminals.
b. To make decisions about the kinds of punishments we impose upon criminals, we must first understand why we punish criminals.
c. In order for us to be able to decide about the kinds of punishments we impose upon people convicted of crimes, we must first understand why people should be punished.
d. Beginning with understanding why we punish, we can then as a society make decisions about the kinds of punishments we impose upon criminals.
e. Deciding upon the kinds of punishments we impose upon criminals, as a society, we must first understand why punishment is imposed upon criminals.

57. Known as the Australian Eleanor Roosevelt, Jessie Street lived a life in privilege while at the same time devoting her efforts to working for the rights of the disenfranchised, including workers, women, refugees, and Aborigines.

a. lived a life in privilege while at the same time devoting
b. lived a life of privilege while simultaneously she devoted
c. lived a life of privilege while devoting
d. lived a life in privilege and devoting at the same time
e. lived a life of privilege and wealth while at the same time devoted

58. The main reason for the decline in worldwide illiteracy rates, which have dropped over the last 20 years, is the sharp increase of literacy rates among young women, which is the result of campaigns to increase educational opportunities for girls.

a. The main reason for the decline in worldwide illiteracy rates, which have dropped over the last 20 years,
b. Declining over the last 20 years, worldwide illiteracy rates have fallen for one main reason, which
c. Declining over the last 20 years, the main reason for the fall in illiteracy rates
d. The main reason worldwide illiteracy rates, having dropped over the last 20 years,
e. The main reason for the decline in worldwide illiteracy rates over the last 20 years

59. Probably as old as human society, and defined as "the willful, malicious, and repeated following and harassing of another person," is stalking.

- **a.** Probably as old as human society, and defined as "the willful, malicious, and repeated following and harassing of another person," is stalking.
- **b.** Stalking is probably as old as human society and is defined as "the willful, malicious, and repeated following and harassing of another person."
- **c.** Probably as old as human society, the definition of stalking is "the willful, malicious, and repeated following and harassing of another person."
- **d.** "The willful, malicious, and repeated following and harassing of another person" is the definition of stalking, which is probably as old as human society.
- **e.** Probably as old as human society, stalking is defined as "the willful, malicious, and repeated following and harassing of another person."

60. Typically people think of genius, whether it manifests itself in Mozart composing symphonies at age five or Einstein's discovery of relativity, as having a quality not just of the supernatural but also they are eccentric.

- **a.** as having a quality not just of the supernatural but also they are eccentric.
- **b.** as having two qualities, being that they are both supernatural as well as eccentric.
- **c.** as having a quality not just of the supernatural but also of the eccentric.
- **d.** as having a quality not just of the supernatural but also another quality, that is, eccentricity.
- **e.** as it has two qualities, not only supernatural but as well eccentric.

61. The financial hub of a business management information system (MIS) is accounting, the system of recording, analyzing, and reporting economic transactions.

- **a.** The financial hub of a business management information system (MIS) is accounting, the system of recording, analyzing, and reporting economic transactions.
- **b.** The financial hub of a business management information system (MIS) is accounting, it is the system of recording, analyzing, and reporting economic transactions.
- **c.** The financial hub of a business management information system (MIS), which is accounting, is the system of recording, analyzing, and used to report economic transactions.
- **d.** A system of recording, analyzing, and reporting economic transactions, the financial hub of a business management information system (MIS) is accounting.
- **e.** A system of accounting is a business management information system (MIS)'s financial hub, in that it is used to record, analyze, and report economic transactions.

62. The poet William Blake believed that true religion reveals through art, not through nature.

- **a.** reveals through
- **b.** is revealed through
- **c.** reveals in
- **d.** is revealed by
- **e.** reveals

63. Although they are not considered the most highest evolved of the cephalopods, cuttlefish are extremely intelligent.

a. the most highest evolved
b. the more higher evolved
c. the most highly evolving
d. the most highly evolved
e. the most evolutionarily high

64. Athletes who suffer from asthma need to work in the conjunction of a doctor who understands the disease and can design a proper training regimen.

a. to work in the conjunction of a doctor who
b. to work in conjunction with a doctor that
c. to work in conjunction with a doctor who
d. to work in conjunction of a doctor that
e. to work at the conjunction of a doctor who

65. Although on the one hand it is true that the lack of computer-related skills accounts for and explains many of the problems in today's job market, there is meanwhile a lack of skilled labor in many different fields.

a. Although on the one hand it is true that the lack of computer-related skills accounts for and explains many of the problems in today's job market, there is meanwhile a lack of skilled labor in many different fields.
b. While the lack of computer-related skills accounts for many of the problems in today's job market, the lack of skilled labor is evident in many different fields.
c. A lack of skilled labor affects all fields, not just computer-related, the problems in today's job market shows.
d. While the lack of computer-related skills accounts for many of the problems in today's job market, many different fields are also experiencing a shortage of skilled labor.
e. Lacking computer-related skills, today's job market has many problems, and other fields also lack skilled labor.

66. Like Carl Jung, Joseph Campbell believed that the archetypal story of the hero who ventures from the safety of his village, endures many trials and triumphs, and returns with knowledge or goods that will save or enlighten his people, is part of the collective unconscious of all humankind.

a. enlighten his people, is part of
b. enlighten his people; is part of
c. enlighten his people, are part of
d. enlighten his people, who are part of
e. enlighten his people, being in part

67. The Competitive Civil Service system is designed to give applicants fair and equal treatment and to ensure that federal applicants are hired based in objective criteria.

a. are hired based in
b. are hired on
c. are hired based on
d. are hired based by
e. are hired through employment of

68. Often attractive and charming, and always inordinately self-confident, people which suffer from anti-social personality disorder demonstrate a disturbing emotional shallowness.

a. people which suffer from
b. people are suffering from
c. people that suffer from
d. people who suffer from
e. people suffer from

69. Brought on by weightlessness in protracted space flight, besides the obvious hazards of meteors, rocky debris, and radiation, astronauts also have to deal with muscle atrophy.

a. Brought on by weightlessness in protracted space flight, besides the obvious hazards of meteors, rocky debris, and radiation, astronauts also have to deal with muscle atrophy.
b. Besides the obvious hazards of meteors, rocky debris, and radiation in protracted space flight, astronauts also have to deal with muscle atrophy, which is brought on by weightlessness.
c. In protracted space flight, besides the obvious hazards of meteors, rocky debris, and radiation, astronauts also have to deal with muscle atrophy brought about through weightlessness.
d. Besides the obvious hazards of protracted space flight, which include meteors, rocky debris, and radiation, astronauts also have to deal with another problem, which is the muscle atrophy that occurs after an extended period of weightlessness.
e. Besides the obvious hazards of meteors, rocky debris, and radiation, astronauts in protracted space flight also have to deal with muscle atrophy brought on by weightlessness.

70. The atmosphere forms a gaseous envelope around the earth, protecting it from the cold of space, harmful ultraviolet light, and meteors that are large, but not the largest.

a. and meteors that are large, but not the largest.
b. and all but the largest meteors.
c. and most meteors, except those that are very large.
d. and large meteors, excepting the largest.
e. and with the exception of the largest, meteors.

71. They were <u>in mind, of a like manner</u> about how to handle Carson's breach of contract.

a. in mind, of a like manner
b. likened of mind
c. in a likened mind
d. of a like-mindedness
e. of a like mind

72. Ralph Waldo Emerson, <u>the renowned poet, essayist, and transcendentalist,</u> believed that the universe is a transcendent "over-soul" and that every living thing is a part of this "blessed Unity."

a. the renowned poet, essayist, and transcendentalist
b. the poet, essayist, and transcendentalist who was renowned
c. the renowned poet as well as an essayist, who was also a transcendentalist
d. who was a renowned poet and was also an essayist and transcendentalist
e. being renowned as a poet, essayist, and transcendentalist

73. <u>Recombinant DNA technology allows scientists to cut segments of DNA from one type of organism and combine them with the genes of a second organism, also called genetic engineering.</u>

a. Recombinant DNA technology allows scientists to cut segments of DNA from one type of organism and combine them with the genes of a second organism, also called genetic engineering.
b. Allowing scientists to cut segments of DNA from one type of organism and combine them with the genes of a second organism, recombinant DNA technology is also called genetic engineering.
c. Recombinant DNA technology, also called genetic engineering, allows scientists to cut segments of DNA from one type of organism and combine them with the genes of a second organism.
d. Recombinant DNA technology, also called genetic engineering, allows scientists the cutting of segments of DNA from one type of organism and the combination of them with the genes of a second organism.
e. Recombinant DNA technology, which is also known in more familiar terminology as genetic engineering, allows scientists the opportunity to cut segments of DNA from one type of organism and combine them with the genes of a second organism.

74. Millions of people in the United States are affected by <u>eating disorders, more than 90%</u> of those afflicted are adolescents or young women.

a. eating disorders, more than 90%
b. eating disorders; more than 90%
c. eating disorders, of which more than 90%
d. eating disorders. Ninety percent more
e. eating disorders, over 90%

75. When a normally functioning immune system attacks a nonself molecule, the system has the ability to "remember" the specifics of the foreign body, and upon subsequent encounters with the same species of molecules, it reacts accordingly.

a. it reacts
b. the foreign body reacts
c. the molecules react
d. the immune system reacts
e. the species react

▶ Answer Explanations

Reading Comprehension

1. d. This choice offers the best title for the passage, which explains why the "worriers in Washington" may have nothing to fear after all. Choice **a** is incorrect because the passage is not about the relationship between the AARP and Social Security or the AARP's position on Social Security issues. Choice **b** is incorrect because the passage actually argues the opposite: that most baby boomers will continue to pay into Social Security long after the traditional age of retirement. Choice **c** is true, but it is just one specific fact cited within the passage to support the main idea. Choice **e** is also true, but the passage explains why the economists' fears are unfounded.

2. c. The AARP study cited in the third paragraph reveals that 87% of the baby boomers surveyed "planned to continue working for pay" once they reach retirement age. The passage does not state that the government raised the retirement age (choice **a**). Choices **b** and **e** are incorrect because the AARP survey also notes that "between 25% and 44% of respondents reported they are not financially prepared to retire," which means they will need supplemental income. A desire to remain active in their community (choice **d**) is one of the reasons many baby boomers will continue to work, but it is the *fact* that they will continue to work (not *why* they will continue to work) that allays the fear of a bankrupt system.

3. b. The survey statistics demonstrate that most baby boomers will keep working, so the Social Security system will not encounter a sudden massive strain as baby boomers reach the retirement age. Choice **a** is incorrect because although the number of baby boomers is cited (80,000,000), no other figure is cited in comparison. One statistic from the survey suggests that many baby boomers have not planned well for retirement (choice **c**), but several other statistics are also cited, so this cannot be the main purpose. The passage states that the survey was designed in part to measure baby boomers' optimism (choice **d**), but the passage does not cite results of questions in that category. Choice **e** is incorrect for the same reason.

4. a. The survey found that a quarter to nearly a half of all respondents planned to keep working because "they are not financially prepared to retire." This suggests that many baby boomers do not have adequate savings. Nothing in the survey results suggests a fear of retirement (choice **b**). Also, nothing in the passage suggests that baby boomers are unaware of the cost of retirement (choice **c**). The passage does not assess how realistic baby boomers' goals are (choice **d**) and makes no reference to politicians (choice **e**) other than the vague "worriers in Washington," a group that could include economists, lobbyists, and many other kinds of people.

5. c. Although the passage does demonstrate the fragility of an endangered species (choice **a**) and the importance of effective wildlife management (choice **b**), the main goal is to argue that mixing species is the *wrong* way to attempt to preserve an endangered species. This is expressed clearly in the final paragraph: "We cannot and should not create genetically mixed species as a means of achieving a compromise between the needs of development and a species' survival." The passage does show that the mixing of species was successful (choice **d**), but the passage criticizes this point. The author is critical of land development in areas with specific endangered species, but this is not the focus of the passage, so choice **e** is incorrect.

6. b. The main idea of the passage is that efforts to preserve species through interbreeding will only backfire, pushing a particular endangered species farther down the road to extinction. The passage's statistics show how the interbreeding has accomplished this in the case of the Florida panther. The Texas panther is not described, so choice **a** is incorrect. The author does not attack general wildlife protection policies—indeed, no policies are mentioned, only the specific handling of this panther population—so choice **c** is incorrect. Human encroachment was a main threat to the panthers (choice **d**), but the author did not discuss how encroachment harmed the species. Only a brief history of panthers in Florida is provided, so choice **e** is incorrect.

7. e. The end of the first paragraph provides the clue to this answer. The Texas panther was introduced because "pressure from development caused officials to grow impatient and shift their strategies and goals." This suggests that interbreeding was brought in as a quick fix so that the panther population could grow quickly and development in the area could be approved once the population was stabilized. The author is clearly against interbreeding, but nothing indicates that the author would prefer extinction (choice **a**). The passage suggests that wildlife protection and development are often in conflict, but does not suggest that they are incompatible (choice **b**). Development corporations pressured officials to act quickly, but the author does not state that wildlife protection agencies are in the pocket of development corporations (choice **c**). Nothing suggests how government officials feel about the results of the interbreeding, so choice **d** is also incorrect.

8. a. Several sentences point the blame at government officials. The first sentence states that the panther "is nearing extinction with the help of scientists and government officials." The last sentence in the first paragraph reveals that officials opted for interbreeding because "pressure from development caused [them] to grow impatient." Finally, the third paragraph tells us that the interbreeding was "a compromise between the needs of development and a species' survival." Thus, the blame rests on officials who bowed to pressure from developers. The author does not state that developers are encroaching upon protected areas (choice **b**), and although fingers are pointed at scientists in the first sentence, nothing indicates that scientists suggested the solution (choice **c**). Choices **d** and **e** are incorrect because the passage does not mention advocates of species preservation or suggests that agencies did not act quickly enough. Rather, the problem is that agencies wanted to act *too* quickly.

9. c. The last paragraph expresses the author's fear that the "success" in Florida "could portend a tragic trend in wildlife management" and that "species tampering . . . will irrevocably transform our national landscape." Thus, he fears that this approach will become a standard in wildlife preservation. Nothing suggests that he is a former member of any agency, so choice **a** is incorrect. The author clearly does not want to compromise a species' integrity, so choice **b** is incorrect. The author does not state that he believes in a conspiracy of genetic experiments, so choice **d** is incorrect. Finally, the realism of "sustainable numbers" statistics is not discussed, so choice **e** is incorrect.

10. a. The passage states that Hogarth's prints were "scathing depictions of all levels of English society," and it offers examples of several different kinds of moral corruption (the apprentice who "engages in many unsavory activities" and the wealthy Tom Rakewell who spends his money foolishly, marries for money, and gambles). Because of these examples, you know choice **b** is incorrect. Hogarth's work may have been controversial (choice **c**), but this is not indicated in the passage. The passage also does not imply that his works offended his wealthy patrons (choice **d**). You might also infer that his works are very valuable (choice **e**), but the passage does not mention this either.

11. d. The second sentence provides the answer: Hogarth "was renowned for prints that revealed the moral lapses of eighteenth-century England." The passage does not indicate that Hogarth was the first to tell stories through prints (choice **a**) or that he defied authorities by portraying particular subjects in his prints (choice **b**). His prints may have often revealed the hardships of life in his time (choice **c**), but the example of *The Rake's Progress* also shows that he dealt with the life of the privileged who often did not have to experience those hardships. The passage says that Hogarth pointed out problems in his society, but nothing indicates that his work inspired change in his society (choice **e**).

12. b. The series describes the different outcomes of two men who start off in similar circumstances as apprentices but arrive at vastly different ends. The most logical conclusion to draw is that the choices the men make regarding their behavior determine the difference in their outcomes—one succeeds in business and politics, whereas the other lives a life of corruption and dies a criminal. The passage does not mention that people were too quick to judge each other (choice **a**); the alderman's job was to judge his former apprentice who was guilty of murder, so the judgment does not appear to be hasty. Nothing suggests that the corrupt apprentice reflects that corruption was common among apprentices in Hogarth's day, so choice **c** is incorrect. The morally incorruptible apprentice becomes a successful politician, but it is a leap of false logic to assume that all successful politicians are morally incorruptible, so choice **d** is incorrect. Finally, the passage does not provide any description of the alderman's emotions as he sentences his former coworker, so choice **e** is also incorrect.

13. e. The successful apprentice in *Industry and Idleness* conveys that diligence and industriousness (*plus* moral behavior) leads to great distinction (choice **a**), but this idea is too limiting to be the main lesson of Hogarth's work, as it does not apply to *The Rake's Progress.* Similarly, wealth may have had to do with Tom Rakewell's moral corruption (choice **b**), although that is not clear from the description, and wealth is not a factor in the apprentice's downfall in *Industry and Idleness*, so this is incorrect. Hogarth's work seems to encourage the judgment of others based on their moral behavior, and the descriptions of his work suggest that he does not take into account particular circumstances, so choice **c** is incorrect. The passage does not claim that the corrupt apprentice or Rakewell were "born bad," so choice **d** is incorrect. The successful apprentice's focus on diligence, the title of the series, the corrupt apprentice's loss of work, and Rakewell's poor choices make **e** the best choice.

14. c. The second paragraph states that "Employers are pushing the drive toward interim staffing in order to maintain maximum flexibility." This narrows the choices to **c** and **d**. The following sentence reveals that **c** is the correct answer: "Companies can be more innovative and flexible in their planning cycles if they have the option to hire employees on an as-needed basis."

15. d. Although the passage describes the benefits of interim staffing, it does not attempt to persuade employers to use interim staffing (choice **a**). It is clear from the first paragraph that the passage is explanatory in nature. The last sentence—"The reasons for these changes in staffing norms is generated at both the employer and employee level"—tells us that the passage will explain how employers and employees are driving the increase in interim staffing. The differences between temporary and permanent staffing are briefly discussed (choice **b**), but these are details of the passage, not its main point. Likewise, the kinds of companies that benefit from interim staffing are briefly discussed (choice **c**), but they are also details within the passage. One of the differences noted is that interim staffers do not get benefits, but the author does not attempt to persuade employers to provide benefits to interim staff (choice **e**).

16. b. The focus of the passage is the change in the labor market, and the goal is to explain this change, so statistics illustrating the change would significantly enhance the text. An interview with an interim employee (choice **a**) would be interesting and relevant, but it would not enhance the main goal as much as choice **b**. Again, because the passage does not argue whether interim employees should have benefits, choice **c** is incorrect. Choice **d** would add a minor detail to the passage that would not enhance the text as much as choice **b**. According to the passage, flexibility in hiring is the main benefit of interim staffing, not cost savings, so choice **e** is not the best choice.

17. a. The passage gives a wide range of examples of interim positions—from receptionists to CFOs—so this is the most logical conclusion. Nothing suggests that interim employees are less qualified (indeed, the passage states that "a more highly trained professional is being sought for interim work"), so choice **b** is incorrect. The passage does not attempt to predict whether the trend toward interim staffing is already at its peak or whether it will continue to gain momentum, so choices **c** and **d** are incorrect. The passage focuses on interim staffing as a solution to the personal needs of employees and the flexibility and budgeting needs of employers, so choice **e** is incorrect.

18. b. The main idea is expressed at the beginning of the third paragraph: "Perhaps it's time to consider creating special group homes as a means of providing these children with stable and safe environments." The first two paragraphs describe the problems with foster care, whereas the last two show how group homes would address those problems. The passage does argue that the current foster care system is at least to some extent a failure (choice **a**), but that is part of the larger argument that something else must be done. The passage refers to prisons in the last paragraph, but this is to compare the treatment of children in foster care with the treatment of inmates in prison, not to compare group homes to prisons (choice **c**). The passage argues that children in foster care need more stability (choice **d**), but this is one of the supporting ideas, not the main idea. The author may feel that no system is perfect (choice **e**) and acknowledges that group homes are not a perfect solution, but again, this is a detail within the passage, not the overall main idea.

19. a. The third paragraph lists the advantages that a group home system would have over foster care. The passage doesn't mention that group homes would enable children to be reunited more quickly with their parents (choice **a**), a factor that is unaffected by either foster care or group homes. The paragraph specifically mentions the other benefits listed in choices **b** through **e**.

20. c. In the last paragraph, the author acknowledges that "For some, the idea of a government agency housing, clothing, and feeding needy children may sound extreme." This suggests that the idea will be resisted. The author does not appear to think that this idea is long overdue (choice **a**); the author says "perhaps it is time" to consider group homes, not "it is high time" or some other phrase that would suggest impatience. The author is not close-minded enough to suggest that group homes are the only option (choice **b**). The statement "There must be a better means of caring for these children" and the word "perhaps" indicate that the author is thinking about options and possibilities. The author would probably agree that the idea of creating group homes should be researched (choice **d**), but the passage does not indicate this point. Finally, the author suggests that the basic rights that should not be denied to children are food, clothes, and shelter—not orphanages themselves, so choice **e** is incorrect.

21. d. The final sentence suggests that prison inmates—who are provided with food, shelter, and clothing—are sometimes better cared for than children in foster care, who may not get the attention and care they need for their physical and emotional well being. Nothing states that the author was in prison (choice **a**) or was a foster child (choice **c**). The author also does not suggest that foster parents are often too lenient (choice **b**). Because the author is advocating the creation of group homes to provide better care than the current foster care system, choice **e** is also incorrect.

22. c. Listed among the benefits of a group home is the fact that children would "develop relationships with others experiencing the trauma of being separated from their parents." This suggests that children would find comfort in being with others in similar circumstances. This inference is especially logical given the passage's emphasis in the second paragraph on how foster care isolates children who have been taken from their parents. The passage does not mention the quality of education that would be provided to children in group homes, so choice **a** is incorrect. Choice **b** is incorrect because the author does not state how much attention children would get in the group home and because there is no standard for how much attention children get in foster care (some likely get inordinate amounts of attention, whereas others are neglected). The cost of either childcare option is not discussed, so choice

d is incorrect. Finally, because the passage does not discuss the management of the group home system, and because it is logical to conclude that a government-run group home system would also be heavily bureaucratic in nature, choice **e** is also incorrect.

23. e. The second sentence says that PCOS is "little understood" and "often goes undetected and is frequently misdiagnosed." Thus, many women who have the syndrome do not even know they have it. One symptom of PCOS is infertility, but not all women who have PCOS are infertile, so choice **a** is incorrect. The passage tells us that new research has debunked the theory that male hormones in the blood cause the disease, so choice **b** is incorrect. Nothing in the passage suggests that women who have the syndrome overreact (choice **c**) or cannot afford treatment (choice **d**).

24. c. The second paragraph discusses the symptoms and complications of the disease. Notice how the author lists seven physical symptoms in just one sentence, whereas two full sentences are devoted to psychological issues: the impact of these symptoms on a woman's self-esteem and the stress and depression caused by the symptoms. Infertility (choice **a**), obesity and its attendant problems (choice **b**), and skin rashes and acne (choice **d**) are all physical symptoms listed in the first sentence of the second paragraph. Choice **e** is incorrect because the syndrome does not cause the sudden onset of diabetes; it only creates "an increased risk of diabetes."

25. b. Because PCOS is "little understood" and because so many varied symptoms could also be symptoms of other ailments, the disease is often misdiagnosed. The passage does not suggest that doctors ignore the symptoms (choice **a**), that doctors believe the symptoms are psychosomatic (choice **e**), or that not enough attention is given to women's health issues (choice **c**). The symptoms of PCOS symptoms are not compared to the symptoms of diabetes, so choice **d** is incorrect.

Critical Reasoning

26. c. Choice **c** is not helpful in accounting for Vonnegut's early reluctance to be identified as a science-fiction writer because it is not relevant. The other choices are directly related to the phenomenon and help us understand why he did not originally want to be called a science-fiction writer but now welcomes the categorization.

27. a. The argument that American society is violent and many Americans feel isolated and stressed (conclusion) because they have rejected the practice of extended families (premise) is based on several assumptions about extended families (e.g., that they ease stress and engender a sense of belonging), about Americans (e.g., that they feel isolated and alone), and about the effects of isolation and stress. It may be true that many Americans value independence more than interdependence, but that assumption is not directly related to the argument. It does not serve as a link between the premise and the conclusion.

28. e. The evidence in the passage points to one conclusion: that the *Star Wars* films appeal to audience-goers of all ages. The passage tells us that the prequels are even more successful than the originals and that the films are popular among "young children, teenagers, and adults alike." This suggests that viewers of all ages appreciate the themes in the films. The passage does not compare the quality or marketing of the prequels to the sequels, so choices **a** and **b** are incorrect. It does not discuss the special effects in the film, so choice **c** is incorrect. Fans of the original film may have wanted more *Star Wars* stories, but the passage does not state this, so choice **d** is not a logical conclusion to the argument.

29. b. The passage argues that foods with little or no fat leave people feeling unsatisfied, so they are likely to eat more than they would of foods that have a substantial fat content. Although the evidence suggests that eating a low-fat diet is better than a no-fat diet (choice **a**), choice **b** is a more logical conclusion, especially because the focus in the passage is how much we eat. The health value of potato chips, which are only used as an example, is not discussed, so choice **c** is incorrect. Choice **d** is incorrect because the passage suggests that weight control is a matter of what kind of foods people eat, not the suppression of cravings. The passage does not state that fat-free foods should be banned from stores, so **e** is not a logical conclusion.

30. d. The huge difference in results after the robots were reprogrammed makes **d** the most logical conclusion: Sharing information can dramatically improve the productivity of a group. Choice **a** is incorrect for several reasons. First, self-interest and sharing aren't exclusively human behaviors; animals are also driven by self-interest, and many animals also share (information, food, etc.). Second, the robots were programmed, not *taught*. The experiment doesn't really show that the robots *learned* anything; they did what they were programmed to do, and as a result, they were more successful. Choice **b** is incorrect because the passage does not suggest that the robots were incorrectly programmed in the first experiment. Nothing indicates how the researchers felt about the results, so choice **c** is not a logical conclusion. Although the robots were far less productive when they were self-interested, choice **e** is not logical because they did indeed gather some pucks and because in many instances self-interest can result in highly productive behavior (e.g., self-preservation).

31. b. The lack of good music (choice **a**) may help account for older bands making a comeback, but this is not the best explanation. More convincing is the notion that older bands were able to blend their old sounds with new sounds to appeal to a wide audience—people who enjoyed their older music and people who enjoy the sounds of contemporary music. This would help explain their renewed popularity, because they still have a core of older fans as well as a large contingent of newer fans (younger listeners who were not necessarily familiar with their older music). Choice **c** is incorrect because a nostalgia for the 1960s and 1970s would mean the bands' older music would be in demand, not their new music. Choice **d** is incorrect because this does not account for their lapse into "relative obscurity." Choice **e** is incorrect for the same reason as **c**—if a new generation of listeners discovered classic rock, then they would be more interested in the bands' older work.

32. c. Jensen and Ling did not have to be in direct competition with each other; indeed, they did not even have to know the other business existed. Rather, this argument hinges on other important assumptions. Clearly, the most important assumption is **a**, that the business leader's personality is the main factor in the business's success or failure. The premises focus on the personality traits of Jensen and Ling and jump to the conclusion that their personalities made the difference in their business success. Choice **b** is incorrect for the same reason; it also forms a logical link between the premises and the conclusion. Choices **d** and **e** are incorrect because they state assumptions that are essential in making this an apples-to-oranges comparison. Whatever their personality differences, this comparison does not work if Jensen and Ling were not similarly equipped (with education and experience) and in comparable businesses operating under comparable circumstances.

33. e. This statement would actually *support* the argument that angels exist. All of the other choices, however, offer valid objections to the argument.

34. d. Including the fact that the poverty line is regularly *raised* to account for inflation would significantly strengthen the conclusion that more families were living in poverty in 1990 despite the lower percentage of families under the poverty line. Choice **a** is an opinion that expresses anger at statistical manipulation but does not provide a premise that would further support the conclusion. Choice **b** offers information that might help account for a normal difference in the number of families living in poverty, but the passage doesn't argue that fewer families were in poverty in 1990; rather, it argues the opposite. Choice **c** is essentially irrelevant. Democrats and Republicans may have certain agendas and institute certain social policies, but this is not relevant unless the reader knows a specific Democratic or Republican measure taken to affect the poverty level. Choice **e** suggests that many more poor people needed assistance in 1990 than 1980, but it is essentially irrelevant without further information showing the correlation between welfare recipients and the poverty line; it may be an apples-to-oranges comparison. You would need to know if any significant changes in welfare policy occurred in the interim.

35. a. Kylie's stomachache could have been caused by any number of factors other than the food at Joe's. Perhaps she ate or drank something that evening that did not agree with her. Perhaps she was nervous or anxious about something and that caused her stomach to be upset. Perhaps she caught the stomach flu. Reversing causation is not possible, so choice **b** is incorrect. The argument does not necessarily assume she wouldn't have gotten sick eating the same food at Moe's (choice **c**); the passage doesn't say what she ate or whether she even could have eaten the same thing at Moe's. The only assumption here is that she was sickened by the food at Joe's. The argument does not specify the type of illness (choice **d**) or describe how long it lasted (choice **e**), but these are not the best criticisms of the argument. Knowing more about the kind of illness she had might help us rule out food poisoning or other food-related illnesses, but the best criticism is clearly **a**.

36. c. Because she has never had the jitters before, it is important for Brianais to try to do something to stop them. Therefore, this is not a criticism of her plan of action. The other options, however, all point out reasons why her plan of action may not be effective. If the jitters are caused by lack of sleep (choice **a**) or anxiety (choice **e**), then her plan will fail. Similarly, if her jitters worsen by a total withdrawal from caffeine (choice **b**), her plan will also fail. The fact that Brianais often gets the jitters when she drinks too much coffee (choice **d**) suggests that Brianais does not need to stop drinking coffee altogether; she just needs to cut back to her regular amount.

37. c. The unstated assumption that connects the premise to the conclusion in this argument is that Grammy nominations and record sales are accurate measures of an artist's greatness. Obviously, this is a highly debatable assumption, but it does provide the necessary link between the premise and the conclusion. The success of Jones's previous albums (choice **a**) and his next album (choice **c**) are irrelevant to the conclusion, which is focused on his success *today*. Jones may or may not win those Grammy awards (choice **d**), but that is essentially irrelevant as well; it does not logically connect the premise to the conclusion. Jones's popularity with both fans and critics (choice **e**) is important, but it likewise does not provide a logical connection.

38. **a.** Anuj's plan of action is based on the assumption that he will have the same success with the diet pill as his acquaintances. In order for this to be true, however, **a** must also be true—he must have a similar body type, exercise regimen, and diet. If, for example, he does not exercise but those people who lost weight with the pill did, he might not have the same results. Anuj may have to avoid certain foods (choice **b**) or take the pill at the same time each day (choice **c**) in order for it to be most effective, but these assumptions do not underlie his belief that he will have the same results as the others. Choice **d** is incorrect because the passage does not state what sort of diet the others had, and again this plan of action rests upon the assumption that he will have similar results. Anuj should probably monitor his weight loss carefully (choice **e**), but this is just common sense and not relevant to his plan of action.

39 **d.** The fact that her apartment building was constructed prior to 1940 is essentially irrelevant to her sleep difficulties in her apartment. All of the other factors, however, could logically account for her sleep difficulties and the fact that they disappeared once she moved.

40. **b.** Perhaps something was wrong with Toby, causing him to deviate from his normal course of action, but there are many other plausible explanations, including his decision to avoid foods high in cholesterol (choice **a**), a simple desire for a change of pace (choice **c**), a decision to go on a diet and eat foods lower in fat (choice **d**), or a decision to eat only vegetarian foods (choice **e**).

41. **d.** The relationship that Zsa Zsa has with her competitors will have little effect on her plan of action. Rather, her plan rests on the other assumptions provided. If she is to succeed in creating a niche for herself in the neighborhood, she needs to have a large enough population of young people (choice **a**), provide the styles and services those clients desire (choice **b**), offer those styles and services at prices her clients can afford (choice **c**), and offer styles and services not available at her competitors (choice **e**).

42. **c.** The fact that Dr. Frankenstein brings a creature to life but then abandons that creature, refusing to take responsibility for his creation, tells us that one of *Frankenstein*'s main themes is scientific responsibility. This would help explain why college professors concerned about scientific responsibility would choose this book. The other choices may be interesting and informative, but they do not help you evaluate the argument because they do not provide information that enables you to ascertain the relevance of the conclusion.

43. **e.** Brandon does not directly address the issue of whether or not animals have rights. Instead, he brings in another issue—whether or not animals would kill him if they were hungry for food—and thus shifts the argument to *his* pain rather than the right of animals to be free of pain. Thus, the best criticism of this argument is that Brandon brings in a *red herring*. Brandon's response is not based on any assumption about human beings' right to kill animals, so choice **a** is incorrect. He does give one specific example (lions), so choice **b** is incorrect. He does not attack Arthur, so choice **c** is incorrect. Finally, he does not make an absolute statement including all animals, so choice **d** is also incorrect.

44. **d.** If pet owners cannot completely control their pets' behaviors, then this undermines the conclusion that pet owners should be 100% accountable for their pets' actions. The other choices, however, all make claims that support the argument for accountability.

45. a. The problem with this statement is that it may reverse causation. Perhaps Lotta made new friends after she came out of her shell, but it is equally possible that Lotta's new friends helped her come out of her shell. Lotta's accomplishments at work may have helped her come out of her shell (choice **b**), but that is not a relevant criticism of the argument; it has nothing to do with the question of making friends after coming out her shell. The level of intimacy of her new friendships (choice **c**) is also irrelevant to an analysis of the argument because it does not make any claims about the depth of the relationships. If Lotta often has periods of introversion (choice **d**), then she also has periods of coming out of her shell, so this is not relevant (again, it does not address the cause/effect issue). If Lotta is very likeable (choice **e**), it might explain an ease in making new friends or the number of new friends, but it does not connect the two pieces of the statement.

46. c. All of the choices except **c** provide information that would help evaluate the conclusion that using midwives could save millions of dollars a year in healthcare costs. Only choice **c** is irrelevant. The author's own experience with a midwife may or may not be typical and does not address the issue of whether or not midwives are more cost effective.

47. a. The issue in the argument is whether increased speed limits are dangerous, so the argument should focus on proving that this is the case. The fact that the argument does not discuss why the speed limit was originally set at 55 mph is essentially irrelevant, so it is not a valid criticism of the argument. All of the other options, however, express valid criticisms and point out significant flaws in the reasoning.

48. d. The conclusion of the argument is that we should expect an unusually cold winter because we are in the twelfth year of a cycle in which every twelfth year is unusually cold. Although the 12-year cycle might indeed have existed for the last 36 years, it goes against our understanding of weather that such a pattern will continue. In all likelihood, the fact that the twelfth year has been unusually cold for the last 36 years is coincidence, not a set meteorological pattern. Thus, the information that would most strengthen the argument is predictions from the National Weather Center, which uses advanced forecasting technology and analysis of existing weather patterns to predict the weather and could estimate the general tenor of the approaching season. The charts in choices **a** through **c** would be useful in proving that such a pattern has existed the last 36 years, but they do not provide strong evidence of the weather to come. A discussion of weather patterns (choice **e**) would be informative, but it would not strengthen the argument about the approaching winter weather.

49. b. The information provided in the passage leads to the conclusion that objects should be dispersed evenly around the room. This would "encourage the free flow of energy" and reduce clutter, because objects would not be crammed together. Proper ventilation (choice **a**) may indeed improve the flow of energy, but that cannot be concluded from the passage. The passage does not indicate where square objects should be placed (choice **c**), whether walls should be kept bare (choice **d**), or whether light colored paints are best (choice **e**), so these choices are incorrect.

50. a. This argument assumes that the main concern of the Task Force is its own existence. The speaker assumes that the Task Force will present findings that would ensure that the Task Force is not disbanded. The passage did not identify the speaker's relationship to the leader of the Task Force (choice **b**) or indicate that the speaker was not asked to join the Task Force (choice **c**). Neither of these assumptions make a logical connection between the premise and conclusion of the argument. It is possible that the speaker's leadership ability will be questioned by the Task Force findings (choice **d**) or that the Task Force wants to hire more police officers (choice **e**), but these two assumptions also do not link the premise and conclusion.

Sentence Correction

51. c. Choices **a, b,** and **d** have problems with word order. In choices **a** and **d**, the modifier *presumed to be genetic or partially genetic in origin* is misplaced. In **b**, the subject and predicate are reversed. Choice **e** is unnecessarily wordy and redundant.

52. a. The original is the most clear and correct version. Choices **b** and **c** are unnecessarily wordy, and **c** also creates a sentence fragment with the semicolon. Choice **d** is awkward and unclear, and the use of *since* in choice **e** is illogical.

53. b. The correct idiom is *hazard a guess.* All of the other choices incorrectly express the idiom. In addition, the idiom completes an independent clause, and *we need more data to draw a real conclusion* is also an independent clause; they cannot be separated with a comma, so choices **a** and **d** are also incorrect.

54. d. This choice is nearly identical to **a**, except that choice **a** makes a mistake in subject-verb agreement (*have* instead of *has*, which must be singular to agree with *each*). Choice **b** reverses the subject and predicate, creating awkward word order. Choice **c** disrupts the parallel structure of the list, and choice **e** is slightly wordy and less direct than choice **d**.

55. c. *Errors* is a plural noun, so it should be modified by *fewer*, not *less*. Thus, choices **a, b,** and **e** are incorrect. Choice **e** also reverses the word order, placing the modifier *less* after the noun. Choice **d** is incorrect because it is less concise than choice **c** and the placement of *20% to 30%* in parenthesis is slightly awkward and less direct than in choice **c.**

56. b. Choices **a**, **c**, and **d** are wordy and redundant, with **a** being the most problematic. Choice **e** changes *to make decisions* into *deciding*, creating an awkward sentence because the sentence opens with a participle rather than an infinitive clause, suggesting action already in progress rather than action that will be taken once reasons for punishment are understood.

57. c. The correct idiom is to live a *life of privilege*, so choices **a** and **d** are incorrect. Choice **b** is wordy (*simultaneously* repeats *while* and *she* is repeated unnecessarily), as is choice **e** (*wealth* is redundant with *life of privilege*).

58. e. This is the most correct and concise version. Choices **a**, **b**, and **d** are less concise, and **d** creates an illogical sentence by changing *have* to *having*. Choice **c** is incorrect because *declining over the last 20 years* is misplaced and as a result modifies *main reason.*

59. e. Choice **a** reverses the subject and predicate. Choice **b** is correct but is less effective than choice **e** because it sets up the two items of information as equal—that stalking is *probably as old as human society* and its definition. Choice **e** uses *probably as old as human society* as an introduction to the focus of the sentence—the definition of stalking. Choice **e** is also more direct and does not need to repeat the verb *is.* Choice **c** uses the phrase *the definition of stalking is* rather than the more direct *stalking is defined as.* Choice **d** puts the definition before the word being defined, which is less effective, making readers wait until they have finished the definition to find out what is being defined.

60. **c.** This choice maintains the parallel structure necessary in a *not only/but also* construction. Choices **a** and **d** disrupt the parallel structure, and **d** is also wordy. Choice **b** uses the grammatically incorrect phrase *being that.* Choice **e** has two problems. First, it creates an illogical sentence by changing *as having* to *as it has.* If you eliminate the *whether* clause in the middle of the sentence, the core sentence would read *Typically people think of genius as it has two qualities, not only supernatural but as well eccentric.* Second, it changes *not only/but also* to *not only/but as well,* an incorrect idiom.

61. **a.** Choice **b** is a run-on sentence. Choice **c** inserts an unnecessary *which* clause, making the sentence unnecessarily wordy. Choice **d** misplaces the modifier *a system of recording, analyzing, and reporting economic transactions,* which should be as close as possible to *accounting.* Choice **e** has awkward word order and the indirect and bulky phrase *in that it is.*

62. **b.** Choices **a**, **c**, and **e** are incorrect because the helping verb *is* is required to make the sentence logical. Choice **e** is also missing the preposition *through,* which is necessary for the correct meaning as suggested by the context of the sentence. Choice **d** uses the preposition *by* instead of *through,* which is inconsistent with the final phrase and also less correct as suggested by the context of the sentence.

63. **d.** Choice **a** uses a double superlative, combining *most* and a modifier with *-est.* Choice **b** uses a double comparison as well, using *more* and a modifier with *-er.* Choice **c** incorrectly uses *evolving* instead of *evolved,* changing a modifier to a verb and making the sentence illogical. Choice **e** makes *evolutionarily* an adverb, which creates an awkward and unclear sentence.

64. **c.** The proper idiom is *in conjunction with.* Choices **a** and **e** are therefore incorrect. Choices **b** and **d** are incorrect because the pronoun *who,* not *that,* must be used to refer to *doctor.*

65. **d.** Choice **a** is wordy and redundant. Choice **b** is correct, but it is less effective than choice **d** because the word choice and sentence structure are less sophisticated. Choice **c** has an error in subject-verb agreement (*problems . . . shows*) and has awkward word order. Choice **e** has a misplaced modifier; because of its placement, *lacking computer-related skills* modifies *today's job market.*

66. **a.** This is a complicated sentence, and many phrases and clauses separate the subject *story* from the verb *is* (this subject-verb pair is not the main subject of the sentence but the subject and verb in the *that* clause describing what Jung and Campbell believed). Because *story* is the subject, choice **c** is incorrect; the verb must be singular. Choices **d** and **e** are incorrect because they do not provide a verb to complete the clause; rather, they create an additional clause or phrase. Choice **b** creates a sentence fragment by inserting a semicolon after *people.*

67. **c.** The correct idiom is *based on,* so all other choices are incorrect.

68. **d.** The pronoun *who* should be used to refer to people. Choices **a** and **c** are therefore incorrect. The clause *who suffer from antisocial personality disorder* is necessary to describe which people *demonstrate a disturbing emotional shallowness.* Choices **b** and **e** do not use a pronoun to create such a clause, making the sentence unclear and/or illogical.

69. **e.** Choices **a**, **b**, and **c** misplace the modifier *in protracted space flight*, which should follow *astronauts*, and **a** also misplaces *brought on by weightlessness*, which should follow *atrophy*. Choice **c** also makes an error in the idiom *brought on by*. Choice **d** is wordy.

70. **b.** All of the other choices are unnecessarily wordy and/or less direct. Choices **a** and **e** also disrupt the parallel structure of the list. Choice **e** is also awkward.

71. **e.** The correct idiom is *of a like mind*. All other choices are therefore incorrect.

72. **a.** This is the most concise version. Choice **b** disrupts the parallel structure by turning the modifier *renowned* into a clause. Choices **c** and **d** are wordy. Choice **e** incorrectly uses *being* to create an awkward sentence.

73. **c.** Choice **a** misplaces the modifier *also called genetic engineering*, which should immediately follow *recombinant DNA technology*. Choice **b** turns what should be the predicate of the sentence (the main action and focus of the sentence) into a huge introductory phrase, shifting the emphasis onto *also called genetic engineering*, which becomes the new predicate. Choice **d** incorrectly uses the wordy and indirect phrases *the cutting of* instead of the infinitive *to cut* and *the combination of them with* instead of *combine them with*. Choice **e** is wordy.

74. **b.** Choice **a** is a run-on sentence, which choice **b** corrects by changing the comma to a semicolon. Choice **c** creates a wordy and awkward sentence. Choice **d** changes the meaning of the sentence and makes it unclear—90% more *of what?* Choice **e** is also a run-on.

75. **d.** Choice **a** is an unclear sentence because *it* could refer to several antecedents, including *foreign body*, *molecules*, *immune system*, and *species*. The correct antecedent is *immune system*. Choice **e** also has an error in subject-verb agreement (*species* requires a singular verb—*reacts*).

CHAPTER

12 Verbal Section Glossary

active voice when the subject is performing the action (as opposed to *passive voice*)

ad hominem a logical fallacy in which the arguer attacks a person rather than the person's claim

agreement the state of being balanced in number (e.g., singular subjects and singular verbs; plural antecedents and plural pronouns)

antecedent the word or phrase to which a pronoun refers (e.g., *Jane kissed her son*)

argument a set of claims with a conclusion (main claim) and one or more premises supporting that conclusion

begging the question a logical fallacy in which the conclusion repeats the premise

bias a strong inclination or preference for one person, position, or point of view over others

cause a person, thing, or action that makes something happen

chronological order when events are arranged by time (the order in which the events occurred or will occur)

claim a statement with a truth value

clause a group of words containing a subject and predicate (e.g., *as he came running*)

comparative the adjective form showing the greater degree in quality or quantity, which is formed by adding *-er* (e.g., *happier*) or *less* (e.g., *less beautiful*)

comparison the discovery of similarities between two or more items or ideas
complex sentence a sentence with at least one dependent and one independent clause
compound sentence a sentence with at least two independent clauses
conclusion in critical reasoning, the main claim of an argument (the assertion it aims to prove)
conjunctive adverb a word or phrase that often works with a semicolon to connect two independent clauses and show the relationship to one another (e.g., *however, therefore, likewise*)
contraction a word that uses an apostrophe to show that a letter or letters have been omitted (e.g., *can't*)
contrast the discovery of differences between two or more items or ideas
coordinating conjunction one of seven words—*and, but, for, nor, or, so,* and *yet*—that serve to connect two independent clauses
dependent clause a clause that has a subordinating conjunction and expresses an incomplete thought
diction word choice
direct object the person or thing that receives the action of the sentence
effect an event or change created by an action
fragment an incomplete sentence (it may or may not have a subject and predicate)
gerund the noun form of a verb, which is created by adding *-ing* to the verb base
helping verb (auxiliary verb) verbs that help indicate exactly when an action will take place, is taking place, did take place, should take place, might take place, and so on.
independent clause a clause that expresses a complete thought and can stand on its own
indirect object the person or thing that receives the direct object
infinitive the base form of a verb plus the word *to* (e.g., *to go*)
intransitive verb a verb that does not take an object (the subject performs the action on his-/her-/itself)
logical reasonable, based upon reasoning and good common sense, not emotional
logical fallacy a flaw or error in reasoning
main idea the controlling idea of a passage
mechanics the rules governing punctuation, capitalization, and spelling
modifier a word or phrase that describes or qualifies a person, place, thing, or action
non sequitur a logical fallacy in which the connection between a premise and conclusion is unstated; jumping to conclusions
order of importance when ideas are arranged by rank, from most to least important or least to most important
paragraph one or more sentences about one main idea, set off by indenting the first line
participial phrase the adjective form of a verb, which is created by adding *-ing* to the verb base
passive voice when the subject of the sentence is being acted upon (passively receives the action)
past participle the verb form expressing what happened in the past, formed by a past-tense helping verb plus the simple past-tense form of the verb
phrase a group of words that do not contain both a subject and a predicate (e.g., *in the box, will be going*)
post hoc, ergo propter hoc a logical fallacy that assumes X caused Y just because X preceded Y
predicate the part of the sentence that tells us what the subject is or does
premise a claim given in support of a conclusion in an argument

present participle the verb form expressing what is happening now, which is formed by a present-tense helping verb and *-ing* form of the main verb
proper noun a noun that identifies a specific person, place, or thing (e.g., *Elm Street*)
qualifier a word or phrase that limits the scope of a claim (e.g., *never, always*)
red herring a logical fallacy in which the arguer brings in an irrelevant issue to divert the argument
redundancy the unnecessary repetition of words or ideas (e.g., *Lana's mentally out of her mind!*)
run-on a sentence that has two or more independent clauses without the proper punctuation or connecting words (e.g., *subordinating conjunction*) between them
slippery slope a logical fallacy that presents an *if/then* situation as an absolute
straw man a logical fallacy in which the opponent's position is distorted, oversimplified, exaggerated, or otherwise misrepresented
style the manner in which something is done; in writing, the combination of a writer's sentence structure and word choice
subject the person, place, or thing that performs the action of the sentence
subjunctive the verb form that indicates something that is wished for or contrary to fact
subordinating conjunction a word or phrase that introduces an adverb clause, making the clause dependent and showing its relationship to another (usually independent) clause (e.g., *because, since, while*)
superlative the adjective form showing the greatest degree in quality or quantity, which is formed by adding *-est* (e.g., *happiest*), *most* (e.g., *most boring*), or *least*
thesis the main idea or theme of a passage
tone the mood or attitude conveyed by words or speech
topic sentence a sentence that expresses the main idea of a paragraph
transition a word or phrase used to move from one idea to the next and show the relationship between those ideas (e.g., *however, next, in contrast*)
transitive verb a verb that takes an object (someone or something receives the action of the verb)
wordiness the use of several words when a few words can more clearly and concisely express the same idea (e.g., *the pen that belongs to Jill*)

PART

III

The GMAT Analytical Writing Assessment

CHAPTER

13 Analytical Writing Assessment Pretest

In the following chapters, you will learn all about the GMAT® Analytical Writing Assessment (AWA) section: the kinds of topics you will be asked to write about, how you will be expected to write about those topics, and how your essays will be scored. You will also review strategies for effective analytical writing and learn specific tips and strategies that can be used on the exam.

Before you begin the AWA review, take the following pretest. Use this practice test to help you determine how much preparation you need for this section of the exam.

▶ Pretest

The following AWA pretest contains two essay prompts, one of each kind of prompt you will see on the actual exam. This pretest is designed to give you a sense of what to expect and help you assess your strengths and weaknesses for this portion of the exam. When you are finished, compare your results to the scoring guide and sample essays in the answer key. Use the results to plan your study time effectively and determine the areas where you need the most careful review and practice.

Test-Taking Tip

When practicing essays on your computer, be sure to turn off the spell check and grammar check; the word-processing program on the GMAT exam will not include either of these features.

To practice the timing of the GMAT exam, spend 30 minutes on each essay. On the test, you will have to write both essays in one hour, so do both essays consecutively for the most realistic practice test scenario. Make every effort to write your essays on a computer with a basic word processor. The more practice you have composing and revising on the computer, the more comfortable you will be on the exam.

If you cannot practice composing on a computer, use the following lined paper to write your responses. Also, be sure you have scratch paper available so that you can brainstorm and outline your essays.

DO NOT READ THE ESSAY PROMPTS UNTIL YOU ARE READY TO BEGIN THE PRETEST. READ ONLY THE FIRST PROMPT. READ THE SECOND PROMPT ONLY AFTER YOU HAVE COMPLETED THE FIRST ESSAY AND ARE READY TO BEGIN THE SECOND.

▶ Analysis of an Issue

"Successful corporations have a moral responsibility to contribute to society by supporting education, nonprofit services, or the arts."

Discuss the extent to which you agree or disagree with this opinion. Support your position with reasons and/or examples from your own experience, observations, or reading. Complete your essay in 30 minutes.

► Analysis of an Argument

The following idea was proposed in a meeting of the owners of an upmarket restaurant.

> *"The only way to expand our customer base is to move to a location that gives us much more exposure. In our current location, we don't get enough business because we are too isolated. We should find a space next to another store or near a transportation hub."*

Discuss how well-reasoned you find this argument. In your essay, be sure to analyze the argument's logic and use of evidence. For example, you may need to consider whether the assumptions that underlie the argument are sound or whether counterarguments or alternative explanations would weaken the conclusion. You may also discuss the kind of evidence that would strengthen or refute the argument, what revisions to the argument would make it more reasonable, or what information, if anything, would help you better evaluate the argument. Complete your essay in 30 minutes.

▶ Answer Explanations

The following model essays earn a 6 on the AWA section, the top score on the written exam. Both essays have most or all of the following characteristics:

CONTENT	DEVELOPMENT	ORGANIZATION	EXPRESSION	CONVENTIONS
The content of your written response shows an understanding and interpretation of the issue or argument and the task presented in the prompt.	The development of your written response gives a clear and logical explanation of ideas using specific and relevant support.	The organization of your written response shows a coherent, orderly, and well-reasoned approach.	The expression of your ideas reflects an awareness of audience, a command of vocabulary and sentence structure, and an ability to use language to convey purpose.	The use of standard English in your written response exhibits the correct use of spelling, punctuation, paragraph organization, capitalization, and grammar.
■ Forms a thesis statement that reveals an in-depth understanding of the issue or argument. ■ Presents a sophisticated and insightful analysis of the issue or argument.	■ Develops ideas clearly and fully. ■ Provides a wide range of relevant and specific evidence to support the thesis statement.	■ Maintains the focus of the thesis statement. ■ Uses a logical and coherent structure. ■ Applies skillful writing devices and transitions.	■ Exhibits a mature, sophisticated use of language that is precise and engaging. ■ Has a voice and a sense of awareness of audience and purpose. ■ Varies the structure and length of sentences to enhance meaning.	■ Shows control of the conventions of standard English. ■ Has few, if any, errors even when using sophisticated language.

▶ Sample Essay—Analysis of an Issue (Score: 6)

All for-profit corporations have a moral responsibility to contribute to society by supporting education, nonprofit services, or the arts. In today's increasingly global marketplace, companies that embrace their social responsibilities and empower their leaders and employees to serve local and world communities will reap rewards now and for years to come. These companies will realize that they will reap long-term benefits in morale and bottom-line growth and sustainability by giving their personnel the opportunity to work toward higher goals (social responsibilities) and to make a difference in their lives and the lives of the people around them.

Every organization has a legal responsibility to serve its immediate (or local) community as a productive "citizen" by obeying and upholding the laws that govern its operations and by giving its employees a safe place to work. Yet, a select group of modern companies take their social responsibilities a step further, moving beyond mere compliance and into a heightened awareness of social responsibility. These companies operate under "enlightened self-interest." They realize that what is good for the community and for society is good for the company, and they spend a tremendous amount of effort and money incorporating social programs into their corporate infrastructures and even encouraging and rewarding social involvement and leadership.

These companies go beyond merely making grants to nonprofit groups or arts programs. Even more importantly, in addition to monetary gifts to these types of social organizations, they set up hearty volunteerism programs through which employees at all levels are encouraged to participate in organized volunteer activities. Typically, they match skills to needs. For instance, researchers at a pharmaceutical company might be organized to help tutor students in science.

Although some may argue that corporations have a responsibility only to their stakeholders and their bottom line and do not legally have a responsibility to "do good" in society, they miss the point that social responsibility is in the best interest of the company. Companies that actively participate in social programs aimed at curbing crime, fighting poverty and illiteracy, and teaching skills to those in need reap bottom-line benefits from their social programs every day. These programs not only have a positive impact on the local communities where they are enacted, but they also continue to deliver dividends to the organization in positive public relations, building the image of the company in the eyes of the community and developing a more effective employee base.

Corporations that contribute to society benefit on the inside as well. Employees involved in volunteerism programs are more motivated to perform in their business environment because their commitment to others improves morale and fulfills an important psychological need. These same employees build leadership skills and interpersonal skills while performing their volunteer work, and these skills are not left at home. Furthermore, employees are more likely to feel strong loyalty to a company that helps them improve others and themselves.

In summary, corporations that take their moral responsibility to contribute to society seriously and develop corporate programs such as volunteerism programs will fare better than their counterparts who shirk their social duties. A healthy community equals a healthy business.

▶ Sample Essay—Analysis of an Argument (Score: 6)

Location is everything . . . or is it? The owners of an upmarket restaurant are considering a proposal to move next to another store or near a transportation hub in order to expand their customer base. Without offering any evidence, the proposal concludes that moving to a location that offers more exposure is the only way to increase exposure and clientele. Although moving to a new location is certainly one method that could improve the restaurant's patron base, it is not the only method, nor does it guarantee that numbers would improve. The owners must weigh the costs of moving against staying in their current location and using other techniques to improve business.

The first issue is whether location could help expand the customer base. Certainly in the real-estate market, the mantra is "location, location, location." If a new restaurant is placed near another store, customers may plan to stop in for a meal before or after shopping or running errands. Similarly, proximity to a transportation hub could increase patronage because more people would be aware of its existence and its location would provide convenient access for customers. But a restaurant's location is only one factor that patrons consider when choosing to spend a large amount of money on a meal. For most people, food quality and service are most important. Atmosphere and cleanliness are other persuasive factors. If a restaurant has excellent food served in a clean, comfortable setting at reasonable prices, chances are patrons will come, even if the restaurant is a little out of the way.

Another issue the owners should review is how the cost of a move would affect the bottom line. First, how would new lease or mortgage payments vary from the current costs? Second, moving is an expensive venture, particularly when it involves a lot of furniture and fragile objects such as dishes that need to be packed securely. The owners could be faced with some or all of the following costs: renting trucks, paying movers, buying boxes, purchasing insurance for items in transit, and paying overtime to staff to assist with the move. An even bigger expense could be the loss of income while the move is being made because the restaurant would have to shut down to pack, move, and get reestablished in the new location.

Because location isn't everything and moving costs are so high, the owners should seriously examine ways to increase the customer base from their current location. First, however, they need to determine the true cause of their lack of business. If people just are not impressed with the food or if they feel the price is too high, moving is not going to solve anything and might only exacerbate the problem. If, on the other hand, the owners determine (via customer survey/comment cards or other feedback mechanism) that the restaurant's isolated location *is* the problem, they can draw in new customers in many ways and make people aware of their existence. For example, they could send flyers with special discounts to names on purchased mailing lists or to previous customers, publish ads with coupons to attract new and existing customers, and invite restaurant reviewers from area newspapers to generate interest.

With these considerations, I think the owners would be wise to inventory the current customer satisfaction and attempt to increase business from their present location rather than trying to improve business with a move. If customers are currently not satisfied with food quality, price, or service, moving to a new location is not likely to generate more business, despite the increased exposure. Moving will also increase short-term costs and does not guarantee that a new location will bring more customers. Location is not the only factor these owners need to consider when aiming to expand their customer base, and even if it is the problem, a move is not the only or best answer.

CHAPTER

14 About the Analytical Writing Assessment

The first part of the GMAT® exam is the Analytical Writing Assessment (AWA): a two-part essay exam designed to measure your ability to think critically and convey your ideas effectively in writing. The AWA consists of two separate writing questions: an Analysis of an Argument and an Analysis of an Issue. You will have 30 minutes to write each essay.

▶ Analysis of an Issue

For the Analysis of an Issue essay, you will be presented with a short statement (one to three sentences) about an issue, and you will be asked to take a position on the issue. Your essay should clearly state your opinion and support that opinion with specific reasons and examples.

Issue Topics

The issue topics can be about anything, including business, social, political, or ethical matters. Whatever their subject matter, issue topics will be general enough so that all test takers can form a reasonable opinion on the issue. You will not need prior or specialized knowledge of the subject to write an effective essay. For example, you do not need specific knowledge of how successful corporations work to answer the Analysis of an Issue prompt from the pretest. Indeed, this prompt is a good example of how open AWA issue questions usually are. Notice, for example, the number of terms that can be defined in many ways, leaving the prompt open to a wide range of responses:

> *"Successful corporations have a moral responsibility to contribute to society by supporting education, nonprofit services, or the arts."*

What makes a successful corporation? What sort of responsibility is needed? What kind of contribution must be made? What kind of support is required? This prompt can generate many different responses depending upon the focus each writer chooses.

Here is a sampling of the kinds of general issues you might see on the AWA:

- what schools should teach students (e.g., ethics versus academics)
- the best methods for protecting the environment
- the best way to motivate employees
- the keys to success
- the best way to improve employee-supervisor relations
- the impact of technology, consumerism, globalism, mass media, or other predominant features of our culture or times
- the responsibilities of government, corporations, or individuals
- the best preparation for the workforce
- corporate policies, especially regarding employees, privacy, and the environment
- healthcare
- advances in science and technology, especially those that impact the workplace

Analyzing the Issue

The AWA is designed to measure both your writing and analytical skills. Thus, to receive a high score on this essay, you must show evidence that you have carefully considered all sides of the issue and the pros and cons of your position. As you plan your response, consider the following questions:

- What positions can be taken on the issue?
- What are the pros and cons of each major position?

This does not mean that a good Analysis of an Issue essay will explain each position and present all of the pros and cons for each side; not enough time is available for such a comprehensive review. However, your essay should do the following:

- **Acknowledge** the other side, especially powerful counterarguments that might be made by the opposition
- **Concede** any serious drawbacks or flaws in your position

For example, the Analysis of an Issue essay in the pretest skillfully acknowledged the opposition and then presented a rebuttal to that position:

> Although some may argue that corporations have a responsibility only to their stakeholders and their bottom line and do not legally have a responsibility to "do good" in society, they miss the point that social responsibility is in the best interest of the company. Companies that actively participate in social programs aimed at curbing crime, fighting poverty and illiteracy, and teaching skills to those in need reap bottom-line benefits from their social programs every day. These programs not only have a positive impact on the local communities where they are enacted, but they also continue to deliver dividends to the organization in positive public relations, building the image of the company in the eyes of the community and developing a more effective employee base.

▶ Analysis of an Argument

For your Analysis of an Argument essay, you will be presented with a short argument (one paragraph that is one to five sentences long). Your task will be to critique the reasoning behind that argument. In this essay, you should not offer your opinion of the *issue* in the argument; instead, you must offer your assessment of the *argument* by evaluating the logic (or lack thereof) of the claims.

Argument Topics

The argument in your writing prompt can also be about any topic, although a majority of the topics are somehow related to business. Once again, you will not need to have any specific knowledge about that topic to respond effectively in an essay. For example, the Analysis of an Argument prompt in the pretest is business related, but you do not need to know anything about owning a restaurant to successfully critique the argument. You just need to be able to analyze the argument and present your analysis in an organized and engaging manner.

The following is a sampling of the kinds of general subjects you might find in argument prompts on the AWA:

- strategies for improving business or services
- which products or services to choose
- how to spend funds or save money
- health and environmental issues
- societal trends

AWA Prompt List

Want to see the AWA writing prompts from last year's GMAT exam? You can download a complete list of the 2001–2002 AWA essay prompts from the website www.mba.com/mba/TaketheGMAT/Tools/AWATopics2001.htm.

Analyzing the Argument

On the analysis level, your readers will be looking for evidence that you have considered the following questions:

- What assumptions underlie the argument? Are they reasonable or problematic? If they are problematic, why?
- What is the conclusion of the argument? Is it a logical conclusion based on the evidence?
- Does the argument have any logical fallacies?
- What evidence would help strengthen the argument?
- Are there counterarguments or alternative explanations that would weaken the conclusion?
- Is there any information that would help you better evaluate the conclusion?

Although the arguments on the AWA may be somewhat logical, they will usually have at least one significant flaw that you will need to recognize. The argument may do the following:

- be based on problematic assumptions
- jump to conclusions
- compare apples to oranges
- ignore alternative explanations
- show poor reasoning

The argument from the pretest, for example, was based on the problematic assumption that location is everything and a move was therefore necessary to improve business. This ignored alternative explanations for the lack of business, including the possibility that customers were simply dissatisfied with the food, price, or service. It also did not consider other possibilities for attracting customers to the current location. Finally, it neglected to consider the high cost of the move.

A solid grasp of critical reasoning skills is essential not only for the critical reasoning questions on the Verbal section but also for an effective analysis of the argument on the AWA. To review critical reasoning skills, see pages 87–107.

What Makes a Good Essay?

To earn a 4, 5, or 6 on the AWA, your essays will need to have the following six characteristics:

- A clear main idea (thesis). Do you have something to say? In the issue essay, have you taken a clear position? In the argument essay, have you expressed your main assessment of the argument?
- Sufficient development. Have you explained your position or your judgment of the argument?
- Strong support. Have you supported your ideas with specific reasons and examples?
- Effective organization. Have you presented your ideas and support in a logical order?
- Clear, controlled sentences. Do your ideas come across clearly in properly constructed sentences?
- Grammatical correctness. Have you followed the conventions of standard written English?

Remember that this is an analytical writing assessment. An essay may be beautifully written, but if it doesn't show evidence of critical reasoning, it will not receive a top score.

▶ How the Essays Are Scored

Two independent readers will score each AWA essay holistically on a scale of 0 (lowest) to 6 (highest). Readers will take into consideration the overall effectiveness of each essay, including its content, style, and grammatical correctness. An essay that expresses sophisticated ideas in sentences full of errors will not receive a top score, but that same essay can earn a 6 even if it has a couple of grammatical mistakes or an awkwardly phrased sentence.

A holistic approach means that readers will be looking for the following elements:

- the level of critical thinking evident in your ideas
- effective organization
- sufficient development of ideas
- strong and sufficient support of ideas
- effective word choice and sentence structure
- clear and controlled sentences
- a command of the conventions of standard written English

Your AWA score will be the average of all four scores, two for each essay. If two scores for one essay differ by more than one point, a third independent reader will rate your essay and all five scores will be averaged for your total AWA score.

Getting to Know E-rater®

As we noted in the first chapter, one of your readers will be a college or university faculty member specially trained to review GMAT essays. The other reader, however, is likely to be a computer program called E-rater®,

Follow Directions

Your essay will not be scored if you write on a topic other than what was assigned. It is extremely important that you respond to the prompt you are given. Never write about a different topic.

which "reads" the essays looking for very specific elements. E-rater cannot understand your ideas and will not grasp the nuances of your argument and style. Rather, it looks for evidence that you have presented a logical, well-organized argument in clear and controlled sentences. Although some might argue that this is a highly superficial way to score an essay, the general writing elements that E-rater will be assessing are the same elements that human readers—who really only have a few minutes to devote to each essay—are also looking for. These elements include the following:

- the number and length of paragraphs and other indications of logical grouping of ideas
- transitions and other words and phrases that suggest the development and organization of ideas (e.g., *in addition, more important*)
- variety in sentence structure (varied sentence length and combinations of phrases and clauses)
- correct grammar and mechanics (punctuation, capitalization, and spelling)

Keep It Simple

Because you only have a half-hour to write each essay, because human readers must read AWA essays quickly, and because E-rater is designed to look for fundamental structural elements, a simple, straightforward presentation of your ideas using all of the signposts possible is the best way to write on this exam. Don't try to write an elaborate, complicated essay, and do not try to gain points by showing off sophisticated stylistic techniques. Aim for simplicity and clarity throughout your essays.

Instead of *implying* your main idea, for example, make sure you have a clear thesis statement for your essay and topic sentences for each paragraph. Choose a simple, easily recognizable organizational pattern for your ideas. Use transitions between sentences and paragraphs, even if the connections seem obvious to you. Avoid stylistic techniques that you might sometimes use for emphasis. For example, sometimes a one-word sentence or paragraph can have great impact as a stylistic technique. However, E-rater is likely to see it as a grammatical error (sentence fragment) or an underdeveloped paragraph. Instead, stick to a more traditional sentence or paragraph length.

The GMAT Scoring Rubric

Although scoring an essay is far more subjective than correcting a multiple-choice exam, the GMAC has developed a detailed **scoring rubric** to guide its human readers through the essay-scoring process. This rubric lists the specific criteria that essays should meet for each score. The following shows a scoring rubric modeled after the official GMAT scoring guide. Be sure to review the scoring guide carefully. The more you know about what is expected of you in the essay, the better you will be able to meet those expectations.

SCORE	CONTENT	DEVELOPMENT	ORGANIZATION	EXPRESSION	CONVENTIONS
	The content of your written response shows an understanding and interpretation of the issue or argument and the task presented in the prompt.	The development of your written response gives a clear and logical explanation of ideas using specific and relevant support.	The organization of your written response shows a coherent, orderly, and well-reasoned approach.	The expression of your ideas reflects an awareness of audience, a command of vocabulary and sentence structure, and an ability to use language to convey purpose.	The use of standard English in your written response exhibits the correct use of spelling, punctuation, paragraph organization, capitalization, and grammar.
6	■ Forms a thesis statement that reveals an in-depth understanding of the issue or argument. ■ Presents a sophisticated and insightful analysis of the issue or argument.	■ Develops ideas clearly and fully. ■ Provides a wide range of relevant and specific evidence to support the thesis statement.	■ Maintains the focus of the thesis statement. ■ Uses a logical and coherent structure. ■ Applies skillful writing devices and transitions.	■ Exhibits a mature, sophisticated use of language that is precise and engaging. ■ Has a voice and a sense of awareness of audience and purpose. ■ Varies the structure and length of sentences to enhance meaning.	■ Shows control of the conventions of standard English. ■ Has few, if any, errors even when using sophisticated language.
5	■ Forms a thesis statement that reveals a thorough understanding of the issue or argument and the task presented in the prompt. ■ Presents a clear and thoughtful analysis of the issue or argument.	■ Develops ideas clearly and consistently. ■ Makes reference to relevant and specific evidence that supports the thesis statement.	■ Maintains the focus of the thesis statement. ■ Uses a logical sequence of ideas. ■ Applies the appropriate writing devices and transitions.	■ Uses language that is fluent and original. ■ Has an awareness of audience and purpose. ■ Varies the structure and length of sentences to control the rhythm and pacing.	■ Shows control of the conventions of standard English, but may have some errors, especially when using sophisticated language or sentence structure.

4	■ Forms a thesis statement that shows a basic understanding of the issue or argument and the task presented in the prompt. ■ Presents a reasonable analysis, often of the most obvious aspects of the issue or argument.	■ Develops some ideas more fully than others. ■ Provides some specific and relevant evidence to support the thesis statement.	■ Maintains a clear and appropriate focus throughout most of the essay. ■ Uses a logical sequence of ideas but may lack consistency.	■ Uses appropriate language. ■ Shows some awareness of audience and purpose. ■ Occasionally varies the sentence structure and length.	■ Shows incomplete control of standard English. ■ Has some errors but they do not interfere with comprehension.
3	■ Forms a thesis statement that shows a basic understanding of the issue or argument and the task presented in the prompt. ■ Presents an incomplete analysis of the issue or argument or neglects important aspects of the analysis.	■ Develops ideas briefly. ■ Provides some evidence and support material to support the thesis statement.	■ Creates, but does not maintain an appropriate focus. ■ Uses a basic structure but may include some inconsistencies or irrelevancies.	■ Uses very basic vocabulary. ■ Demonstrates little sense of audience or purpose. ■ Attempts to vary the sentence structure or length but has uneven success.	■ Attempts to control standard English but has some errors that interfere with comprehension.

2	■ Expresses a confused or incomplete understanding of the issue or argument and the task presented in the prompt. ■ Makes little attempt to analyze the issue or argument or presents a fundamentally flawed analysis.	■ Is a combination of incomplete or undeveloped ideas. ■ Uses references that are vague, irrelevant, repetitive, or unsubstantiated.	■ Suggests some organization but lacks an appropriate focus. ■ Suggests a focus but lacks organization.	■ Uses language that is often simple and imprecise or that may be unsuitable for the audience or purpose. ■ Shows little awareness of how to use sentences to achieve a rhythmic effect.	■ Shows little control of standard English. ■ Has frequent errors that interfere with comprehension.
1	■ Gives minimal or no evidence of understanding of the issue or argument. ■ Makes little or no attempt to analyze the issue or argument.	■ Has minimal evidence of development.	■ Shows no focus or organization.	■ Uses language that is very limited, incoherent, and/or inappropriate. ■ Shows little or no ability to vary the sentence structure or length.	■ Is limited, making the assessment of conventions unreliable. ■ Is illegible or not recognized as English.
0	■ If response is totally unrelated to the topic, incoherent, or blank, the essay will be given a 0.				

Get Real Scores for Your Practice Essays

For a fee of $20, you can complete an official practice AWA and have it scored by the GMAC in the same way your GMAT AWA will be scored. For more information, visit the GMAC website at www.mba.com/mba/Store/products/EssayInsight.htm.

How Long Should the Essays Be?

Although length is not a guarantee of a high score—you could write 500 words of fluff—the length of the essay and the score are related. In general, longer essays are more effective because they take the time to sufficiently develop and support their ideas.

As a general guide, you will need to write at least four or five paragraphs to have a strong, sufficiently developed essay. This includes an introductory paragraph that states your main idea, two or three paragraphs developing and supporting that main idea, and a brief concluding paragraph. Your essay should run approximately 400 to 600 words with an average of three to five sentences per paragraph. But remember, this is just a general guide. An essay with seven or eight shorter paragraphs might be just as effective as an essay with four longer ones. Keep these paragraph suggestions in mind, but focus on developing and supporting your ideas.

CHAPTER

15 Guide to Effective Writing

You have probably written dozens, maybe even hundreds, of essays in your academic career, so you might feel that you have already heard all there is to say about writing effective essays. In a way, you are right. Most of what you read in the rest of this section will probably not be new to you. However, good writers are always returning to the fundamental elements of effective writing. Sometimes a subject that you didn't quite understand before will suddenly make sense because it is explained in a different way or presented in a new context. So read the rest of this chapter with an open mind. At the least, you will review the fundamentals of effective analytical writing and get some specific tips for doing well on the AWA. At the most, you will learn new strategies and techniques that will dramatically improve your writing skills.

▶ The Writing Process

Experienced writers know that good writing doesn't happen all at once; rather, it develops in stages. That's because writing is a *process*, not just a *product*—a process of determining how to best communicate ideas to an audience for a purpose. It is difficult to produce good writing without going through each step in the process.

A Word about Essays

The word *essay* has its roots in the Old French word *essai,* meaning *trial* or *attempt,* and the Latin *exagium,* meaning *weighing.* Thus, essay can be defined as follows:

- a trial or attempt to accomplish or perform something, an undertaking
- a short prose composition on any subject

Essays—those short prose compositions—are really *attempts* to accomplish something: to convey ideas to an audience for a specific purpose. In the process, the writer *weighs* his or her ideas and explores different possibilities.

Over the centuries, essay styles may have changed, but the standard form of the essay remains the same:

- an introduction that presents the topic and thesis
- a body that develops and supports that thesis
- a conclusion that restates the main idea

This standard structure has many variations, and these variations can be highly effective and make the reading process more interesting. But remember, because of the time constraint and the fact that one of your readers is a computer, it's best to stick to the old standard.

The writing process can be divided into four steps:

1. Planning
2. Drafting
3. Revising
4. Editing

When you are under pressure to write a winning essay in just 30 minutes, you may be tempted to skip these steps and just write your essay in one shot. You might end up with a successful essay with this approach, but your chances of doing well on the AWA—indeed, on any writing task—will increase dramatically if you take the time to work through each step. Even though you only have 30 minutes, the 10 to 15 minutes you spend planning and proofreading your essay will be time well-spent. In fact, for essay exams, the planning stage is so important that the stage is divided into four separate steps, which are discussed in this section.

Planning

Good writing requires preparation. The planning stage (often called **prewriting**) includes all of the steps that writers take to prepare for their writing task. These include *incubation, brainstorming,* and *outlining.*

Incubation is perhaps an unconventional term to describe the process of mulling over ideas without actually writing anything down. It's the back-burner thinking that often takes place even without your full awareness. For example, you might have read an essay assignment and set it aside to complete later. While you were out running errands, doing the dishes, or waiting for the train, you suddenly came up with ideas for your essay because part of your brain had been thinking about this topic.

Unfortunately, on the AWA, you do not have the time to incubate. As soon as you get your prompt, you will have to start brainstorming ideas.

Brainstorming refers to the process of coming up with ideas, such as support for an essay, solutions to a problem, or gifts for a birthday. The key to a successful brainstorm is to be open to all ideas. At this important stage, don't censor yourself. Write down whatever comes to mind. The more freedom you give yourself to think, the more ideas will come to you. The more ideas you get on paper, the more freedom you will have to pick the best (strongest) support for your thesis.

Several brainstorming techniques can help you generate ideas and examples to support your thesis, including **freewriting**, **listing**, and **mapping**.

Freewriting is a technique that is useful any time you are having trouble coming up with ideas and is particularly helpful if you are having trouble getting started. This brainstorming technique is exactly what it says: *free writing*. Write down whatever comes to mind about the question or topic. Don't worry about grammar or structure; write in your native language or your personal shorthand if you like. *Just write.* If you keep your hands moving for even two or three minutes, you are bound to come up with some good ideas. Here's a freewriting example for the Analysis of an Argument essay from the pretest:

> Location location location they say but that's not the only thing that matters. I go out of my way to a place if it has food I like (ex, Carmello's). Maybe there are other factors keeping customers away (food, cost, service, atmosphere, other competition) maybe they just need to be more aggressive in getting customers to their door. Maybe too pricey for mediocre food, so moving won't matter. Moving—expenses—especially for closing down during the move.

Listing is probably the most common brainstorming technique and particularly useful if you are a linear thinker. Simply list on a piece of paper (or on the computer screen) all of the ideas that come to mind in relation to your topic. Here's how the writer of the Analysis of an Argument essay used listing to brainstorm ideas:

New location:
near hub = convenience
near stores = people eat after shopping
higher rent
maybe more competition
moving costs

Old location:
other factors?
  food
  service
  price
  atmosphere
survey customers
restaurant reviews
ads

Mapping enables you to make connections among ideas as you brainstorm. For visual learners, this is often the most effective brainstorming technique because relationships among ideas are clear and serve as triggers for other ideas. Here's how the same brainstorm might appear as a map:

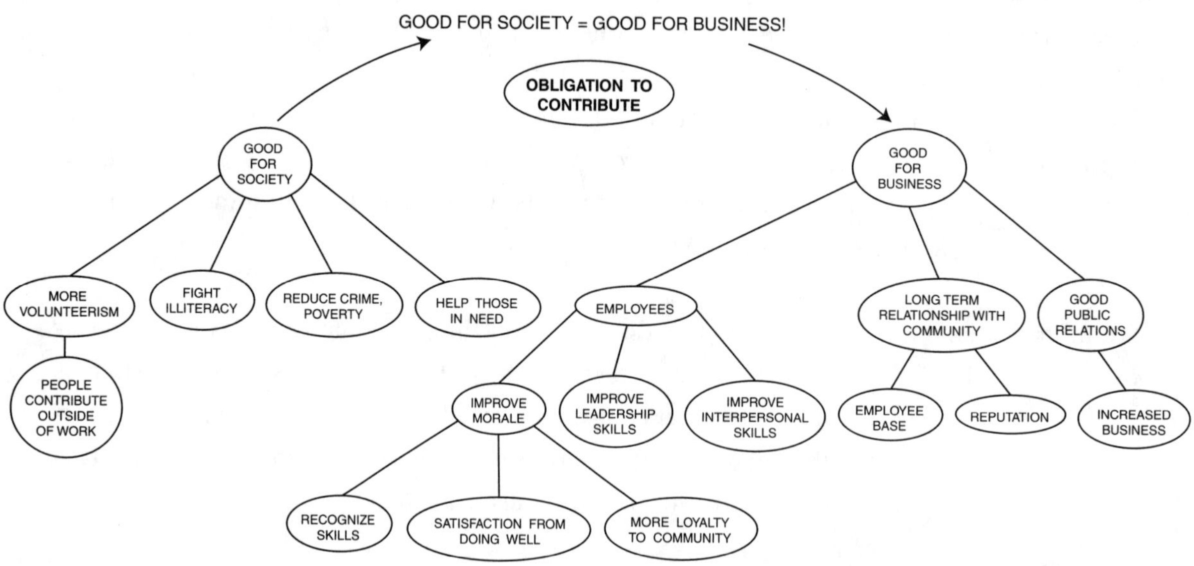

Drafting is the process of actually writing the essay. As you know from your own experience, drafts can come in many varieties, from the very rough to the highly polished. On an at-home essay, you have the freedom to write roughly and polish your essay in several revision stages until your essay says what you want it to say and the way you want to say it.

However, on an essay exam, your first draft is essentially your *only* draft. That is why, as we have already noted, the planning stage is so important. The better you plan your essay, the more complete and effective your draft will be.

Revising and Editing

To **revise** means to carefully read over your essay and make changes to improve it. **Revising** focuses on improving the *content* (what you say) and *style* (how you say it). In other words, when you revise, you concentrate on the big picture: how you organize and present your ideas in your essay. **Editing,** on the other hand, deals with *grammar* (correct sentences), *mechanics* (correct spelling, capitalization, and punctuation), and *usage* (correct use of idioms).

Editing is very important; your writing should be as clear and correct as possible. Errors in grammar, usage, and mechanics can make your sentence unclear and frustrate your readers. However, as a general rule, it doesn't make much sense to carefully proofread each sentence before you revise. After all, you may realize that you need to rewrite, add, or delete entire sentences or paragraphs.

REVISING ISSUES	EDITING ISSUES
thesis	grammar
support	usage
organization	punctuation
focus/unity	capitalization
sentence structure	spelling
style	

How to Divide Your Time on an Essay Exam

As you know from your own experience, writing an essay in 30 minutes is very different from writing an essay at home over the course of a week or two. When you are writing an essay outside of class, you have the time to write and revise several drafts. Even if you are typically a one-draft writer, you know you have the option of devoting considerable time and energy to revising.

In an essay exam situation, however, you do not have the luxury of extended revision time after you draft, so you need to approach the writing process in a slightly different way. Because you cannot count on having the time to revise for major issues, you must be extra careful to plan your essay wisely.

On an essay exam, use this general rule of thumb for dividing your time:

- one-fourth of the time planning
- one-half of the time writing
- one-fourth of the time revising and editing

The 30 minutes you spend on each AWA essay can be divided as follows:

- 7–8 minutes planning
- 15 minutes writing
- 7–8 minutes revising and editing

Although no essay will be perfect (and is not expected to be), in general, the more time you spend planning, the less time you will need to spend revising.

1, 2, 1, 3, 2, 4?

Although the process of writing can be broken down into four consecutive steps, they do not necessarily occur in a linear fashion. In fact, writing is really a richly layered process in which two or more steps might take place simultaneously or the steps might take place out of order. You might revise sections as you draft, for example, or draft new sections after a period of extensive revision. Many writers also edit as they draft and revise if they catch themselves making a mistake.

That said, the process still works best in the general order of planning, drafting, revising, and editing. It is fine if some overlapping occurs, but don't skip a step or completely reverse the order of stages.

▶ Seven Steps for Writing a Strong AWA Essay

The following section takes the four steps of the writing process and breaks them down into seven steps for writing on an essay exam. These steps will help you write a strong, effective essay on the AWA section of the GMAT exam:

Step 1: Understand the writing prompt.
Step 2: Formulate a clear thesis.
Step 3: Brainstorm support for your thesis.
Step 4: Create a detailed outline.
Step 5: Write your essay.
Step 6: Revise.
Step 7: Edit carefully.

Step 1: Understand the Writing Prompt

Before you can plan your essay, you need to be sure you clearly understand the essay prompt. As noted earlier, it is essential that you respond accurately to the writing prompt you are given on the exam. If you write about a different topic, *you will not receive credit for your essay.* It's therefore critical to understand the argument or issue presented in the prompt and how you are expected to respond to that prompt.

You already know that your Analysis of an Argument essay must critique the reasoning of the argument in the prompt and that your Analysis of an Issue essay must present your position on an issue. It is critical to take the time to read the argument and issue carefully several times before you begin to write. They are only a few sentences long, so it will only take a minute or two to ensure that you understand your topic.

In addition, be clear about what you are supposed to do in your essay. After the issue or argument, you will find a brief set of instructions. On most exams, they will be very similar to the instructions on the pretest. The key words in each set of directions have been underlined.

Analysis of an Issue

Discuss the extent to which you agree or disagree with the opinion expressed above. Support your position with reasons and/or examples from your own experience, observations, or reading.

Analysis of an Argument

Discuss how well reasoned you find this argument. In your essay, be sure to analyze argument's logic and use of evidence. For example, you may need to consider whether the assumptions that underlie the argument are sound or whether counterarguments or alternative explanations would weaken the conclusion. You may also discuss the kind of evidence that would strengthen or refute the argument, what revisions to the argument would make it more reasonable, or what information, if anything, would help you better evaluate the argument.

Occasionally, an issue prompt will include a slightly different set of directions such as the following:

"True freedom is the ability to make choices based upon happiness, not necessity."

Explain what you think this quotation means and discuss the extent to which you agree or disagree with this opinion. Support your position with reasons and/or examples from your own experience, observations, or reading.

This topic requires the additional task of explaining the meaning of the quotation. Be sure to read the directions carefully, so you address each part of the directions in the prompt.

Step 2: Formulate a Clear Thesis

Before you begin to write, you need a clear sense of what you are going to say in response to the prompt. As soon as possible, formulate a tentative **thesis**—a sentence that expresses your main idea or the argument you are going to make and support in your essay.

A thesis does not just repeat or paraphrase the question or prompt; it does not simply make general statements about the topic or state how others might respond to the question. A good thesis takes a position and makes a clear assertion about the subject. For example, for the Analysis of an Issue prompt, the following sentences are *not* thesis statements (they do not answer the question):

"Successful corporations have a moral responsibility to contribute to society by supporting education, nonprofit services, or the arts."

- Many successful corporations contribute to society.
- Do successful corporations have a moral responsibility to contribute to society?
- Corporations can contribute to society in many ways, including supporting education and the arts.

The following sentences, however, *are* thesis statements. Notice how they respond directly to the question and make a clear assertion about the subject:

- All for-profit corporations have a moral responsibility to contribute to society by supporting education, nonprofit services, or the arts.
- For-profit corporations have much to gain by supporting education, nonprofit services, or the arts, but they do not have a moral responsibility to do so.

To determine your thesis for your Analysis of an Issue essay, in most cases, you will simply need to state whether you agree or disagree with the statement in the prompt.

Developing a thesis for your Analysis of an Argument prompt will be somewhat more complicated. First, you need to examine the argument and determine its main flaw or the element around which your discussion will focus. Your thesis should summarize your assessment of the argument. For example, notice how the Analysis of an Argument essay from the pretest presents a clear, two-part thesis that identifies the problem with the conclusion and the argument's lack of attention to alternate possibilities:

> Although moving to a new location is certainly one method that could improve the restaurant's patron base, it is not the only method, nor does it guarantee that numbers would improve. The owners must weigh the costs of moving against staying in their current location and using other techniques to improve business.

As noted earlier, the writing process is not necessarily linear, and you may need to brainstorm ideas before you determine your thesis. For example, you may need to make several notes about the argument before you determine the focus of your evaluation.

Step 3: Brainstorm Support for Your Thesis

Once you have formulated a tentative thesis, decide how you will support your answer. On a piece of scrap paper, list at least three to five reasons, examples, or specific details to support your thesis or events to develop your story.

Because you are still in the planning stage, write down whatever comes to mind. Remember, you don't have to include everything you list in your essay. The more you put down, the more ideas you can choose from to develop and support your thesis.

For example, here's how the writer of the Analysis of an Issue essay in the pretest brainstormed support for his essay:

Enlightened Self-Interest

↓ Good for Society
Good for the Company

↓ Economic 1st
Social 2nd — Those in Need
Long Term

Growth → Public Relations

Volunteerism → Good Name
Good Business

Increased Morale
Build Leadership Skills
Interpersonal Skills
Build Long-Term Community Relationships

- Crime
- Poverty
- Illiteracy

Healthy Community = Good/Healthy Business!

Step 4: Create a Detailed Outline

The next step is perhaps the most critical part of planning during an essay exam. Because your time is limited, you will only be able to make limited revisions after you write the draft. That means your draft must be very strong from the start. Creating a detailed outline gives you the opportunity to make sure your essay will be both well organized and well developed.

To ensure that you have both strong support and sufficient development of ideas, organize your ideas in a two-tiered outline. For each main supporting idea, list at least one specific detail or example. Imagine that each paragraph is a mini-essay, with its own thesis (topic sentence) and support (specific examples and details). A sufficiently detailed outline will offer a point to guide you through just about every sentence in the body of the essay.

1. Introduction
2. Support #1
   a. specific reason/example
   b. specific reason/example
   c. specific reason/example

3. Support #2
   a. specific reason/example
   b. specific reason/example
   c. specific reason/example
4. Support #3
   a. specific reason/example
   b. specific reason/example
   c. specific reason/example
5. Conclusion

This basic outline has three main supporting points with room to develop each of those supporting ideas with specific reasons and examples. For example, look carefully at how the writer of the Analysis of an Argument essay outlined her essay:

1. Intro: location isn't everything
2. Why move?
   a. Attract customers shopping/running errands
   b. Convenience
   c. Exposure
3. Why not move?
   a. Location not only factor
   b. Cost of move
      i. Packing, renting truck, etc.
      ii. Higher rent
      iii. Closing down
4. Root of problem?
   a. May be other causes
   b. Survey customers
   c. If location, then other options
      i. Advertise
      ii. Coupons
      iii. Reviews
5. Conc: check cust satisf'n 1st; if location, try other things before move

Organize Your Support

Obviously, you know where to put your introductory and concluding paragraphs. But how do you organize the ideas in the body of your essay? In the Reading Comprehension section review (pages 69–85), you reviewed the four most common organizational patterns: chronology, comparison and contrast, cause and effect, and order of importance. Most texts use a combination of these and other strategies, with one overall organizing principle and several other strategies within individual sentences and paragraphs.

Three-Part Essay Structure

Keep your essay simple and clear by following the standard three-part essay structure:

- **Introduction.** Tell your readers what you are going to tell them. (State your thesis.)
- **Body.** Tell them. (Develop your ideas and provide specific support for your thesis.)
- **Conclusion.** Tell them what you have told them. (Restate your thesis.)

The following table lists seven organizational patterns and their organizing principles. Your overall principle depends on your specific subject and purpose. Determine which pattern will best help you convey your ideas clearly.

PATTERN	ORGANIZING PRINCIPLE
chronology	time or sequence (first, second, etc.)
comparison and contrast	similarities and/or differences
cause and effect	agent of change/result of change
order of importance	rank (most to least important or least to most important)
spatial	physical location (e.g., top to bottom or front to back)
analysis or classification	parts, types, or groups of X
problem/solution	problem and solution(s)

Notice how the Analysis of an Argument outline combines several organizational strategies, including problem/solution and cause and effect. Beginning with the perceived solution (moving to a new location), the writer points out flaws in that plan. Then she evaluates the cause of the problem and proposes other possible solutions. Within paragraphs, examples are listed in order of importance.

Revise Your Outline

As we noted earlier, revision normally takes place *after* the drafting stage. However—and this is a big *however*—the guidelines are a little different on a timed essay exam, especially when the time is so short. Because your time is so limited, some revising should actually take place *before* you write, while you are outlining your essay. As you outline, make sure you have a clear thesis that addresses the writing prompt, sufficient and relevant support, and logical organization. More important, make sure your outline addresses everything you are supposed to do in the essay. Does it address counterarguments? Have you considered the assumptions that underline the argument? Now is the time to make sure these fundamental elements are in place.

Step 5: Write Your Essay

Now that you have a clear, detailed outline, you can begin to write, starting with your introduction.

Introduction

First impressions count, and that's why introductions are so important in writing. A good introduction does three things:

- Indicates what the essay is about (its topic) and what the writer is going to say about the topic (its main idea)
- Grabs the reader's attention
- Establishes the tone of the passage

Techniques for grabbing attention include opening with one of the following:

- a question
- a quotation
- a surprising fact or statement
- an imaginary situation or scenario
- an anecdote
- interesting background information
- a new twist on a familiar phrase

For example, notice how the Analysis of an Argument essay from the pretest grabs the reader's attention by asking a question that calls the real estate mantra into doubt:

> Location is everything . . . or is it? The owners of an upmarket restaurant are considering a proposal to move next to another store or near a transportation hub in order to expand their customer base . . .

If you can *quickly* think of a catchy way to begin your essay, terrific. But if you can't, don't spend precious minutes trying to come up with the perfect opening line. You don't have the time. Remember, you only have 30 minutes for the whole essay—planning, writing, revising, and editing. You need to start writing as soon as you organize your thoughts.

One good way to jump right in is to *paraphrase* (repeat in your own words) or summarize the argument or issue in the prompt and state your thesis. The Analysis of an Issue sample essay opens with a clear thesis that paraphrases the issue. The second and third sentences then outline the major points that will be covered in the essay:

> All for-profit corporations have a moral responsibility to contribute to society by supporting education, nonprofit services, or the arts. In today's increasingly global marketplace, companies that

Be Flexible

As you write your essay, follow your outline, but be flexible. Writing is a process of discovery, and as you write, you may suddenly realize you have something else important to say. Just because it isn't in your outline doesn't mean you shouldn't use it. If it adds strong support to your thesis, include it. Similarly, if, as you are writing, you realize that an idea from your outline isn't as relevant or convincing as you thought, or that it's in the wrong place, make the change. Your outline should guide you as you write, but it should not keep you from making effective changes.

> embrace their social responsibilities and empower their leaders and employees to serve local and world communities will reap rewards now and for years to come. These companies will realize that they will reap long-term benefits in morale and bottom-line growth and sustainability by giving their personnel the opportunity to work toward higher goals (social responsibilities) and to make a difference in their lives and the lives of the people around them.

If you are feeling really pressured for time, you can always simply quote from the prompt, as in the following example:

> It has been argued that "true freedom is the ability to make choices based upon happiness, not necessity." I agree with this statement.

When you have finished your essay, you can go back and revise for a more sophisticated introduction if you have time.

A standard introduction that simply rephrases the prompt and states your thesis may not win any awards for ingenuity, but it will get the job done by introducing the topic and presenting your thesis to the reader.

Body

Once you have written your introduction, write the body of your essay paragraph by paragraph, following your outline. Make sure each paragraph has a clear topic sentence and specific support. (See pages 72–75 for a review of topic sentences.) Do not forget about transitions between paragraphs. Key words and phrases such as *more important*, *similarly*, and *in addition* will guide your reader through your argument.

For your convenience, we have reprinted this list of common transitions from the Verbal section review:

IF YOU WANT TO	USE THESE TRANSITIONAL WORDS AND PHRASES		
introduce an example	for example	for instance	that is
	in other words	in particular	specifically
	in fact	first (second) of all	

IF YOU WANT TO	USE THESE TRANSITIONAL WORDS AND PHRASES		
show addition	and	in addition	also
	again	moreover	furthermore
show emphasis	indeed	in fact	certainly
acknowledge another point of view	although	though	granted
	despite	even though	
show rank	more important	above all	first and foremost
	most important	first, second, third	
show cause	because	since	created (by)
show effect	therefore	hence	so
	consequently	as a result	
show comparison	likewise	similarly	like
	in the same way	in a like manner	just as
show contrast	unlike	however	on the other hand
	whereas	instead	rather
	but	on the contrary	conversely
	in contrast	yet	
show the passage of time	then	next	later
	after	before	during
	meanwhile	while	soon
	eventually	finally	afterward
	in the meantime	immediately	suddenly

Conclusion

After writing the supporting paragraphs, write a brief conclusion. Conclusions, like introductions, should be powerful. After all, people tend to remember most what comes first and last, and the final words have the power to ring in readers' ears for a long time afterward. A good conclusion will do the following:

- Restate the main idea and its core support.
- Provide a sense of closure (does not "open a new can of worms" by introducing a new topic).
- Arouse readers' emotions to make the ending and main idea memorable. To make conclusions memorable, you can use the following techniques:
  - a quotation
  - a question
  - an anecdote

Who Is Your Audience?

Although you know that technically your only audience will be a college or university faculty member and E-rater®, on the AWA (as in most essays you have written for school), you will be expected to write for a **general audience.** Assume your essay will be read by an audience of your peers and everyday people with a general college education and a wide variety of interests and backgrounds.

You will need an appropriate **level of formality** for this audience. Treat your readers with respect, but do not put them off by sounding too formal or pretentious. Avoid informal language or jargon (technical or specialized language); let your writing be natural without being too informal.

Your audience also determines the **level of detail** and **specificity** in your essay. Because you are writing for a general audience and not friends, you cannot assume that readers know the context of your ideas and experiences. For example, if you are arguing that Internet sites should be censored, do not assume that readers have seen the kind of sites you are talking about. You will need to briefly describe those sites to give your readers sufficient context.

- a prediction
- a solution or recommendation
- a call to action

In your final paragraph, restate your thesis, *but not in exactly the same words.* Make sure you don't introduce any new topics. Instead, make readers feel as if you have covered your topic thoroughly and that they have gotten something meaningful from reading your essay. Notice how the writer of the Analysis of an Issue essay accomplishes this and ends with a short, memorable sentence that embodies the theme of the essay:

> In summary, corporations that take their moral responsibility to contribute to society seriously and develop corporate programs such as volunteerism programs will fare better than their counterparts who shirk their social duties. A healthy community equals a healthy business.

Step 6: Revise

Once all of your ideas are down on paper, it's time to revise. Even if you only have five minutes left, you still have time to check for the following elements:

- **Is your thesis strong and clear and stated at the beginning of your essay?** If not, write a thesis statement and fit it into your introduction.
- **Do you have strong and sufficient support with specific reasons and examples?** If your support seems weak, add another example. If your support seems too general, add a specific example.
- **Do you maintain focus in your essay? Do all of your paragraphs support your thesis, and do all of your sentences within each paragraph support the topic sentence?** If a paragraph or sentence seems to lose focus, delete it or make the connection clear.

Write First, Revise Second, and Edit Last

Because you are under considerable time pressure on an essay exam, you must keep moving. Don't get stuck on trying to find just the right word or cadence to your sentence. For now, approximate; get as close to your idea as possible. Get all of your ideas down first, and then go back and refine your sentences. Likewise, don't spend precious time proofreading until you have finished your essay. You don't want to waste time editing sentences that you might change or delete when you revise.

- **Are your ideas presented in a logical order?** If not, move paragraphs or sentences around to make the organization more effective.
- **Do you have strong transitions between ideas, especially between paragraphs?** If not, add key transitional words.
- **Have you paragraphed effectively?** Are any paragraphs too long or too short? Look for a logical place to divide a very long paragraph into two or combine two short paragraphs.
- **Can you combine any sentences for more variety in sentence structure or otherwise improve the fluency of your essay?** If your sentence patterns sound monotonous, try combining shorter sentences or turning clauses into modifiers.
- **Can you make any changes in word choice so that your sentences are more concise and precise?** Eliminate wordiness and redundancy. Replace weak words with more precise and powerful ones.

In the following section, you will see how the writer of the Analysis of an Issue sample essay revised his draft. Notice how he made changes on several levels, including a few minor edits along the way:

> All for-profit corporations have a moral responsibility to contribute to society by supporting education, nonprofit services, or the arts. In today's increasingly global marketplace, companies that embrace their social responsibilities and empower their leaders and employees to serve local and world communities will reap rewards now and for years to come. These companies will realize ~~find that they will reap~~ long-term benefits in morale and bottom line growth and sustainability by giving their personnel the opportunity to work toward higher goals (social responsibilities) and to make a difference in their lives and the lives of the people around them.
>
> Every organization has a legal responsibility to serve its immediate (or local) community as a productive "citizen" by obeying and upholding the laws, that ~~which~~ govern its operations, and by giving its employees a ~~"save"~~ safe place to work. Yet, a select group of modern companies take their social responsibilities a step further, moving beyond mere compliance and into a heightened awareness of social responsibility. These companies operate under "enlightened self-interest." They realize that what is good for the community and for society is good for the company and they spend a tremendous amount of effort and money incorporating social programs into their corporate infrastructures and even encouraging and rewarding social involvement and leadership.

These companies go beyond merely making grants to non-profit groups or arts programs. Even more important, in addition to monetary gifts ~~They may continue to make grants and gifts~~ to these types of social organizations, ~~more important~~ they setup hearty volunteerism programs~~,~~ ~~where~~ through which employees at all levels are encouraged to participate in organized volunteer activities ~~programs~~. Typically, they match skills to needs. For instance, researchers at a pharmaceutical company might be organized to help tutor students in science. ~~they organize employees with teaching skills to help out in local schools or in private tutoring.~~

Although some may argue that corporations have a responsibility only to their stakeholders~~,~~ and their bottom line ~~only,~~ and do not legally have a responsibility to "do good" in society, they miss the point that social responsibility is in the best interest of the company. Companies that actively participate in social programs aimed at curbing crime, fighting poverty and illiteracy, ~~and educating~~ and teaching skills to those in need, reap bottom-line benefits from their social programs every day. These programs not only have a positive impact on the local communities where they are enacted, but they also continue to deliver dividends to the organization in positive public relations, building the image of the company in the eyes of the community and developing a more effective employee base.

Corporations that contribute to society benefit on the inside as well. Employees involved in volunteerism programs are more motivated to perform in their business environment because their commitment to others improves morale and fulfills an important ~~as moral is increased and~~ ~~ps~~psychological need~~s are met~~. These same employees build leadership skills and interpersonal skills while performing their volunteer work, and these skills are not left at home. Furthermore, employees are more likely to feel strong loyalty to a company that helps improve their community and themselves. ~~by building long-term community relations with these types of programs, the organization is increasing its long-term sustainability, as it can call upon its community base for future employees and leaders.~~

In summary, corporations that take their moral responsibility to contribute to society seriously and develop corporate programs such as volunteerism programs will ~~fair~~ fare better than their counterparts who shirk their social duties. A healthy community equals healthy business.

Step 7: Edit Carefully

Last but not least—for it is very important to write correctly—take a few minutes to check for grammatical or mechanical errors in your essay. Although no one expects a 30-minute essay to be perfect, mistakes can interfere with the clarity of your ideas, and the more errors you have in your essay, the less likely you will earn a top score. In fact, too many errors can dramatically overshadow the quality of your content. Indeed, if you only have two or three minutes left after you complete your draft, spend those two or three minutes revising and editing with a focus on catching grammatical errors. You do not have time to look at the bigger picture, so just do whatever you can to improve your essay as you read it through.

▶ Writing with Style

Style refers to the manner in which something is done. For example, people all buy and wear clothes that fit their own personal style—the way they like to look and feel when they are dressed. The same is true of writing; each writer has his or her own individual style, and the more you understand stylistic techniques, the more effectively you can express yourself in writing.

As we noted earlier in the Sentence Correction section review, style in writing is controlled primarily by two elements: word choice and sentence structure. Together, these two elements determine the tone, level of formality, and level of detail, creating the overall feel of the text. To keep your sentences clear and effective, use the following guidelines for writing with style:

1. Be concise.
2. Be precise.
3. Avoid ambiguity.
4. Use the active voice.
5. Use variety in sentence structure.
6. Avoid jargon and pretentious language.

These guidelines are discussed in detail on pages 129–136 in the verbal section review. However, because word choice and sentence structure are so important, they deserve extra attention with an additional review.

Word Choice

One of the most empowering decisions writers make is a constant one: **word choice**. As you write, you are always thinking about the right words to express your ideas. The "right" word has three essential characteristics:

- It expresses the idea you wish to convey.
- It is exact (precise).
- It is appropriate for the audience and tone.

For example, take a look at the following sentence:

The argument is <u>good</u>.

Good is not an effective word choice; it doesn't really tell us much about the argument. How is it good? In what way? To what degree? A more precise word can make a tremendous difference:

The argument is <u>persuasive</u>.
The argument is <u>logical</u>.
The argument is <u>incisive</u>.

Each of these underlined adjectives has much more impact than the adjective *good.* These exact modifiers create a vivid picture; they tell the reader more precisely what is good about the argument and how it is effective.

Use exact verbs, nouns, adjectives, and adverbs throughout your essay. The more precise you can be, the more impact your writing will have.

Appropriate Level of Formality

Your audience determines your level of formality, and this is also controlled by word choice. The level of formality can range from the very informal (slang) to the very formal (esoteric and ceremonial) to everything in between. Writers use word choice and sentence structure to manipulate the level of formality. Here are two examples:

> **A:** *It was so cool. I mean, I never saw anything like it before. What a great flick! You have to check it out.*
> **B:** *It was really an impressive film, unlike anything I've ever seen before. You should definitely go see it.*

These two sentences are drastically different in style and, in particular, in the level of formality. Although they both tell the same story and use the personal first-person *I,* each writer has a different relationship with the reader. The word choice and style—the short sentences and the very casual language—indicate that the writer of passage A has a more informal, more friendly relationship with the reader than the writer of passage B. The emotion of the writer in passage A is much more transparent, too, because the language is more informal and natural. You get the idea that passage A is addressed to a close friend, whereas passage B might be addressed to a colleague or supervisor.

In your essay, be sure to write at an appropriate level of formality. Do not use slang, but do not be excessively formal either. For example, the following sentence is too informal and slangy for the general audience of the GMAT exam:

> *The restaurant owners would be nuts to just get up and move. They have other things that they should check out first.*

Be more formal without overstepping the bounds into pretentious or ceremonial language as this writer does:

> *The restaurant owners would be unwise to move without first considering other alternatives to improving their business.*

Consistent and Appropriate Tone

A consistent and appropriate **tone** is another essential element of effective writing. **Tone** is *the mood or attitude conveyed by words or speech.* Think, for example, of all the different ways to say "sure" or "hello." How you say the word conveys so much of its meaning.

When we speak, we create tone by how quickly or slowly we say a word, how loudly or softly we say it, and how we use facial expressions and body language. When we write, though, our readers can't *hear* how our words sound, and they certainly can't see our facial expressions or body language. However, we can use word choice to convey our tone. For example, if you are describing a humorous event, you might use the phrase *topsy-turvy* rather than *chaotic* or *disorganized.* Similarly, if you are describing an unpleasant event, you might use the word *tumultuous* or *helter-skelter* to convey the same idea.

Punctuation is also an important tool in creating tone. For example, look carefully at this pair of sentences:

Wait, I'm coming with you.
Wait—I'm coming with you!

Although the words in the sentences are exactly the same, the tone is quite different. In this example, it's not word choice but punctuation that changes the tone. The first sentence is calm and neutral. The second sentence, on the other hand, is emotional and excited. The first sentence, with its comma and period, does not express emotion. The second sentence clearly expresses more urgency and excitement, thanks to the dash and exclamation point.

People use an endless variety of tones when they speak. Likewise, people use an endless variety of tones when they write, from cheerful to somber, uplifting to bleak, sincere to sarcastic, and everything in between. On the GMAT exam, however, you will have little room to play with tone. Given the kinds of essays you have to write on the AWA, and given the elements your readers will be looking for as they score your writing, your best bet is to stick to a serious, respectful tone throughout your essay.

Sentence Variety and Techniques for Emphasis

A strong GMAT essay also demonstrates an ability to manipulate sentence structure and punctuation for effect. Sentence structure, as noted earlier, is an important element of style. If all of your sentences have the same pattern, you will end up with monotonous and dry writing, such as the following passage:

> Corporations have a moral responsibility to contribute to society. They should support education, nonprofit services, or the arts. They will empower their leaders and employees to serve their community by doing so. They will also reap rewards in the short and long term. They will improve morale and grow their bottom line.

Unsophisticated and quite dull, isn't it? This is because all of the sentences are short and share the same structure; they all start with *corporations/they* + helping verb + present tense verb. This is quite different from **parallel structure**, which is the repetition of sentence pattern to create rhythm within a sentence or paragraph. (See page 118 for a review of parallel structure.) This kind of repetition only creates monotony and shows a lack of flexibility in creating sentence patterns. Here's the same paragraph, but it has been revised to show variety in sentence structure:

Corporations have a moral responsibility to contribute to society by supporting education, nonprofit services, or the arts. By doing so, they empower their leaders and employees to serve their community, and they will reap rewards in the short and long term, including increased morale and a stronger bottom line.

Notice how much more interesting this paragraph is now. The five sentences have been combined into two, and only one sentence starts with the subject. Many of the short sentences have been turned into clauses and phrases, creating varied sentence patterns.

Sentence structure and punctuation can also be used to create emphasis and enhance meaning. Often, the best place to put sentence elements that you want to emphasize is at the end (the "save the best for last" approach). What comes last is what lingers the longest in the readers' mind.

He is tall, dark, and handsome. (The emphasis is on *handsome.* If *tall* was the most important characteristic, then that should come last.)
She is smart, reliable, and experienced. (The emphasis is on *experienced*; if *smart* is the most important characteristic, then that should be last in the list.)

This also works with the *not only/but also* construction. In this sentence, the word order puts the emphasis on the corporation's obligation to employees and stockholders:

Successful corporations have an obligation to the general public as well as to their employees and stockholders.

By revising the sentence so that *public* is the last element, the emphasis is properly shifted on the obligation to society:

Successful corporations have an obligation not only to their employees and stockholders but also to the general public.

You can also use a dash to set off part of a sentence for emphasis:

Successful corporations are not only obligated to their employees and stockholders—they are also obligated to the general public.

In the previous example, the stress on the last element is heightened by the dash, which emphasizes the importance of this obligation to society.

Do Not Repeat Yourself

On the sentence level, in general, less is more. The fewer words you use to get your point across, the better. **Redundancy** is the unnecessary repetition of ideas. **Wordiness** is the use of several words when a few can express the same idea more clearly and concisely. Avoid both of these as you write your essay.

Wordiness and redundancy typically result from three different causes:

- The use of unnecessary words or phrases

  Redundant: *The owners must think about and consider the costs and expenses of moving.*

  Concise: *The owners must consider the costs of moving.*

  Wordy: *The restaurant may need improvement in the areas of food or service.*

  Concise: *The restaurant may need to improve its food or service.*

- The use of wordy phrases instead of adjectives or adverbs

  Wordy: *A survey would show in a clear way whether the restaurant needs to improve its food or service.*

  Concise: *A survey would clearly show whether the restaurant needs to improve its food or service.*

- The use of the passive instead of active voice

  Passive: *Moving to improve business was an idea considered by the owners of the restaurant.*

  Active: *The owners of the restaurant* considered *the idea of moving to improve business.*

Do not skimp on details, but do not waste words either.

For a more detailed review of ways to eliminate redundancy and reduce wordiness, see pages 129–131.

▶ Writing Correctly: The Conventions of Standard Written English

One of the main elements upon which your essay will be judged is its adhesion to the conventions of standard written English. This means that your sentences should be grammatically correct, use proper idioms and sentence structure, and be free of errors in **mechanics**—punctuation, spelling, and capitalization. The essentials of grammar and usage were covered in the Verbal section review on pages 109–136. This section will list the grammar rules you need to remember and review the guidelines for punctuation, capitalization, and spelling.

Rules for Grammar and Usage

1. The basic word order for sentences is subject-predicate: subject, verb, indirect object, and object.
2. Make sure sentences have both a subject and a predicate *and* express a complete thought.
3. Respect sentence boundaries. Don't let two or more independent clauses run together.
4. Keep modifiers as close as possible to the words they modify.

5. Use parallel structure for any series of actions or items or the *not only/but also* construction.
6. Make sure verbs agree in number with their subjects.
7. Keep verb tenses consistent.
8. Use the correct subject or object form of personal pronouns. Determine whether a pronoun is functioning as a subject or object in the sentence.
9. Use apostrophes with pronouns to show contraction only. Pronouns do not need apostrophes to show possession.
10. Use *who* for people, *that* for things, and *which* for nonessential clauses that do not refer to people.
11. Pronouns must agree in number and person with their antecedents.
12. Be consistent in pronoun point of view.
13. Use *less* for singular nouns representing quantity or degree. Use *fewer* for plural nouns.
14. Use *good* and *bad* to describe nouns and pronouns; use *well* and *badly* to describe verbs.
15. In comparisons, add *-er* or *-est* for short modifiers. For longer words, use *more/most* or *less/least* before the modifier.
16. Do not use double comparisons or double negatives.
17. Use idioms correctly.

Punctuation

Punctuation marks are the symbols used to separate sentences, express emotions, and show relationships between objects and ideas. Correct punctuation clarifies meaning and adds drama and style to sentences. Poor punctuation, on the other hand, can confuse your readers and distort your intended meaning. For example, take a look at the following two versions of the same sentence:

Don't bother Xavier.
Don't bother, Xavier.

The same words are used, but the two sentences have very different meanings because of punctuation. In the first sentence, the comma indicates that the speaker is telling *us* not to bother Xavier. In the second sentence, the speaker is telling *Xavier* not to bother. Here is another example of how punctuation can drastically affect meaning:

You should eat Zak so you can think clearly during your interview.

Because this sentence is missing some essential punctuation, the sentence says something very different from what the author intended. The speaker isn't telling us to eat Zak; rather, she is telling Zak to eat. The sentence should be revised as follows:

You should eat, Zak, so you can think clearly during your interview.

As you saw earlier, punctuation also has another important function: It enables writers to express a variety of tones and emotions.

Punctuation Guidelines

There are many rules for punctuation, and the better you know them, the more correctly and effectively you can punctuate your sentences. This table lists the main punctuation marks and guidelines for when to use them:

IF YOUR PURPOSE IS TO	USE THIS PUNCTUATION	EXAMPLE
End a sentence.	**period** [.] **question mark** [?] **exclamation point** [!]	Most sentences end in a period. *I feel tired today.* However, if you are posing a question, use a question mark. *Should the voting age be raised to 21?* Exclamation points should be used sparingly for emphasis. *"What a beautiful dress!"*
Connect complete sentences (two independent clauses).	**semicolon** [;] **comma** [,] and a **conjunction** [and, or, nor, for, so, but, yet] **dash** [—] (less common, but more dramatic)	A semicolon can connect two sentences; it is an excellent way to show that two ideas are related. *Leslie is coming, but Huang is staying home.* *Hurry up—we're late!*
Connect items in a list.	**comma** [,] but if one or more items in that list already has a comma, use a **semicolon** [;]	*His odd shopping list included batteries, a box of envelopes, and a can of beans.* *The castaways included a professor, who was the group's leader; an actress; and a millionaire and his wife.*
Introduce a list of three or more items.	**colon** [:]	*There are three things I want to do before I die: go on a cruise, go skydiving, and surf.*
Introduce an explanation (what follows explains or answers what precedes).	**colon** [:]	*You know what they say about real estate:* *Location is everything.*
Introduce a quotation (words directly spoken).	**colon** [:] or **comma** [,]	*She yelled, "Let's get out of here!" He said only one word: "Believe."*
Indicate a quotation.	**quotation marks** [" "]	*"To be or not to be?" is one of the most famous lines from Hamlet.*
Indicate a question.	**question mark** [?]	*What time is it? "How much longer?" he asked.*

IF YOUR PURPOSE IS TO	USE THIS PUNCTUATION	EXAMPLE
Connect two words that work together as one object or modifier.	hyphen [-]	*mother-in-law, turn-of-the-century poet, French-fried potatoes*
Separate a word or phrase for emphasis.	dash [—]	*I never lie—never. We're late—very late!*
Separate a word or phrase that is relevant but not essential information.	commas [,]	*Elaine, my roommate, is from Chicago. Her nickname as a child, her mother told me, was "Boo-boo."*
Separate a word or phrase that is relevant but secondary information.	parenthesis [()]	*There is an exception to every rule (including this one).*
Show possession or contraction.	apostrophe [']	*Why is Lisa's wallet in Ben's backpack?*

Comma Rules

Although you won't drop from a score of 6 to 5 because of a couple of misplaced commas, the correct use of commas is important. The presence and placement of commas can dramatically affect a sentence's meaning and can make the difference between clarity and confusion in your sentences. The previous chart lists four different uses of commas, but there are several others. Here is a complete list of comma rules. The better you know them, the more clear, correct, and controlled your sentences will be.

Use a comma in the following ways:

1. With a coordinating conjunction to separate two complete sentences. Note that a comma is *not* required if both parts of the sentence are four words or less:

   Let's eat first, and then we will go to a movie.

   I'm definitely older, but I don't think I'm much wiser.

   I love him and he loves me.

2. To set off introductory words, phrases, or clauses.

   Next 4th of July, I plan to watch the fireworks from the rooftop.

   Wow, that sure looks good!

   Because the game was cancelled, Jane took the kids bowling.

3. To set off a direct address, interjection, or transitional phrase.

Well, Jeb, it looks like we will be stuck here for a while.

His hair color is a little, um, unusual.

My heavens, this is spicy chili!

Sea horses, for example, are unusual in that the males carry the eggs.

4. Between two modifiers that could be replaced by *and.*

He is a quiet, shy person.

(Both *quiet* and *shy* modify *person.*)

Incorrect: *Denny's old, stamp collection is priceless.*

Correct: *Denny's old stamp collection is priceless.*

(You cannot put *and* between *old* and *stamp*; *old* describes *stamp* and *stamp* modifies *collection.* They do not modify the same noun.)

5. To set off information that is relevant but not essential (nonrestrictive).

Essential, not set off:

The woman who wrote Happy Moon *is coming to our local bookstore.*

(We need this information to know which woman we're talking about.)

Nonessential, set off by commas:

The dog, lost and confused, wandered into the street.

(The fact that the dog was lost and confused is not essential to the sentence.)

Essential, not set off:

Witnesses who lie under oath will be prosecuted.

Nonessential, set off by commas:

Leland, who at first refused to testify, later admitted to lying under oath.

6. To separate items in a series.

The price for the cruise includes breakfast, lunch, dinner, and entertainment.

The recipe calls for fresh cilantro, chopped onions, diced tomatoes, and lemon juice.

7. To set off most quotations. As a general rule, short quotations are introduced by commas, whereas long quotations (several sentences or more) are introduced by colons. All speech in dialogue should be set off by commas.

"Let's get going," he said excitedly.

Emmanuel Kant is famous for the words, "I think, therefore I am."

Joseph said, "Please forgive me for jumping to conclusions."

8. To set off parts of dates, numbers, titles, and addresses.

She was born on April 30, 2002.

Please print 3,000 copies.

Tiberio Mendola, M.D., is my new doctor.

Please deliver the package to me at 30 Willow Road, Trenton, NJ.

9. To prevent confusion, as in cases when a word is repeated.

What it is, is a big mistake.

After I, comes J.

Capitalization

Capitalization is an important tool to help us identify (1) the beginning of a new sentence and (2) proper nouns and adjectives. Here are six rules for correct capitalization:

1. Capitalize the first word of a sentence.

Please close the door.

What are you trying to say?

If you are quoting a full sentence within your own sentence, use a capital letter, unless you introduce the quote with that.

According to the study, "A shocking three out of four students admitted to cheating."

The study claims that "a shocking three out of four students admitted to cheating."

If you have a full sentence within parentheses, that sentence should be capitalized as well (and the end punctuation mark should be within the parentheses).

ABC Corporation regularly contributes to the We Care Fund (including an impressive donation of $10,000 in 2002).

ABC Corporation regularly contributes to the We Care Fund. (They donated an impressive $10,000 in 2002.)

2. Capitalize proper nouns. A proper noun is the name of a specific person, place, or thing (as opposed to a *general* person, place, or thing).

CAPITALIZE (SPECIFIC)	DON'T CAPITALIZE (GENERAL)
Jennifer Johnson (specific person)	the woman
Business Law (specific class)	my law class
Main Street (specific street)	on the street
Frosted Flakes® (specific brand)	good cereal
Caspian Sea (specific sea)	deep sea/ocean
Lincoln Memorial (specific monument)	impressive memorial/monument
U.S.S. Cole (specific ship)	naval carrier
Dade Management School (specific school)	my graduate school
Precambrian Age (specific time period)	long ago
Data Corporation (specific company)	that company

Exceptions: Do not capitalize words such as *river, street,* and so on in plural proper nouns as they are generic: the Pacific and Indian oceans.

3. Capitalize the days of the weeks and months of the year, but *not* the seasons.

It was a warm spring day in May.

Wednesday is the first official day of autumn.

4. Capitalize the names of countries, nationalities, languages, religions, and geographical locations (but *not* geographical directions).

He has traveled to Brazil and Tunisia.

She is half Chinese, half French.

She is from the South. Drive south for five miles.

We speak Spanish at home.

He is a devout Catholic.

5. Capitalize titles that come *before* proper names.

Judge Lydia Ng	*Lydia Ng, judge in the Fifth District*
Professor Lee Chang	*Lee Chang, professor of physical science*
Vice President Tilda Stanton	*Tilda Stanton, vice president*

6. Capitalize titles of publications, including books, stories, poems, plays, articles, speeches, essays, and other documents, as well as works of art, including films, paintings, and musical compositions.

Pablo Picasso's painting Guernica *captures the agony of the Spanish Civil War.*

Read Susan Sontag's essay "On Photography" for class tomorrow.

The Declaration of Independence is a sacred document.

Spelling

Although a few misspellings will probably have little impact on your AWA score, misspelled words can interfere with clarity, and if your reader's pet peeve is misspelled words, a few spelling errors may have more influence on your score than they deserve. To that end, review these spelling rules, especially the correct use of contractions and homonyms. A list of frequently misspelled words is included at the end of this chapter.

Basic Spelling Guidelines

Here are ten guidelines for correct spelling. Please remember that *there are exceptions to every rule.* If spelling is one of your weaknesses, spend extra time reviewing these rules and the list of frequently misspelled words that appears at the end of this chapter.

1. Form plurals of regular nouns by adding *-s* or *-es.*

job	*jobs*
house	*houses*
beach	*beaches*

2. Change the spelling of words with the following endings when forming plurals:

f →	*v*
thief	*thieves*
wolf	*wolves*

but not

belief	*beliefs*
chief	*chiefs*

consonant + y	→	*ie*
family		*families*
party		*parties*

but not vowel + *y:*

toy		*toys*
monkey		*monkeys*
sis	→	*ses*
basis		*bases*
hypothesis		*hypotheses*
on	→	*a*
criterion		*criteria*
phenomenon		*phenomena*
us	→	*i*
nucleus		*nuclei*
radius		*radii*

3. Double consonants when adding *-ing, -ed, -er,* or *-est* when:

- the verb stem contains one vowel + one consonant in one syllable

grab	*grabbing*	*grabbed*
trip	*tripping*	*tripped*

- the verb stem contains two or more syllables with one vowel + consonant in the final stressed syllable

prefer	*preferring*	*preferred*
control	*controlling*	*controlled*

(but not travel, traveling, traveled because the stress is on the first syllable)

- the suffix *-er* or *-est* is added to one-syllable adjectives ending in one vowel + consonant

big	*bigger*	*biggest*
hot	*hotter*	*hottest*

- adding *-ly* to an adjective ending in *l*

joyful	*joyfully*
successful	*successfully*

4. Change final *y* to *ie* on certain verb forms when verb ends in consonant + y:

cry	*cries*	*crying*	*cried*
study	*studies*	*studying*	*studied*

5. Change final *y* to *i* in two-syllable adjectives when adding a suffix:

happy	*happier*	*happiest*
silly	*sillier*	*silliest*
friendly	*friendlier*	*friendliest*

6. In general, *i* comes before *e* except after *c*, unless the syllable sounds like *ay:*

believe	*receive*	*sleigh*
niece	*deceive*	*neighbor*

Exceptions:

science
species
height
foreign

7. Keep a silent -*e* when adding an -*ly* suffix or a suffix beginning with a consonant:

state	*stately*	*statement*
rude	*rudely*	*rudeness*

8. Drop a silent -*e* before a suffix beginning with a vowel:

admire	*admirable*
approximate	*approximation*

9. Drop -*le* in adjectives when adding -*ly:*

admirable	*admirably*
sensible	*sensibly*

10. With adjectives ending in -*ic*, add -*ally* to form the adverb:

tragic	*tragically*
comic	*comically*

Contractions and Possessives

Confusion between contractions and possessives results in some of the most common spelling mistakes. **Contractions** are words that use an **apostrophe** to show that a letter or letters have been omitted from the word(s). **Possessive pronouns** indicate ownership of objects and ideas. They do *not* take an apostrophe.

POSSESSIVE PRONOUN	MEANING	EXAMPLE
its	belonging to it	The dog chased its tail.
your	belonging to you	Your time is up.
their	belonging to them	Their words were comforting.
whose	belonging to who	Whose tickets are these?

CONTRACTION		
it's	it is	It's time to eat.
you're	you are	You're not going to believe your eyes.
they're	they are	They're getting their tickets now.
who's	who is/who has	Who's got my tickets?

Whenever you come across a question with a contraction, read it as two words. If it doesn't make sense, then you need a possessive pronoun, not a contraction. Eliminate the apostrophe.

Homonyms

Homonyms are words that sound alike but have different spellings and meanings. Here are some of the most common homonyms:

accept except	to take or receive leave out
affect effect	(v.) to have an influence (n.) the result or impact of something
all ready already	fully prepared previously
bare bear	(adj.) uncovered; (v.) to uncover (n.) animal; (v.) to carry or endure
brake break	(v.) to stop; (n.) device for stopping (v.) to fracture or rend; (n.) a pause or temporary stoppage
buy by	(v.) to purchase (prep.) next to or near, through

cite	(v.) to quote or mention as an example
sight	(n.) something seen or visible; the faculty of seeing
site	(n.) location; (v.) to locate
desert	(n.) dry area; (v.) to abandon
dessert	(n.) sweet course at the end of a meal
every day	(adv.) each day
everyday	(adj.) ordinary, daily
fair	(adj.) light in color; favorable; just, unbiased; (n) gathering or exhibition for sale of goods, shows, and entertainment
fare	(n.) price charged for a passenger to travel; food provided; (v) to progress (*we fared well on our journey*)
hear	(v.) to perceive with the ears
here	(adv.) in this place
know	(v.) to understand, be aware of
no	(adj./adv.) negative—opposite of *yes*
loose	(adj.) not tight, not confined
lose	(v.) to misplace; to fail to win
may be	(v.) might be (possibility)
maybe	(adv.) perhaps
morning	(n.) the first part of the day
mourning	(n.) grieving
passed	(v.) past tense of *pass* (to go by)
past	(adv.) beyond; (n.) events that have already occurred
patience	(n.) quality of being patient, able to wait
patients	(n.) people under medical care
personal	(adj.) private or pertaining to the individual
personnel	(n.) employees
presence	(n.) condition of being
presents	(n.) gifts
principal	(adj.) most important; (n.) head of a school
principle	(n.) fundamental truth

right	(adj.) correct; (adv.) opposite of *left*
rite	(n.) ceremony
write	(v.) produce words on a surface
scene	(n.) setting or view
seen	(v). past participle of see
than	(conj.) used to compare *(he is taller than I)*
then	(adv.) at that time, therefore (*first this, then that; if you think it's good, then I'll do it)*
their	(pn.) possessive form of *they*
there	(adv.) location; in that place
through	(prep.) in one side and out the other; by means of
threw	(v. past tense of *throw*
to	(prep.) in the direction of
too	(adv.) in addition, excessive
two	number
waist	(n.) part of the body
waste	(v.) to squander; (n.) trash
weak	(adj.) feeble
week	(n.) seven days
weather	(n.) climatic conditions
whether	(conj.) introducing a choice
which	(adj./pn.) what, that
witch	(n.) woman with supernatural powers

Unfortunately, the only thing you can do to master homonyms is to memorize the correct meanings and spellings. Try using mnemonic devices to remember which word is which. For example,

stationary versus stationery: Remember that "station**ery**" is the one to write on because it is spelled with an "er" like the lett**er** you are writing.

(See page 25 in Chapter 2 for more about mnemonic devices.)

For a list of over 700 pairs of homonyms, visit www.cooper.com/alan/homonym_list.html. You can also find homonym quizzes and worksheets at http://www.edhelper.com/language/Homonyms.htm.

▶ 150 Most Commonly Misspelled Words

absence
abundance
accidentally
accommodate
acknowledgment
acquaintance
aggravate
alibi
alleged
ambiguous
analysis
annual
argument
awkward
basically
boundary
bulletin
calendar
canceled
cannot
cemetery
coincidence
collegiate
committee
comparative
completely
condemn
congratulations
conscientious
consistent
convenient
correspondence
deceive
definitely
dependent
depot
descend
desperate
development
dilemma
discrepancy
eighth
eligible
embarrass
equivalent
euphoria
existence
exuberance
feasible
February
fifth
forcibly
forfeit
formerly
fourth
fulfill
grateful
grievance
guarantee
guidance
harass
hindrance
ideally
implement
independence
indispensable
inoculate
insufficient
interference
interrupt
jealousy
jewelry
judgment
leisure
length
lenient
liaison
lieutenant
lightning
loophole
losing
maintenance
maneuver
mathematics
millennium
minuscule
miscellaneous
misspell
negotiable
ninth
occasionally
occurred
omission
opportunity
outrageous
pamphlet
parallel
perceive
permanent
perseverance
personnel
possess
potato
precede
preferred
prejudice
prevalent
privilege
procedure
proceed
prominent
pronunciation
quandary
questionnaire

receipt
receive
recommend
reference
referred
regardless
relevant
religious
remembrance
reservoir
responsible
restaurant
rhythm
ridiculous
roommate
scary
scissors
secretary
separate
souvenir
specifically
sufficient
supersede
temperament
temperature
truly
twelfth
ubiquitous
unanimous
usually
usurp
vacuum
vengeance
visible
Wednesday
wherever

CHAPTER

16 Tips and Strategies for the AWA

The following section offers specific tips and strategies to use on the AWA during the exam. Practice these strategies as you complete the sample essay prompts that follow.

General Writing Strategies

- Remember the general guideline for dividing your time on an essay exam: use about one-fourth of the time to plan, one-half of the time to write, and one-fourth of the time to revise and edit.
- Look for key words in the essay prompt to be sure you address all aspects of the assignment.
- The key to brainstorming is to avoid censoring yourself. Keep an open mind and write down whatever ideas come to you. You do not have to use everything in your essay.
- Remember that your brainstorming and outline are for your eyes only. Use whatever brainstorming and outlining techniques you find most useful.
- On an essay exam, every minute counts. Don't wait around for ideas to come to you. If you are having trouble coming up with ideas, use brainstorming techniques such as listing and freewriting to get ideas down on paper.

- A good thesis makes an assertion about the topic; it does not just repeat the topic or ask a question. Make sure your thesis takes a clear position on the issue or argument.
- Your planning time is probably the most crucial part of an essay exam. Create a detailed outline to organize your ideas. Revise your outline before you begin writing to make sure you have sufficient support and specific examples and that you have addressed all of the elements in the prompt.
- Make sure you have at least two or three supporting ideas for your thesis. If no other organizational pattern makes sense, put them in order of importance, with your most important idea last.
- Remember, it's important to get going and keep moving. If you can't think of the exact word or phrase you are looking for, approximate. You can come back to fix it later if you have time. For now, writing something that is close enough must be good enough so you can get the rest of your ideas down.
- Remember to keep it simple. Your time is limited, and your readers will be looking for basic structural and organizational elements. Don't worry about impressing your readers with sophisticated organization or style; you don't need anything out of the ordinary to impress your readers. A formulaic but clear essay will do better than one that is overly complex.
- Remember that first impressions are important, but it's more important to finish your essay. Don't get hung up trying to write a perfect introduction. Simply summarize the argument or issue and state your thesis. If you have time later, you can come back and write a catchier introduction.
- Signpost, signpost, signpost. Use strong transitions throughout your essay to make the relationships between ideas clear. Remember that both your human reader and E-rater® will be looking for these guides.
- A specific fact or detail has more power than a general statement. Include specific examples whenever possible.
- In general, unless you have less than five minutes left, revise first and then edit. Save your grammar and spelling check until after you have made "big picture" changes to your essay. If you are nearly out of time, read through your essay quickly and make any revisions or editorial changes.
- If a sentence seems unclear to you, it may be that you are trying to do too much in one sentence. Try breaking it up into two simpler sentences that are more clear.
- Remember the guidelines for effective style: be precise, be concise, use the active voice, vary the sentence structure, and avoid jargon and pretentious language. Make sure you use an appropriate level of formality and a serious, respectful tone throughout your essay.
- Correct punctuation is important, but don't get hung up on trying to determine whether you need a comma or a semicolon. Make your choice quickly and move on to the next issue.
- If you are unsure about capitalization, ask yourself whether the word in question is something *specific* or *general.* If it is a specific person, place, or thing, then it probably should be capitalized. Remember, in this regard, *specific* means *particular* or *individual,* not *detailed.* For example, a poodle is a specific type of dog, but it is not capitalized because it doesn't refer to a specific (individual or particular) dog. *Rover,* however, should be capitalized because Rover is a specific (individual or particular) dog.
- If you have the time, read your essay *backward* line by line. This will enable you to spot errors that you might miss reading straight through.

▶ Analyzing the Issue

- Remember that in the Analysis of an Issue essay, there is no correct answer. A good essay will take a clear position and support that position. Don't be afraid to say what you think. Just be sure to back up your opinion.
- A strong issue essay will address counterarguments. Take a minute to imagine how someone taking the opposite point of view would support that position. Acknowledge key concerns and then show why your position has more merit.

▶ Analyzing the Argument

The argument you are presented with on the GMAT exam may have many different problems. To address all of the different possibilities, break down your analysis into two steps: (1) what the argument has and (2) what it might be missing:

1. **What is already there?** Check the premises and conclusion. Are the premises (stated and unstated) logical? Do they lead logically to the conclusion? Is the evidence strong and convincing? Are there any fallacies in the argument?
2. **What might be missing?** What alternative explanations or counterarguments are missing from the argument? What evidence would strengthen the conclusion? What missing information would help you better evaluate the argument?

CHAPTER

17 AWA Practice

The following practice section contains ten prompts for the Analysis of an Issue section and ten prompts for the Analysis of an Argument section. Use these prompts to practice your timed writing skills for the AWA. Give yourself 30 minutes for each essay. Sample essay responses are provided after the sample prompts.

To create a realistic testing scenario, it is important that you *do not* read the prompts until you are ready to begin your timed session. Even a quick glance at the topic will give you the opportunity to start developing ideas for an essay. Remember, you will not have any incubation period on the GMAT® exam; you will only receive your topic when your timed writing session begins.

You will have to write two essays in a row on the GMAT exam, so practice doing one of each kind of essay consecutively. The first few times you may find that you lose steam on the second essay; after all, writing two essays in just one hour is hard work. But the more you practice, the easier it will become, and the more comfortable you will be with pacing yourself through the writing process.

It is also critical that you use a computer with a basic word processor to practice writing the essays. You will *not* have the option of writing the essays by hand on the AWA, so you must be comfortable composing and revising on the computer. Be sure to turn off the spell check and grammar check; the word-processing program on the GMAT exam will not include either of these features. Have several sheets of scratch paper available so that you can brainstorm and outline your essays.

▶ Analysis of an Issue Sample Prompts

1. *A leader who is respected is more powerful than one who is feared.*

Discuss the extent to which you agree or disagree with this opinion. Support your position with reasons and/or examples from your own experience, observations, or reading. Complete your essay in 30 minutes.

2. *The main goal of education should be to teach students to be good citizens, not to prepare them for the workplace.*

Discuss the extent to which you agree or disagree with this opinion. Support your position with reasons and/or examples from your own experience, observations, or reading. Complete your essay in 30 minutes.

3. *One of the problems with our society is that we have created such a large divide between the home and the workplace. Even if people bring their work home from the office, their professional life has little connection to their home life.*

Discuss the extent to which you agree or disagree with this opinion. Support your position with reasons and/or examples from your own experience, observations, or reading. Complete your essay in 30 minutes.

4. *Every employee deserves a certain amount of privacy in the workplace, whether that means a private office or cubicle or the ability to make private phone calls or send personal e-mails.*

Discuss the extent to which you agree or disagree with this opinion. Support your position with reasons and/or examples from your own experience, observations, or reading. Complete your essay in 30 minutes.

5. *Without competition, people stop trying to improve and become complacent. Competition is therefore good for individuals and businesses alike.*

Discuss the extent to which you agree or disagree with this opinion. Support your position with reasons and/or examples from your own experience, observations, or reading. Complete your essay in 30 minutes.

6. *Success requires sacrifice. You cannot be successful in your professional life without sacrificing something in your personal life.*

Discuss the extent to which you agree or disagree with this opinion. Support your position with reasons and/or examples from your own experience, observations, or reading. Complete your essay in 30 minutes.

7. *Art reminds us of our humanity and connection to others. We all need some form of art in our lives to keep us human.*

Explain what you think is meant by the previous statement and discuss the extent to which you agree or disagree with this opinion. Support your position with reasons and/or examples from your own experience, observations, or reading. Complete your essay in 30 minutes.

8. *A creative person can succeed, but not without diligence. Diligence is the most important factor in success.*

Discuss the extent to which you agree or disagree with this opinion. Support your position with reasons and/or examples from your own experience, observations, or reading. Complete your essay in 30 minutes.

9. *Today's highest paid teachers are those who teach high school and college students. But the most important years in a human being's educational development are the earliest years. Therefore, early childhood educators should receive the highest salaries.*

Discuss the extent to which you agree or disagree with this opinion. Support your position with reasons and/or examples from your own experience, observations, or reading. Complete your essay in 30 minutes.

10. *You must be committed to your goals and beliefs, but not be inflexible. An unwillingness to change course or to compromise will lead to your downfall.*

Discuss the extent to which you agree or disagree with this opinion. Support your position with reasons and/or examples from your own experience, observations, or reading. Complete your essay in 30 minutes.

▶ Analysis of an Argument Sample Prompts

1. The following appeared in an article in a trade magazine for the advertising industry.

Because of the increasing diversity of the American population, new products and services must appeal and be marketed to a very specific group or subculture within society. These days, attempting to appeal to the public at large is a losing proposition.

Discuss how well reasoned you find this argument. In your essay, be sure to analyze the argument's logic and use of evidence. For example, you may need to consider whether the assumptions that underlie the argument are sound or whether counterarguments or alternative explanations would weaken the conclusion. You may also discuss the kind of evidence that would strengthen or refute the argument, what revisions to the argument would make it more reasonable, or what information, if any, would help you better evaluate the argument. Complete your essay in 30 minutes.

2. The following appeared in an editorial in a local newspaper.

For over a decade, Main Street has suffered from a lack of business. People do not like to shop on Main Street, and store turnover has been relentless. What Main Street needs is a face-lift. We should make a number of small improvements that will make Main Street a more pleasant place to shop, such as better lighting, more benches and potted plants along the sidewalks, and improved parking, which has always been a problem for shoppers along Main Street. These small but important changes will attract both new businesses and new customers to Main Street.

Discuss how well reasoned you find this argument. In your essay, be sure to analyze the argument's logic and use of evidence. For example, you may need to consider whether the assumptions that underlie the argument are sound or whether counterarguments or alternative explanations would weaken the conclusion. You may also discuss the kind of evidence that would strengthen or refute the argument, what revisions to the argument would make it more reasonable, or what information, if any, would help you better evaluate the argument. Complete your essay in 30 minutes.

3. The following appeared in a plan proposed to the board of directors of Fresh Food Corporation.

To distinguish our stores from our competitors and draw more customers into Fresh Food stores, we should donate a portion of each purchase to a well-known nonprofit organization each year. With the right publicity, people will begin to choose us over our competitors because they will feel good about buying from Fresh Food, even if our products cost a little more.

Discuss how well reasoned you find this argument. In your essay, be sure to analyze the argument's logic and use of evidence. For example, you may need to consider whether the assumptions that underlie the argument are sound or whether counterarguments or alternative explanations would weaken the conclusion. You may also discuss the kind of evidence that would strengthen or refute the argument, what revisions to the argument would make it more reasonable, or what information, if any, would help you better evaluate the argument. Complete your essay in 30 minutes.

4. The following was proposed at a town meeting in North Hillsborough.

North Hillsborough has seen a record increase in crime in the last five years, while the crime rate in South Hillsborough has seen a slight decline. North Hillsborough has only five police officers, while South Hillsborough has eight. Clearly we need more police officers if we want to reduce crime in North Hillsborough.

Discuss how well reasoned you find this argument. In your essay, be sure to analyze the argument's logic and use of evidence. For example, you may need to consider whether the assumptions that underlie the argument are sound or whether counterarguments or alternative explanations would weaken the conclusion. You may also discuss the kind of evidence that would strengthen or refute the argument, what revisions to the argument would make it more reasonable, or what information, if any, would help you better evaluate the argument. Complete your essay in 30 minutes.

5. The following was proposed at a meeting of the marketing team for Zinger mints.

Our newest competitor, Mint Magic candies, hits the stores next week. The best way to keep our market share is to develop an ad campaign saying that our mints simply taste better than theirs.

Discuss how well reasoned you find this argument. In your essay, be sure to analyze the argument's logic and use of evidence. For example, you may need to consider whether the assumptions that underlie the argument are sound or whether counterarguments or alternative explanations would weaken the conclusion. You may also discuss the kind of evidence that would strengthen or refute the argument, what revisions to the argument would make it more reasonable, or what information, if any, would help you better evaluate the argument. Complete your essay in 30 minutes.

6. The following appeared in a report from human resources to the president of Aberdeen Manufacturing.

In a recent survey, 46% of our employees indicated that they would be "very interested" in the option of a four-day, 40-hour workweek. Since this is less than half of our employees, we should not offer this option, because it would not be worth the administrative cost and effort.

Discuss how well reasoned you find this argument. In your essay, be sure to analyze the argument's logic and use of evidence. For example, you may need to consider whether the assumptions that underlie the argument are sound or whether counterarguments or alternative explanations would weaken the conclusion. You may also discuss the kind of evidence that would strengthen or refute the argument, what revisions to the argument would make it more reasonable, or what information, if any, would help you better evaluate the argument. Complete your essay in 30 minutes.

7. The following appeared in a letter to the editor of a local newspaper.

We can all do something to improve the economy: Support our local small business owners. Instead of going to a big chain store to buy your coffee, office supplies, or toothpaste and shampoo, shop at your local coffee shop, stationery store, or pharmacy. Big chain stores have forced thousands of smaller stores out of business, increasing unemployment and weakening the economy. They don't deserve our patronage.

Discuss how well reasoned you find this argument. In your essay, be sure to analyze the argument's logic and use of evidence. For example, you may need to consider whether the assumptions that underlie the argument are sound or whether counterarguments or alternative explanations would weaken the conclusion. You may also discuss the kind of evidence that would strengthen or refute the argument, what revisions to the argument would make it more reasonable, or what information, if any, would help you better evaluate the argument. Complete your essay in 30 minutes.

8. The following appeared in a letter to the editor of a business magazine.

Some people feel that businesses should aim to create a more egalitarian office environment by giving everyone equal-sized office space, for example, and seeking input from even the very lowest-level employees. But businesses are built upon and thrive on hierarchy. People who think a workplace can be egalitarian are simply fooling themselves. Hierarchy should be acknowledged and reinforced in the business environment.

Discuss how well reasoned you find this argument. In your essay, be sure to analyze the argument's logic and use of evidence. For example, you may need to consider whether the assumptions that underlie the argument are sound or whether counterarguments or alternative explanations would weaken the conclusion. You may also discuss the kind of evidence that would strengthen or refute the argument, what revisions to the argument would make it more reasonable, or what information, if any, would help you better evaluate the argument. Complete your essay in 30 minutes.

9. The following was proposed by a husband to his wife.

Our neighbors, the Hansons, got a phonics program for their son Jimmy, and he was reading by age four. If we get a phonics program for Junior, he will also be able to read by age four.

Discuss how well reasoned you find this argument. In your essay, be sure to analyze the argument's logic and use of evidence. For example, you may need to consider whether the assumptions that underlie the argument are sound or whether counterarguments or alternative explanations would weaken the conclusion. You may also discuss the kind of evidence that would strengthen or refute the argument, what revisions to the argument would make it more reasonable, or what information, if any, would help you better evaluate the argument. Complete your essay in 30 minutes.

10. The following appeared in a letter to the editor of a city newspaper.

The philosopher George Santayana once wrote, "Those who cannot remember the past are condemned to repeat it." We should place a greater emphasis on learning history in school so that our future citizens do not make the same mistakes that have been made in the past.

Discuss how well reasoned you find this argument. In your essay, be sure to analyze the argument's logic and use of evidence. For example, you may need to consider whether the assumptions that underlie the argument are sound or whether counterarguments or alternative explanations would weaken the conclusion. You may also discuss the kind of evidence that would strengthen or refute the argument, what revisions to the argument would make it more reasonable, or what information, if any, would help you better evaluate the argument. Complete your essay in 30 minutes.

▶ Answers and Explanations

Here are sample essays for ten of the practice prompts (five Analysis of an Issue prompts and five Analysis of an Argument prompts). These ten essays would receive the top score of 6 because they have most or all of the following characteristics:

CONTENT	DEVELOPMENT	ORGANIZATION	EXPRESSION	CONVENTIONS
The content of your written response shows an understanding and interpretation of the issue or argument and the task presented in the prompt.	The development of your written response gives a clear and logical explanation of ideas using specific and relevant support.	The organization of your written response shows a coherent, orderly, well-reasoned approach.	The expression of your ideas reflects an awareness of audience, a command of vocabulary and sentence structure, and an ability to use language to convey purpose.	The use of standard English in your written response exhibits the correct use of spelling, punctuation, paragraph organization, capitalization, and grammar.
▪ Forms a thesis statement that reveals an in-depth understanding of the issue or argument ▪ Presents a sophisticated and insightful analysis of the issue or argument	▪ Develops ideas clearly and fully ▪ Provides a wide range of relevant and specific evidence to support the thesis statement	▪ Maintains the focus of the thesis statement ▪ Uses a logical and coherent structure ▪ Applies skillful writing devices and transitions	▪ Exhibits a mature, sophisticated use of language that is precise and engaging ▪ Has a voice and a sense of awareness of audience and purpose ▪ Varies the structure and length of sentences to enhance meaning	▪ Shows control of the conventions of standard English ▪ Has few, if any, errors even when using sophisticated language

The following sample essays are correct in spelling, grammar, and mechanics. Remember, however, that you can have a few mistakes and still score a 6.

Analysis of an Issue Sample Essays

Prompt #2:

The main goal of education should be to teach students to be good citizens, not to prepare them for the workplace.

Does a country need good citizens? Certainly, it does. But should the main goal of education be to teach students to be good citizens? No. While nurturing good citizens should be a primary goal, it should not be more important than preparing students for the workforce.

Upon graduation, most students head out into the workforce. At this crucial moment in their lives, what is more important: their citizenship or their ability to become gainfully employed? As important as good citizenship is, it does not pay the bills, and a society full of citizens who cannot support themselves will have many serious problems.

Indeed, preparing young people for the workplace by providing them with analytical and technical skills is essential for economic growth. Today more than ever, economic success is created and maintained by individuals who can run small businesses, make scientific advances, manage information, and labor in increasingly technical manufacturing settings. A country of good citizens who lack the skills necessary to maintain a stable economy will struggle financially and, therefore, socially and politically. How will the government fund programs and provide necessary services to its citizens? How much will those good citizens suffer if the country cannot support itself or has to compete with other countries for resources? How would it defend itself in a time of war without a prepared, well-funded military?

However, this does not mean that education should focus primarily on workforce preparation. Economic stability is not the only factor in a society's success. For people to want to live and work in a society, they must learn about and value the core beliefs of that society. Likewise, they must understand and participate in the workings of that society. They must also respect and value their fellow citizens and their environment. They must, in short, be good citizens, and it should be the duty of our schools to teach them how to be.

In the United States of America, for example, children are taught the Pledge of Allegiance from the earliest days of kindergarten; they are taught to respect the flag and all that it stands for. In later grades, those children learn about the U.S. government, election processes, legal system, and tax system. This knowledge will help to create good citizens who can serve on a jury or in the military, understand their duty to pay taxes, vote to elect officials, and develop projects and programs that support and improve their communities.

For the United States to maintain its success and achieve its goals in technological growth, space travel, military operations, environmental issues, and hundreds of other areas, we need educated citizens who are well prepared for the workplace. A thriving, skilled workforce bolsters the economy and keeps money circulating—money that funds our government through taxes. Without financially successful citizens, the country's sources of revenue would soon diminish.

Thus, the main goal of education should not be primarily to prepare students for the workforce *or* teach them to be good citizens but rather to prepare students for the workforce *while* teaching them to be good citizens. To continue to succeed in our increasingly global world, to maintain our country's standard of living, and to keep America a place where people *want* to live and work, our schools must prepare good citizens and educated workers.

Prompt #4:

Every employee deserves a certain amount of privacy in the workplace, whether that means a private office or cubicle or the ability to make private phone calls or e-mails.

The issue of employee privacy in the workplace is a sensitive topic for both employees and employers. Employers often feel that private matters interfere with work and do not belong in the workplace, but the reality is that employees sometimes need to make personal calls, send private e-mails, or discuss private matters with colleagues. Further, a little privacy can often go a long way to improving employee productivity. In my opinion, employees deserve to make personal calls and send private e-mails, within guidelines, and they deserve additional privacy for their work if it can improve job performance.

An employee deserves a private office if the actual job requires the privacy of a room and a door. For example, when I worked as a professional trainer at a regional bank's corporate headquarters, I had to discuss training skill levels with employees who attended my classes. As I only had a cubicle, we had to discuss their performance within listening range of other employees. Any type of employee evaluation is a private matter and should take place behind closed doors. In addition, many employees work on projects that require the discussion of sensitive issues with clients either in person or on the phone. These employees should have offices where this kind of work can take place in privacy.

Private office space is often limited, but that doesn't mean employees can't have at least some degree of privacy. Cubicles or other privacy-providing devices can often help employees focus on work and improve job performance. In a separate area of the bank where I was employed, the clerical staff members had their desks positioned in a large open area. They had no means of attaining privacy either for work or personal matters. They were free to chat easily throughout the day, but usually chatted more than they worked. The installation of cubicles quieted the area and significantly improved work efficiency.

One of the most complex workplace privacy issues is e-mail. Do employees have the right to send personal e-mails from the workplace? Do employers have the right to read employee e-mails? Unlike phone calls that must sometimes be made during the day to tend to family matters, e-mails—because they leave a written record in cyberspace—create liability issues for the employer. Although I dislike the idea of "Big Brother" watching, I believe it is fair for an employer to monitor e-mail activity on business e-mail accounts. However, it is imperative that employees know that their e-mails may be monitored.

On the other hand, I do not believe employers have the right to read employee e-mails sent from personal accounts. If I access my Hotmail or Yahoo e-mail account from work during my break, for example, I should be free to write whatever I want to whomever I please without the possibility of my employer reading my message. Of course, as a responsible employee, I must be careful not to send private e-mails of this sort on company time, and my employer has every right to establish a policy limiting such e-mails to break time.

Where the issue of privacy seems most clear to me is in regard to private telephone calls, which employees do deserve. All employees, at one point or another, need to make or receive personal calls during business hours, whether it is to make a doctor appointment or to assist a family member, and they should be allowed to make these calls in private. Of course, the number and duration of these calls should be limited, and if they interfere with work or abuse the privilege, the employee deserves to be reprimanded, but the employer does not have a right to listen in on these phone calls. Instead, employers should make sure personal call guidelines are clear (e.g., that long-distance calls will be tracked and billed to employees), and private space for such calls should be provided in a break room, office, or other area.

We all value our privacy, and a certain degree of privacy in the workplace is necessary to keep employees satisfied and productive. Allowing personal phone calls and e-mails according to reasonable guidelines and providing private workspace is a small concession to employee satisfaction and productivity.

Prompt #5:

Without competition, people stop trying to improve and become complacent. Competition is therefore good for individuals and businesses alike.

From a child's first science fair to man's first steps on the moon, competition has spurred people to do their best. Competition can be the best motivation for individuals and businesses alike to accomplish great goals. Without competition, we lose the incentive to do better and we become complacent. Indeed, both individuals and businesses benefit from competition.

A sense of competition has been the key to improving business at our local home and garden store, which is part of a national chain. Until recently, the large store was the only one to offer a wide array of home and garden products to our small city. But shoppers found a disinterested staff of people who were unwilling to help beyond pointing to an aisle. Complaints to local management were not taken seriously. As a result, complacency was negatively affecting business. Many people chose to drive out of town to shop at a place that seemed to care more for its customers.

The recent arrival of an equally large competitor has brought some much-needed change to the first store. Now customers see willingness from staff to answer questions and to assist in finding items. Store management is motivated to address customer concerns and complaints. New competition has improved the way the store does business and has allowed it to keep some of its former customers instead of sending them all to the competitor.

Here is another example of how competition benefits a business, its employees, and customers. One of my previous employers was a retail clothing store. Members of the sales staff were given quotas, and the quotas were posted on charts for everyone to see. At the end of each day, actual sales figures were recorded on the quota chart. The daily competition motivated sales staff to try harder to increase sales by asking customers if they wanted to purchase an extra tie, shirt, or maybe a pair of socks. The store reaped large profits, and the staff enjoyed bonuses for increased sales.

Of course, it is true that some people have an overdeveloped sense of competition. For them, everything is a contest, and they can make life difficult for themselves and everyone around them. It is also true that some people simply do not do well in competitive situations, while others have lost the will to compete after having lost too many times. But most of us do have a healthy sense of competition, and most of us learn to better ourselves after the experience of a loss. More importantly, most of us have accomplished things we never thought possible because we were determined to beat the competition.

As school students, we are spurred to do our best in science fairs to compete for first place ribbons. Students go on to compete as members of the band, math team, or any sports team. As adults, we compete in the workplace for a variety of reasons—to gain clients, improve sales, earn grants, or to garner recognition. Our society revolves around competition, whether we are in school, at work, or watching professional sports and reality shows on television. Competition motivates individuals and businesses to do their very best; it fosters creativity and hard work. Without it, we quickly fall into complacency, which leads us to settle for less than we can achieve.

Prompt #8:

A creative person can succeed, but not without diligence. Diligence is the most important factor in success.

If a creative person never applies herself, how is she to succeed? What good are the creative forces if no effort is made to create? I agree a creative person needs diligence to succeed. However, I think diligence is just one of the possible factors contributing to success, not necessarily the most important factor.

Artist Mary Engelbreit began drawing and painting as a young child and grew to become a talented artist. As a young woman she wanted to illustrate children's books, but found a limited response to her requests for work. Yet she was diligent and kept creating her art, despite the rejections. She soon found a receptive market for her distinctive artwork in the field of greeting cards.

Today Mary Engelbreit owns a large, flourishing company and is responsible for the creative design of the successful magazine *Home Companion*, home décor accessories, greeting cards, and numerous other licensed products, all of which utilize her colorful artwork. If she had not worked hard to promote her art and ideas, she would not be so successful today.

But is diligence the only factor in Engelbreit's success? No, it is not. While she is a naturally creative person, without natural talent, Engelbreit probably would not have found a market for her art, no matter how hard she tried. There must be something valuable in her work, whether it is a distinguishing style, emotive force, or unique vision, to make others appreciate her art. Her diligence was instrumental in getting her work recognized, but the root of her success is her natural talent.

Belief in one's talent is another important factor in an artist's success. Time and again, great artists will describe how their work was rejected over and over and over, but they ignored rejection letters and the critics who told them they didn't have talent. Imagine, for example, if Thomas Edison believed the educators who threw him out of school and told him he would never amount to anything. Imagine if director Stanley Kubrick had listened to critics who panned works like *2001: A Space Odyssey* because they didn't grasp the film's brilliance. But Edison and Kubrick kept at their work, believing in themselves and their talents, and this belief fueled their diligence.

Another element of success is often luck. I once asked a college president how he became so successful in his career. He listed the following reasons: intelligence, hard work, determination, and luck. He explained there were several points in his career where luck was his only explanation as to why he advanced to another level. When discussing the road to success, many famous actors and singers describe their lucky breaks, the audition nearly missed or the chance meeting with a producer.

Success is the result of many factors ranging from natural creative talent, to luck, to intelligence, to diligence. Diligence is certainly an important factor, but it is not the only one. A creative person will not be successful if he or she is not diligent about creating work, whether it is paintings, symphonies, novels, sculptures, or any other creative endeavor. Without the effort to produce, the creative person will have nothing to share and thus no chance of success.

Prompt #9:

Today's highest paid teachers are those who teach high school and college students. But the most important years in a human being's educational development are the earliest years. Therefore, early childhood educators should receive the highest salaries.

When looking at teacher salaries, it is true that "today's highest paid teachers are those who teach high school and college students." And although the earliest years in a human being's educational development are so important because they serve as building blocks to later learning, one cannot diminish the importance of education attained at the high school and college levels. Furthermore, I disagree with the claim that "early childhood educators should receive the highest salaries." I believe that all levels of educational development are important, and early childhood teachers do not merit the highest pay simply because they teach children during the most formative years.

The learning that takes place in the first few years of school sets the stage for learning later in life. The fundamentals of critical academic skills, including reading, math, spatial relations, problem solving, and interpersonal relations, are taught in preschool and kindergarten. These skills are the building blocks of all future learning. One could therefore argue that these early years are the most crucial years in a child's academic development, and in a sense, they are right—for without these building blocks, higher learning could not take place. But does that mean that the teachers of these fundamental—but also most simple—skills deserve the highest salaries? No, it does not.

Although students are beyond the "crucial early years" in primary and secondary school, what they learn is of great importance. Reading and learning about our world and its people, science, and math at the secondary level help prepare students to think critically. They need to be taught to receive detailed information (by reading, for example), to analyze that information, and then to make rational decisions. This process is emphasized at the high school and college levels to prepare students for future careers. So while talented educators at the elementary schools are crucial to teaching the basic educational and lifetime skills, educators in high schools and colleges are necessary to teach analytical and career skills. Indeed, teachers are important at all levels for they all teach varied yet necessary information and skills.

How, then, should salary be determined? A standard method should be utilized for teachers at all levels. Most learning institutions already do this to some degree, determining salary based on a teacher's education and years of experience. A teacher with more years of experience should be compensated more than a newcomer to the field. Likewise, a teacher with an advanced degree should be paid more because he or she can teach a subject in greater depth than a less qualified colleague. That is why most of today's highest paid teachers happen to be those at the high school and college level. Those teachers typically require more education and/or more experience to meet the demands of teaching more difficult subjects that must be explored with greater scrutiny. Most college professors, for example, have their Ph.D. while only a small percentage of early childhood educators have their masters.

Any learning, whether at the elementary, secondary, or college level, is important. Whether they are teaching my kindergartner to combine three letters to form a word or someday preparing her to enter the workforce, teachers of all subjects and at all levels should be valued for the expertise they provide. But they should not be paid equally. The more their education and experience, and the more challenging their subject, the higher their salaries should be.

Analysis of an Argument Sample Essays

Prompt #1:

Because of the increasing diversity of the American population, new products and services must appeal and be marketed to a very specific group or subculture within society. These days, attempting to appeal to the public at large is a losing proposition.

The previous argument states that because of the increasing diversity of American society, new products and services should be marketed to very specific groups of people. It also states that marketing to the public at large "is a losing proposition." The assumption is that, with so many different cultures in America, a company has to target a specific customer within society because a company can no longer appeal to people from many different backgrounds. While some businesses do succeed by appealing to a very specific customer, other businesses are currently succeeding by appealing to the public at large. One must look at the products and services offered to determine target audiences and marketing approaches. Other factors that will determine a product or service's level of success include pricing, customer demographics, and customer demand.

An example of a business that can succeed by appealing to a specific group or subculture is the small grocery store that offers foods and products for a targeted customer. For example, a recent article in *Southern Living* magazine highlighted the success of a Cuban market in North Carolina. A growing Cuban population and difficulty finding specific foods spurred the owner to open his store, and his business is profitable. He has found a perfect niche, marketing specialty products to a targeted group of people.

On the other hand, appealing to the public at large has brought huge success to companies such as SmartMart and Video Emporium. Neither business targets a specific subculture; yet both are far from losing propositions. SmartMart offers a huge variety of products, but their products are used by many, if not most, subcultures of society. Items such as cleaning products, paper goods, clothing, and toys appeal to the masses. While Video Emporium's business is limited to the rental and sale of videos, DVDs, and video games, its inventory is large and wide, including movies and films that appeal to people of all ages, interests, and persuasions. As a result, Video Emporium stores can be found in most cities across the country.

In all cases, pricing, high-quality products and service, customer demand, and demographics are important to the marketing and success of any business. Marketing to a specific group of society will only be profitable if the products are in demand and the specific customer base is substantial enough to support business goals. Conversely, marketing to the masses is not a losing effort if the products are of general interest, the pricing is affordable, and the population base can support the sales needed to keep the business running.

Thus, while the growing diversity of our country has spurred the growth of new products and services offered directly to specific groups, some businesses will continue to find success when offering products to the population at large. Attempting to appeal to the masses is not necessarily a losing proposition. Products, service, demand, and demographics have to be considered when determining the target market for a business.

Prompt #3:

To distinguish our stores from our competitors and draw more customers into Fresh Food stores, we should donate a portion of each purchase to a well-known nonprofit organization each year. With the right publicity, people will begin to choose us over our competitors because they will feel good about buying from Fresh Food, even if our products cost a little more.

According to the previous argument, Fresh Food stores should begin donating a portion of each purchase to a well-known nonprofit organization to draw in more customers. The assumption is that if people are aware of Fresh Food's charitable donations, they will feel good about shopping there and will be willing to spend more money for Fresh Food's products. Although some customers may view charitable practices as favorable, higher prices may deter a larger percentage of customers who are unwilling to pay more. While price is usually one of the leading factors determining where people shop, consumers also take into consideration the quality and availability of inventory, location, organization, cleanliness, and even the return policy. If pricing disparities are too great and if these additional factors are not favorable, Fresh Food will be unable to draw more customers by promoting its charitable contributions.

The first issue is whether customers would want to shop at Fresh Food simply because it shares profits with a charity. Most people would view Fresh Food's efforts as commendable. Certainly, it makes good business sense to offer nonprofit donations, not just from a tax standpoint but for the positive image it promotes for the company. Consumers may feel an even greater loyalty to the store if those contributions are made on a local level, so the consumers see their money benefiting their own community.

On the other hand, product pricing is almost always the biggest factor consumers use to make purchase decisions. Pricing is so important that many large retailers, such as Low Price King, will meet or beat a competitor's price if a customer presents an advertisement depicting the lower price. With consumers placing such a great emphasis on pricing, Fresh Food will alienate customers who choose to buy products at the lowest cost. In addition, some consumers may feel they would rather choose their own charities and spend less for Fresh Food's products.

Additionally, Fresh Food must analyze the other critical factors consumers consider when choosing a store. Customers also care about product quality and variety, inventory availability, store organization (e.g., its cleanliness and wide aisles for shopping carts), special services offered (such as a snack bar or one-hour photo), location, safety, and parking convenience.

For example, take the successful retailer Bull's-eye. Bull's-eye stores do donate a portion of each purchase to charities. In many instances, Bull's-eye's prices are higher than its main competitors', SmartMart and Z-mart, for comparable products. So why would a customer choose Bull's-eye over the other stores? It is not just because Bull's-eye donates to charities. Bull's-eye has to surpass the other stores in most of the previous categories so customers will be more willing to pay higher prices at Bull's-eye. Indeed, Bull's-eye typically offers a wider selection of products of slightly higher quality than its competitors in an atmosphere that feels more like a department store than a discount retail chain. Because of these elements, Bull's-eye's consumers are willing to pay a little more, and they have the added benefit of knowing some of their money goes to a charity.

Therefore, Fresh Food needs a complete comparison between itself and its competition before it begins donating to charities and raising its prices. All of the critical factors consumers consider need to be addressed. In order to overcome price disparities with similar competitors, Fresh Food will have to convince the customer that the shopping experience as a whole is better at Fresh Food. When reminded that donations are being made to charities, customers will feel even better about shopping at Fresh Food.

Prompt #5:

Our new competition, Mint Magic candies, hits the stores next week. The best way to keep our market share is to develop an ad campaign saying that our mints simply taste better than theirs.

Zinger mints will soon face competition from Mint Magic candies. Worried that new competition could affect market share, Zinger's marketing team wisely met to develop a strategy. However, the team's suggestion to develop an ad campaign saying Zinger mints simply taste better than Mint Magic mints is not the best approach. Of the many possible strategies, calling attention to the competition's mints might tempt consumers to try both and compare for themselves. The Zinger marketing team needs to develop other marketing approaches.

If the Zinger company runs ads mentioning the competitor's brand name, Zinger is inadvertently spending its own money to familiarize the public with the names of both mints, not just its own. Because Mint Magic is sure to launch its own campaign, Zinger mints should not add to the media attention. Worse, such an ad campaign could lead customers to try the new mint to compare taste, especially because a negative campaign against the competition suggests to consumers that Zinger management is worried that Mint Magic candies really *are* better than Zinger mints.

Consequently, Zinger mints should design a marketing strategy based on the merits of its own product. For instance, the campaign could remind customers how tasty Zinger mints have always been or use a nostalgic approach, perhaps showing different generations of a family enjoying the mints. Or the company could rerun ads that were used extensively enough in the past that consumers recognize them from childhood. The marketing team needs to create a sense of loyalty in its existing customers and describe the mints in such a tantalizing way that it attracts new customers.

The arrival of a new competitor could also be a good time for Zinger mints to try some new marketing methods to maintain or even increase its market share. For example, a Zinger mints sales promotion offering coupons in Sunday newspapers could coincide with the launch of Mint Magic. The timing might also be right for the company to introduce some additional new flavors or similar products. Adding to the product line may help to offset the loss of original mint customers to the competition. But to retain existing customers, the original Zinger mints should remain unchanged, or Mint Magic could lose customers the way Super Cola did when it tried to replace Original Cola with New Cola.

In conclusion, although the Zinger mint company is right to be concerned about a new competitor's arrival, the best approach to keeping market share is to foster existing customer loyalty. A campaign that claims Zinger mints taste better than the new mints is a risky proposition that could send customers to Mint Magic. Instead, Zinger ads need to focus on the merits of its own product.

Prompt #6:

In a recent survey, 46% of our employees indicated that they would be "very interested" in the option of a four-day, 40-hour workweek. Since this is less than half of our employees, we should not offer this option, since it would not be worth the administrative cost and effort.

It goes without saying that happy employees do better work and are more productive than unhappy employees. So although a recent human resource report dismissed offering the option of a four-day, 40-hour workweek, it seems to have come to the wrong conclusion.

The report argues that since less than half of Aberdeen's employees were "very interested," the option was not worth the administrative cost and effort. But before the president of Aberdeen Manufacturing decides whether or not to follow the report's recommendation, he or she should evaluate what the actual costs would be, determine how important such an option really is to the 46% of employees, and consider the consequences of alienating those workers.

Though 46% is not quite the majority, the discontent of that large percent of employees could have a huge impact on the overall atmosphere of the workplace. If those employees really hoped for the implementation of the modified workweek, what would the ramifications be when they learned the option would not be considered? Certainly their attitudes toward the company, and ultimately their work, could suffer. Their negative attitudes could spread to many other employees. The belief that the human resources and management personnel are not listening tends to make employees feel unimportant and unvalued, which in turn lessens the value those employees give to their work.

Further, Aberdeen's president cannot make a good decision about the modified workweek without information that is not specified in the argument. We do not know what percentage of employees may feel "somewhat interested" and how many responded that they were "not interested." If even a small percentage of employees said they were "somewhat interested," then indeed a majority of workers have a desire to at least have more dialogue about the modified workweek option. Perhaps a more detailed survey to more accurately determine level of interest is in order.

Even without another survey, Aberdeen Manufacturing should explore the administrative costs and implications of implementing the option for the sake of the 46% who were "very interested." The human resource professionals would find it valuable and inexpensive to consult with human resource peers at other companies that use the four-day, 40-hour schedule, and there is likely to be a good deal of literature on the subject in professional journals. These peers and journal articles could explain best practices and the expected costs of such an implementation. Also, human resources should ask employees through a simple e-mail or other surveying process for their suggestions on how the modified workweek could best be implemented. After all, employees with a vested interest may have some of the most helpful suggestions.

Thus, it would be unwise for Aberdeen to ignore the desire of nearly half of its employees to explore a four-day, 40-hour workweek option. True, 46% is not technically a majority, but it is only common sense to assume that more than half of the employees are at least "somewhat interested" in the proposal. Chances are good that Aberdeen could keep administrative costs to a minimum by following best practices already established in the industry, so high administrative cost seems a poor excuse. By not pursuing the option further, Aberdeen Manufacturing would send the message that it undervalues its employees, and that is sure to have negative consequences on the work atmosphere and later on the bottom line of the company.

Prompt #9:

Our neighbors, the Hansons, got a phonics program for their son Jimmy, and he was reading by age four. If we get a phonics program for Junior, he will also be able to read by age four.

The father making the previous argument might be wise to get a phonics program for Junior to help his son learn how to read, but he would also be wise to realize that he might not get the same results as the Hansons. Just because Jimmy was reading at age four does not mean that Junior will also be reading by age four. The father's argument seems to assume that the phonics program is the only factor that will determine when Junior will be able to read. Clearly, there are many problems with this assumption, because many factors affect Junior's reading ability.

First, the father seems to believe that the phonics program alone is what taught Jimmy to read at an early age. But we don't know if Jimmy's parents helped to build his reading skills in other ways. This information is crucial to evaluating the father's argument. Perhaps Jimmy was enrolled in a preschool that focused on early reading skills. Perhaps Jimmy's parents or caregiver worked with him regularly to teach him phonics. Perhaps Jimmy had a private tutor to help him develop his reading readiness. Although the phonics program may certainly have helped Jimmy learn to read, we don't know what other teaching took place.

If we knew that the phonics program was the *only* tool the Hansons used to help Jimmy learn to read, then the father's argument would have more merit. But even if this is the case, there are still other important factors to consider.

For one thing, would Junior's parents purchase the same phonics program as the Hansons? The argument doesn't specify. Junior's father only states that they should by "a" phonics program. There are many phonics programs out on the market. Some of them are excellent; others are likely to be largely inadequate. If the father wants the same results as the Hansons, he needs to get a program of comparable quality.

Likewise, Junior's parents would need to work with him the same amount of time and in the same way that the Hansons worked with Jimmy in order to get the same results. If the Hansons spent ten hours each week working with Jimmy on the phonics program and Junior's parents only spent one or two hours a week, that could account for a drastic difference in reading ability.

Another important question is the age at which the children begin the phonics program (assuming the program is the same). If Jimmy started the program at age three, that would give him a full year to work with the program and develop his reading skills. On the other hand, if Junior is already three and a half, he has considerably less time to master those same skills, and his father should not expect his son to learn the same material in half the time.

Of course, this line of reasoning is based on another problematic assumption, which is that the children themselves are comparable in terms of their reading readiness, their interest in learning to read, and their general ability to learn new concepts. For example, perhaps Jimmy had been able to recognize the letters of the alphabet months before he started the phonics program, while Junior is still just learning to recite his ABCs. In this case, Junior has a good deal of work to do before he can begin sounding out words with the phonics program.

Likewise, Junior must be interested in learning how to read. If he is not, and his parents push him too hard, he is likely to withdraw from the process, and his parents will find themselves frustrated trying to meet a goal (Junior reading by age four) with a child who is not interested in meeting that goal. If Jimmy's interest in learning to read was strong, that could have had a significant impact on how much and how quickly he learned with the phonics program.

Finally, another important factor is the children's ability to learn. Even if both children started at the same age, with the same basic reading readiness skills and the same level of interest, they may not have the same ability to learn new concepts. Junior might struggle in areas in which Jimmy accelerated, and vice versa.

In short, the father's argument rests on the assumption that the learning situations for Jimmy and Junior are entirely comparable. But because there are so many variables to consider, such as reading readiness, other reading preparation activities, and each child's ability to learn, Junior's father cannot logically assume Junior will have the same success as Jimmy simply by purchasing a phonics program.

PART

IV The GMAT Quantitative Section

CHAPTER

18 Quantitative Pretest

The entire GMAT® quantitative part of the exam takes place in one section of the test. This section contains 37 questions and must be completed in 75 minutes. Therefore, the test taker can spend about two minutes per question, on average. The questions in this section consist of two different multiple-choice formats: problem solving and data sufficiency. Each type of question has five possible choices for answers. These questions test a person's knowledge of mathematical concepts and their applications, along with thinking and reasoning skills. Examinees will be asked to recall the mathematics that they learned in middle school and high school and apply these skills in an advanced manner for the questions on the test. Although scrap paper is allowed, the use of calculators is prohibited on the GMAT exam.

Since the Quantitative section is only administered as a CAT, this section will be taken on a computer. As each person takes the exam, the computer randomly generates the sequence of questions administered based on the participant's ability. The test begins with a question of average difficulty. If the question is answered correctly, points are added to the score and a more difficult question follows. If the question is answered incorrectly, there is no penalty, but an easier question follows. Keep in mind that harder questions carry more weight and will result in a higher score. Because of the CAT format, each question must be answered and confirmed before proceeding to the next question. Since randomly guessing an incorrect answer will lower your score, making an educated guess by eliminating one or more of the answer choices should result in a better score. Your score is based on both the number of questions you answer and the level of difficulty of the questions; the more difficult questions you answer, the better.

Even though the Quantitative section is administered on a computer, minimal computing skills are necessary. Free GMAT tutorials can be downloaded from various Internet sites and taken ahead of time. The testing site also offers a tutorial that can be completed immediately before commencing the test. These skills, such as using the mouse and the HELP feature, should be practiced before beginning the test. Once you start a particular section of the exam, the clock cannot be stopped. Time spent asking for help will be counted in the total time for that particular section.

The quantitative portion will not test how well you recall a lot of facts and figures; instead, it will test how well you use your existing knowledge of math and how well you apply it to various situations. In addition, this section of the test will not evaluate your personality, work ethic, or ability to work with others. Although the problems may seem difficult at times, they will not be assessing the undergraduate work you may have completed in college or any particular course you may have taken; the math will be high school level. Even though the test is used as a precursor for business school, the questions will not require knowledge of business-related skills.

This section of the test contains a number of trial questions that are being field-tested for future use. These particular questions will not be counted toward your total score; however, the actual questions are not distinguished from the trial questions. Do your best on all of the questions and treat them as if they all count.

▶ Problem Solving Questions

ANSWER SHEET

1.	ⓐ	ⓑ	ⓒ	ⓓ	ⓔ	8.	ⓐ	ⓑ	ⓒ	ⓓ	ⓔ	15.	ⓐ	ⓑ	ⓒ	ⓓ	ⓔ
2.	ⓐ	ⓑ	ⓒ	ⓓ	ⓔ	9.	ⓐ	ⓑ	ⓒ	ⓓ	ⓔ	16.	ⓐ	ⓑ	ⓒ	ⓓ	ⓔ
3.	ⓐ	ⓑ	ⓒ	ⓓ	ⓔ	10.	ⓐ	ⓑ	ⓒ	ⓓ	ⓔ	17.	ⓐ	ⓑ	ⓒ	ⓓ	ⓔ
4.	ⓐ	ⓑ	ⓒ	ⓓ	ⓔ	11.	ⓐ	ⓑ	ⓒ	ⓓ	ⓔ	18.	ⓐ	ⓑ	ⓒ	ⓓ	ⓔ
5.	ⓐ	ⓑ	ⓒ	ⓓ	ⓔ	12.	ⓐ	ⓑ	ⓒ	ⓓ	ⓔ	19.	ⓐ	ⓑ	ⓒ	ⓓ	ⓔ
6.	ⓐ	ⓑ	ⓒ	ⓓ	ⓔ	13.	ⓐ	ⓑ	ⓒ	ⓓ	ⓔ	20.	ⓐ	ⓑ	ⓒ	ⓓ	ⓔ
7.	ⓐ	ⓑ	ⓒ	ⓓ	ⓔ	14.	ⓐ	ⓑ	ⓒ	ⓓ	ⓔ						

Directions: Solve the problem and choose the letter indicating the best answer choice. The numbers used in this section are real numbers. The figures used are drawn to scale and lie in a plane unless otherwise noted.

1. If both the length and the width of a rectangle are tripled, then the area of the rectangle is
  a. two times larger.
  b. three times larger.
  c. five times larger.
  d. six times larger.
  e. nine times larger.

2. If a set of numbers consists of $\frac{1}{4}$ and $\frac{1}{6}$, what number can be added to the set to make the average (arithmetic mean) also equal to $\frac{1}{4}$?

a. $\frac{1}{6}$

b. $\frac{1}{5}$

c. $\frac{1}{4}$

d. $\frac{1}{3}$

e. $\frac{1}{2}$

3. Given integers as the measurements of the sides of a triangle, what is the maximum perimeter of a triangle where two of the sides measure 10 and 14?

a. 34
b. 38
c. 44
d. 47
e. 48

4. In 40 minutes, Diane walks 2.5 miles and Sue walks 1.5 miles. In miles per hour, how much faster is Diane walking?

a. 1
b. 1.5
c. 2
d. 2.5
e. 3

5. If $x \neq -2$, then $\frac{5x^2 - 20}{5x + 10} =$

a. $x - 2$
b. $x - 10$
c. $5x + 2$
d. $x + 2$
e. $5x - 2$

6. If five less than y is six more than $x + 1$, then by how much is x less than y?

a. 6
b. 7
c. 10
d. 11
e. 12

7. If x dozen eggs cost y dollars, what is the cost, C, of z dozen eggs?

a. $C = xyz$

b. $C = \frac{xy}{z}$

c. $C = \frac{yz}{x}$

d. $C = xy + z$

e. $C = x + y + z$

8. At a certain high school, 638 students are taking biology this year. Last year 580 students took biology. Which of the following statements is NOT true?

a. There was a 10% increase in students taking biology.
b. There were 90% more students taking biology last year.
c. There were 10% fewer students taking biology last year.
d. The number of students taking biology this year is 110% of the number from last year.
e. The number of students taking biology last year was about 91% of the students taking biology this year.

9. Two positive integers differ by 7. The sum of their squares is 169. Find the larger integer.

a. 4
b. 5
c. 9
d. 12
e. 14

10. Quadrilateral WXYZ has diagonals that bisect each other. Which of the following could describe this quadrilateral?

I. parallelogram
II. rhombus
III. isosceles trapezoid

a. I only
b. I and II only
c. I and III only
d. II and III only
e. I, II, and III

► Data Sufficiency Questions

Directions: Each of the following problems contains a question that is followed by two statements. Select your answer using the data in statement (1) and statement (2) and determine whether they provide enough information to answer the initial question. If you are asked for the value of a quantity, the information is sufficient when it is possible to determine only one value for the quantity. The five possible answer choices are as follows:

a. Statement (1), BY ITSELF, will suffice to solve the problem, but NOT statement (2) by itself.
b. Statement (2), BY ITSELF, will suffice to solve the problem, but NOT statement (1) by itself.
c. The problem can be solved using statement (1) and statement (2) TOGETHER, but not ONLY statement (1) or statement (2).
d. The problem can be solved using EITHER statement (1) only or statement (2) only.
e. The problem CANNOT be solved using statement (1) and statement (2) TOGETHER.

The numbers used are real numbers. If a figure accompanies a question, the figure will be drawn to scale according to the original question or information, but it will not necessarily be consistent with the information given in statements (1) and (2).

11. Is k even?
(1) $k + 1$ is odd.
(2) $k + 2$ is even.

12. Is quadrilateral ABCD a rectangle?
(1) $m\angle ABC = 90^\circ$
(2) $AB = CD$

13. Sam has a total of 33 nickels and dimes in his pocket. How many dimes does he have?
(1) There are more than 30 nickels.
(2) He has a total of \$1.75 in his pocket.

14. If x is a nonzero integer, is x positive?
(1) x^2 is positive.
(2) x^3 is positive.

15. The area of a triangle is 36 square units. What is the height?
(1) The area of a similar triangle is 48 square units.
(2) The base of the triangle is half the height.

16. What is the value of x?
(1) $x^2 = -6x - 9$
(2) $2y - x = 10$

17. What is the slope of line *m*?

(1) It is parallel to the line $2y = 3 + x$.

(2) The line intersects the *y*-axis at the point (0, 5).

18. If two triangles are similar, what is the perimeter of the smaller triangle?

(1) The sum of the perimeters of the triangles is 30.

(2) The ratio of the measures of two corresponding sides is 2 to 3.

19. While shopping, Steve spent three times as much money as Judy, and Judy spent five times as much as Nancy. How much did Nancy spend?

(1) The average amount of money spent by the three people was \$49.

(2) Judy spent \$35.

20. A cube has an edge of *e* units and a rectangular prism has a base area of 25 and a height of *h*. Is the volume of the cube equal to the volume of the rectangular prism?

(1) The value of *h* is equal to the value of *e*.

(2) The sum of the volumes is 250 cubic units.

▶ Answer Explanations to the Pretest

1. e. Suppose that the length of the rectangle is 10 and the width is 5. The area of this rectangle would be $A = lw = 10 \times 5 = 50$. If both the length and width are tripled, then the new length is $10 \times 3 = 30$ and the new width is $5 \times 3 = 15$. The new area would be $A = lw = 30 \times 15 = 450$; 450 is nine times larger than 50. Therefore, the answer is **e**.

2. d. Let *x* equal the number to be added to the set. Then $\frac{\frac{1}{4} + \frac{1}{3} + x}{3}$ is equal to $\frac{1}{4}$. Use the LCD of 12 in the numerator so the equation becomes $\frac{\frac{3}{12} + \frac{2}{12} + x}{3} - \frac{\frac{5}{12} + x}{3} = \frac{1}{4}$. Cross-multiply to get $4(\frac{5}{12}) + 4x = 3$, which simplifies to $\frac{5}{3} + 4x = 3$. Subtract $\frac{5}{3}$ from each side of the equation to get $4x = \frac{4}{3}$. Divide each side by 4. $\frac{4x}{4} = \frac{\frac{4}{3}}{4}$. $x = \frac{4}{3} \div 4 = \frac{4}{3} \times \frac{1}{4} = \frac{1}{3}$. Another way to look at this problem is to see that $\frac{1}{4} = \frac{3}{12}$ and $\frac{1}{6} = \frac{3}{12}$. Since you want the average to be $\frac{1}{4} = \frac{3}{12}$, then the third number would have to be $\frac{4}{12} = \frac{1}{3}$ to make this average.

3. d. Use the triangle inequality, which states that the sum of the two smaller sides of a triangle must be greater than the measure of the third side. By adding the two known sides of $10 + 14 = 24$, this gives a maximum value of 23 for the third side because the side must be an integer. Since the perimeter of a polygon is the sum of its sides, the maximum perimeter must be $10 + 14 + 23 = 47$.

4. b. Since the distance given is out of 40 minutes instead of 60, convert each distance to hours by using a proportion. For Diane, use $\frac{2.5}{40} = \frac{x}{60}$. Cross-multiply to get $40x = 150$. Divide each side by 40. Diane walks 3.75 miles in one hour. For Sue, repeat the same process using $\frac{1.5}{40} = \frac{x}{60}$. Cross-multiply to get $40x = 90$ and divide each side by 40. So Sue walks 2.25 miles in one hour. $3.75 - 2.25 = 1.5$.

Diane walks 1.5 miles per hour faster than Sue.

5. a. Factor the expression and cancel out common factors.

$\frac{5x^2 - 20}{5x + 10} = \frac{5(x^2 - 4)}{5(x + 2)} = \frac{5(x + 2)(x - 2)}{5(x + 2)} = (x - 2)$. The expression reduces to $x - 2$.

6. e. Translate the sentence into mathematical symbols and use an equation. *Five less than y* becomes $y - 5$, and *six more than* $x + 1$ becomes $x + 1 + 6$. Putting both statements together results in the equation $y - 5 = x + 1 + 6$. This simplifies to $y - 5 = x + 7$. Since you need to find how much is x less than y, solve the equation for x by subtracting 7 from both sides. Since $x = y - 12$, x is 12 less than y, which is choice **e**.

7. c. Substitution can make this type of problem easier. Assume that you are buying 10 dozen eggs. If this 10 dozen eggs cost \$20, then 1 dozen eggs cost \$2. This is the result of dividing \$20 by 10, which in this problem is $\frac{y}{x}$. If $\frac{y}{x}$ is the cost of 1 dozen eggs, then if you buy z dozen eggs, the cost is $\frac{y}{x} \times z$, which is the same as choice **c**, $C = \frac{yz}{x}$.

8. b. Use the proportion for the percent of change. $638 - 580 = 58$ students is the increase in the number of students. $\frac{58}{580} = \frac{x}{100}$. Cross-multiply to get $580x = 5{,}800$ and divide each side by 580. $x = 10$. Therefore, the percent of *increase* is 10%. The only statement that does not support this is **b** because it implies that fewer students are taking biology this year.

9. d. Let $x =$ the smaller integer and let $y =$ the larger integer. The first sentence translates to $y - x = 7$ and the second sentence translates to $x^2 + y^2 = 169$. Solve this equation by solving for y in the first equation ($y = x + 7$) and substituting into the second equation.

	$x^2 + y^2 = 169$
	$x^2 + (x + 7)^2 = 169$
Use FOIL to multiply out $(x + 7)^2$:	$x^2 + x^2 + 7x + 7x + 49 = 169$
Combine like terms:	$2x^2 + 14x + 49 = 169$
Subtract 169 from both sides:	$2x^2 + 14x + 49 - 169 = 169 - 169$
	$2x^2 + 14x - 120 = 0$
Factor the left side:	$2(x^2 + 7x - 60) = 0$
	$2(x + 12)(x - 5) = 0$
Set each factor equal to zero and solve $2 \neq 0$ $x + 12 = 0$.	$x - 5 = 0$
	$x = -12$ or $x = 5$

Reject the solution of -12 because the integers are positive. Therefore, the larger integer is $5 + 7 = 12$. A much easier way to solve this problem would be to look at the answer choices and find the solution through trial and error.

10. b. The diagonals of both parallelograms and rhombuses bisect each other. Isosceles trapezoids have diagonals that are congruent, but do not bisect each other.

11. d. Either statement is sufficient. If $k + 1$ is odd, then one less than this, or k, must be an even number. If $k + 2$ is even and consecutive even numbers are two apart, then k must also be even.

12. e. Neither statement is sufficient. Statement (1) states that one of the angles is 90 degrees, but this alone does not prove that all four are right angles. Statement (2) states that one pair of nonadjacent sides are the same length; this also is not enough information to prove that both pairs of opposite sides are the same measure.

13. b. Since statement (1) says there are more than 30 nickels, assume there are 31 nickels, which would total \$1.55. You would then need two dimes to have the total equal \$1.75 from statement (2). Both statements together are sufficient.

14. b. Substitute possible numbers for x. If $x = 2$, then $(2)^2 = 4$. If $x = -2$, then $(-2)^2 = 4$, so statement (1) is not sufficient. Substituting into statement (2), if $x = -2$, then $(-2)^3 = (-2)(-2)(-2) = -8$; the value is negative. If $x = 2$, then $2^3 = 2 \times 2 \times 2 = 8$; the value is positive. Therefore, from statement (2), x is positive.

15. b. Using statement (2), the formula for the area of the triangle, $A = \frac{1}{2}bh$, can be used to find the height. Let $b =$ the base and $2b =$ the height. $36 = \frac{1}{2}(2b)(b) = b^2$. Therefore, the base is 6 and the height is 12. The information in statement (1) is not necessary and insufficient.

16. a. Statement (1) only has one variable. This quadratic equation can be put in standard form ($x^2 + 6x + 9 = 0$) and then solved for x by either factoring or using the quadratic formula. Since statement (2) has variables of both x and y, it is not enough information to solve for x.

17. a. Parallel lines have equal slopes. Using statement (1), the slope of the line can be found by changing the equation $2y = 3 + x$ to slope-intercept form, $y = \frac{1}{2} + 3$. The slope is $\frac{1}{2}$. Statement (2) gives the y-intercept of the line, but this is not enough information to calculate the slope of the line.

18. c. Statement (1) is insufficient because the information does not tell you anything about the individual triangles. Statement (2) gives information about each triangle, but no values for the perimeters. Use both statements and the fact that the ratio of the perimeters of similar triangles is the same as the ratio of their corresponding sides. Therefore, $2x + 3x = 30$. Since this can be solved for x, the perimeters can be found. Both statements together are sufficient.

19. d. Either statement is sufficient. If the average dollar amount of the three people is \$49, then the total amount spent is $49 \times 3 = \$147$. If you let $x =$ the amount that Nancy spent, then $5x$ is the amount Judy spent and $3(5x) = 15x$ is the amount that Steve spent. $x + 5x + 15x + 21x$. $\frac{147}{21} = \$7$. Using statement (2), if Judy spent \$35, then Nancy spent \$7 ($35 \div 5$).

20. **c.** Statement (1) alone will not suffice. For instance, if an edge = 3 cm, then $3^3 \neq 25 \times 3$. Recall that volume is length times width times height. However, if you assume the volumes are equal, the two volume formulas can be set equal to one another. Let x = the length of the cube and also the height of the rectangular prism. Since volume is basically length times width times height, then $x^3 = 25x$. $x^3 - 25x = 0$. Factor to get $x(x - 5)(x + 5) = 0$. Solve for x to get $x = 0, -5$, or 5. Five is the length of an edge and the height. Statement (2) is also needed to solve this problem; with the information found from statement (1), statement (2) can be used to verify that the edge is 5; therefore, it follows that the two volumes are equal.

CHAPTER

19 About the Quantitative Section

The math concepts tested on the GMAT® Quantitative section basically consist of arithmetic, algebra, and geometry. Questions of each type will be mixed throughout the session, and many of the questions will require you to use more than just one concept in order to solve it. The majority of the questions will need to be solved using arithmetic. This area of mathematics includes the basic operations of numbers (addition, subtraction, multiplication, and division), properties and types of numbers, number theory, and counting problems.

Algebra will also be included in a good portion of the section. Topics include using polynomials, combining like terms, using laws of exponents, solving linear and quadratic equations, solving inequalities, and simplifying rational expressions.

Geometric concepts will appear in many of the questions and may be integrated with other concepts. These concepts require the knowledge and application of polygons, plane figures, right triangles, and formulas for determining the area, perimeter, volume, and surface area of an object. Each of these concepts will be discussed in detail in Chapter 22.

A portion of the questions will appear in a word-problem format with graphs, logic problems, and other discrete math areas scattered throughout the section. Remember that a few of the questions are experimental and will not be counted in your final score; however, you will not be able to tell which questions are experimental.

The Quantitative section tests your overall understanding of basic math concepts. The math presented in this section will be comparable to what you encountered in middle school and high school, and the question level may seem similar to that on the SAT® exam or ACT Assessment®. Even though the questions are presented in different formats, reviewing some fundamental topics will be very helpful. This section tests your ability to use critical thinking and reasoning skills to solve quantitative problems. You will want to review how to solve equations, how to simplify radicals, and how to calculate the volume of a cube. However, the majority of the questions will also ask you to take the problem one step further to assess how well you apply and reason through the material.

The two types of questions in the Quantitative section are problem solving and data sufficiency. You have already seen both types of questions in the pretest. Each type will be explained in more detail in the next section.

▶ About the Types of Questions

The two types of questions—problem solving and data sufficiency—each contains five answer choices. Both types of questions will be scattered throughout the section. Problem solving questions test your basic knowledge of math concepts—what you should have learned in middle school and high school. Most of these questions will ask you to take this existing knowledge and apply it to various situations. You will need to use reasoning skills to analyze the questions and determine the correct solutions. The majority of the questions will contain a multistep procedure. When answering problem-solving questions, try to eliminate improbable answers first to increase your chances of selecting the correct solution.

A Sample Problem Solving Question

Directions: Solve the problem and choose the letter indicating the best answer choice. The numbers used in this section are real numbers. The figures used are drawn to scale and lie in a plane unless otherwise noted.

Given integers as the lengths of the sides of a triangle, what is the maximum perimeter of a triangle where two of the sides measure 10 and 14?

a. 27
b. 28
c. 48
d. 47
e. 52

Answer: **d.** Use the triangle inequality, which states that the sum of the two smaller sides of a triangle must be greater than the measure of the third side. By adding the two known sides of $10 + 14 = 24$, this gives a maximum value of 23 for the third side because the side must be an integer. Since the perimeter of a polygon is the sum of its sides, the maximum perimeter must be $10 + 14 + 23 = 47$.

The other type of question in this section is data sufficiency. Data sufficiency questions give an initial question or statement followed by two statements labeled (1) and (2). Given the initial information, you must determine whether the statements offer enough data to solve the problem. The five possible answer choices are as follows:

a. Statement (1), BY ITSELF, will suffice to solve the problem, but NOT statement (2) by itself.
b. Statement (2), BY ITSELF, will suffice to solve the problem, but NOT statement (1) by itself.
c. The problem can be solved using statement (1) and statement (2) TOGETHER, but not ONLY statement (1) or statement (2).
d. The problem can be solved using EITHER statement (1) only or statement (2) only.
e. The problem CANNOT be solved using statement (1) and statement (2) TOGETHER.

This type of question measures the test taker's ability to examine and interpret a quantitative problem and distinguish between pertinent and irrelevant information. To solve this particular type of problem, the test taker will have to be able to determine at what point there is enough data to solve a problem. Since these questions are seldom used outside of the GMAT exam, it is important to familiarize yourself with the format and strategies used with this type of question as much as possible before taking the exam.

Strategies can be used when answering data sufficiency questions. For example, start off by trying to solve the question solely by using statement (1). If statement (1) contains enough information to do so, then your only choice is between **a** (statement [1] only) or **d** (each statement alone contains enough information). If statement (1) is not enough information to answer the question, your choices boil down to **b** (statement [2] only), **c** (the statements need to be used together), or **e** (the problem cannot be solved using the information from both statements, and more information is needed).

A Sample Data Sufficiency Question

Directions: The following problem contains a question followed by two statements. Select your answer using the data in statement (1) and statement (2) and determine whether they provide enough information to answer the initial question. If you are asked for the value of a quantity, the information is sufficient when it is possible to determine only one value for the quantity.

a. Statement (1), BY ITSELF, will suffice to solve the problem, but NOT statement (2) by itself.
b. Statement (2), BY ITSELF, will suffice to solve the problem, but NOT statement (1) by itself.
c. The problem can be solved using statement (1) and statement (2) TOGETHER, but not ONLY statement (1) or statement (2).
d. The problem can be solved using EITHER statement (1) only or statement (2) only.
e. The problem CANNOT be solved using statement (1) and statement (2) TOGETHER.

The numbers used are real numbers. If a figure accompanies a question, the figure will be drawn to scale according to the original question or information, but it will not necessarily be consistent with the information given in statements (1) and (2).

If x is a nonzero integer, is x positive?
(1) x^2 is positive.
(2) x^3 is positive.

Answer: **b.** Substitute possible numbers for x. If $x = 2$, then $(2)^2 = 4$. If $x = -2$, then $(-2)^2 = 4$, so statement (1) is not sufficient. Substituting into statement (2), if $x = -2$, then $(-2)^3 = (-2)(-2)(-2) = -8$; the value is negative. If $x = 2$, then $2^3 = 2 \times 2 \times 2 = 8$; the value is positive. Therefore, from statement (2), x is positive.

CHAPTER

20 ▶ Arithmetic

The following lessons are designed to review the basic mathematical concepts that you will encounter on the GMAT® Quantitative section and are divided into three major sections: arithmetic, algebra, and geometry. The lessons and corresponding questions will help you remember a lot of the primary content of middle school and high school math. Please remember that the difficulty of many of the questions is based on the manner in which the question is asked, not the mathematical concepts. These questions will focus on critical thinking and reasoning skills. Do not be intimidated by the math; you have seen most of it, if not all of it, before.

▶ Types of Numbers

You will encounter several types of numbers on the exam:

- **Real numbers.** The set of all rational and irrational numbers.
- **Rational numbers.** Any number that can be expressed as $\frac{a}{b}$, where $b \neq 0$. This really means "any number that can be written as a fraction" and includes any repeating or terminating decimals, integers, and whole numbers.

- **Irrational numbers.** Any nonrepeating, nonterminating decimal (i.e., $\sqrt{2}$, π, 0.343443444 . . .).
- **Integers.** The set of whole numbers and their opposites { . . . , –2, –1, 0, 1, 2, 3, . . . }.
- **Whole numbers.** {0, 1, 2, 3, 4, 5, 6, . . . }.
- **Natural numbers** also known as the **counting numbers.** {1, 2, 3, 4, 5, 6, 7, . . . }.

▶ Properties of Numbers

Although you will not be tested on the actual names of the properties, you should be familiar with the ways each one helps to simplify problems. You will also notice that most properties work for addition and multiplication, but not subtraction and division. If the operation is not mentioned, assume the property will not work under that operation.

Commutative Property

This property states that even though the order of the numbers changes, the answer is the same. This property works for addition and multiplication.

Examples

$a + b = b + a$	$ab = ba$
$3 + 4 = 4 + 3$	$3 \times 4 = 4 \times 3$
$7 = 7$	$12 = 12$

Associative Property

This property states that even though the grouping of the numbers changes, the result or answer is the same. This property also works for addition and multiplication.

$a + (b + c) = (a + b) + c$	$a(bc) = (ab)c$
$2 + (3 + 5) = (2 + 3) + 5$	$2 \times (3 \times 5) = (2 \times 3) \times 5$
$2 + 8 = 5 + 5$	$2 \times 15 = 6 \times 5$
$10 = 10$	$30 = 30$

Identity Property

Two identity properties exist: the Identity Property of Addition and the Identity Property of Multiplication.

Addition

Any number plus zero is itself. Zero is the additive identity element.

$a + 0 = a$ $\qquad$ $5 + 0 = 5$

MULTIPLICATION

Any number times one is itself. One is the multiplicative identity element.

$a \times 1 = a$ $\qquad$ $5 \times 1 = 5$

Inverse Property

This property is often used when you want a number to cancel out in an equation.

ADDITION

The additive inverse of any number is its opposite.

$a + (-a) = 0$ $\qquad$ $3 + (-3) = 0$

MULTIPLICATION

The multiplicative inverse of any number is its reciprocal.

$a \times \frac{1}{a} = 1$ $\qquad$ $6 \times \frac{1}{6} = 1$

Distributive Property

This property is used when two different operations appear: multiplication and addition or multiplication and subtraction. It basically states that the number being multiplied must be multiplied, or distributed, to each term within the parentheses.

$a(b + c) = ab + ac$ $\quad$ or $\quad$ $a(b - c) = ab - ac$
$5(a + 2) = 5 \times a + 5 \times 2$, which simplifies to $5a + 10$
$2(3x - 4) = 2 \times 3x - 2 \times 4$, which simplifies to $6x - 8$

► Order of Operations

The operations in a multistep expression must be completed in a specific order. This particular order can be remembered as **PEMDAS.** In any expression, evaluate in this order:

P	Parentheses/grouping symbols first
E	then Exponents
MD	Multiplication/Division in order from right to left
AS	Addition/Subtraction in order from left to right

Keep in mind that division may be done before multiplication and subtraction may be done before addition, depending on which operation is first when working from left to right.

Examples

Evaluate the following using the order of operations:

1. $2 \times 3 + 4 - 2$
2. $3^2 - 16 - (5 - 1)$
3. $[2\,(4^2 - 9) + 3] - 1$

Answers

1. $2 \times 3 + 4 - 2$

$6 + 4 - 2$	Multiply first.
$10 - 2$	Add and subtract in order from left to right.
8	

2. $3^2 - 16 + (5 - 1)$

$3^2 - 16 + (4)$	Evaluate parentheses first.
$9 - 16 + 4$	Evaluate exponents.
$-7 + 4$	Subtract and then add in order from left to right.
-3	

3. $[2\,(4^2 - 9) + 3] - 1$

$[2\,(16 - 9) + 3] - 1$	Begin with the innermost grouping symbols and follow PEMDAS. (Here, exponents are first within the parentheses.)
$[2\,(7) + 3] - 1$	Continue with the order of operations, working from the inside out (subtract within the parentheses).
$[14 + 3] - 1$	Multiply.
$[17] - 1$	Add.
16	Subtract to complete the problem.

▶ Special Types of Defined Operations

Some unfamiliar operations may appear on the GMAT exam. These questions may involve operations that use symbols like #, $, &, or @. Usually, these problems are solved by simple substitution and will only involve operations that you already know.

Example

For $a \# b$ defined as $a^2 - 2b$, what is the value of $3 \# 2$?

a. -2
b. 1
c. 2
d. 5
e. 6

For this question, use the definition of the operation as the formula and substitute the values 3 and 2 for a and b, respectively. $a^2 - 2b = 3^2 - 2(2) = 9 - 4 = 5$. The correct answer is **d**.

▶ Factors, Multiples, and Divisibility

In the following section, the principles of factors, multipliers, and divisibility are covered.

Factors

A whole number is a factor of a number if it divides into the number without a remainder. For example, 5 is a factor of 30 because $30 \div 5 = 6$ without a remainder left over.

On the GMAT exam, a factor question could look like this:

If x is a factor of y, which of the following may not represent a whole number?

a. xy

b. $\frac{x}{y}$

c. $\frac{y}{x}$

d. $\frac{yx}{x}$

e. $\frac{xy}{y}$

This is a good example of where substituting may make a problem simpler. Suppose $x = 2$ and $y = 10$ (2 is a factor of 10). Then choice **a** is 20, and choice **c** is 5. Choice **d** reduces to just y and choice **e** reduces to just x, so they will also be whole numbers. Choice **b** would be $\frac{2}{10}$, which equals $\frac{1}{5}$, which is not a whole number.

Prime Factoring

To prime factor a number, write it as the product of its prime factors. For example, the prime factorization of 24 is

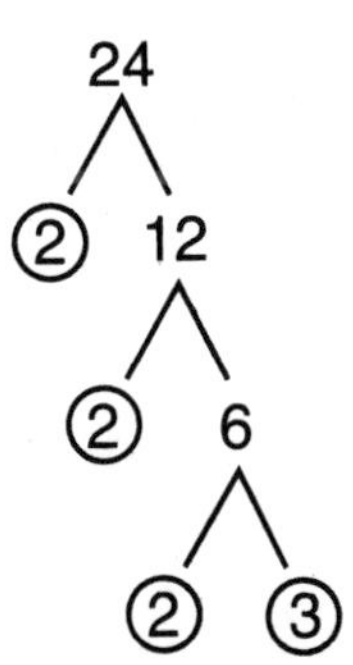

$24 = 2 \times 2 \times 2 \times 3 = 2^3 \times 3$

Greatest Common Factor (GCF)

The greatest common factor (GCF) of two numbers is the largest whole number that will divide into either number without a remainder. The GCF is often found when reducing fractions, reducing radicals, and factoring. One of the ways to find the GCF is to list all of the factors of each of the numbers and select the largest one. For example, to find the GCF of 18 and 48, list all of the factors of each:

18: 1, 2, 3, 6, 9, 18
48: 1, 2, 3, 4, 6, 8, 12, 16, 24, 48

Although a few numbers appear in both lists, the largest number that appears in both lists is 6; therefore, 6 is the greatest common factor of 18 and 48.

You can also use prime factoring to find the GCF by listing the prime factors of each number and multiplying the common prime factors together:

The prime factors of 18 are $2 \times 3 \times 3$.
The prime factors of 48 are $2 \times 2 \times 2 \times 2 \times 3$.
They both have at least one factor of 2 and one factor of 3. Thus, the GCF is $2 \times 3 = 6$.

Multiples

One number is a multiple of another if it is the result of multiplying one number by a positive integer. For example, multiples of three are generated as follows: $3 \times 1 = 3$, $3 \times 2 = 6$, $3 \times 3 = 9$, $3 \times 4 = 12$, . . . Therefore, multiples of three can be listed as {3, 6, 9, 12, 15, 18, 21, . . . }

Least Common Multiple (LCM)

The least common multiple (LCM) of two numbers is the smallest number that both numbers divide into without a remainder. The LCM is used when finding a common denominator when adding or subtracting fractions. To find the LCM of two numbers such as 6 and 15, list the multiples of each number until a common number is found in both lists.

6: 6, 12, 18, 24, 30, 36, 42, . . .
15: 15, 30, 45, . . .

As you can see, both lists could have stopped at 30; 30 is the LCM of 6 and 15. Sometimes it may be faster to list out the multiples of the larger number first and see if the smaller number divides evenly into any of those multiples. In this case, we would have realized that 6 does not divide into 15 evenly, but it does divide into 30 evenly; therefore, we found our LCM.

Divisibility Rules

To aid in locating factors and multiples, some commonly known divisibility rules make finding them a little quicker, especially without the use of a calculator.

- **Divisibility by 2.** If the number is even (the last digit, or units digit, is 0, 2, 4, 6, 8), the number is divisible by 2.
- **Divisibility by 3.** If the sum of the digits adds to a multiple of 3, the entire number is divisible by 3.
- **Divisibility by 4.** If the last two digits of the number form a number that is divisible by 4, then the entire number is divisible by 4.
- **Divisibility by 5.** If the units digit is 0 or 5, the number is divisible by 5.
- **Divisibility by 6.** If the number is divisible by both 2 and 3, the entire number is divisible by 6.
- **Divisibility by 9.** If the sum of the digits adds to a multiple of 9, the entire number is divisible by 9.
- **Divisibility by 10.** If the units digit is 0, the number is divisible by 10.

▶ Prime and Composite Numbers

In the following section, the principles of prime and composite numbers are covered.

Prime Numbers

These are natural numbers whose only factors are 1 and itself. The first ten prime numbers are 2, 3, 5, 7, 11, 13, 17, 19, 23, and 29. Two is the smallest and the only even prime number. The number 1 is neither prime nor composite.

Composite Numbers

These are natural numbers that are not prime; in other words, these numbers have more than just two factors. The number 1 is neither prime nor composite.

Relatively Prime

Two numbers are relatively prime if the GCF of the two numbers is 1. For example, if two numbers that are relatively prime are contained in a fraction, that fraction is in its simplest form. If 3 and 10 are relatively prime, then $\frac{3}{10}$ is in simplest form.

▶ Even and Odd Numbers

An even number is a number whose units digit is 0, 2, 4, 6, or 8. An odd number is a number ending in 1, 3, 5, 7, or 9. You can identify a few helpful patterns about even and odd numbers that often arise on the Quantitative section:

odd + odd = even	odd × odd = odd
even + even = even	even × even = even
even + odd = odd	even × odd = even

When problems arise that involve even and odd numbers, you can use substitution to help remember the patterns and make the problems easier to solve.

▶ Consecutive Integers

Consecutive integers are integers listed in numerical order that differ by 1. An example of three consecutive integers is 3, 4, and 5, or –11, –10, and –9. Consecutive *even* integers are numbers like 10, 12, and 14 or –22, –20, and –18. Consecutive *odd* integers are numbers like 7, 9, and 11. When they are used in word problems, it is often useful to define them as x, $x + 1$, $x + 2$, and so on for regular consecutive integers and x, $x + 2$, and $x + 4$ for even or odd consecutive integers. Note that both even and odd consecutive integers have the same algebraic representation.

▶ Absolute Value

The absolute value of a number is the distance a number is away from zero on a number line. The symbol for absolute value is two bars surrounding the number or expression. Absolute value is always positive because it is a measure of distance.

$|4| = 4$ because 4 is four units from zero on a number line.

$|-3| = 3$ because –3 is three units from zero on a number line.

▶ Operations with Real Numbers

For the quantitative exam, you will need to know how to perform basic operations with real numbers.

Integers

This is the set of whole numbers and their opposites, also known as *signed numbers*. Since negatives are involved, here are some helpful rules to follow.

Adding and Subtracting Integers

1. If you are adding and the signs are the same, add the absolute value of the numbers and keep the sign.
a. $3 + 4 = 7$ **b.** $-2 + -13 = -15$

2. If you are adding and the signs are different, subtract the absolute value of the numbers and take the sign of the number with the larger absolute value.
a. $-5 + 8 = 3$ **b.** $10 + -14 = -4$

3. If you are subtracting, change the subtraction sign to addition, and change the sign of the number following to its opposite. Then follow the rules for addition:

a. $-5 + -6 = -11$ **b.** $-12 + (+7) = -5$

Remember: When you subtract, you add the opposite.

MULTIPLYING AND DIVIDING INTEGERS

1. If an even number of negatives is used, multiply or divide as usual, and the answer is positive.

a. $-3 \times -4 = 12$ b. $(-12 \div -6) \times 3 = 6$

2. If an odd number of negatives is used, multiply or divide as usual, and the answer is negative.

a. $-15 \div 5 = -3$ **b.** $(-2 \times -4) \times -5 = -40$

This is helpful to remember when working with powers of a negative number. If the power is even, the answer is positive. If the power is odd, the answer is negative.

Fractions

A fraction is a ratio of two numbers, where the top number is the *numerator* and the bottom number is the *denominator.*

REDUCING FRACTIONS

To reduce fractions to their lowest terms, or simplest form, find the GCF of both numerator and denominator. Divide each part of the fraction by this common factor and the result is a reduced fraction. When a fraction is in reduced form, the two remaining numbers in the fraction are *relatively prime.*

a. $\frac{6}{9} = \frac{2}{3}$ **b.** $\frac{32x}{4xy} = \frac{8}{y}$

When performing operations with fractions, the important thing to remember is when you need a common denominator and when one is not necessary.

ADDING AND SUBTRACTING FRACTIONS

It is very important to remember to find the least common denominator (LCD) when adding or subtracting fractions. After this is done, you will be only adding or subtracting the numerators and keeping the common denominator as the bottom number in your answer.

a. $\frac{2}{5} + \frac{2}{3}$

$LCD = 15$

$\frac{2 \times 3}{5 \times 3} + \frac{2 \times 5}{3 \times 5}$

$\frac{6}{15} + \frac{10}{15} = \frac{16}{15}$

b. $\frac{3}{y} + \frac{4}{xy}$

$LCD = xy$

$\frac{3 \times x}{y \times x} + \frac{4}{xy} = \frac{3x + 4}{xy}$

Multiplying Fractions

It is not necessary to get a common denominator when multiplying fractions. To perform this operation, you can simply multiply across the numerators and then the denominators. If possible, you can also cross-cancel common factors if they are present, as in example **b.**

a. $\frac{1}{3} \times \frac{2}{3} = \frac{2}{9}$

b. $\frac{12}{25} \times \frac{5}{3} = \frac{\cancel{12}^{4}}{\cancel{25}_{5}} \times \frac{\cancel{5}^{1}}{\cancel{3}} = \frac{4}{5}$

Dividing Fractions

A common denominator is also not needed when dividing fractions, and the procedure is similar to multiplying. Since dividing by a fraction is the same as multiplying by its reciprocal, leave the first fraction alone, change the division to multiplication, and change the number being divided by to its reciprocal.

a. $\frac{4}{5} \div \frac{4}{3} = \frac{\cancel{4}^{1}}{5} \times \frac{3}{\cancel{4}_{1}} = \frac{3}{5}$

b. $\frac{3x}{y} \div \frac{12x}{5xy} = \frac{\cancel{3}^{1}\cancel{x}^{1}}{\cancel{y}_{1}} \times \frac{5x\cancel{y}^{1}}{\cancel{12}_{4}\cancel{x}_{1}} = \frac{5x}{4}$

Decimals

The following chart reviews the place value names used with decimals. Here are the decimal place names for the number 6384.2957.

6	3	8	4	.	2	9	5	7
THOUSANDS	HUNDREDS	TENS	ONES	DECIMAL POINT	TENTHS	HUNDREDTHS	THOUSANDTHS	TEN THOUSANDTHS

It is also helpful to know of the fractional equivalents to some commonly used decimals and percents, especially because you will not be able to use a calculator.

$0.1 = 10\% = \frac{1}{10}$

$0.\overline{3} = 33\frac{1}{3}\% = \frac{1}{3}$

$0.4 = 40\% = \frac{2}{5}$

$0.5 = 50\% = \frac{1}{2}$

$0.\overline{6} = 66\frac{2}{3}\% = \frac{2}{3}$

$0.75 = 75\% = \frac{3}{4}$

Adding and Subtracting Decimals

The important thing to remember about adding and subtracting decimals is that the decimal places must be lined up.

a. $\begin{array}{r} 3.6 \\ +5.61 \\ \hline 9.21 \end{array}$ **b.** $\begin{array}{r} 5.984 \\ -2.34 \\ \hline 3.644 \end{array}$

Multiplying Decimals

Multiply as usual, and count the total number of decimal places in the original numbers. That total will be the amount of decimal places to count over from the right in the final answer.

$$\begin{array}{r} 34.5 \\ \times 5.4 \\ \hline 1,380 \\ +\ 17,250 \\ \hline 18,630 \end{array}$$

Since the original numbers have two decimal places, the final answer is 186.30 or 186.3 by counting over two places from the right in the answer.

Dividing Decimals

Start by moving any decimal in the number being divided by to change the number into a whole number. Then move the decimal in the number being divided into the same number of places. Divide as usual and keep track of the decimal place.

$1.53 \div 5.1$

$$5.1\overline{)1.53} \Rightarrow \begin{array}{r} .3 \\ 51\overline{)15.3} \\ -15.3 \\ \hline 0 \end{array}$$

Ratios

A *ratio* is a comparison of two or more numbers with the same unit label. A ratio can be written in three ways:

$a: b$

a to b

or $\frac{a}{b}$

A *rate* is similar to a ratio except that the unit labels are different. For example, the expression 50 miles per hour is a rate—50 miles/1 hour.

Proportion

Two ratios set equal to each other is called a *proportion.* To solve a proportion, cross-multiply.

$$\frac{4}{5} = \frac{10}{x}$$

Cross multiply to get:

$$4x = 50$$

$$\frac{4x}{4} = \frac{50}{4}$$

$$x = 12\frac{1}{2}$$

Percent

A ratio that compares a number to 100 is called a *percent.*

To change a decimal to a percent, move the decimal two places to the right.

$.25 = 25\%$

$.105 = 10.5\%$

$.3 = 30\%$

To change a percent to a decimal, move the decimal two places to the left.

$36\% = .36$

$125\% = 1.25$

$8\% = .08$

Some word problems that use percents are commission and rate-of-change problems, which include sales and interest problems. The general proportion that can be set up to solve this type of word problem is $\frac{\text{Part}}{\text{Whole}} = \frac{\%}{100}$, although more specific proportions will also be shown.

Commission

John earns 4.5% commission on all of his sales. What is his commission if his sales total \$235.12?

To find the part of the sales John earns, set up a proportion:

$$\frac{\text{part}}{\text{whole}} = \frac{\text{change}}{\text{original cost}} = \frac{\%}{100}$$

$$\frac{x}{235.12} = \frac{4.5}{100}$$

Cross multiply.

$$100x = 1058.04$$

$$\frac{100x}{100} = \frac{1058.04}{100}$$

$$x = 10.5804 \approx \$10.58$$

Rate of Change

If a pair of shoes is marked down from \$24 to \$18, what is the percent of decrease?

To solve the percent, set up the following proportion:

$$\frac{\text{part}}{\text{whole}} = \frac{\text{change}}{\text{original cost}} = \frac{\%}{100}$$

$$\frac{24 - 18}{24} = \frac{x}{100}$$

$\frac{6}{24} = \frac{x}{100}$ Cross multiply.

$$24x = 600$$

$$\frac{24x}{24} = \frac{600}{24}$$

$x = 25\%$ decrease in price

Note that the number 6 in the proportion setup represents the discount, not the sale price.

Simple Interest

Pat deposited \$650 into her bank account. If the interest rate is 3% annually, how much money will she have in the bank after 10 years?

Interest = Principal (amount invested) × Interest rate (as a decimal) × Time (years) or $I = PRT$.

Substitute the values from the problem into the formula $I = (650)(.03)(10)$.

Multiply $\quad I = 195$

Since she will make \$195 in interest over 10 years, she will have a total of \$195 + \$650 = \$845 in her account.

Exponents

The exponent of a number tells how many times to use that number as a factor. For example, in the expression 4^3, 4 is the *base number* and 3 is the *exponent,* or *power.* Four should be used as a factor three times: $4^3 = 4 \times 4 \times 4 = 64$.

Any number raised to a negative exponent is the reciprocal of that number raised to the positive exponent: $3^{-2} = (\frac{1}{3})^2 = \frac{1}{9}$

Any number to a fractional exponent is the root of the number: $25^{\frac{1}{2}} = \sqrt{25} = 5$

$$27^{\frac{1}{3}} = \sqrt[3]{27} = 3$$

$$256^{\frac{1}{4}} = \sqrt[4]{256} = 4$$

Any nonzero number with zero as the exponent is equal to one: $140^0 = 1$.

Square Roots and Perfect Squares

Any number that is the product of two of the same factors is a perfect square.

$1 \times 1 = 1, 2 \times 2 = 4, 3 \times 3 = 9, 4 \times 4 = 16, 5 \times 5 = 25, \ldots$

Knowing the first 20 perfect squares by heart may be helpful. You probably already know at least the first ten.

1, 4, 9, 16, 25, 36, 49, 64, 81, 100, 121, 144, 169, 196, 225, 256, 289, 324, 361, 400

Radicals

A square root symbol is also known as a radical sign. The number inside the radical is the radicand.

To simplify a radical, find the largest perfect square factor of the radicand

$\sqrt{32} = \sqrt{16} \times \sqrt{2}$

Take the square root of that number and leave any remaining numbers under the radical.

$\sqrt{32} = 4\sqrt{2}$

To add or subtract square roots, you must have like terms. In other words, the radicand must be the same. If you have like terms, simply add or subtract the coefficients and keep the radicand the same.

Examples

1. $3\sqrt{2} + 2\sqrt{2} = 5\sqrt{2}$

2. $4\sqrt{2} - \sqrt{2} = 3\sqrt{2}$

3. $6\sqrt{2} + 3\sqrt{5}$ cannot be combined because they are not like terms.

Here are some rules to remember when multiplying and dividing radicals:

Multiplying: $\sqrt{x} \times \sqrt{y} = \sqrt{xy}$

$\sqrt{2} \times \sqrt{3} = \sqrt{6}$

Dividing: $\sqrt{\frac{x}{y}} = \frac{\sqrt{x}}{\sqrt{y}}$

$\sqrt{\frac{25}{16}} = \frac{\sqrt{25}}{\sqrt{16}} = \frac{5}{4}$

Counting Problems and Probability

The probability of an event is the number of ways the event can occur, divided by the total possible outcomes.

$$P(E) = \frac{\text{Number of ways the event can occur}}{\text{Total possible outcomes}}$$

The probability that an event will NOT occur is equal to $1 - P(E)$.

The *counting principle* says that the product of the number of choices equals the total number of possibilities. For example, if you have two choices for an appetizer, four choices for a main course, and five choices for dessert, you can choose from a total of $2 \times 4 \times 5 = 40$ possible meals.

The symbol $n!$ represents *n factorial* and is often used in probability and counting problems. $n! = (n) \times (n-1) \times (n-2) \times \ldots \times 1$. For example, $5! = 5 \times 4 \times 3 \times 2 \times 1 = 120$.

Permutations and Combinations

Permutations are the total number of arrangements or orders of objects when the order matters. The formula is ${}_nP_r = \frac{n!}{(n-r)!}$, where n is the total number of things to choose from and r is the number of things to arrange at a time. Some examples where permutations are used would be calculating the total number of different arrangements of letters and numbers on a license plate or the total number of ways three different people can finish first, second, and third in a race.

Combinations are the total number of arrangements or orders of objects when the order does not matter. The formula is ${}_nC_r = \frac{n!}{r!(n-r)!}$, where n is the total number of objects to choose from and r is the size of the group to choose. An example where a combination is used would be selecting people for a committee.

Statistics

Mean is the average of a set of numbers. To calculate the mean, add all the numbers in the set and divide by the number of numbers in the set. Find the mean of 2, 3, 5, 10, and 15.

$$\frac{2 + 3 + 5 + 10 + 15}{5} = \frac{35}{5}$$

The mean is 7.

Median is the middle number in a set. To find the median, first arrange the numbers in order and then find the middle number. If two numbers share the middle, find the average of those two numbers.

Find the median of 12, 10, 2, 3, 15, and 12.
First put the numbers in order: 2, 3, 10, 12, 12, and 15.

Since an even number of numbers is given, two numbers share the middle (10 and 12). Find the average of 10 and 12 to find the median.

$$\frac{10 + 12}{2} = \frac{22}{2}$$

The median is 11.

Mode is the number that appears the most in a set of numbers and is usually the easiest to find.

Find the mode of 33, 32, 34, 99, 66, 34, 12, 33, and 34.
Since 34 appears the most (three times), it is the mode of the set.

NOTE: It is possible for there to be no mode or several modes in a set.
Range is the difference between the largest and the smallest numbers in the set.

Find the range of the set 14, –12, 13, 10, 22, 23, –3, 10.
Since –12 is the smallest number in the set and 23 is the largest, find the difference by subtracting them.
23 – (–12) = 23 + (+12) = 35. The range is 35.

CHAPTER

21 ▶ Algebra

▶ Translating Expressions and Equations

Translating sentences and word problems into mathematical expressions and equations is similar to translating two different languages. The key words are the vocabulary that tells what operations should be done and in what order. Use the following chart to help you with some of the key words used on the GMAT® quantitative section.

$+$	$-$	$\times$	$\div$	$=$
SUM MORE THAN ADDED TO PLUS INCREASED BY	DIFFERENCE LESS THAN SUBTRACTED FROM MINUS DECREASED BY FEWER THAN	PRODUCT TIMES MULTIPLIED BY	QUOTIENT DIVIDED BY	EQUAL TO TOTAL

The following is an example of a problem where knowing the key words is necessary:

Fifteen less than five times a number is equal to the product of ten and the number. What is the number?
Translate the sentence piece by piece:

Fifteen less than five times the number	equals	the product of 10 and x.
$5x - 15$	$=$	$10x$

The equation is	$5x - 15 = 10x$
Subtract $5x$ from both sides:	$5x - 5x - 15 = 10x - 5x$
Divide both sides by 5:	$\frac{-15}{5} = \frac{5x}{5}$
	$-3 = x$

It is important to realize that the key words *less than* tell you to subtract from the number and the key word *product* reminds you to multiply.

▶ Combining Like Terms and Polynomials

In algebra, you use a letter to represent an unknown quantity. This letter is called the *variable.* The number preceding the variable is called the *coefficient.* If a number is not written in front of the variable, the coefficient is understood to be one. If any coefficient or variable is raised to a power, this number is the *exponent.*

$3x$	Three is the coefficient and x is the variable.
xy	One is the coefficient, and both x and y are the variables.
$-2x^3y$	Negative two is the coefficient, x and y are the variables, and three is the exponent of x.

Another important concept to recognize is *like terms.* In algebra, like terms are expressions that have exactly the same variable(s) to the same power and can be combined easily by adding or subtracting the coefficients.

Examples

$3x + 5x$	These terms are like terms, and the sum is $8x$.
$4x^2y + -10x^2y$	These terms are also like terms, and the sum is $-6x^2y$.
$2xy^2 + 9x^2y$	These terms are not like terms because the variables, taken with their powers, are not exactly the same. They cannot be combined.

A *polynomial* is the sum or difference of many terms and some have specific names:

$8x^2$	This is a *monomial* because there is one term.
$3x + 2y$	This is a *binomial* because there are two terms.
$4x^2 + 2x - 6$	This is a *trinomial* because there are three terms.

▶ Laws of Exponents

- When multiplying like bases, add the exponents: $x^2 \times x^3 = x^{2+3} = x^5$
- When dividing like bases, subtract the exponents: $\frac{x^5}{x^2} = x^{5-2} = x^3$
- When raising a power to another power, multiply the exponents: $(x^2)^3 = x^{2\times 3} = x^6$
- Remember that a fractional exponent means the root: $\sqrt{x} = x^{\frac{1}{2}}$ and $\sqrt[3]{x} = x^{\frac{1}{3}}$

The following is an example of a question involving exponents:

Solve for x: $2^{x+2} = 8^3$.

a. 1
b. 3
c. 5
d. 7
e. 9

The correct answer is **d.** To solve this type of equation, each side must have the same base. Since 8 can be expressed as 2^3, then $8^3 = (2^3)^3 = 2^9$. Both sides of the equation have a common base of 2, so set the exponents equal to each other to solve for x. $x + 2 = 9$. So, $x = 7$.

▶ Solving Linear Equations of One Variable

When solving this type of equation, it is important to remember two basic properties:

- If a number is added to or subtracted from one side of an equation, it must be added to or subtracted from the other side.
- If a number is multiplied or divided on one side of an equation, it must also be multiplied or divided on the other side.

Linear equations can be solved in four basic steps:

1. Remove parentheses by using distributive property.
2. Combine like terms on the same side of the equal sign.
3. Move the variables to one side of the equation.
4. Solve the one- or two-step equation that remains, remembering the two previous properties.

Examples

Solve for x in each of the following equations:

a. $3x - 5 = 10$

Add 5 to both sides of the equation: $3x - 5 + 5 = 10 + 5$

Divide both sides by 3: $\frac{3x}{3} = \frac{15}{3}$

$x = 5$

b. $3(x - 1) + x = 1$

Use distributive property to remove parentheses:

$3x - 3 + x = 1$

Combine like terms: $4x - 3 = 1$

Add 3 to both sides of the equation: $4x - 3 + 3 = 1 + 3$

Divide both sides by 4: $\frac{4x}{4} = \frac{4}{4}$

$x = 1$

c. $8x - 2 = 8 + 3x$

Subtract $3x$ from both sides of the equation to move the variables to one side:

$8x - 3x - 2 = 8 + 3x - 3x$

Add 2 to both sides of the equation: $5x - 2 + 2 = 8 + 2$

Divide both sides by 5: $\frac{5x}{5} = \frac{10}{5}$

$x = 2$

▶ Solving Literal Equations

A literal equation is an equation that contains two or more variables. It may be in the form of a formula. You may be asked to solve a literal equation for one variable in terms of the other variables. Use the same steps that you used to solve linear equations.

Example

Solve for x in terms of a and b: $2x + b = a$

Subtract b from both sides of the equation: $2x + b - b = a - b$

Divide both sides of the equation by 2: $\frac{2x}{2} = \frac{a-b}{2}$

$x = \frac{a-b}{2}$

▶ Solving Inequalities

Solving inequalities is very similar to solving equations. The four symbols used when solving inequalities are as follows:

- $<$ is less than
- $>$ is greater than
- $\leq$ is less than or equal to
- $\geq$ is greater than or equal to

When solving inequalities, there is one catch: If you are multiplying or dividing each side by a negative number, you must reverse the direction of the inequality symbol. For example, solve the inequality $-3x + 6 \leq 18$:

1. First subtract 6 from both sides: $-3x + 6 - 6 \leq 18 - 6$
2. Then divide both sides by –3: $\frac{-3x}{-3} \leq \frac{12}{-3}$
3. The inequality symbol now changes: $x \geq -4$

Solving Compound Inequalities

A compound inequality is a combination of two inequalities. For example, take the compound inequality $-3 < x + 1 < 4$. To solve this, subtract 1 from all parts of the inequality. $-3 - 1 < x + 1 - 1 < 4 - 1$. Simplify. $-4 < x < 3$. Therefore, the solution set is all numbers between –4 and 3, not including –4 and 3.

▶ Multiplying and Factoring Polynomials

When multiplying by a monomial, use the distributive property to simplify.

Examples

Multiply each of the following:

1. $(6x^3)(5xy^2) = 30x^4y^2$ (Remember that $x = x^1$.)

2. $2x(x^2 - 3) = 2x^3 - 6x$

3. $x^3(3x^2 + 4x - 2) = 3x^5 + 4x^4 - 2x^3$

When multiplying two binomials, use an acronym called **FOIL.**

F Multiply the **f**irst terms in each set of parentheses.

O Multiply the **o**uter terms in the parentheses.

I Multiply the **i**nner terms in the parentheses.

L Multiply the **l**ast terms in the parentheses.

Examples

1. $(x - 1)(x + 2) = x^2 + 2x - 1x - 2 = x^2 + x - 2$

F O I L

2. $(a - b)^2 = (a - b)(a - b) = a^2 - ab - ab - b^2$

F O I L

Factoring Polynomials

Factoring polynomials is the reverse of multiplying them together.

Examples

Factor the following:

1. $2x^3 + 2 = 2(x^3 + 1)$ Take out the common factor of 2.

2. $x^2 - 9 = (x + 3)(x - 3)$ Factor the difference between two perfect squares.

3. $2x^2 + 5x - 3 = (2x - 1)(x + 3)$ Factor using FOIL backwards.

4. $2x^2 - 50 = 2(x^2 - 25) = 2(x + 5)(x - 5)$ First take out the common factor and then factor the difference between two squares.

▶ Solving Quadratic Equations

An equation in the form $y = ax^2 + bx + c$, where a, b, and c are real numbers, is a quadratic equation. In other words, the greatest exponent on x is two.

Quadratic equations can be solved in two ways: factoring, if it is possible for that equation, or using the quadratic formula.

By Factoring

In order to factor the quadratic equation, it first needs to be in standard form. This form is $y = \mathbf{a}x^2 + \mathbf{b}x + \mathbf{c}$. In most cases, the factors of the equations involve two numbers whose sum is **b** and product is **c**.

Examples

Solve for x in the following equation:

1. $x^2 - 25 = 0$

This equation is already in standard form. This equation is a special case; it is the difference between two perfect squares. To factor this, find the square root of both terms.

The square root of the first term x^2 is x.

The square root of the second term 25 is 5.

Then two factors are $x - 5$ and $x + 5$.

The equation	$x^2 - 25 = 0$
then becomes	$(x - 5)(x + 5) = 0$
Set each factor equal to zero and solve	$x - 5 = 0$ or $x + 5 = 0$
	$x = 5$ or $x = -5$

The solution is $\{5, -5\}$.

2. $x^2 + 6x = -9$

This equation needs to be put into standard form by adding 9 to both sides of the equation. $x^2 + 6x + 9 = -9 + 9$

$$x^2 + 6x + 9 = 0$$

The factors of this trinomial will be two numbers whose sum is 6 and whose product is 9. The factors are $x + 3$ and $x + 3$ because $3 + 3 = 6$ and $3 \times 3 = 9$.

The equation becomes	$(x + 3)(x + 3) = 0$
Set each factor equal to zero and solve	$x + 3 = 0$ or $x + 3 = 0$
	$x = -3$ or $x = -3$

Because both factors were the same, this was a perfect square trinomial. The solution is $\{-3\}$.

3. $x^2 = 12 + x$

This equation needs to be put into standard form by subtracting 12 and x from both sides of the equation. $x^2 - x - 12 = 12 - 12 + x - x$

$$x^2 - x - 12 = 0$$

Since the sum of 3 and –4 is –1, and their product is –12, the equation factors to $(x + 3)(x - 4) = 0$

Set each factor equal to zero and solve: $x + 3 = 0$ or $x - 4 = 0$

$x = -3$ or $x = 4$

The solution is $\{-3, 4\}$.

By Quadratic Formula

Solving by using the quadratic formula will work for any quadratic equation, especially those that are not factorable.

Solve for x:

$x^2 + 4x = 1$

Put the equation in standard form. $x^2 + 4x - 1 = 0$

Since this equation is not factorable, use the quadratic formula by identifying the value of a, b, and c and then substituting it into the formula. For this particular equation, $a = 1$, $b = 4$, and $c = -1$.

$$x = \frac{-b \pm \sqrt{b^2 - 4ac}}{2a}$$

$$x = \frac{-4 \pm \sqrt{4^2 - 4(1)(-1)}}{2(1)}$$

$$x = \frac{-4 \pm \sqrt{16 + 4}}{2}$$

$$x = \frac{-4 \pm \sqrt{20}}{2}$$

$$x = \frac{-4}{2} \pm \frac{2\sqrt{5}}{2}$$

$$x = -2 \pm \sqrt{5}$$

The solution is $\{-2 + \sqrt{5}, -2 - \sqrt{5}\}$.

The following is an example of a word problem incorporating quadratic equations:

A rectangular pool has a width of 25 feet and a length of 30 feet. A deck with a uniform width surrounds it. If the area of the deck and the pool together is 1,254 square feet, what is the width of the deck?

Begin by drawing a picture of the situation. The picture could be similar to the following figure.

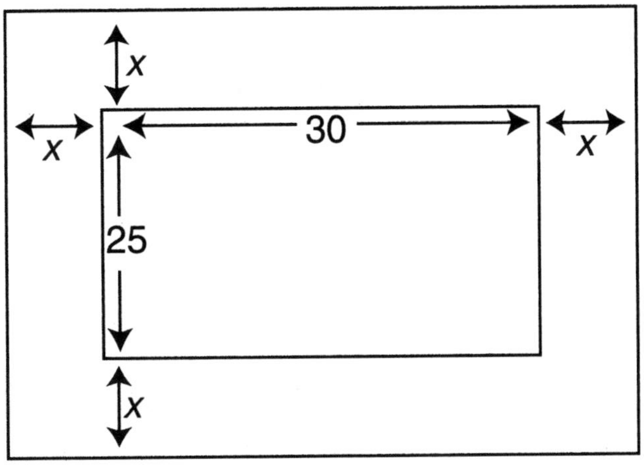

Since you know the area of the entire figure, write an equation that uses this information. Since we are trying to find the width of the deck, let $x =$ the width of the deck. Therefore, $x + x + 25$ or $2x + 25$ is the width of the entire figure. In the same way, $x + x + 30$ or $2x + 30$ is the length of the entire figure.

The area of a rectangle is length × width, so use $A = l \times w$.

Substitute into the equation:	$1{,}254 = (2x + 30)(2x + 25)$
Multiply using FOIL:	$1{,}254 = 4x^2 + 50x + 60x + 750$
Combine like terms:	$1{,}254 = 4x^2 + 110x + 750$
Subtract 1,254 from both sides:	$1{,}254 - 1{,}254 = 4x^2 + 110x + 750 - 1{,}254$
	$0 = 4x^2 + 110x - 504$
Divide each term by 2:	$0 = 2x^2 + 55x - 252$
Factor the trinomial:	$0 = (2x + 63)(x - 4)$
Set each factor equal to 0 and solve	$2x + 63 = 0$ or $x - 4 = 0$
	$2x = -63 \quad x = 4$
	$x = -31.5$

Since we are solving for a length, the solution of –31.5 must be rejected. The width of the deck is 4 feet.

▶ Rational Expressions and Equations

Rational expressions and equations involve fractions. Since dividing by zero is undefined, it is important to know when an expression is undefined.

The fraction $\frac{5}{x-1}$ is undefined when the denominator $x - 1 = 0$; therefore, $x = 1$.

You may be asked to perform various operations on rational expressions. See the following examples.

Examples

1. Simplify $\frac{x^2b}{x^3b^2}$.

2. Simplify $\frac{x^2 - 9}{3x - 9}$.

3. Multiply $\frac{4x}{x^2 - 16} \times \frac{x + 4}{2x^2}$.

4. Divide $\frac{a^2 + 2a}{a^2 + 3a + 2} \div \frac{a^2 - 3a}{2a + 2}$.

5. Add $\frac{1}{xy} + \frac{3}{y}$.

6. Subtract $\frac{x + 6}{x} - \frac{x - 2}{3x}$.

7. Solve $\frac{2}{3}x + \frac{1}{6}x = \frac{1}{4}$.

8. Solve $\frac{1}{x} = \frac{1}{4} + \frac{1}{6}$.

Answers

1. $\frac{\cancel{x^2}\cancel{b}}{\cancel{x^3}\cancel{b^2}} = \frac{1}{xb}$

2. $\frac{(x + 3)\cancel{(x - 3)}}{3\cancel{(x - 3)}} = \frac{(x + 3)}{3}$

3. $\frac{\cancel{4}x\cancel{(x + 4)}}{\cancel{2}\cancel{x^2}(x - 4)\cancel{(x + 4)}} = \frac{2}{x(x - 4)}$

4. $\frac{\cancel{a}\cancel{(a + 2)}}{\cancel{(a + 1)}\cancel{(a + 2)}} \times \frac{2\cancel{(a + 1)}}{\cancel{a}(a - 3)} = \frac{2}{a - 3}$

5. $\frac{1 + 3x}{xy}$

6. $\frac{3x + 18 - x + 2}{3x} = \frac{2x + 20}{3x}$

7. Multiply each term by the LCD = 12.

$$8x + 2x = 3$$
$$10x = 3$$
$$x = \frac{10}{3}$$

8. Multiply each term by the LCD = 12*x*.

$$3x + 2x = 12$$
$$5x = 12$$
$$x = \frac{12}{5} = 2.4$$

▶ Coordinate Graphing

The coordinate plane is divided into four quadrants that are created by the intersection of two perpendicular signed number lines: the *x*- and *y*-axes. The quadrants are numbered I, II, III, and IV as shown in the diagram.

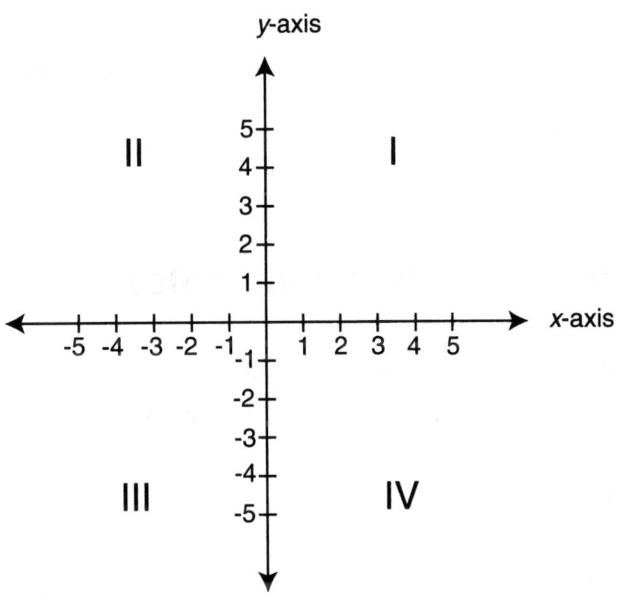

Each location in the plane is named by a point (*x*, *y*). These numbers are called the *coordinates* of the point. Each point can be found by starting at the intersection of the axes, the origin, and moving *x* units to the right or left and *y* units up or down. Positive directions are to the right and up and negative directions are to the left and down.

When graphing linear equations (slope and *y*-intercept), use the $y = mx + b$ form, where *m* represents the slope of the line and *b* represents the *y*-intercept.

Slope

The *slope* between two points (x_1, y_1) and (x_2, y_2) can be found by using the following formula:

$$\frac{\text{change in } y}{\text{change in } x} = \frac{y_1 - y_2}{x_1 - x_2}$$

Here are a few helpful facts about slope and graphing linear equations:

- Lines that slant up to the right have a positive slope.
- Lines that slant up to the left have a negative slope.
- Horizontal lines have a slope of zero.
- Vertical lines have an undefined slope or no slope.
- Two lines with the same slope are parallel and will never intersect.
- Two lines that have slopes that are negative reciprocals of each other are perpendicular.

To find the *midpoint* between any two points (x_1, y_1) and (x_2, y_2), use the following formula:

$$\left(\frac{x_1 + x_2}{2}, \frac{y_1 + y_2}{2}\right)$$

To find the *distance* between any two points (x_1, y_1) and (x_2, y_2), use the following formula:

$$\sqrt{(x_1 - x_2)^2 + (y_1 - y_2)^2}$$

▶ Systems of Equations with Two Variables

When solving a system of equations, you are finding the value or values where two or more equations equal each other. This can be done in two ways algebraically: by elimination and by substitution.

Elimination Method

Solve the system $x - y = 6$ and $2x + 3y = 7$.

Put the equations one above the other, lining up the *x*s, *y*s, and the equal sign.

$$\begin{aligned} x - y &= 6 \\ 2x + 3y &= 7 \end{aligned}$$

Multiply the first equation by –2 so that the coefficients of x are opposites. This will allow the xs to cancel out in the next step. Make sure that ALL terms are multiplied by –2. The second equation remains the same.

$$-2\,(x - y = 6) \Rightarrow -2x + 2y = -12$$
$$2x + 3y = 7 \Rightarrow 2x + 3y = 7$$

Combine the new equations vertically.

$$\begin{aligned} -2x + 2y &= -12 \\ 2x + 3y &= 7 \\ 5y &= -5 \end{aligned}$$

Divide both sides by 5.

$$\frac{5y}{5} = \frac{-5}{5}$$

$$y = -1$$

To complete the problem, solve for x by substituting –1 for y into one of the original equations.

$$\begin{aligned} x - y &= 6 \\ x - (-1) &= 6 \\ x + 1 &= 6 \\ x + 1 - 1 &= 6 - 1 \\ x &= 5 \end{aligned}$$

The solution to the system is $x = 5$ and $y = -1$, or $(5, -1)$.

Substitution Method

Solve the system $x + 2y = 5$ and $y = -2x + 7$

Substitute the second equation into the first for y.

$$x + 2(-2x + 7) = 5$$

Use distributive property to remove the parentheses.

$$x + -4x + 14 = 5$$

Combine like terms. Remember $x = 1x$.

$-3x + 14 = 5$

Subtract 14 from both sides and then divide by -3.

$-3x + 14 - 14 = 5 - 14$

$\frac{-3x}{-3} = \frac{-9}{-3}$

$x = 3$

To complete the problem, solve for y by substituting 3 for x in one of the original equations.

$y = -2x + 7$
$y = -2\,(3) + 7$
$y = -6 + 7$
$y = 1$

The solution to the system is $x = 3$ and $y = 1$, or $(3, 1)$.

▶ Problem Solving with Word Problems

You will encounter a variety of different types of word problems on the GMAT quantitative section. To help with this type of problem, first begin by figuring out what you need to solve for and defining your variable as that unknown. Then write and solve an equation that matches the question asked.

Mixture Problems

How many pounds of coffee that costs \$4.00 per pound need to be mixed with 10 pounds of coffee that costs \$6.40 per pound to create a mixture of coffee that costs \$5.50 per pound?

a. 4
b. 6
c. 8
d. 10
e. 16

For this type of question, remember that the total amount spent in each case will be the price per pound times how many pounds are in the mixture. Therefore, if you let x = the number of pounds of \$4.00 coffee, then \$4.00(x) is the amount of money spent on \$4.00 coffee, \$6.40(10) is the amount spent on \$6.40 coffee, and \$5.50(x + 10) is the total amount spent. Write an equation that adds the first two amounts and sets it equal to the total amount.

$$4.00(x) + 6.40(10) = 5.50(x + 10)$$

Multiply through the equation: $4x + 64 = 5.5x + 55$

Subtract $4x$ from both sides: $4x - 4x + 64 = 5.5x - 4x + 55$

Subtract 55 from both sides: $64 - 55 = 1.5x + 55 - 55$

Divide both sides by 1.5: $\frac{9}{1.5} = \frac{1.5x}{1.5}$

$6 = x$

You need 6 pounds of the \$4.00 per pound coffee. The correct answer is **b**.

Distance Problems

Most problems that involve motion or traveling will probably use the formula *distance* = *rate*×*time.*

Wendy drove 4 hours in a car to reach a conference she was attending. On her return trip, she followed the same route but the trip took her $1\frac{1}{2}$ hours longer. If she drove 220 miles to conference, how much slower was her average speed on the return trip?

a. 10
b. 15
c. 25
d. 40
e. 55

Use the formula *distance* = *rate* × *time* and convert it to $\frac{distance}{time}$ = *rate*. Remember that the distance was 220 miles for each part of the trip. Since it took her 4 hours to reach the conference, then $4 + 1\frac{1}{2} = 5\frac{1}{2}$ hours for the return trip. $\frac{220}{5.5}$ = 40 miles per hour. However, the question did not ask for the speed on the way back; it asked for the difference between the speed on the way there and the speed on the way home. The speed on the way there would be $\frac{220}{4}$ = 55 miles per hour and 55 – 40 = 15 miles per hour slower on the return trip. The correct answer is **b**.

Ratio Word Problems

You can often use the ratio to help.

> Three-fifths of the employees at Company A work overtime each week and the other employees do not. What is the ratio of employees who do not work overtime to the employees that do?
> **a.** 2 to 5
> **b.** 3 to 5
> **c.** 2 to 3
> **d.** 3 to 2
> **e.** 5 to 2

This is a case where the part is the employees who work overtime and the whole is the total number of employees. Using $\frac{\text{Part}}{\text{Whole}} : \frac{3}{5} = \frac{\text{employees who work overtime}}{\text{total employees}}$. Then this must imply that $\frac{2}{5} = \frac{\text{employees who do not work overtime}}{\text{total employees}}$. Therefore, the ratio $\frac{2}{3} = \frac{\text{employees who do not work overtime}}{\text{employees who do not work overtime}}$, which is equivalent to choice **c**. Be careful; you were not looking for the ratio of employees who do not work overtime to the total employees, which would have been choice **a**.

Work Problems

For this particular type of problem, think about how much of a job will be completed in one hour.

> Jason can mow a lawn in 2 hours. Ciera can mow the same lawn in 4 hours. If they work together, how many hours will it take them to mow the same lawn?
> **a.** 1 hour 20 minutes
> **b.** 1 hour 30 minutes
> **c.** 1 hour 45 minutes
> **d.** 2 hours 20 minutes
> **e.** 3 hours

Think about how much of the lawn each person completes individually. Since Jason can finish in 2 hours, in 1 hour he completes $\frac{1}{2}$ of the lawn. Since Ciera can finish in 4 hours, then in 1 hour she completes $\frac{1}{4}$ of the lawn. If we let $x =$ the time it takes both Jason and Ciera working together, then $\frac{1}{x}$ is the amount of the lawn they finish in 1 hour working together. Then use the equation $\frac{1}{2} = \frac{1}{4} = \frac{1}{x}$ and solve for x.

$$\frac{1}{2} = \frac{1}{4} = \frac{1}{x}$$

Multiply each term by the LCD of $4x$: $4x(\frac{1}{2}) + 4x(\frac{1}{4}) = 4x(\frac{1}{x})$

The equation becomes $2x + x = 4$
Combine like terms: $3x = 4$

Divide each side by 3: $\frac{3x}{3} = \frac{4}{3}$

Therefore $x = 1\frac{1}{3}$ hours

Since $\frac{1}{3}$ of an hour is $\frac{1}{3}$ of 60 minutes, which is 20 minutes, the correct answer is **a**.

▶ Functions

Functions are a special type of equation often in the form $f(x)$. Suppose you are given a function such as $f(x) = 3x + 2$. To evaluate $f(4)$, substitute 4 into the function for x.

$$f(x) = 3x + 2$$
$$f(4) = 3(4) + 2$$
$$= 12 + 2$$
$$= 14$$

CHAPTER

22 Geometry

This section reviews some of the terms that you should be familiar with for the Quantitative section. Be aware that the test will probably not ask you for a particular definition; instead, it will ask you to apply the concept to a specific situation. An understanding of the vocabulary involved will help you do this. Here are a few basic terms:

- A **point** is a location in a plane.
- A **line** is an infinite set of points contained in a straight path.
- A **line segment** is part of a line; a segment can be measured.
- A **ray** is an infinite set of points that start at an endpoint and continue in a straight path in one direction only.
- A **plane** is a two-dimensional flat surface.

► Angles

Two rays with a common endpoint, called a *vertex*, form an angle. The following figures show the different types of angles:

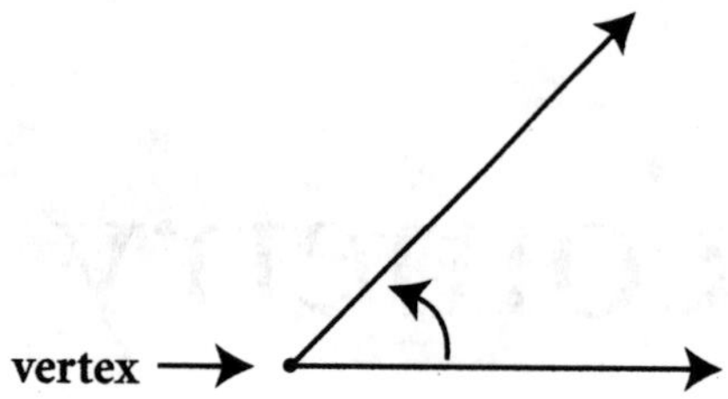

Acute
The measure is between 0 and 90 degrees.

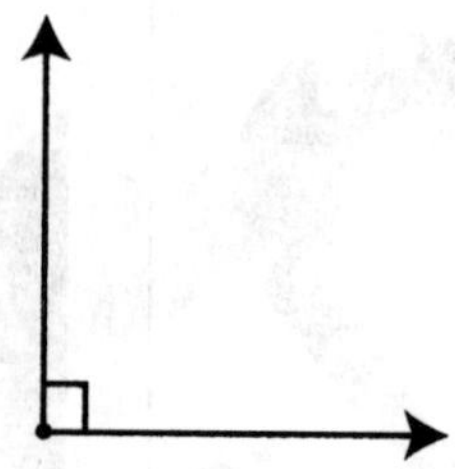

Right
The measure is equal to 90 degrees.

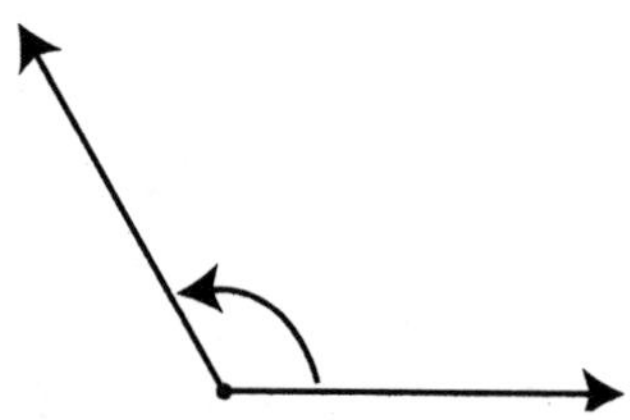

Obtuse
The measure is between 90 and 180 degrees.

Straight
The measure is equal to 180 degrees.

Here are a few tips to use when determining the measure of the angles.

- A pair of angles is *complementary* if the sum of the measures of the angles is 90 degrees.
- A pair of angles is *supplementary* if the sum of the measures of the angles is 180 degrees.
- If two angles have the same measure, then they are *congruent*.
- If an angle is *bisected*, it is divided into two congruent angles.

Lines and Angles

When two lines intersect, four angles are formed.

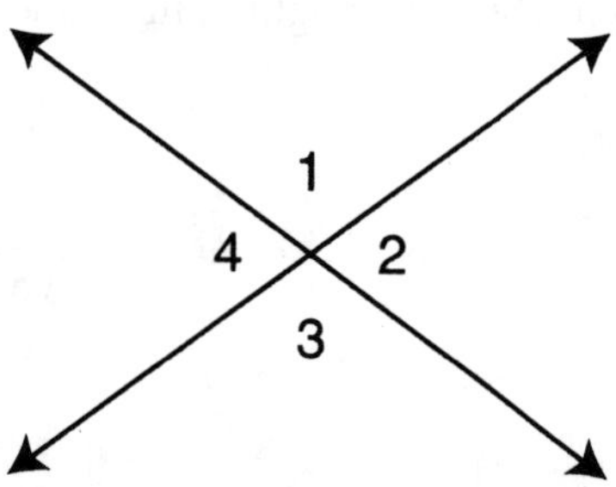

Vertical angles are the nonadjacent angles formed, or the opposite angles. These angles have the same measure. For example, m $\angle 1 =$ m $\angle 3$ and m $\angle 2 =$ m $\angle 4$.

The sum of any two *adjacent angles* is 180 degrees. For example, m $\angle 1 +$ m $\angle 2 = 180$. The sum of all four of the angles formed is 360 degrees.

If the two lines intersect and form four right angles, then the lines are *perpendicular.* If line m is perpendicular to line n, it is written $m \perp n$. If the two lines are in the same plane and will never intersect, then the lines are *parallel.* If line l is parallel to line p, it is written $l \parallel p$.

Parallel Lines and Angles

Some special angle patterns appear when two parallel lines are cut by another nonparallel line, or a transversal. When this happens, two different-sized angles are created: four angles of one size, and four of another size.

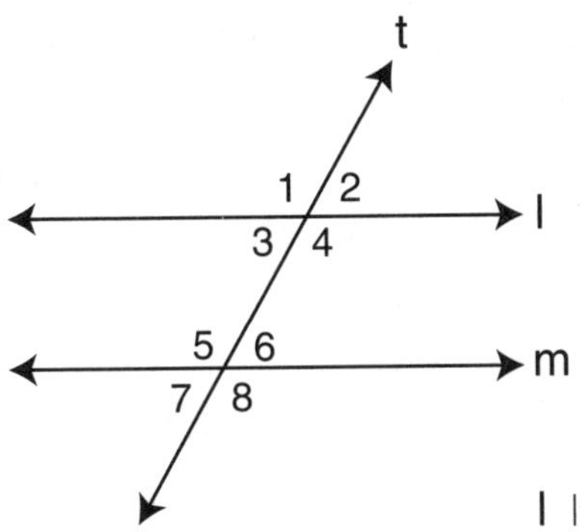

l || m
t is the transversal

- **Corresponding angles.** These are angle pairs 1 and 5, 2 and 6, 3 and 7, and 4 and 8. Within each pair, the angles are congruent to each other.
- **Alternate interior angles.** These are angle pairs 3 and 6, and 4 and 5. Within the pair, the angles are congruent to each other.
- **Alternate exterior angles.** These are angle pairs 1 and 8, and 2 and 7. Within the pair, the angles are congruent to each other.
- As in the case of two intersecting lines, the **adjacent angles** are supplementary and the **vertical angles** have the same measure.

▶ Polygons

A polygon is a simple closed figure whose sides are line segments. The places where the sides meet are called the *vertices* of the polygon. Polygons are named, or classified, according to the number of sides in the figure. The number of sides also determines the sum of the number of degrees in the interior angles.

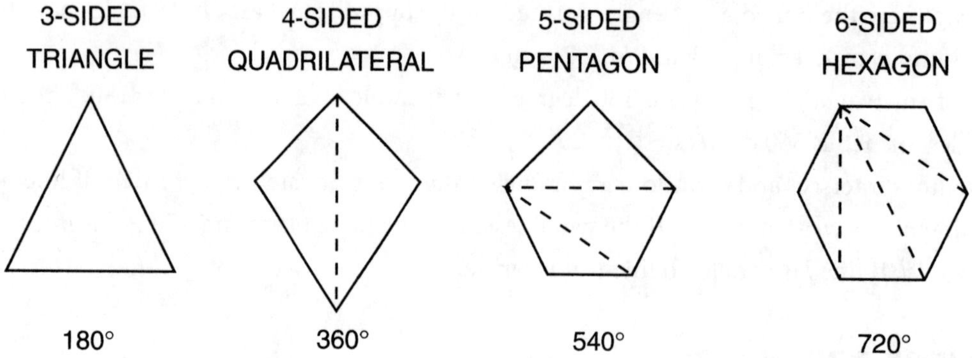

The total number of degrees in the *interior angles* of a polygon can be determined by drawing the non-intersecting diagonals in the polygon (the dashed lines in the previous figure). Each region formed is a triangle; there are always two fewer triangles than the number of sides. Multiply 180 by the number of triangles to find the total degrees in the interior vertex angles. For example, in the pentagon, three triangles are formed. Three times 180 equals 540; therefore, the interior vertex angles of a pentagon is made up of 540 degrees. The formula for this procedure is 180 $(n - 2)$, where n is the number of sides in the polygon.

The sum of the measures of the *exterior angles* of *any* polygon is 360 degrees.

A *regular polygon* is a polygon with equal sides and equal angle measure.

Two polygons are *congruent* if their corresponding sides and angles are equal (same shape and same size).

Two polygons are *similar* if their corresponding angles are equal and their corresponding sides are in proportion (same shape, but different size).

▶ Triangles

Triangles can be classified according to their sides and the measure of their angles.

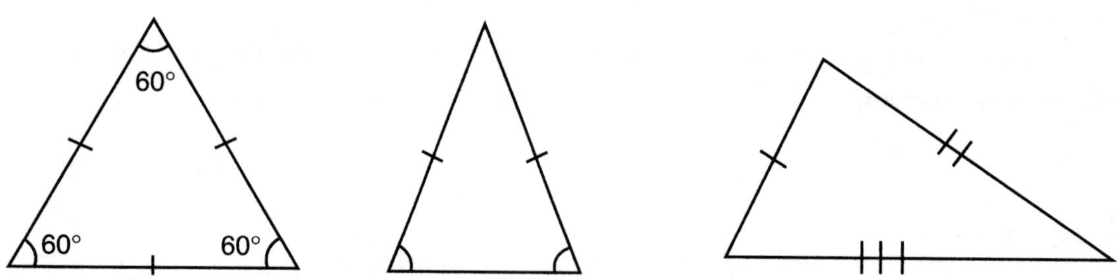

Equilateral
All sides are congruent.
All angles are congruent.
This is a **regular** polygon.

Isosceles
Two sides are congruent.
Base angles are congruent.

Scalene
All sides have a different measure.
All angles have a different measure.

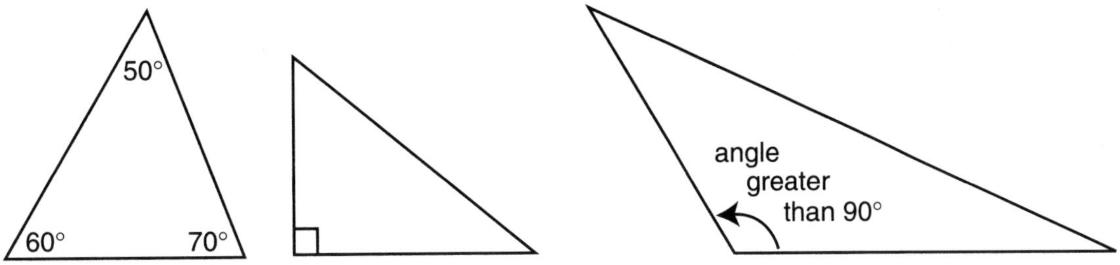

Acute

The measure of each angle is less than 90 degrees.

Right

It contains one 90-degree angle.

Obtuse

It contains one angle that is greater than 90 degrees.

Triangle Inequality

The sum of the two smaller sides of any triangle must be larger than the third side. For example, if the measures 3, 4, and 7 were given, those lengths would not form a triangle because $3 + 4 = 7$, and the sum must be greater than the third side. If you know two sides of a triangle and want to find a third, an easy way to handle this is to find the sum and difference of the two known sides. So, if the two sides were 3 and 7, the measure of the third side would be between $7 - 3$ and $7 + 3$. In other words, if x was the third side, x would have to be between 4 and 10, but not including 4 or 10.

Right Triangles

In a right triangle, the two sides that form the right angle are called the *legs* of the triangle. The side opposite the right angle is called the *hypotenuse* and is always the longest side of the triangle.

Pythagorean Theorem

To find the length of a side of a right triangle, the Pythagorean theorem can be used. This theorem states that the sum of the squares of the legs of the right triangle equal the square of the hypotenuse. It can be expressed as the equation $a^2 + b^2 = c^2$, where a and b are the legs and c is the hypotenuse. This relationship is shown geometrically in the following diagram.

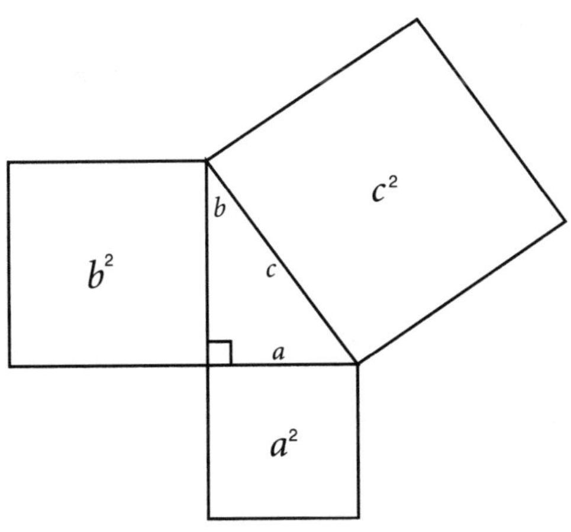

Example

Find the missing side of the right triangle *ABC* if the m$\angle C = 90°$, $AC = 6$, and $AB = 9$.

Begin by drawing a diagram to match the information given.

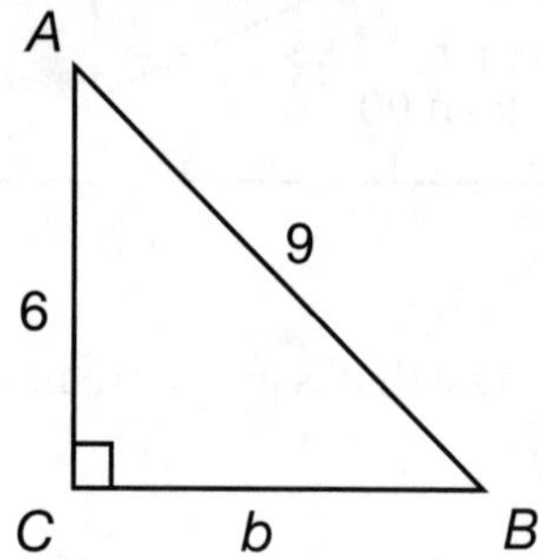

By drawing a diagram, you can see that the figure is a right triangle, *AC* is a leg, and *AB* is the hypotenuse. Use the formula $a^2 + b^2 = c^2$ by substituting $a = 6$ and $c = 9$.

$a^2 + b^2 = c^2$

$6^2 + b^2 = 9^2$

$36 + b^2 = 81$

$36 - 36 + b^2 = 81 - 36$

$b^2 = 45$

$b = \sqrt{45}$ which is approximately 6.7

Special Right Triangles

Some patterns in right triangles often appear on the Quantitative section. Knowing these patterns can often save you precious time when solving this type of question.

45-45-90 Right Triangles

If the right triangle is isosceles, then the angles' opposite congruent sides will be equal. In a right triangle, this makes two of the angles 45 degrees and the third, of course, 90 degrees. In this type of triangle, the measure of the hypotenuse is always $\sqrt{2}$ times the length of a side. For example, if the measure of one of the legs is 5, then the measure of the hypotenuse is $5\sqrt{2}$.

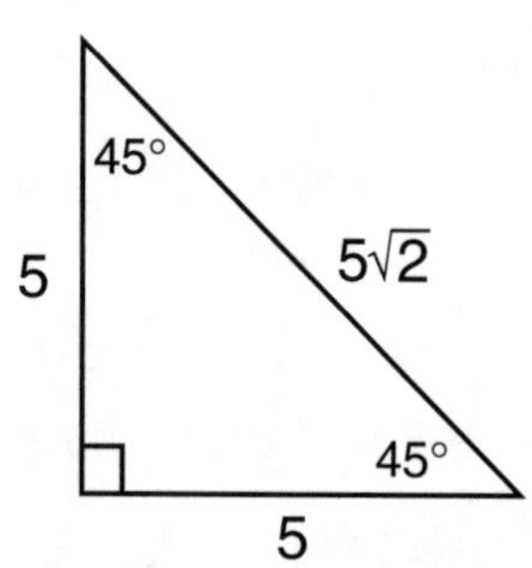

30-60-90 Right Triangles

In this type of right triangle, a different pattern occurs. Begin with the smallest side of the triangle, which is the side opposite the 30-degree angle. The smallest side multiplied by $\sqrt{3}$ is equal to the side opposite the 60-degree angle. The smallest side doubled is equal to the longest side, which is the hypotenuse. For example, if the measure of the hypotenuse is 8, then the measure of the smaller leg is 4 and the larger leg is $4\sqrt{3}$

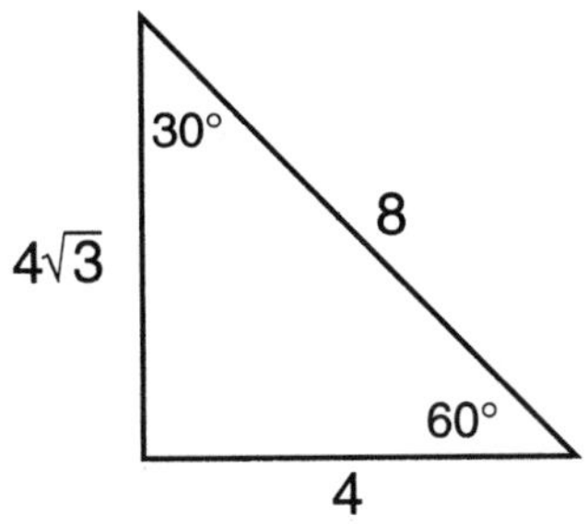

Pythagorean Triples

Another pattern that will help with right-triangle questions is Pythagorean triples. These are sets of whole numbers that always satisfy the Pythagorean theorem. Here are some examples those numbers:

3–4–5
5–12–13
8–15–17
7–24–25

Multiples of these numbers will also work. For example, since $3^2 + 4^2 = 5^2$, then each number doubled (6–8–10) or each number tripled (9–12–15) also forms Pythagorean triples.

► Quadrilaterals

A quadrilateral is a four-sided polygon. You should be familiar with a few special quadrilaterals.

Parallelogram

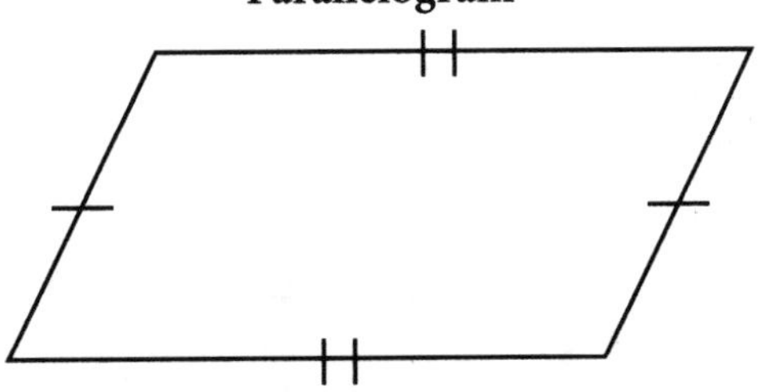

This is a quadrilateral where both pairs of opposite sides are parallel. In addition, the opposite sides are equal, the opposite angles are equal, and the diagonals bisect each other.

Rectangle

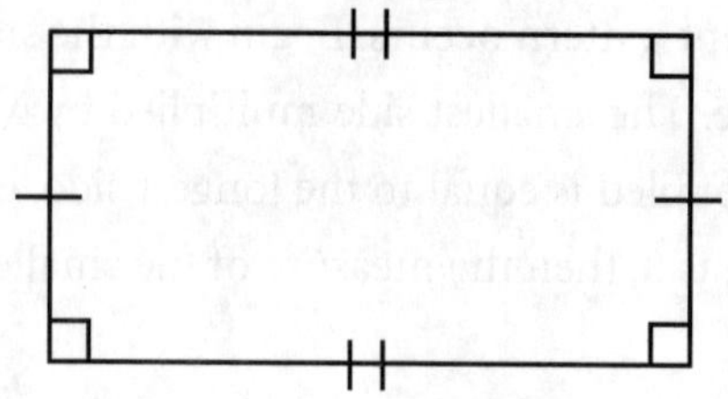

This is a parallelogram with right angles. In addition, the diagonals are equal in length.

Rhombus

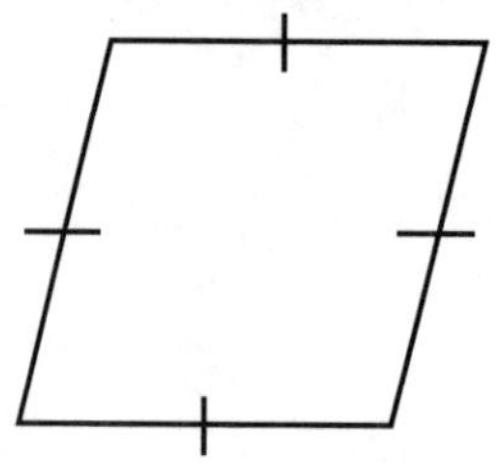

This is a parallelogram with four equal sides. In addition, the diagonals are perpendicular to each other.

Square

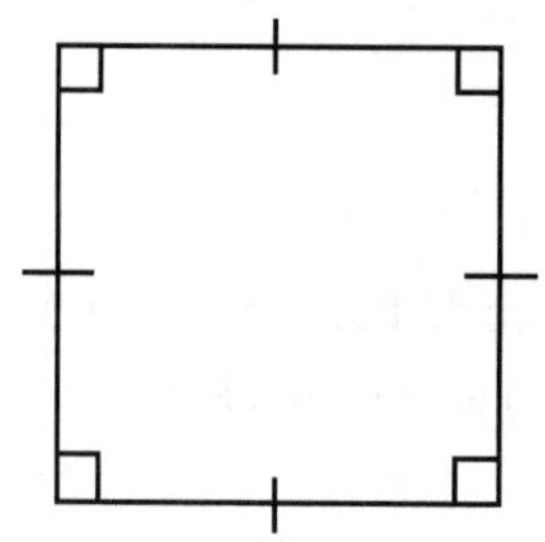

This is a parallelogram with four right angles and four equal sides. In addition, the diagonals are perpendicular and equal to each other.

▶ Circles

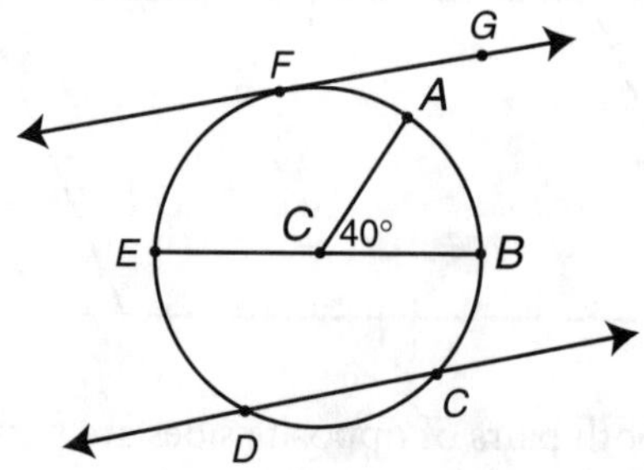

- Circles are typically named by their center point. This circle is circle *C*.

- The distance from the center to a point on the circle is called the *radius*, or *r*. The radii in this figure are *CA*, *CE*, and *CB*.
- A line segment that has both endpoints on the circle is called a *chord*. In the figure, the chords are $\overline{BE}$ and $\overline{CD}$.
- A chord that passes through the center is called the *diameter*, or *d*. The length of the diameter is twice the length of the radius. The diameter in the previous figure is $\overline{BE}$.
- A line that passes through the circle at one point only is called a *tangent*. The tangent here is line *FG*.
- A line that passes through the circle in two places is called a *secant*. The secant in this figure is line *CD*.
- A *central angle* is an angle whose vertex is the center of the circle. In this figure, $\angle ACB$, $\angle ACE$, and $\angle BCE$ are all central angles. (Remember, to name an angle using three points, the middle letter must be the vertex of the angle.)
- The set of points on a circle determined by two given points is called an *arc*. The measure of an arc is the same as the corresponding central angle. Since the m $\angle ACB = 40$ in this figure, then the measure of arc *AB* is 40 degrees.
- A *sector* of the circle is the area of the part of the circle bordered by two radii and an arc (this area may resemble a slice of pie). To find the area of a sector, use the formula $\frac{x}{360} \times \pi 6^2$, where *x* is the degrees of the central angle of the sector and *r* is the radius of the circle. For example, in this figure, the area of the sector formed by $\angle ACB$ would be $= \frac{460}{360} \times \pi 6^2$

$$= \frac{1}{9} \times 36\pi$$

$$= 4\pi$$

- *Concentric circles* are circles that have the same center.

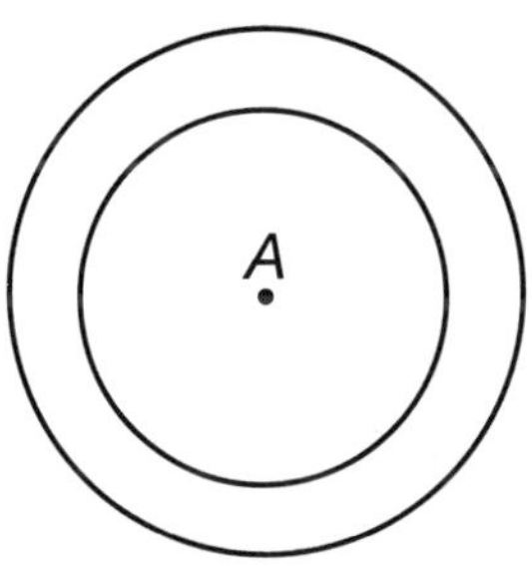

▶ Measurement and Geometry

Here is a list of some of the common formulas used on the GMAT exam:

- The *perimeter* is the distance around an object.

Rectangle	$P = 2l + 2w$
Square	$P = 4s$

- The *circumference* is the distance around a circle.

Circle	$C = \pi d$

- *Area* refers to the amount of space inside a two-dimensional figure.

Parallelogram	$A = bh$
Triangle	$A = \frac{1}{2}bh$
Trapezoid	$A = \frac{1}{2}h\,(b_1 + b_2)$, where b_1 and b_2 are the two parallel bases
Circle	$A = \pi r^2$

- The *volume* is the amount of space inside a three-dimensional figure.

General formula	$V = Bh$, where B is the area of the base of the figure and h is the height of the figure
Cube	$V = e^3$,where e is an edge of the cube
Rectangular prism	$V = lwh$
Cylinder	$V = \pi r^2 h$

- The *surface area* is the sum of the areas of each face of a three-dimensional figure.

Cube	$SA = 6e^2$, where e is an edge of the cube
Rectangular solid	$SA = 2(lw) + 2\,(lh) + 2(wh)$
Cylinder	$SA = 2\pi r^2 + dh$

Circle Equations

The following is the equation of a circle with a radius of r and center at (h, k):

$$(x - h)^2 + (y - k)^2 = r^2$$

The following is the equation of a circle with a radius of r and center at $(0, 0)$:

$$x^2 + y^2 = r^2$$

CHAPTER

23 Tips and Strategies for the Quantitative Section

The following bullets summarize some of the major points discussed in the lessons and highlight critical things to remember while preparing for the Quantitative section. Use these tips to help focus your review as you work through the practice questions.

- When multiplying or dividing an even number of negatives, the result is positive, but if the number of negatives is odd, the result is negative.
- In questions that use a unit of measurement (such as meters, pounds, and so on), be sure that all necessary conversions have taken place and that your answer also has the correct unit.
- Memorize frequently used decimal, percent, and fractional equivalents so that you will recognize them quickly on the test.
- Any number multiplied by zero is equal to zero.
- A number raised to the zero power is equal to one.
- Remember that division by zero is undefined.
- For complicated algebra questions, substitute or plug in numbers to try to find an answer choice that is reasonable.

- When given algebraic expressions in fraction form, try to cancel out any common factors in order to simplify the fraction.
- When multiplying like bases, add the exponents. When dividing like bases, subtract the exponents.
- Know how to factor the difference between two squares: $x^2 - y^2 = (x + y)(x - y)$.
- Use FOIL to help multiply and factor polynomials. For example, $(x + y)^2 = (x + y)(x + y) = x^2 + xy + xy + y^2 = x^2 + 2xy + y^2$.
- When squaring a number, two possible choices result in the same square (i.e., $2^2 = 4$ and $[-2]^2 = 4$).
- Even though the total interior degree measure increases with the number of sides of a polygon, the sum of the exterior angles is *always* 360 degrees.
- Know the rule for 45–45–90 right triangles: The length of a leg multiplied by $\sqrt{2}$ is the length of the hypotenuse.
- Know the rule for 30–60–90 right triangles: The shortest side doubled is the hypotenuse and the shortest side times $\sqrt{3}$ is the side across from the 60-degree angle.
- The incorrect answer choices for problem solving questions will often be the result of making common errors. Be aware of these traps.
- To solve the data-sufficiency questions, try to solve the problem first using only statement (1). If that works, the correct answer will be either **a** or **d**. If statement (1) is not sufficient, the correct answer will be **b, c,** or **e.**
- To save time on the test, memorize the directions and possible answer choices for the data-sufficiency questions.
- With the data-sufficiency questions, stop as soon as you know if you have enough information. You do not actually have to complete the problem.
- Although any figures used will be drawn to scale, be wary of any diagrams in data-sufficiency problems. The diagram may or may not conform with statements (1) and (2).
- Familiarize yourself with the monitor screen and mouse of your test-taking station before beginning the actual exam. Practice basic computer skills by taking the tutorial before the actual test begins.
- Use the available scrap paper to work out problems. You can also use it as a ruler on the computer screen, if necessary. Remember, no calculators are allowed.
- The HELP feature will use up time if it is used during the exam.
- A time icon appears on the screen, so find this before the test starts and use it during the test to help pace yourself. Remember, you have on average about two minutes per question.
- Since each question must be answered before you can advance to the next question, on problems you are unsure about, try to eliminate impossible answer choices before making an educated guess from the remaining selections.
- Only confirm an answer selection when you are sure about it—you cannot go back to any previous questions. Reread the question a final time before selecting your answer.
- Spend a bit more time on the first few questions—by getting these questions correct, you will be given more difficult questions. More difficult questions score more points.

CHAPTER

24 Quantitative Practice Test

The following Quantitative section practice test contains 80 multiple-choice questions that are similar to the questions you will encounter on the GMAT® exam. These questions are designed to give you a chance to practice the skills you have learned in a format that simulates the actual exam. Answer these practice questions carefully. Use the results to assess your strengths and weaknesses and determine which areas, if any, you need to study further.

With 80 questions, this practice section has more than twice the number of questions you will see on the actual exam. To practice the timing of the GMAT exam, complete the entire practice section in 162 minutes (2 hours and 42 minutes).

Record your answers on the answer sheet provided. Make sure you mark your answer clearly in the circle that corresponds to the question.

Remember that the GMAT exam is a CAT, and you will not be able to write anywhere on the exam. To mimic the exam environment, do not write on the test pages. Make any notes or calculations on a separate sheet of paper.

ANSWER SHEET

1. (a) (b) (c) (d) (e)	28. (a) (b) (c) (d) (e)	55. (a) (b) (c) (d) (e)
2. (a) (b) (c) (d) (e)	29. (a) (b) (c) (d) (e)	56. (a) (b) (c) (d) (e)
3. (a) (b) (c) (d) (e)	30. (a) (b) (c) (d) (e)	57. (a) (b) (c) (d) (e)
4. (a) (b) (c) (d) (e)	31. (a) (b) (c) (d) (e)	58 (a) (b) (c) (d) (e)
5. (a) (b) (c) (d) (e)	32. (a) (b) (c) (d) (e)	59. (a) (b) (c) (d) (e)
6. (a) (b) (c) (d) (e)	33. (a) (b) (c) (d) (e)	60. (a) (b) (c) (d) (e)
7. (a) (b) (c) (d) (e)	34. (a) (b) (c) (d) (e)	61. (a) (b) (c) (d) (e)
8. (a) (b) (c) (d) (e)	35. (a) (b) (c) (d) (e)	62. (a) (b) (c) (d) (e)
9. (a) (b) (c) (d) (e)	36. (a) (b) (c) (d) (e)	63. (a) (b) (c) (d) (e)
10. (a) (b) (c) (d) (e)	37. (a) (b) (c) (d) (e)	64 (a) (b) (c) (d) (e)
11. (a) (b) (c) (d) (e)	38. (a) (b) (c) (d) (e)	65. (a) (b) (c) (d) (e)
12. (a) (b) (c) (d) (e)	39. (a) (b) (c) (d) (e)	66. (a) (b) (c) (d) (e)
13. (a) (b) (c) (d) (e)	40. (a) (b) (c) (d) (e)	67. (a) (b) (c) (d) (e)
14. (a) (b) (c) (d) (e)	41. (a) (b) (c) (d) (e)	68. (a) (b) (c) (d) (e)
15. (a) (b) (c) (d) (e)	42. (a) (b) (c) (d) (e)	69. (a) (b) (c) (d) (e)
16. (a) (b) (c) (d) (e)	43. (a) (b) (c) (d) (e)	70. (a) (b) (c) (d) (e)
17. (a) (b) (c) (d) (e)	44. (a) (b) (c) (d) (e)	71. (a) (b) (c) (d) (e)
18. (a) (b) (c) (d) (e)	45. (a) (b) (c) (d) (e)	72. (a) (b) (c) (d) (e)
19. (a) (b) (c) (d) (e)	46. (a) (b) (c) (d) (e)	73. (a) (b) (c) (d) (e)
20. (a) (b) (c) (d) (e)	47. (a) (b) (c) (d) (e)	74. (a) (b) (c) (d) (e)
21. (a) (b) (c) (d) (e)	48. (a) (b) (c) (d) (e)	75. (a) (b) (c) (d) (e)
22. (a) (b) (c) (d) (e)	49. (a) (b) (c) (d) (e)	76. (a) (b) (c) (d) (e)
23. (a) (b) (c) (d) (e)	50. (a) (b) (c) (d) (e)	77. (a) (b) (c) (d) (e)
24. (a) (b) (c) (d) (e)	51. (a) (b) (c) (d) (e)	78. (a) (b) (c) (d) (e)
25. (a) (b) (c) (d) (e)	52. (a) (b) (c) (d) (e)	79. (a) (b) (c) (d) (e)
26. (a) (b) (c) (d) (e)	53. (a) (b) (c) (d) (e)	80. (a) (b) (c) (d) (e)
27. (a) (b) (c) (d) (e)	54. (a) (b) (c) (d) (e)	

Directions: Solve the problem and choose the letter indicating the best answer choice. The numbers used in this section are real numbers. The figures used are drawn to scale and lie in a plane unless otherwise noted.

1. If the least common multiple of two prime numbers x and y is 10, where $x > y$, then the value of $2x + y$ is

a. 7
b. 9
c. 11
d. 12
e. 21

2. What is the product of 6% and 14%?

a. 0.00084
b. 0.0084
c. 0.084
d. 0.84
e. 8.4

3. A taxicab fare costs x dollars for the first quarter of a mile and $\frac{1}{4}x$ dollars for each quarter of a mile after that. How much will the total cost be for a $2\frac{1}{2}$ mile ride?

a. $3x$

b. $\frac{13}{4}x$

c. $10x$

d. $\frac{5}{4}x$

e. $2.5x$

4. Which of the following measures could form the sides of a triangle?

I. 3, 3, 5
II. 6, 6, 12
III. 1, 2, 3

a. I only
b. II only
c. III only
d. I and II only
e. II and III only

5. Scott's average (arithmetic mean) golf score on his first four rounds was 78. What score does he need on his fifth round to drop his average score by 2 points?

a. 68
b. 72
c. 78
d. 88
e. 312

6. Celeste worked for h hours each day for d consecutive days. If she earns \$9.50 per hour, what is the total amount she earned?

a. $\frac{9.50}{d} + h$

b. $9.50 + d + h$
c. $9.50 + dh$
d. $9.50h + d$
e. $9.50dh$

7. A certain jacket was marked down 20% the first week and another 20% the next week. What percent of the regular price was the final cost of the jacket after the two markdowns?

a. 30%
b. 36%
c. 40%
d. 60%
e. 64%

8. If 20 typists can type 48 letters in 20 minutes, then how many letters will 30 typists working at the same rate complete in 1 hour?

a. 63
b. 72
c. 144
d. 216
e. 400

9. What is the final balance of a bank account after two years if the starting balance is $1,000 at an annual rate of 5%, using simple interest? Assume no other money was withdrawn or deposited.

a. $50
b. $100
c. $1,050
d. $1,100
e. $1,150

10. Which of the following has the smallest numerical value?

a. $2^3 \times 2^2$
b. 2^6
c. $2^5 \times 2^1$
d. $(2^2)^3$
e. $2^3 \times 3^3$

11. How many liters of a 40% iodine solution need to be mixed with 35 liters of a 20% iodine solution to create a 35% iodine solution?

a. 35
b. 49
c. 100
d. 105
e. 140

12. If it takes Steve 6 hours to tile a floor and Cheryl 4 hours to tile the same floor, how long would it take both Steve and Cheryl to tile the floor if they worked together?

a. 2 hours 12 minutes
b. 2 hours 24 minutes
c. 3 hours
d. 3 hours 12 minutes
e. 10 hours

13. Given the area of the three squares, find the perimeter of △ABC.

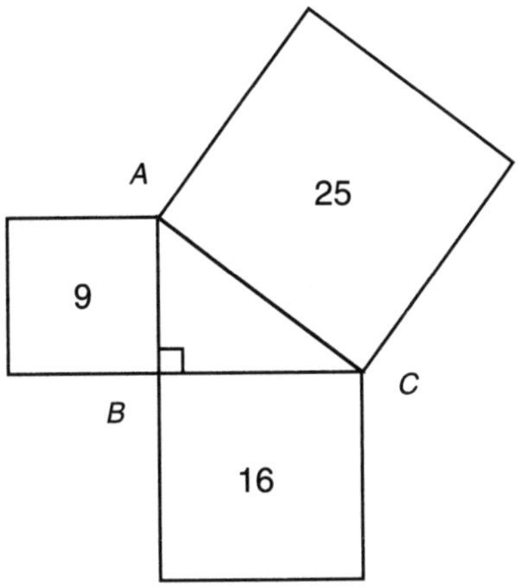

a. 12
b. 12.5
c. 19.5
d. 20
e. 25

14. During a sale, the price of a pair of shoes is marked down 10% from the regular price. After the sale ends, the price goes back to the original price. What is the percent of increase to the nearest percent from the sale price back to the regular price for the shoes?

a. 9%
b. 10%
c. 11%
d. 15%
e. 90%

15. How many degrees is the smaller angle?

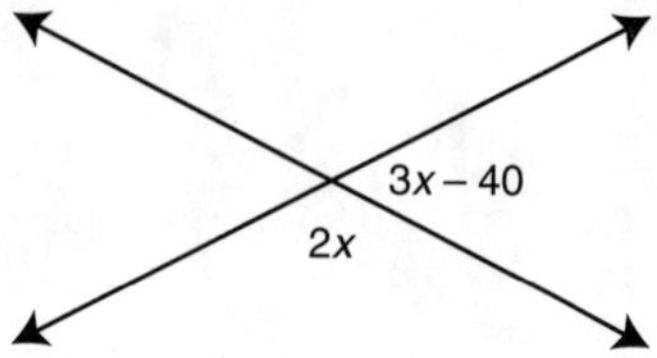

NOTE: FIGURE NOT DRAWN TO SCALE

a. 44
b. 88
c. 92
d. 132
e. 180

16. If the average (arithmetic mean) of x, $x + 2$, and $x + 4$ is 33, what is the value of x?

a. 30
b. 31
c. 32
d. 32
e. 37

17. If it costs d dollars to make the first 100 copies of a poster and e dollars for each poster after that, what is the total cost of 125 posters?

a. $25d + 100e$
b. $100d + 25e$
c. $125de$
d. $d + 25$e
e. $\frac{125}{de}$

18. If the volume of a cube is x^3 cubic units, what is the number of square units in the surface area of the cube?

a. x^2
b. x^3
c. x^6
d. $6x^2$
e. $6x^3$

19. If $x - 3$ is a multiple of two, what is the next larger multiple of two?

a. $2x$
b. $x - 2$
c. $x - 1$
d. $x - 5$
e. $x + 2$

20. If $3^{x+1} = 81$, then $x - 1 =$

a. 2
b. 3
c. 4
d. 9
e. 27

21. For dinner at a restaurant, there are x choices of appetizers, $y + 1$ main courses, and z choices of dessert. How many total possible choices are there if you choose 1 appetizer, 1 main course, and 1 dessert for your meal?

a. $x + y + z + 1$
b. $xyz + xz$
c. $xy + z + 1$
d. $xyz + 1$
e. $xyz + \frac{1}{2}$

22. If $x \$ y$ is defined as $2(x + y)^2$, then what is the value of $2 \$ 3$?

a. 25
b. 36
c. 50
d. 100
e. 144

23. If x, y, and z are real numbers, which is always true?

I. $x(yz) = (xy)z$
II. $\frac{x}{y} = \frac{y}{z}$
III. $z(x + y) = zx + zy$
a. I only
b. II only
c. I and II only
d. I and III only
e. I, II, and III

24. If $y = 6^x$, then $6y$ equals

a. 6^x

b. 6^{x+1}

c. $6^x + 6$

d. $6x$

e. $6^x - 1$

25. What is the smallest of six consecutive odd integers whose average (arithmetic mean) is $x + 2$?

a. $x - 5$

b. $x - 3$

c. $x - 1$

d. x

e. $x + 1$

26. The product of a and b is equal to 11 more than twice the sum of a and b. If $b = 7$, what is the value of $b - a$?

a. 2

b. 5

c. 7

d. 24

e. 35

27. $\left[\sqrt[3]{(\sqrt{x})^2}\right]^3 =$

a. $\sqrt{x}$

b. $3\sqrt{x}$

c. x

d. x^2

e. x^3

28. The instructions state that Cheryl needs $\frac{4}{9}$ square yards of one type of material and $\frac{2}{3}$ square yards of another type of material for a project. She buys exactly that amount. After finishing the project, however, she has $\frac{8}{18}$ square yards left that she did not use. What is the total amount of square yards of material Cheryl used?

a. $\frac{1}{12}$

b. $\frac{1}{9}$

c. $\frac{2}{3}$

d. $1\frac{1}{9}$

e. $2\frac{1}{9}$

29. Which of the following values of x would satisfy the inequality $x > 1$?

I. $x = (\frac{1}{2})^3$

II. $x = (\frac{-4}{3})^2$

III. $x = (\frac{-1}{3})^{-2}$

a. I only
b. II only
c. II and III only
d. I and III only
e. I, II, and III

30. John is three times as old as Sam. If John will be twice as old as Sam in six years, how old was Sam two years ago?

a. 2
b. 4
c. 6
d. 8
e. 16

31. Given a spinner with four sections of equal size labeled A, B, C, and D, what is the probability of NOT getting an A after spinning the spinner two times?

a. $\frac{9}{16}$
b. $\frac{1}{8}$
c. $\frac{1}{4}$
d. $\frac{1}{2}$
e. $\frac{15}{16}$

32. A case of 12 rolls of paper towels sells for \$9. The cost of one roll sold individually is \$1. What is the percent of savings per roll for the 12-roll package over the cost of 12 rolls purchased individually?

a. 9%
b. 11%
c. 15%
d. 25%
e. 90%

33. How many different committees can be formed from a group of two women and four men if three people are on the committee and at least one member must be a woman?

a. 6
b. 8
c. 10
d. 12
e. 16

34. Susan spent one-third of her money on books and half of the remaining money on clothing. She then spent three-fourths of what she had left on food. She had \$5 left over. How much money did she start with?

a. \$60
b. \$80
c. \$120
d. \$160
e. \$180

35. A truck travels 20 miles due north, 30 miles due east, and then 20 miles due north. How many miles is the truck from the starting point?

a. 20.3
b. 70
c. 44.7
d. 50
e. 120

36. $\frac{(\frac{1}{2}) \times (\frac{2}{5})}{.04} =$

a. .20
b. .5
c. 2
d. 5
e. 20

37. A rectangular swimming pool is 20 feet by 28 feet. A deck that has uniform width surrounds the pool. The total area of the pool and deck is 884 square feet. What is the width of the deck?

a. 2 feet
b. 2.5 feet
c. 3 feet
d. 4 feet
e. 5 feet

38. If a person randomly guesses on each question of a test with n questions, what is the probability of guessing half of the questions correctly if each question has five possible answer choices?

a. $5n$
b. $(\frac{5}{2})n$
c. $(\frac{1}{5})^n$
d. $(\frac{1}{5})^{\frac{n}{2}}$
e. $(\frac{1}{5})^{2n}$

39. Two integers are in the ratio of 1 to 4. If 6 is added to the smaller number, the ratio becomes 1 to 2. Find the larger integer.

a. 4
b. 6
c. 12
d. 24
e. 30

40. The measure of the side of a square is tripled. If x represents the perimeter of the original square, what is the value of the new perimeter?

a. $3x$
b. $4x$
c. $9x$
d. $12x$
e. $27x$

▶ Data Sufficiency Questions

Directions: Each of the following problems contains a question that is followed by two statements. Select your answer using the data in statement (1) and statement (2), and determine whether they provide enough information to answer the initial question. If you are asked for the value of a quantity, the information is sufficient when it is possible to determine only one value for the quantity. The five possible answer choices are as follows:

a. Statement (1), BY ITSELF, will suffice to solve the problem, but NOT statement (2) by itself.
b. Statement (2), BY ITSELF, will suffice to solve the problem, but NOT statement (1) by itself.
c. The problem can be solved using statement (1) and statement (2) TOGETHER, but not ONLY statement (1) or statement (2).
d. The problem can be solved using EITHER statement (1) only or statement (2) only.
e. The problem CANNOT be solved using statement (1) and statement (2) TOGETHER.

The numbers used are real numbers. If a figure accompanies a question, the figure will be drawn to scale according to the original question or information, but will not necessarily be consistent with the information given in statements (1) and (2).

41. What is the value of $x + 2y$?
(1) $2x + 4y = 20$
(2) $y = 5 - \frac{1}{2}x$

42. Is $r - 5$ a real number?
(1) r is a rational number.
(2) $\sqrt{r}$ is an irrational number.

43. Is rectangle $ABCD$ a square?
(1) m $\angle ABC = 90$
(2) $AC \perp CD$

44. What is the measure of an interior vertex angle of a pentagon?
(1) The measure of each adjacent exterior angle is 72.
(2) The pentagon is a regular polygon.

45. What is the value of x?
(1) $x + y = 6$
(2) $2x - y = 9$

46. What is the value of x?

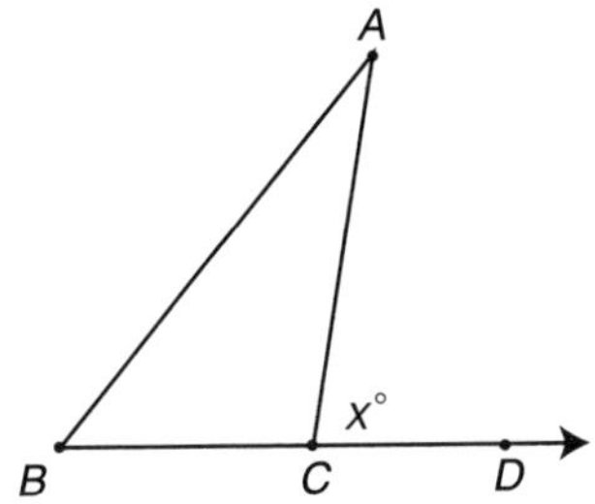

NOTE: FIGURE NOT DRAWN TO SCALE

(1) $m\angle ACB = 30$
(2) $m\angle A + \angle B = 150$

47. It takes Joe and Ted four hours to paint a room when they work together. How long does it take Joe working by himself to paint the same room?
(1) The dimensions of the room are 12' by 12' by 8'.
(2) It takes Ted seven hours to paint the room by himself.

48. Is $xy > 0$?
(1) $x > 1$
(2) $y < 0$

49. Given that C is the center of the circle and $\overline{DB}$ passes through C, what is the area of the sector of the circle?

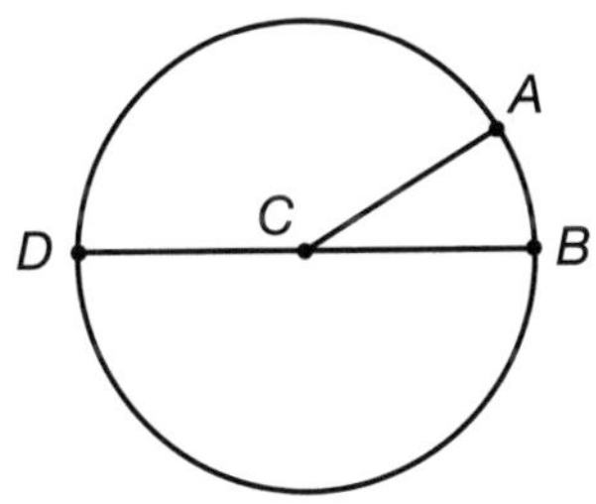

(1) The diameter of the circle is 12.
(2) m $\angle C = 30°$.

50. Points A, B, and C are located in the same plane. What is the distance between point A and point C?
(1) The distance between A and B is 100 cm.
(2) The distance between A and B is twice the distance between B and C.

51. In the following figure, $p \parallel n$. Is x supplementary to y?

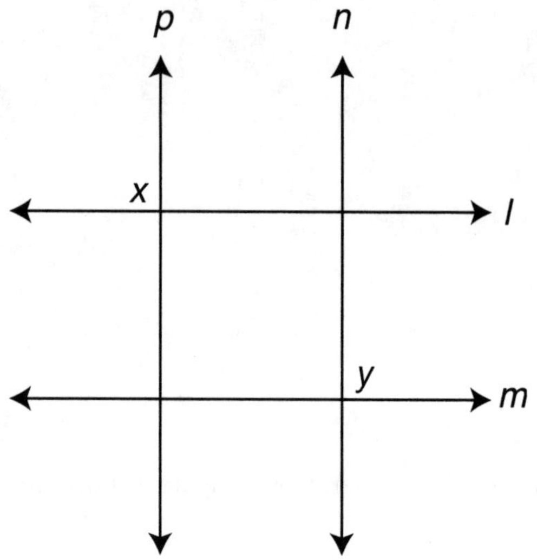

(1) $l \perp p$

(2) $l \parallel m$

52. Which store has a greater discount, store A or store B?

(1) Store B has 20% off all items.

(2) Store A has $20 off all items.

53. Is $x + 1$ a factor of 12?

(1) $x + 1$ is even.

(2) $x + 1$ is a factor of both 2 and 3.

54. What is the value of x?

(1) $22 < 3x + 1 < 28$

(2) x is an integer.

55. If x and y are consecutive even integers, what is the value of xy?

(1) $x + y = 98$

(2) $y - x = 2$

56. What is the numerical value of $x^2 - 25$?

(1) $x - 5 = 3$

(2) $4 - x = 5$

57. A rectangular courtyard with whole-number dimensions has an area of 60 square meters. Find the length of the courtyard.

(1) The width is two more than twice the length.

(2) The length of the diagonal of the courtyard is 13 meters.

58. Is $x + y > 2z$?

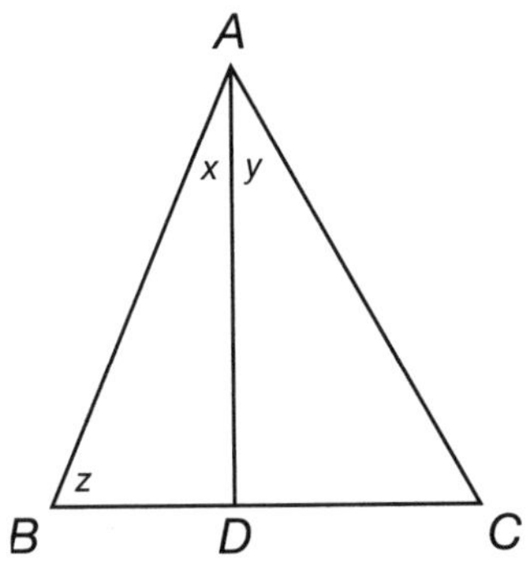

(1) $\triangle ABC$ is equilateral.

(2) $AD \perp BC$

59. The circles in the diagram are concentric circles. What is the area of the shaded region?

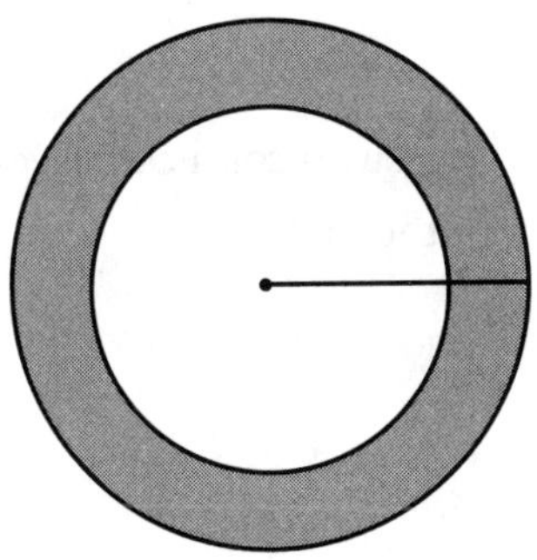

(1) The area of the inner circle is 25π.

(2) The diameter of the larger circle is 20.

60. Find the value of x.

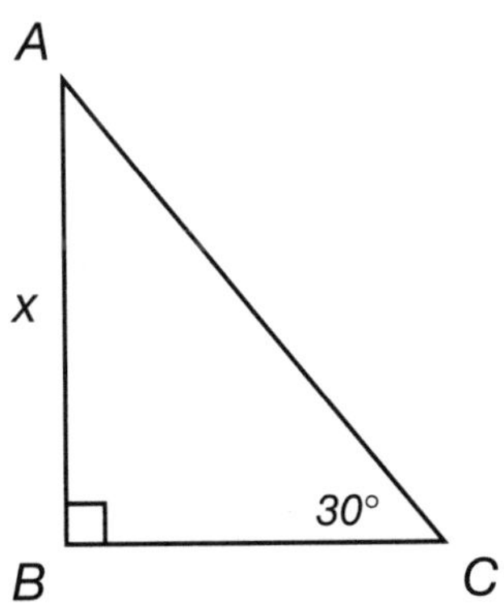

(1) The length of BC is $2\sqrt{3}$.

(2) The length of AC is 4.

61. What is the value of $a + b$?

(1) $a^2 + b^2 = 13$

(2) $2b = \frac{12}{a}$

62. Between what two numbers is the measure of the third side of the triangle?

(1) The sum of the two known sides is 10.

(2) The difference between the two known sides is 6.

63. What is the area of the circle?

(1) The radius is 6.

(2) The circumference is 12π.

64. What is the positive value of z?

(1) $3y + z = 4$

(2) $z^2 - z = 12$

65. Two cars leave the same city traveling on the same road in the same direction. The second car leaves one hour after the first. How long will it take the second car to catch up with the first?

(1) The second car is traveling 10 miles per hour faster than the first car.

(2) The second car averages 60 miles per hour.

66. In right triangle XYZ, the $m\angle y = 90$. What is the length of XZ?

(1) The length of $YZ = 6$.

(2) $m\angle z = 45$

67. Is $\frac{x}{y} > \frac{y}{x}$?

(1) $3x = 6y$

(2) $\frac{x}{y} > 1$

68. What is the total cost of six pencils and four notebooks?

(1) Ten pencils and nine notebooks cost \$11.50.

(2) Twelve pencils and eight notebooks cost \$11.00.

69. What is the ratio of the corresponding sides of two similar triangles?

(1) The ratio of the perimeters of the two triangles is 3:1.

(2) The ratio of the areas of the two triangles is 9:1.

70. What percent of the class period is over?

(1) The time remaining is $\frac{1}{4}$ of the time that has passed.

(2) The class period is 42 minutes long.

71. Daniel rides to school each day on a path that takes him first to a point directly east of his house and then from there directly north to his school. How much shorter would his ride to school be if he could walk on a straight-line path directly to school from his home, instead of east and then north?

(1) The direct straight-line distance from home to school is 17 miles.

(2) The distance he rides to the east is 7 miles less than the distance he rides going north.

72. What is the slope of line m?

(1) Line m intersects the x-axis at the point (4, 0).

(2) The equation of line m is $3y = x - 4$.

73. Jacob is a salesperson. He earns a monthly salary plus a commission on all sales over $4,000. How much did he earn this month?

(1) His monthly salary is $855 and his total sales over $4,000 were $4,532.30.

(2) His total sales for the month were $8,532.30.

74. Is $\triangle ABC$ similar to $\triangle ADE$?

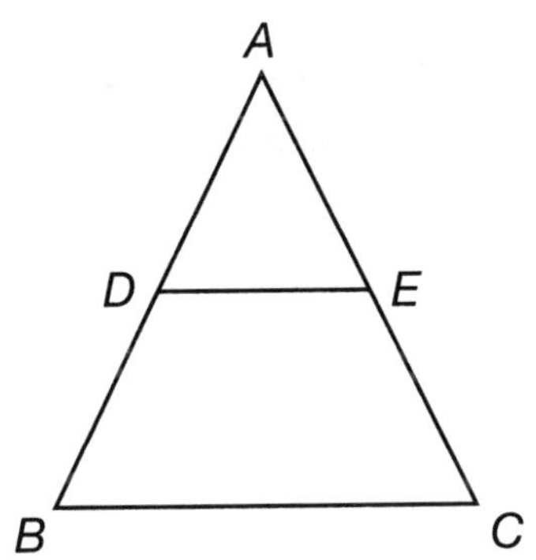

(1) BC is parallel to DE

(2) $AD = AE$

75. The formula for compounded interest can be defined as $A = p\,(1 + r)^n$, where A is the total value of the investment, p is the principle invested, r is the interest rate per period, and n is the number of periods. If a $1,000 principle is invested, which bank gives a better interest rate for a savings account, Bank A or Bank B?

(1) The interest rate at Bank A is 4% compounded annually.

(2) The total amount of interest earned at Bank B over a period of five years is $276.28.

76. A fence has a square gate. What is the height of the gate?
(1) The width of the gate is 30 inches.
(2) The length of the diagonal brace of the gate is 30 $\sqrt{2}$ inches.

77. Find the area of the shaded region.

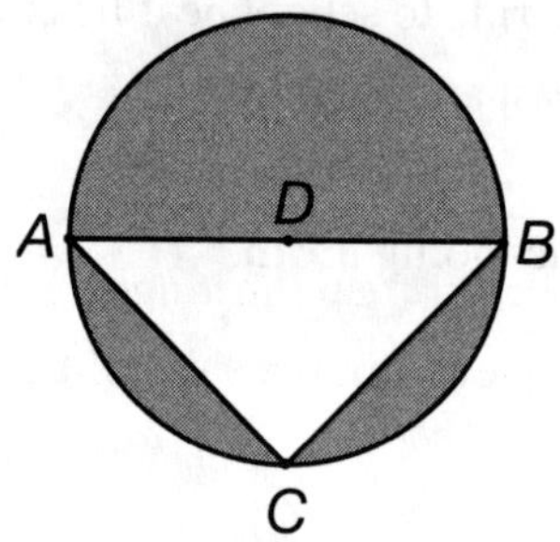

(1) m $\angle A = 43°$.
(2) $AB = 10$ cm.

78. A circle and a straight line are drawn on the same coordinate graph. In how many places do the two graphs intersect?
(1) The equation of the circle is $x^2 + y^2 = 25$.
(2) The y-intercept of the straight line is 6.

79. Michael left a city in a car traveling directly west. Katie left the same city two hours later going directly east traveling at the same rate as Michael. How long after Katie left will they be 350 miles apart?
(1) An hour and a half after Katie left they are 250 miles apart.
(2) Michael's destination is 150 miles farther than Katie's.

80. What is the area of the shaded region?

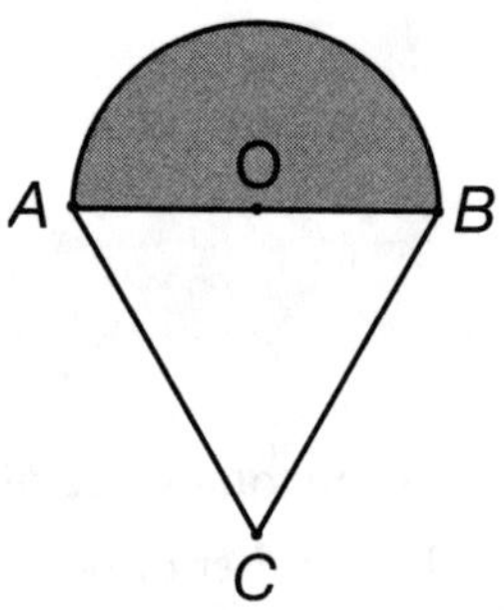

(1) $\triangle ABC$ is equilateral.
(2) The length of $\overline{BC}$ is 16 inches.

▶ Answer Explanations

1. d. The only prime numbers that satisfy this condition are 2 and 5. Since $x > y$, $x = 5$ and $y = 2$. Therefore, by substitution, 2 (5) + 2 = 10 + 2 = 12.

2. b. Convert 6% to its decimal equivalent of 0.06 and 14% to 0.14. The key word "product" tells you to multiply, so $0.06 \times 0.14 = 0.0084$, which is choice **b**.

3. b. $2\frac{1}{2}$ miles divided by $\frac{1}{4}$ is ten quarter miles. Since the first quarter mile costs x amount, the other nine quarter miles cost $\frac{1}{4}x$, so $9 \times \frac{1}{4}x = \frac{9}{4}x$. $x + \frac{9}{4}x = \frac{4}{4}x + \frac{9}{4}x = \frac{13}{4}x$.

4. a. The sum of the measures of the two shorter sides of a triangle must be greater than the longest side. Since 3 + 3 > 5, statement I works. Since 6 + 6 = 12 and 1 + 2 = 3, they do not form the sides of the triangle. The answer is statement I only.

5. a. If the average of four rounds is 78, then the total points scored is $78 \times 4 = 312$. If his score were to drop 2 points, that means his new average would be 76. A 76 average for five rounds is a total of 380 points. The difference between these two point totals is 380 – 312 = 68. He needs a score of 68 on the fifth round.

6. e. Suppose Celeste worked for 8 hours each day for 5 consecutive days. Her total pay would be found by finding her total hours ($8 \times 5 = 40$) and then multiplying 40 by her pay per hour ($9.50). Since you are only multiplying to solve the problem, the expression is $9.50 \times d \times h$ or $9.50dh$.

7. e. To make this problem easier, assume the initial cost of the jacket was $100. The first markdown of 20% would save you $20, bringing the cost of the jacket to $80. For the second markdown, you should be finding 20% of $80, the new cost of the jacket. 20% of 80 = $0.20 \times 80 = 16$. If you save $16 the second time, the final cost of the jacket is 80 – 16 = $64. Since the initial cost was $100, $64 is 64% of this price.

8. d. First calculate the number of letters completed by 30 typists in 20 minutes. Let x = the number of letters typed by 30 typists and set up the proportion $\frac{\text{typists}}{\text{letters}} = \frac{20}{48} = \frac{30}{x}$. Cross-multiply to get $20x = 1{,}440$. Divide both sides by 20 and get $x = 72$. Since 20 minutes is one-third of an hour, multiply $72 \times 3 = 216$ to get the total letters for one hour.

9. d. This problem can be solved by using the simple interest formula: *interest* = *principal* × *rate* × *time*. Remember to change the interest rate to a decimal before using it in the formula. $I = (1{,}000)(0.05)(2)$ = $100. Since $100 was made in interest, the total in the bank account is $1,000 + $100 = $1,100.

10. a. Using the rules for exponents, choice **a** simplifies to 2^5 and choices **b**, **c**, and **d** simplify to $2^6 = 64$. Choice **e** becomes 27×81, which is obviously much larger than 64.

11. **d.** Let x = the number of liters of the 40% solution. Use the equation $0.40x + 0.20(35) = 0.35(x + 35)$ to show the two amounts mixed equal the 35% solution.

Solve the equation: $0.40x + 0.20(35) = 0.35(x + 35)$

Multiply both sides by 100 in order to work with more compatible numbers:

$$40x + 20(35) = 35(x + 35)$$

$$40x + 700 = 35x + 1{,}225$$

Subtract 700 on both sides: $40x + 700 - 700 = 35x + 1{,}225 - 700$

Subtract $35x$ from both sides $40x - 35x = 35x - 35x + 525$

Divide both sides by 5: $\frac{5x}{5} = \frac{525}{5}$

$x = 105$ liters of 35% iodine solution

12. **b.** Let x = the part of the floor that can be tiled in 1 hour. Since Steve can tile a floor in 6 hours, he can tile $\frac{1}{6}$ of the floor in 1 hour. Since Cheryl can tile the same floor in 4 hours, she can tile $\frac{1}{4}$ of the floor in 1 hour. Use the equation $\frac{1}{6} + \frac{1}{4} = \frac{1}{x}$, where $\frac{1}{x}$ represents the part of the floor they can tile in an hour together. Multiply each term by the LCD = $12x$. $12x \times \frac{1}{6} + 12x \times \frac{1}{4} = 12x \times \frac{1}{x}$. The equation simplifies to $2x + 3x = 12$. $5x = 12$. Divide each side by 5 to get $x = \frac{12}{5} = 2.4$ hours. Since 0.4 times 60 minutes equals 24 minutes, the final answer is 2 hours 24 minutes.

13. **a.** The length of one side of a square is equal to the square root of the area of the square. Since the area of the squares is 9, 16, and 25, the lengths of the sides of the squares are 3, 4, and 5, respectively. The triangle is formed by the sides of the three squares; therefore, the perimeter, or distance around the triangle, is $3 + 4 + 5 = 12$.

14. **c.** Suppose that the shoes cost \$10. \$10 – 10% = 10 – 1 = \$9. When the shoes are marked back up, 10% of \$9 is only 90 cents. Therefore, the markup must be greater than 10%. $\frac{\$1}{\$9} = 11\frac{1}{9}\%$, or about 11%.

15. **b.** Note that the figure is not drawn to scale, so do not rely on the diagram to calculate the answer. Since the angles are adjacent and formed by two intersecting lines, they are also supplementary. Combine the two angles and set the sum equal to 180. $2x + 3x - 40 = 180$. Combine like terms and add 40 to both sides. $5x - 40 + 40 = 180 + 40$. $5x = 220$. Divide both sides by 5 to get $x = 44$. Then $2x = 88$ and $3x - 40 = 92$. The smaller angle is 88.

16. **b.** x, $x + 2$, and $x + 4$ are each two numbers apart. This would make $x + 2$ the average of the three numbers. If $x + 2 = 33$, then $x = 31$.

17. **d.** It costs d for the first 100 posters *plus* the cost of 25 additional posters. This translates to $d + 25e$, since e is the cost of each poster over the initial 100.

18. **d.** If the volume of the cube is x^3, then one edge of the cube is x. The surface area of a cube is six times the area of one face, which is x times x. The total surface area is $6x^2$.

19. **c.** The next larger multiple of two would be $x - 3 + 2$, which is $x - 1$. In this case, remember that any even number is a multiple of two and all evens are two numbers apart. If $x - 3$ is a multiple of two, you can assume that it is also an even number. This number plus two would also produce an even number.

20. a. Solve for x first. Since $3^{x+1} = 81$, and 81 is 3^4, make an easier equation just based on the exponents. This would be $x + 1 = 4$. $x = 3$. Therefore, $x - 1 = 3 - 1 = 2$.

21. b. Use the counting principle: Take the number of choices you have for each course and multiply them together to get the total possible combinations. $x \times (y + 1) \times z$. Use the distributive property to simplify to $xyz + xz$.

22. c. For this type of problem, substitute the values you are given for x and y. In this case, $x = 2$ and $y = 3$. The expression becomes $2\,(2 + 3)^2$. Using the order of operations, perform the operation within the parentheses first and then the exponent. $2\,(5)^2 = 2\,(25)$. Multiply to get 50.

23. d. Statement I is an example of the associative property of multiplication and statement III is an example of the distributive property. These properties will hold for any real numbers that are substituted into them. Statement II is not a property of real numbers and may be true for certain numbers, but not for every real number.

24. b. Since $y = 6^x$, multiplying each side of the equation results in $6y = 6\,(6^x)$. Recall that since $6 = 6^1$, $6^x \times 6^1 = 6^{x+1}$ by the laws of exponents.

25. b. Remember that consecutive odd integers are numbers that are two apart in order, like 11, 13, and 15. The average of *six* consecutive odd integers will be an even number. If $x + 2$ is the average, then this value will be at the middle of the integers if they are arranged in order. Therefore, the three consecutive odd integers smaller than this are expressed as $x + 1$, $x - 1$, and $x - 3$ in descending order. The smallest odd integer is $x - 3$.

26. a. Write an equation for the question by translating the first sentence. The product of a and b is ab, and 11 more than twice the sum of a and b translates to $2(a + b) + 11$. The equation is $ab = 2\,(a + b) + 11$. Substitute 7 for b. $7a = 2\,(a + 7) + 11$. This simplifies to $7a = 2a + 14 + 11$ by the distributive property and then becomes $7a = 2a + 25$. Subtract $2a$ from both sides of the equation and then divide each side by 5; $7a - 2a = 2a - 2a + 25$. $\frac{5a}{5} = \frac{25}{5}$. $a = 5$. The value of $b - a = 7 - 5 = 2$.

27. c. Working from the inside out, the square root of x^2 is equal to x. Therefore, the cube root of x^3 is also x. Each operation undoes the other. The expression reduces to just x.

28. c. To solve the problem, you need to add $\frac{4}{9}$ and $\frac{2}{3}$, and then subtract $\frac{8}{18}$ since the amount she has not used is $\frac{8}{18}$, which reduces to $\frac{4}{9}$. If you were to add $\frac{4}{9}$ and $\frac{2}{3}$, and then subtract $\frac{4}{9}$, you would end up with $\frac{2}{3}$.

29. c. Statement I simplifies to $\frac{1}{8}$, which is less than 1. Statement II simplifies to $\frac{16}{9}$, which is greater than 1. In statement III, you need to take the reciprocal of the fraction inside the parentheses (because the exponent is negative) and then evaluate using an exponent of 2. This results in $(-3)^2 = 9$, which is also greater than 1. Both statements II and III would satisfy the inequality $x > 1$.

30. b. Let x = Sam's current age and $3x$ = John's current age. If John will be twice as old as Sam in six years, this sets up the equation $3x + 6 = 2(x + 6)$. Solve this equation for x by using the distributive property on the right side of the equation and then subtracting $2x$ from both sides. $3x + 6 = 2x + 12$. $3x - 2x + 6 = 2x - 2x + 12$. Subtract 6 from both sides. $x + 6 - 6 = 12 - 6$. $x = 6$. Since x is Sam's current age, Sam was four years old two years ago.

31. a. By spinning the spinner two times, the probability of not getting an A is $\frac{3}{4} \times \frac{3}{4} = \frac{9}{16}$.

32. d. If sold by the case, each individual roll cost \$.75 ($\frac{\$9.00}{12} = .75$). To find the percent of savings, compare the savings to the cost of a roll sold individually. $\frac{1.00 - .75}{1.00} = \frac{.25}{1.00} = 0.25 = 25\%$.

33. e. If at least one member must be a woman, the committee will have either one woman and two men or two women and one man. Use combinations because the order does not matter.

Choosing one woman and two men: ${}_2C_1 \times {}_4C_2 = \frac{2}{1} \times \frac{4 \times 3}{2 \times 1} = \frac{24}{2} = 12$..

Choosing two women and one man: ${}_2C_2 \times {}_4C_1 = \frac{2 \times 1}{2 \times 1} = \frac{4}{1} = \frac{8}{2} = 4$.

Since both situations would satisfy the requirement that at least one member is a woman, add the combinations.

$12 + 4 = 16$ total committees

34. a. Start with the money she had left and work backwards. If she had \$5 left over, and had just spent three-fourths of her money on food, then \$5 must be one-fourth of her money. Before buying food she must have had $5 \times 4 = \$20$. She then spent half of her money on clothes; therefore, \$20 was half of her money, giving her \$40 at this point. She then spent one-third of her money on books and had \$40 left over. If \$40 represents two-thirds of her money, then \$60 must be the amount she began with.

35. d. Draw a diagram to show the path of the truck.

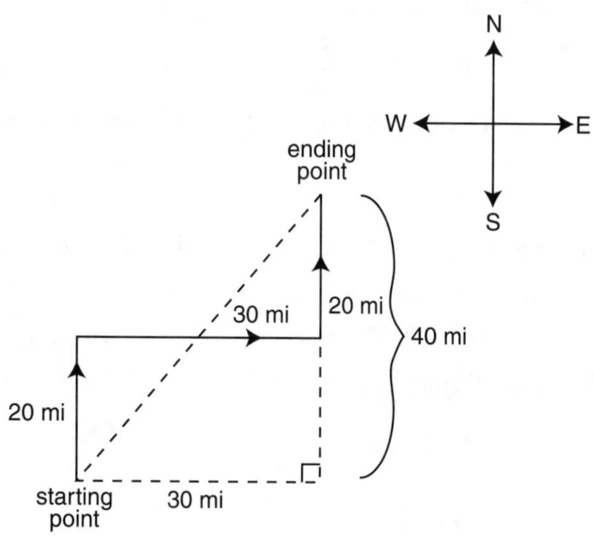

The distance between the starting point and the final destination is a diagonal line. This line is the hypotenuse of a right triangle that has one leg of 40 and the other measuring 30. Use the Pythagorean theorem: $a^2 + b^2 = c^2$. Recall, however, that this is a multiple of the most common Pythagorean triple (3, 4, 5)—namely, 30, 40, 50. The distance is 50 miles.

36. d. $\frac{1}{2} \times \frac{2}{5} = \frac{1}{5} = .2$. 0.2 divided by 0.04 is the same as 20 divided by 4, which is equal to 5.

37. c. Since we are trying to find the width of the deck, let $x =$ the width of the deck. Therefore, $x + x + 20$ or $2x + 20$ is the width of the entire figure. In the same way, $x + x + 28$ or $2x + 28$ is the length of the entire figure.

The area of a rectangle is length × width, so use $A = l \times w$.

Substitute into the equation:	$884 = (2x + 20)(2x + 28)$
Multiply using FOIL:	$884 = 4x^2 + 56x + 40x + 560$
Combine like terms:	$884 = 4x^2 + 96x + 560$
Subtract 884 from both sides:	$884 - 884 = 4x^2 + 96x + 560 - 884$
	$0 = 4x^2 + 96x - 324$
Divide each term by 4:	$0 = x^2 + 24x - 81$
Factor the trinomial:	$0 = (x + 27)(x - 3)$
Set each factor equal to zero and solve:	$x + 27 = 0$ or $x - 3 = 0$
	$x = -27 \quad x = 3$

Since we are solving for a length, the solution of –27 must be rejected. The width of the deck is 3 feet.

38. d. If you are randomly guessing with five possible answer choices, the probability of guessing correct is 1 out of 5, or $\frac{1}{5}$. Since the test has n number of questions and we want to get half of them correct, we want this to happen $\frac{n}{2}$ times. Therefore, the probability would be $\frac{1}{5}$ times itself $\frac{n}{2}$ times, or $(\frac{1}{5})^{\frac{n}{2}}$.

39. d. Let $x =$ the smaller integer. The ratio of 1 to 4 can be written as $1x$ to $4x$ or $\frac{x}{4x}$. Add 6 to the smaller integer, set the ratio equal to $\frac{1}{2}$, and solve. $\frac{x+6}{4x} = \frac{1}{2}$. Cross-multiply to get $2x + 12 = 4x$. Subtract $2x$ from both sides of the equation. $2x - 2x + 12 = 4x - 2x$. $12 = 2x$, so $6 = x$. If the smaller integer is 6, then the larger integer is $6 \times 4 = 24$.

40. a. Since x represents the perimeter of the original square, $3x$ represents the perimeter of the new square. If each side is tripled, the perimeter also triples.

41. d. If you take statement (1) and divide each term by 2, the result is $x + 2y = 10$. Thus, $x + 2y$ is solved for. If you take statement (2) and add $\frac{1}{2}x$ to both sides and multiply each term by 2, the result is also $x + 2y = 10$. Therefore, either statement is sufficient.

42. **d.** Any real number is either rational or irrational and subtracting 5 from any rational or irrational will also be a real number. Statement (1) is sufficient. Statement (2) implies that if the square root of a number is irrational, the original number was either rational or irrational. Statement (2) is sufficient.

43. **b.** Since you know that ABCD is a rectangle, you already know that each vertex angle is 90 degrees. Statement (1) does not tell you any additional information about ABCD. Statement (2) states that the diagonals are perpendicular; a rectangle with perpendicular diagonals is a square. Statement (2) is sufficient.

44. **d.** Either statement is sufficient. Statement (1) is sufficient because if the measure of each adjacent exterior angle is 72, then the measure of the interior angle is $180 - 72 = 108$. Statement (2) is also sufficient. Regular polygons contain congruent sides and congruent angles. If the pentagon is made up of 540 degrees, then $540 \div 5 = 108$ in each angle.

45. **c.** Since this question has two variables and two equations, they can be used together to solve for x and y. If both equations are combined, the result is $3x = 15$. Obviously x and subsequently y can be solved for now, but you do not need to finish the problem once you have reached this conclusion.

46. **d.** In this problem, either statement is sufficient. Angle ACB is supplementary to x, so $180 - 30 = 150$ degrees. Statement (2) says that the sum of the two remote interior angle equal 150 degrees; this is equal to the exterior angle, x. Note that the diagram is not drawn to scale so you should not rely on the diagram to calculate the answer.

47. **b.** The dimensions of the room are not significant and will not help you solve the problem. Statement (2) tells how long it takes Ted to paint the room alone. Using this information, you can set up the equation $\frac{1}{x} + \frac{1}{7} = \frac{1}{4}$. In this equation, x is the time it takes Joe to paint the room, $\frac{1}{x}$ is the part of the room Joe can paint in one hour, $\frac{1}{7}$ is the part of the room Ted can paint in one hour, and $\frac{1}{4}$ is the part of the room they can paint together in one hour. Stop. You have an equation that can be solved, but you do not need to solve it. Statement (2) is sufficient.

48. **c.** Statement (1) and statement (2) together are sufficient. To have a product greater than zero, either x and y are both positive or both negative. You need both statements to be able to tell. The fact that $x > 1$ lets you know that x is positive, and since $y < 0$, y is negative.

49. **c.** To find the area of the sector, use the formula $\frac{x}{360} \times \pi r^2$ where x is the angle measure of the central angle of the sector. The length of the diameter is necessary to find the length of the radius. Statement (1) and statement (2) together are sufficient.

50. **e.** Even though the points are in the same plane, you are not sure if A, B, and C are collinear (contained on the same straight line), or even if B is between A and C. Not enough information is given in either statement.

51. **b.** The fact that l is perpendicular to p indicates that angle x is a right angle, but it tells you nothing about angle y. The fact that l is parallel to m in statement (2) is much more useful. Since p is parallel to n, you can use corresponding angles to figure out that y is equal to the angle adjacent to x. Therefore, x and y are supplementary.

52. **e.** Both statements are irrelevant because you do not know the cost of any of the items at either store.

53. **b.** Statement (1) could mean that $x + 1 = 8$, which is not a factor of 12. If $x + 1$ is a factor of both 2 and 3, then $x = 0$ and $x + 1 = 1$. One is a factor of every number. Statement (2) will suffice by itself.

54. **c.** Solve the compound inequality in statement (1). $22 < 3x + 1 < 28$. Subtract 1 from each part of the inequality. $22 - 1 < 3x + 1 - 1 < 28 - 1$. Divide each part by 3. $\frac{21}{3} < \frac{3x}{3} < \frac{27}{3}$. $7 < x < 9$. The result is that x is some number between 7 and 9; thus, statement (1) is not sufficient. Statement (2), together with statement (1), is sufficient, and the answer is conclusively one value—namely, 8.

55. **a.** Since x and y are consecutive even integers, they are numbers such as 10 and 12 or 32 and 34. Using statement (1), the only two numbers that would satisfy the equation are 48 and 50. Statement (1) is sufficient. Statement (2) just restates the obvious; every two consecutive even integers are two numbers apart. This does not help you solve the problem.

56. **c.** Since $x^2 - 25$ is the difference between two perfect squares, its factors are $(x - 5)$ and $(x + 5)$. Statement (1) gives the value of $x - 5$. Statement (2) can be changed from $4 - x = 5$ to $4 = x + 5$ by adding x to both sides of the equation. Since you now know the numerical value of each factor, you can find the numerical value of $x^2 - 25$.

57. **d.** Let x = the length of the courtyard. Statement (1) states that $2x + 2$ = the width of the courtyard. Using the formula *area* = *length* × *width*, we get the equation $60 = x(2x + 2)$, which can be solved for x. Statement (1) is sufficient. Using statement (2), the diagonal divides the courtyard into two congruent right triangles. If the diagonal is 13 meters, and the dimensions are whole numbers, this must be a 5–12–13 right triangle. The length is 5 meters, and statement (2) is also sufficient.

58. **a.** Statement (1) is sufficient. If the triangle is equilateral, then all sides and all angles are congruent. This would make $x + y = 60$ and $z = 60$; this is enough information to answer the question. From statement (2), you can only tell that $\overline{AD}$ is the altitude drawn to side $\overline{BC}$, and that $\triangle ADB$ and $\triangle ADC$ are both right triangles.

59. **c.** To find the area of the shaded region, you need the area of the inner circle subtracted from the outer circle. Since the formula for the area of a circle is $A = \pi r^2$, you need to know at least the radius of each circle. Statement (1) gives you the area of the inner circle only, but no information about the outer circle. Statement (2) tells you the diameter of the outer circle is 20, so the radius is 10. Both statements are needed to answer the question.

60. **d.** From the diagram, if the measure of angle C is 30 degrees and angle B is a right angle, then $\triangle ABC$ is a 30–60–90 right triangle. Using statement (1), if the measure of BC is $2\sqrt{3}$, then the shortest side x must be $\frac{2\sqrt{3}}{\sqrt{3}}$, which reduces to 2. Using statement (2), if the length of AC is 4 and AC is the hypotenuse of the triangle, then the shortest side of the triangle x is equal to $\frac{4}{2} = 2$. Either statement is sufficient.

61. **c.** Remember that $(a + b)^2 = a^2 + 2ab + b^2$. From statement (1), we know that $a^2 + b^2 = 13$. By cross-multiplying in statement (2), we get $2ab = 12$. Since we know the values of $a^2 + b^2$ and $2ab$, and $(a + b)^2 = a^2 + 2ab + b^2$, we can now take the square root of the sum to find the value of $a + b$.

62. **c.** The sum of the two smaller sides of a triangle must be greater than the longest side. To find the third side, subtract the two known values to get the lower bound and add the two known values to get the upper bound. The value of the third sides must be between these two numbers. Therefore, both statements are necessary.

63. d. The formula for the area of a circle is $A = \pi r^2$, so the radius of the circle must be found in order to use the formula. Statement (1) gives you the radius. Using statement (2), the formula can be found by the fact that the circumference is $\pi \times$ the diameter. If the diameter is 12, then the radius is 6. Stop; you do not actually need to compute the area. Either statement can be used to solve the problem.

64. b. Statement (1) contains two variables; you would need more information to solve for z. Statement (2) can be put into the form $z^2 - z - 12 = 0$. This equation can be solved by either factoring or by using the quadratic formula, and is sufficient to answer the question.

65. c. In this type of question, remember the formula *distance* = *rate* × *time.* Let t = the time it takes the second car to catch up to the first. The fact that the second car is traveling 10 miles per hour faster than the first is not helpful by itself. We need to know more about either the distance traveled or the time traveled. Statement (2) alone also does not give enough information because we do not know the distances traveled. If we use both statements together, the first car's distance is $50\ (t + 1)$ and the second car's distance is $60t$. When the second car catches up, their distances will be the same. Setting the two distances equal to each other gives the equation $50t + 50 = 60t$. We can subtract $50t$ from both sides and divide by 10. $\frac{50}{10} = \frac{10t}{10}$. $t = 5$ hours.

66. c. Statement (1) gives information about one of the three sides of the triangle, but this is not enough to solve for XZ. Statement (2) tells you that the right triangle in this problem is a 45–45–90 right triangle, or an isosceles right triangle. However, this also is not enough information to find XZ. By using the two statements together, if $YZ = 6$, then $XZ = 6\sqrt{2}$.

67. d. Divide both sides of the equation in statement (1) by $3y$. This results in the proportion $\frac{x}{y} = \frac{6}{3}$. Since $\frac{x}{y} = \frac{6}{3}$, $\frac{y}{x} = \frac{3}{6}$. Therefore, the answer to the original question would be yes. Statement (2) tells you that $\frac{x}{y}$ is greater than 1; therefore, it must be an improper fraction. $\frac{y}{x}$ would then be a proper fraction making it less than $\frac{x}{y}$. Either statement is sufficient.

68. b. Statement (2) is the same as the original question doubled. Divide \$11.00 by 2 to answer the question. Statement (1) is not sufficient by itself.

69. d. Either statement is sufficient. The ratio of the perimeters of two similar triangles is equal to the ratio of the corresponding sides. Also, the ratio of the areas of two similar triangles is equal to the squares of the ratios of the corresponding sides.

70. a. Let x equal the amount of time passed. Since the time remaining is $\frac{1}{4}$ of the time that has passed, this time can be represented as $\frac{1}{4}x$.Converting to decimal form may make this problem easier, so change $\frac{1}{4}x$ to $.25x$. Since $1x$ is the time passed and $.25x$ is the time remaining, then $1x + .25x$ is the total time. This is equal to $1.25x$. To calculate the percent of the period that is over, use the proportion $\frac{\text{part}}{\text{whole}} = \frac{\%}{100}$

Now set up a proportion using the time passed as the part and the total time for the class as the whole. $\frac{1}{1.25} = \frac{x}{100}$

Cross-multiply to get $1.25x = 100$.

Divide both sides by 1.25. $\frac{1.25x}{1.25} = \frac{100}{1.25}$

$x = 80\%$

80% of the class period is over.

For this particular question, the number of minutes in the class period is not needed to solve the problem.

71. c. To solve this problem, you need to find the distance east and north that he travels. Since he goes directly east and then directly north, his path forms a right angle, which in turn is part of a right triangle. His straight-line distance to school is the hypotenuse of the right triangle formed by his paths. Although statement (1) gives you the hypotenuse, you do not know enough information to solve for the other sides. Statement (2) gives the relationship between the two legs of the right triangle, but again this is not enough information. Using the information from both statements, you can write an equation using the Pythagorean theorem: $a^2 + b^2 = c^2$. Let x = the distance he travels east and $x + 7$ = the distance he travels north. $x^2 + (x + 7)^2 = 17^2$. This equation can now be solved for the missing legs and therefore the solution to the problem.

72. b. Statement (2) is sufficient. Change the equation to $y = mx + b$ form, where m is the slope of the line and b is the y-intercept. $3y = x - 4$ becomes $\frac{1}{3}x - \frac{4}{3}$. The slope of the line is $\frac{1}{3}$. Statement (1) is not sufficient because we cannot tell the slope of line by only looking at the x-intercept.

73. e. Neither statement is sufficient. The question never states the amount of commission, nor the commission rate, he gets on sales over \$4,000.

74. a. Statement (1) is sufficient. In a triangle, when a line is drawn parallel to a base, the line divides the sides it intersects proportionally. This would make $\triangle ABC$ similar to $\triangle ADE$. Using statement (2), knowing that $AD = AE$ is not enough information to assume that other parts are proportional.

75. c. In order to have enough information to substitute into the formula, you would need both statements. Use $p = \$1,000$, $r = 0.04$ and $n = 5$ to compare Bank A to Bank B. Again, you do not need to actually compute the interest earned once you can answer the question.

76. d. Knowing that the gate is square and the diagonal is $30\sqrt{2}$, the Pythagorean theorem can be used with x as the side of the square. $x^2 + x^2 = (30\sqrt{2})^2$. Or you may recall that the length of a leg will be $\frac{30\sqrt{2}}{\sqrt{2}} = 30$ because it is an isosceles triangle. Thus, statement (2) is sufficient. Since statement (1) gives the width and the gate is a square, then the height is the same as the width. Either statement is sufficient.

77. e. Statement (1) is not sufficient. The fact that angle A is 43 degrees does not give you enough information about the rest of the triangle or the circle. Statement (2) is also not sufficient. Even though the diameter, or $\overline{AD}$, equals 10, you cannot assume that this is the altitude or height of the triangle.

78. e. From statement (1), the circle is centered at the origin and has a radius of 5. This obviously is not sufficient because it does not tell you anything about the line. Even though statement (2) gives you the y-intercept of the line, since you do not know the slope, the line could intersect the circle in 0, 1, or 2 different places. Neither statement is sufficient.

79. a. Using *distance* = *rate* × *time* and the facts from statement (1), you can calculate the time they will be 350 miles apart. You are told that they are traveling at the same rate. To solve for the rate, you can use the equation that relates Michael's distance plus Katie's distance, which equals 250 miles at a time of 1.5 hours. Once the rate is known you can then solve for the time when they are 350 miles apart. Statement (2) is unnecessary information and does not help you to solve for the time.

80. c. Because you know that the triangle is equilateral from statement (1), you also know that each side has the same measure and that each angle is 60 degrees. This does not, however, tell you the length of the diameter or radius of the circle, which you need to know in order to find the area. Statement (2) alone is also insufficient because it tells you the length of one side of the triangle, but no other information about the figure. Using both statements together, the diameter is then 16; thus, the radius is 8. Therefore, the area of the semicircle can be calculated.

CHAPTER

25 Quantitative Section Glossary

binary system one of the simplest numbering systems. The base of the binary system is 2, which means that only the digits 0 and 1 can appear in a binary representation of any number.

circumference the distance around the outside of a circle

composite number any integer that can be divided evenly by a number other than itself and 1. All numbers are either prime or composite.

counting numbers include all whole numbers with the exception of 0

data sufficiency a type of question used on the GMAT® exam that contains an initial question or statement followed by two statements labeled (1) and (2). Test takers are asked to determine whether the statements offer enough data to solve the problem.

decimal a number in the base 10 number system. Each place value in a decimal number is worth ten times the place value of the digit to its right.

denominator the bottom number in a fraction. The denominator of $\frac{1}{2}$ is 2.

diameter a chord that passes through the center of the circle and has endpoints on the circle

difference the result of subtracting one number from another

divisible by capable of being evenly divided by a given number without a remainder

dividend the number in a division problem that is being divided. In $32 \div 4 = 8$, 32 is the dividend.

even number a counting number that is divisible by 2

expanded notation a method of writing numbers as the sum of their units (hundreds, tens, ones, etc.). The expanded notation for 378 is 300 + 70 + 8.

exponent a number that indicates an operation of repeated multiplication. For instance, 3^4 indicates that 3 should be multiplied by itself 4 times.

factor one of two or more numbers or variables that are being multiplied together

fractal a geometric figure that is self-similar; that is, any smaller piece of the figure will have roughly the same shape as the whole.

improper fraction a fraction whose numerator is the same size as or larger than its denominator. Improper fractions are equal to or greater than 1.

integer all of the *whole numbers* and negatives too. Examples are –3, –2, –1, 0, 1, 2, and 3. Note that integers *do not* include fractions or decimals.

multiple of a multiple of a number has that number as one of its factors. The number 35 is a multiple of 7; it is also a multiple of 5.

negative number a real number whose value is less than 0

numerator the top number in a fraction. The numerator of $\frac{1}{4}$ is 1.

odd number a counting number that is not divisible by 2

percent a ratio or fraction whose denominator is assumed to be 100, expressed using the % sign. 98% is equal to $\frac{98}{100}$.

perimeter the distance around the outside of a polygon

polygon a closed two-dimensional shape made up of several line segments that are joined together

positive number a real number whose value is greater than 0

prime number a real number that is divisible by only 2 positive factors: 1 and itself

product the result when two numbers are multiplied together

proper fraction a fraction whose denominator is larger than its numerator. Proper fractions are equal to less than 1.

proportion a relationship between two equivalent sets of fractions in the form $\frac{a}{b} = \frac{c}{d}$

quotient the result when one number is divided into another

radical the symbol used to signify a root operation

radius any line segment from the center of the circle to a point on the circle. The radius of a circle is equal to half its diameter.

ratio the relationship between two things, expressed as a proportion

real numbers include fractions and decimals in addition to *integers*

reciprocal one of two numbers that, when multiplied together, give a product of 1. For instance, since $\frac{3}{2} \times \frac{2}{3}$ is equal to 1, $\frac{3}{2}$ is the reciprocal of $\frac{2}{3}$.

remainder the amount left over after a division problem using whole numbers. Divisible numbers always have a remainder of 0.

root (square root) one of two (or more) equal factors of a number. The square root of 36 is 6, because $6 \times 6 = 36$. The cube root of 27 is 3 because $3 \times 3 \times 3 = 27$.

simplify terms to combine like terms and reduce an equation to its most basic form

variable a letter, often *x*, used to represent an unknown number value in a problem

whole numbers 0, 1, 2, 3, and so on. They do not include negatives, fractions, or decimals.

APPENDIX

A GMAT Online Resources

www.gmac.com/GMAC/default.htm the Graduate Management Admission Council® provides information about the GMAT® exam and business schools nationwide

www.800score.com/gmat-home.html this site offers a variety of online GMAT exam preparation materials and services

www.crack-gmat.com this site offers a variety of GMAT exam preparation materials and online services

www.gmat-mba-prep.com this site provides GMAT exam test-taking strategies, practice tests, and general information

www.princetonreview.com the Princeton Review offers a variety of GMAT exam preparation services and materials

www.kaplan.com Kaplan offers a variety of GMAT exam preparation services and materials

www.gmattutor.com this site offers a wide variety of online GMAT exam preparation services and materials

www.testmagic.com Test Magic offers a variety of online GMAT exam preparation services and materials

http://education.yahoo.com/college/essentials/practice_tests/gmat Yahoo offers a variety of GMAT exam preparation services and materials

www.prep.com this site offers a variety of GMAT exam preparation materials

www.deltacourse.com this site offers online GMAT preparation courses

APPENDIX

B GMAT Print Resources

General

Arco Master the GMAT Cat with CD-ROM (New York: Arco, 2002).

GMAT CAT Success with CD-ROM (New York: Petersons, 2002).

GMAT CAT Success (New York: Petersons, 2002).

Hilbert, Stephen. *Pass Key to the GMAT* (Hauppauge, NY: Barron's Educational Series, 2001).

Kaplan GMAT 2003 (New York: Kaplan, 2002).

Kaplan GMAT/LSAT and GRE 2002 Edition (New York: Kaplan, 2003).

Martz, Geoff, and Robinson, Adam. *Cracking the GMAT with CD-ROM* (New York: Random House, 2002).

The Official Guide for GMAT Review, 10th Edition (Princeton, NJ: Graduate Management Admission, 2000).

Ultimate Prep for the GMAT: A Systematic Approach (Austin: Lighthouse Review, 2002).

Wilmerding, Alex, and others. *The GMAT: Real World Intelligence, Strategies and Experience from the Experts to Prepare You for Everything the Classroom and Textbooks Won't Teach You for the GMAT* (Boston: Aspatore Books, 2002).

▶ Quantitative

LearningExpress. *501 Math Word Problems* (New York: LearningExpress, 2003).
LearningExpress. *Algebra Success in 20 Minutes a Day* (New York: LearningExpress, 2000).
LearningExpress. *Geometry Success in 20 Minutes a Day* (New York: LearningExpress, 2000).
LearningExpress. *Practical Math Success in 20 Minutes a Day* (New York, LearningExpress, 2000).
Stuart, David, and others. *GRE/GMAT Math Workbook* (New York: Kaplan, 2002).
Taylor, N. *Math Collection: SAT & GMAT Practice Problems* (Los Angeles: Unicorn Multi-Media, 2002).

▶ Verbal and Analytical Writing

Bomstad, Linda, O'Toole, Frederick J., and Stewart, Mark Alan. *GMAT CAT: Answers to the Real Essay Questions* (New York: Arco, 2002).
French, Douglas. *Verbal Workout for the GMAT* (New York: Princeton Review, 1999).
LearningExpress. *Reading Comprehension Success in 20 Minutes a Day, 2nd Edition* (New York: LearningExpress, 2001).
LearningExpress. *501 Vocabulary Questions* (New York: LearningExpress, 2003).
LearningExpress. *501 Writing Prompts* (New York: LearningExpress, 2003).
LearningExpress. *Vocabulary and Spelling Success, 3rd Edition* (New York: LearningExpress, 2002).
LearningExpress. *Writing Success in 20 Minutes a Day* (New York: LearningExpress, 2001).
Multhopp, Ingrid. *Kaplan GMAT Verbal Workbook* (New York: Simon & Schuster, 2001).
Palmore, Jo Norris. *Logic and Reading Review for the GRE, GMAT, LSAT, MCAT* (New York: Petersons, 2002).
The Ultimate Verbal and Vocabulary Builder for the SAT, ACT, GRE, GMAT, and LSAT (Austin: Lighthouse Review, 2002).
Writing Skills for the GRE and GMAT Tests (New York: Petersons, 2002).